The Hebrew Letters

by

Gary Kent Spain

Analysis of each letter's meaning, based on Kabbalah's long lost core, reconstructed with the help of the Irish calendar of tree-letters: a brief account of this; a history of letters' shapes in several ancient alphabets[*]; and a parsing of meanings of all Semitic roots used in the Old Testament

---

[*] Egyptian hieroglyphic & hieratic, north & south Semitic, bronze age & Berber Tifinag>> Libyan (Numidian), Greek & Lycian, Meroitic (Nubia), Germanic runes

Salute to One Passed On

My father's turned to mistletoe:
he's rooted in the ground no more
but hovers above the forest floor
below, dissolved into a point,
       like Hebrew yod.
       The other letters
are gathered now to celebrate
such hallowedness: a Greek iota
was he once, teaching his child
and other children how to learn.
When teaching, he was seldom stern.

Table of Contents

Foreword

Patterns in the Wind

The world builds its monuments
To Adam and its monuments
    To Eve.
The world builds its monuments,
But I like not monuments
    That leave

A sour taste in mouth or a
Sourness of spirit
    In a friend,
So I build no monuments
But only leave patterns
    In the wind.

The lever with which I have tackled this project is the reconstructed inner core of the Kabbalah revealed when one puts what has survived of it together with what has survived of Celtic bardic lore in the British Isles. Irish poetic tradition has preserved for us an ancient tree-alphabet that formed a calendar and thus reveals the correct original order of letters about the round of the year and its seasons (the zodiac). The two currents clearly branched off from the same trunk, as indicated by what they have in common; and since each tradition decayed by a different route, when superimposed on each other they miraculously fill each other's holes to reveal an incredible edifice of knowledge built around the sounds of speech, assigning them to the various organs and parts of the body but also, strangely enough, to the chemical 'elements' or atom-types, as well as the four types of elementary particle (the *actual* elements), once letters are assigned the numbers given them in Celtic tradition. Yet without *Sefer Yetzirah* and its division of letters into three mothers, seven doubles, and twelve simples, the deeper significance would remain hidden. The two strands, Celtic and Judaic, are coequal and mutually revelatory.

To clarify, part three is not an analysis of the use of speech-sounds in Semitic languages generally, nor even just in Hebrew and Chaldean (aka Aramaic) generally: it is an analysis of the vocabulary chosen by the poets who wrote the Bible. I feel there would have been a tendency to choose words that reinforced the core meanings of the roots' initial sounds as understood by the bards and prophets of their day. That they wrote in free verse does not make them any less poets in my view. My primary source for the roots is the Davidson *Lexicon*,[1] which apparently reflects an Anglican perspective: it appears to be sufficiently scholarly in approach to serve my purpose.

What passes for Kabbalah today concentrates on Hebrew numbering, using *Gematria* for instance, which equates terms adding to the same number; yet that numbering may be relatively late, a product of Greek influence even. This has led one author to speculate that Kabbalah is actually a Greek thing, considering such origins.[2] Gershom Scholem, the great twentieth-century scholar of Kabbalah, wrote: "As a matter of historical fact, none of these techniques of mystical exegesis [referring to *Gematria*, *Notarikon*, and *Temurah*] can be called Kabbalistic in the strict sense of the word."[3] What use there was of such techniques in the writings of the thirteenth- and fourteenth-century Kabbalists he attributes mainly to the influence of German Hasidim.[4]

It is the more essential *bardic* numbering that opens the floodgates for us. This leads to the conclusion that these numbers, which relate directly to what the letters symbolize, were part of the most ancient strata, whence sprang both the Judaic and Celtic branches of the tradition.

The correlations with atom-types and particle-types is revealed to *us* by comparison with advances in science over only the past few centuries; yet they are built solidly into the structure of the Kabbalah. My guess is that what is revealed shows the level science had reached in the previous civilization, destroyed ten or more millenniums ago by the melting of huge ice packs (end of the last ice age), although this implies the tradition's preservation over many millennia via oral tradition, or else by writings unknown to us.

In its origin, the zodiac is not, as astrologers claim and as generally believed, a mere set of constellations thought to resemble certain figures of mythology. Rather, it is the round of the human form: from aries the head, which represents spring because it is *up*, the direction spring springs; through cancer the breasts, which blossom *out* as does summer; through libra the loins, representing fall, being *down*, the direction leaves and fruit fall; and capricorn the mid-spine (in astrology, the knees), representing winter solstice, winter being when life is most *held back* (or *weak in the knees*) as the sun climbs the steep back of the round (knock-kneed goat capricorn).

Astronomers treat the precession of equinoxes as a *retrograde* revolution of the zodiac (solstices and equinoxes) around the stellar heavens, based on its physical trigger, tidal effects of the moon (two-thirds) and sun (one third). Yet the vast entirety of the stellar heavens actually revolves in the same direction as planets around the *zodiac*, the frame of reference of immediate relevance. This does not of course mean that the farthest stars are traveling *physically* around us at many times the speed of light, only that the continual precession of our zodiac *results* in the heavens revolving in a forward sense around it (every 25,772 years by current calculation), the ultimate relativism perhaps yet ironically a much firmer absolute reference frame, because the actual center of the universe is where intelligence and nature *meet* (in Uprightness).

The symbols of the signs reveal their origin: rams (aries) butt heads; bulls (taurus) have strong necks; the shoulders are twins (gemini); crabs (cancer) walk sideways (cancer being at right angles to aries); and so on. These stations are then *projected onto* the heavens to mark the sun's position at solstices and equinoxes. Believed resemblance of constellations to symbols is merely the stamp sages put on the heavens at a particular juncture. I would even argue that this was done incorrectly and that the actual aries of the *movable* zodiac (the stellar heavens) points to the constellation Virgo—towards the center of the local galactic cluster—as this was the point that crossed over to the intelligent side (signs from libra on) at around the time of Christ, when *gnosis* was revealing the truth of the Triune Self ('disguised' as the Trinity). Let us examine for a moment the division of things into *nature side* and *intelligent side*.

The sign cancer, the breasts, points straight ahead, towards the outer horizon, which is all around us. Straight back *from* straight ahead is capricorn or *back towards us*, towards self: the direction of individual responsibility. The crossover point is libra or straight down. The twelve signs ultimately show the course of progression of every unit in the cosmos, the universe being anthropocentric: from the simplest unit of nature (a fire unit) to the most sophisticated unit of nature, an individual soul (rigorously defined herein) at libra, then on from there, crossing over to the intelligent side to eventually become a *conscious self*.

Of what does this conscious self consist? This can be deduced from a passage in Plato's *Republic* (book V).[5] He says that there is that which abides (the eternal), that which abides and abides not (what has finite duration), and that which abides not (fleeting present instant). Of the first, one can have knowledge; of the second, an opinion; but the third remains utterly dark, this for the simple reason (though not stipulated by him) that by the time attention is turned to it the present instant is gone. Yet it is in the present instant that we must act. Hence the conscious self must obviously consist of a knower, to deal with what is eternal; a thinker, to deal with what has finite duration; and a doer, to act in the present instant. Yet these three distinguishable parts are *one self*, thus explaining the Trinity in simple enough terms as to make centuries of controversy over it seem almost silly. But the original understanding of this was purged from Christianity, by the suppression (and persecution) of the Gnostics.

The Bible—and any competent shaman—will tell you humankind has undergone a Fall. The nature of the Fall can be deduced from the fact that if the present is dark, then the only way a doer can act wisely *in* the present is to follow the guidance of its thinker and knower concerning what has duration *through* the present. Instead, we human doers have succumbed to the illusion that the senses are sufficient to inform us *of* the present, which has led to the atrophying of our ability to 'hear' the admonitions of thinker and knower. We, the doer or Son, feel *cut off* from the higher self—"My God, my God, why hast Thou forsaken me!"—though from *its* point of view, that of Father and Holy Spirit, the self is still One.

My focus is not Christian; rather, it is *Gnostic*. It is true that some forms of Gnosticism vilified the Jewish 'Yahweh', and that any Gnostic worth his-or-her salt sees 'the Creator' in quite a different light than does ordinary theology, Christian *or* Jewish. But the great Christian thinker Johannes Scotus Eriugena himself expressed the view that, since the Creator is eternal, the 'act' of creation is ongoing as well, not just a single event occurring at one particular point of time in the past. After all, the Creator is *us!*—*doers*, who did not just begin evolving from more primitive forms a few million years ago, as the currently held paradigm naively claims, but are made *in the image of the divine*.

In fact to claim the universe had a beginning in time contradicts not just one or two but virtually *all* the conservation laws that consitute science's solid basis! For this reason alone the 'big bang' is pure pseudo-science. Moreover, the current gravitational cosmology it is based on utterly ignores advances in plasma physics showing that stars and galaxies are electric discharges brought about by *magnetic z-pinch*. Since gravity is dozens of orders of magnitude weaker than electromagnetism, it is utterly negligible when dealing with the behavior of stellar plasma.

While the above considerations may be less critical to theologians, creation at a single point in time still presents a contradiction between eternal Creator and momentary crea*tion*. A late friend of mine, an Azerbaijani Jew from Jerusalem—an artist who mended Torah scrolls professionally—told me Genesis carefully interpreted expounds on the *logical*, not necessarily *temporal*, origin of the cosmos. One might suspect as much from light's being created before sun and moon. (He also told me you don't fully grasp the Old Testament till you get its jokes.) Without doubt the story of Adam and Eve and the Fall is a poetic depiction of a process *every one* of us underwent long ago.

Gershom Scholem characterized Kabbalah as *Jewish Gnosticism*, and that is how I see it. I cannot help but see it thus considering the depth of knowledge both scientific and metaphysical built into its structure, once ferreted out by comparison of its two main surviving branches. The intricacy and sophistication of the model preclude any notion I may have made the whole thing up. Frankly, I am not *bright* enough to have done so. But I am bright enough to have noticed certain correlations with what our science has so far revealed, and I have simply pursued these correlations to their logical conclusion.

I begin with a brief exposition of the process by which I penetrated into the mysteries of Kabbalah and the earlier *Ma'aseh Merkavah* or Work of the Chariot: basically a summary of my book *World Egg in the Cauldron of Art*, which expounds on this in detail. It is an overview of the lost core teachings, which also shed light on Orphic and other Mysteries, all the way back to the ancient Egyptians. In part two, I trace the history of each letter in relevant alphabets, in part to show the surprising continuity in interpretation of sounds of speech over vast distances and times. Then in part three I attempt to classify all Semitic roots used in the Old Testament letter by letter, based on facets of that letter detailed earlier, with occasional asides as to how a letter affects the meaning when second or third (most are three-letter roots), though this rarely reveals itself clearly, to me anyway.

It is important to understand that this study of roots is speculative, my categorization of the meanings merely a possible—or probable, I would argue—way of looking at things but in no way the last word. In fact I feel as if I have barely scratched the surface of what there is to be ferreted out. I am no trained linguist (my ability to memorize vocabulary is too lumbering), just a poet fascinated with Hebrew's structure and rich clusters of like meanings in roots starting with the same letter. I am certainly no rabbi—I am not even Jewish. Yet hopefully I have unearthed enough of substance here to deepen understanding and stimulate further study. *My* goal is to not have to repeat the whole process in my next life but start out in youth knowing what I now know.

G.K.Spain
16 February 2023

Part One:

Uncovering the Original Kabbalah

1

The Four Wheels

Invitation

Step outside
For the spirit of the day calls!

The sun conspires
To haul us out of caverns
And carry us away on wings of song!

It was the spring of 1972 when I, a young hippy with a serious interest in metaphysical matters, stumbled across *The White Goddess*, by Robert Graves.[6] In it, he expostulates on the Irish tree-alphabet and its ramifications, including evidence linking it to other ancient cultures and religions. I had already, by that time, studied what survives of Kabbalah enough to know that an important key was missing: assignment of simple letters to the zodiac signs in the *Sefer Yetzirah*, based on their order in the alef-beyt, showed obvious 'tampering' in that the shapes did not fit the parts of the body the signs ostensibly represent; nor was there a phonetic pattern to it.

The Irish tree-alphabet offered a way out of this quandary. Still, it took about a dozen years for me to be sure I had the correlation between alphabets (Irish and Hebrew) correct—not that I spent all those dozen years in study, but I did return to the subject often. With persistence, I was finally satisfied I had it right. But before I expound on that, let me broach the subject of the *Ofanim*.

The first chapter of Ezekiel is held to be the basis of what preceded Kabbalah and formed its conceptual basis: the *Ma'aseh Merkavah*, or Work of the Chariot. Many have speculated as to what Ezekiel's great vision was about, and no-one (that I know of) has come even close to the truth. But the explanation is actually not very complicated, however obscure it has become, the key being: each ". . . as it were a Wheel within a Wheel."

Each is said to have faces of ox, lion, eagle, and man, symbols of what astrology calls the *fixed* signs (taurus-leo-scorpio-aquarius), thus identifying all four Wheels as zodiacs. The first of these Wheels or *Ofanim* is centered atop the ideal Form of standing Upright Sentience, called (in Kabbalah) Adam Qadmon: 'primordial' Adam. This, the divine Form, is both the Ideal towards which every unit of existence strives (the Unmoved Mover) *and* the (normal?) state from which we humans fell. Saying this implies that 'Darwinian evolution'—which was a serious theory, as opposed to a blatant absurdity like the 'big bang'—is incorrect, a conclusion necessitated by the fact that it predicted gradual change over the aeons, whereas the fossil record shows long periods of stasis punctuated by sudden sweeping change. Evidence of sentience (in the form of perfectly machined metal spheres) goes back to the *pre-Jurassic*.[7] This first Wheel is, for us, the Monad, the *omnipresent*, the *all-encompassing*.

The second of the Wheels is also centered atop the head, but in this case of *seated* Adam, of a human being seated (cross-legged) on the ground to meditate. This forms our link *to* the divine, in that when we are seated in meditation the divine Form takes Its seat so to speak *with* us, thus identifying this second Wheel as the Throne world. What this wheel represents is our immediate surroundings: from horizon before, to where we sit, to horizon behind(within). The sky, above us, is unmanifested; whatever is seen *in* that sky also shows us only its bottom half. This Wheel's bottom half thus forms the magic Cauldron of Celtic lore, the motif of its bringing warriors back to life (in the story of Branwen in the *Mabinogian*) simply pointing to the fact that all who die eventually reincarnate on this selfsame earth, their being mute once revived implying the delay in being reborn, meaning we cannot actually converse with them (perhaps implying the 'muteness' of infancy as well). And its seven manifested signs, cancer through capricorn, are the stations of what *Sefer Yetzirah* calls the double letters (the stops). They also must represent the seven *palaces* or *hekhalot*, but I am no expert on that branch of the literature.

The third Wheel is centered at the heart of the human being—or, figuratively, atop the head of the infant in one's lap—and represents the zodiac of the human form, *up* being towards head aries, *down* towards loins libra, *out* towards cancer the breasts, back towards capricorn the mid-spine. This is the Wheel to which *Sefer Yetzirah* assigns the twelve simple letters. Since it sits in the Cauldron like an egg in a nest, it is obviously the World Egg of the Orphic Mysteries; I shall simply call it the Egg.

Finally, the fourth Wheel—each is *half* the height of the preceding Wheel—represents or is centered upon the womb, our doorway into physical existence. It is that world Kabbalah calls *Olam Asiah*, the World of Action, meaning the physical world: when the aries or head of the child in the womb has rotated from pointing up to pointing down, it is ready to be born. The other three Wheels are (in ascending order) the world of *Yetzirah* or Formation; of *Beri'ah* or Creation; and of *Atzilut*, Nearness (to the divine Form) or Emanation, meaning the Sefirot: this first Wheel is where the ten Sefirot originate, though they echo throughout the other three as well, as expressed by the numbered cards (so-called *pips*) of the Tarot of Marseilles.

Let me expound for a moment on this last. Scholars will tell you that the tarot began in northern Italy in the late 1400s, but they are mistaken: the various Italian cities could not even agree on the *order* or *ranking* of the trumps, whereas north of the Alps there was no question of their order being anything other than that of the Tarot of Marseilles. In fact, in online discussion of the subject (at the website Eclectic Tarot) we concluded its trumps probably did not at first have their ranking or numbering, or even titles, printed on them, so familiar must the ranking have been to those who used them. Moreover, there are extremely important details in certain trumps that are not found in *any* other version of 'tarot'. It was undoubtedly the original; the only reason no examples of it survive from the 1400s is that, being the block-printed standard deck, old decks were merely discarded and replaced. Indeed the earliest examples of the Italian cards—as opposed to the set of paintings similar to them that are taken by some scholars as the original yet cannot have been—were found discarded in wells and cisterns. I dare say there is much more archeological activity in northern Italy than in Provence, which explains the finds.

It was in twelfth-century Provence-Languedoc that the Kabbalah itself originally sprang up; this could only have been from the intersection of schools of Jewish esoteric learning (what had survived of *Ma'aseh Merkavah*) and the 'matter of Britain', that is, Celtic bardic lore riding on the back of the Arthurian cycle, which hit the Continent at that time. The Troubadours were particularly taken with the story of Tristan, and Arthurian romance in general was fueled at first by patrons with ties to the region (a daughter of Eleanor of Aquitaine, for example). The process back then of piecing Kabbalah together from the damage done *Ma'aseh Merkavah* by too much secrecy would have been similar to what I have used (minus the chemistry and particle physics) following in their exalted footsteps.

The Tarot of Marseilles embodies the entire world-view of the Kabbalah, albeit not from a Jewish perspective but rather from a Christian Gnostic perspective. For that was the character of the original Celtic Church: it sought to *preserve*, rather than *expunge*, the ancient knowledge druids revered, simply reinterpreting it according to the new dispensation (the knowledge of the Triune Self). Its pip cards represent the reverberation of the ten Sefirot through the four worlds: Clubs or Batons, *Atzilut*; Swords, *Beri'ah*; Cups, *Yetzirah*; and Money (Coins), *Asiah*. Another way of referring to these are: light world, life world, form world, physical world. Court cards (three male, one female) represent the reverberations of the Great Name (יהוה) through the four worlds. The twenty-two trumps represent the twenty-two letters. To assign the letters to trumps using modern methods—in alef-beyt order, starting either with The Fool or I The Mountebank (Magician)—leads nowhere. Occultists' satisfaction with their two *very* different methods of correlation illustrates how uncritical their analysis must be. But once letters' bardic numbers are supplied—five of them secret yet easily ferreted out—the fit is seamless and quite edifying. Still we should give the Hermetic camp credit for recognizing early on the close fit between tarot and Kabbalah.

Another error on the part of some occultists (e.g. Aleister Crowley) was to change courts to include an equal number of males and females, ending up with something unworthy to even be called *tarot* (though Crowley's deck is quite good as *art*). Interpreting the Tarot of Marseilles as a direct expression of British bards' understanding of the Gnostic paradigm (a close parallel to the Judaic) implies over two centuries from the Albigensian Crusade to tarot's first appearance (block printing only reached Europe after Mongols brought it west). That this Gnostic 'heresy' survived such a long interval in the face of the Inquisition (originally formed to exterminate the Cathars) is impressive in itself. But let us leave this for now and return to the subject at hand.

If the simples make a circuit of the third Wheel, and doubles form the manifested half of the second Wheel (an obvious conclusion), what of the three mothers? They bind the Wheels together. Just as the third Wheel contains the fourth in its bottom half, symbol of the dark world of the womb—or of the present instant, also dark—each of the first *three* Wheels has at least one other Wheel in its 'belly': these are the three mothers. We will get to assignment of letters to them in a moment, but first let me expound a bit more on the tree-alphabet.

The order of tree-letters about the round (which form a calendar) is, starting at the winter solstice: B-L-N-F-S-H-D-T-C-M-G-P-R, the penultimate letter being replaced by Ng in ogham. Two letters have duplicates in ogham, S and K (which I prefer to C, which is never soft in Irish): Ss (or St), and Kk or Q. Graves points out that if inscribed on a dolmen (a line from the oldest poem in Gaelic being "Who but I know the secrets of the unhewn dolmen"), the two doubled consonants form the corners, thus: B-L-N-F-S, Ss-H-D-T-K, Kk-M-G-Ng-R (commas indicate the corners). Thus he reasoned if the threshold is the vowels, A-O-U-E-I in seasonal order, then both A and I would also need to be doubled, even though no record survives to prove it (other than the alef-beyt itself, as we shall see). With these two added, the number of letters is the same as the alef-beyt. And however far-fetched one may think his hypothesis, it is confirmed beyond doubt by the coherence and deep ramifications, scientific and otherwise, of what results.

The numbers bards assigned the letters are expressed in *Barddas*[8] (showing the tradition to have been extant in Britain as well as Ireland) by arraying them in *numerical* order thus: A-E-I-O-B-M-P-F-C-G-T-D-N-L-R-S. In addition, Graves says H was assigned 'no value',[9] which identifies it as The Fool. Given the hypothesis above (doubled A and I), this leaves five whose numbers were kept secret. But it is not hard to remedy this: A and I are 1 and 3, so Aa and Ii would be first and third *from the end* (21 and 19); K is 9, so Kk is 18; the opening sequence of vowels implies that U has been displaced from its more natural fifth position, so we place it fifth from the end, 17; which leaves 20 for Ss. (The argument is a little more involved than this, but I state it thus for simplicity's sake.) The corresponding tarot trumps confirm this.

Applying this numbering to their Hebrew equivalents in their restored order (see below) unveils an awesome landscape of hidden knowledge and understanding—insights such as that potassium-chloride marshals the fluids *inside* cells, sodium-chloride the fluids *outside* cells; that sodium directly affects the heart (blood pressure); that calcium in the blood is controlled from the throat (parathyroids); that oxygen is the only atom-type without which there is no *up*; and so on (by atomic number). An even deeper result is clear indication of the four particle types of modern physics (minus the smokescreen of hopelessly flawed quark theory), which occupy the zodiac's four cardinal signs, thereb marking *spin* by height-off-the-ground and average *charge* by horizontal spread. But I jump ahead of myself.

My conclusion after a dozen years of contemplating all this was that the order of simples about the round is, starting at aries the head: samekh-tzaddi-cheyt-vav-ayin-qof-teyt-heh-zayin-yod-lamedh-nun. I shall explain how I arrived at this in a moment. The order of doubles across the seven signs of the Cauldron (cancer through capricorn) follows the calendar order of tree-letters, minus R, the thirteenth month, which thus does not at first glance occupy a sign but gets relegated to the center of the Wheel for the nonce: D-T-K-M-G-P-B. It can be seen from this last that some original phonetic order (as opposed to chaos) spawned this, and indeed, as you are about to see, phonetic order (as opposed to chaos) also spawned the sequence of simples. But first let me point out that the above order of doubles can only be an altered version of an original order with B and P up on the *lip* of the Cauldron—seen here as the mouth—G, K, and (Hebrew) guttural R down in the *gullet* (bottom three signs), and D and T in between, just as the sounds are placed in the mouth. This requires that D and P trade places and R, which we relegated to the center, 'fall' (back) into the bottom sign (libra) once M or mem assumes its proper position as one of the three mothers. Or more precisely, if R can be enticed to resume its original position in the gullet—as opposed to being rolled out on the tip of the tongue, as in Spanish or Arabic—it *frees up* mem to be *just* mother letter mem and not have to fulfill two roles (not that it has any trouble doing so). We have yet to account for reversal of D and P (to position P at the lip or rim) and to show which Wheel each mother letter represents. But first, the simples.

The tricky part of identifying which tree-letter corresponds to which Hebrew letter is to identify the seven bardic vowels. While the alef-beyt is ostensibly twenty-two *consonants*, from its adoption by the Greeks we can identify *some* of the vowels: A, O, U, E are alef (alpha), ayin (omicron), vav (upsilon), heh (epsilon), while iota (yod) must be either I or Ii. It turns out to be the latter, since Ii is mistletoe, rooted in a tree, and yod in square-Hebrew hovers above the line on which one writes. The reason Greek *eta* does not figure as a bardic vowel is that the western Greek heta became our H. And omega plays a different and deeper role, one that will become clear as we discuss the Logos (yes, it is an actual word). Remaining to be assigned are I and Aa.

The first of these is *fairly* easy, but only because we have the Germanic runes to go by: the Elder Futhark has both I and Ii, the latter like our I (a vertical stroke) and named 'ice', thus picturing an icicle (which also 'hovers' in the air); the former still bears the name 'yew' (like tree-letter I) and is shaped as zeta (our Z) would be if carved across the grain of wood (that is, avoiding horizontal strokes), namely ⌡. And indeed Greek zeta is the initial of Zeus (genitive Dios) and thus represents corruption of *d* by *i*—the Indo-European root being **dieus* (Sanskrit *dyaus*). So evidently zeta represents a hardened bardic I, just as the letter *j* does in English.

This leaves Aa and nothing but irreducible consonants to match it to, but it turns out that Aa is a consonant in *all* other alphabets: it is Hebrew teyt, Greek theta, rune **dagaz*, 'day', and so on. And even if I were wrong in this, the upshot (where my logic places it) is confirmed by a passage in the book *Bahir* (see below). We must treat teyt or Aa as a vowel for two purposes: one, to determine what sign it stands for in the zodiac; two, to understand its deeper significance as one of the seven breaths. Graves took Aa to be omega; there may be a connection, but it is not quite that simple. (Omega does relate to the water triad, the one pointing down, which *manifests* in libra or manifested earth, where teyt is.)

Assignment of simples to signs starts with those already so placed by the tree-calendar. Taking tzaddi as Ss—since shin is S, zayin is bardic I, and samekh is xi in Greek, ñ in Lycian, and corresponds to *ogam consaine* Ng, whose place (after G) is taken by P in the *bethluisnion* tree-alphabet—we place tzaddi at S's month, which contains the sign (point) taurus. Lamedh and nun are L and N and thus occupy aquarius and pisces. And cheyt, being H, occupies gemini. Of the five signs on the upper half, this leaves only aries the head to be assigned, which ends up being samekh, whose square-Hebrew shape is that of the head. The sounds of these five signs are arranged as if on the tongue, with voiced sounds behind, unvoiced sounds before, namely *l-n-s-tz-kh*, or in the tree-calendar, L-N-F-Ss-H: out to—*beyond* in the case of F—tongue's tip *voiced*, then back *unvoiced* (F can be voiced or unvoiced, and south Semitic has both a voiced *and* unvoiced samekh).

The version that includes F is an ancient heresy, one 'corrected' by the orthodoxy of the alef-beyt, which no doubt reasoned that F was *beyond* the tongue's tip, not *on* it. Oddly enough, samekh's equivalent in the Celtic sequence was Ng; for the form of samekh in old Hebrew is the same as letter Ng in *ogam consaine*, the fifteen-letter consonants-only version of ogham used in early bronze age Scandinavia. The same shape in the Lycian alphabet of southern Anatolia has the phonetic value *ñ*. When Ng is replaced by P in the bethluisnion tree-alphabet, that alphabet ends up with no Ng and *two* peh-equivalents, F and P. Of these, F was the stand-in for samekh, on the zodiac of the seated torso—at aries, the hub of the Cauldron—while P itself remained out on its rim, with the rest of the doubles.

The seven vowel-equivalents array themselves naturally across the bottom half of the Egg from cancer to capricorn, starting with U and progressing in phonetic order, each doubled vowel following what it doubles: U-O-A-Aa-E-I-Ii. Taking the Egg as the interior of the mouth, U or "oo", farthest forward, is where the front of the mouth constricts; I or "ee", farthest back, where the back of the mouth constricts; and A or "ah", in the middle where the round is at its tallest, is where the mouth is most open. This arrangement places summer's vowel U at summer solstice; autumn's vowel E at mid-autumn (scorpio); winter's vowel I at the sign immediately after that (sagittary)—winter having begun at Samhain (Halloween)—and mistletoe at winter solstice (our Yule). Spring's vowel O *cannot* occupy any sign of spring, because they are not *in* the bottom half, where vowels are stationed: this turns out to be one of the most vital keys to the underlying meaning; but its elucidation must wait yet a bit. Also note how the use of mistletoe in the Æneid to gain entry into the Otherworld (Hades) reinforces its placement here at the conclusion of the manifested half, the entrance into the unmanifested.

It can be seen that the original phonetic logic had *continuous* (continuable) sounds—L-N-F-Ss-H (Hebrew *l-n-s-tz-kh*) plus vowels—on the continuous round, and stops (rolled R being a repeated stop) on the *dis*continuous half-round (Cauldron). But when A, as alef, retreats from its place on the round to act as one of the three mothers, its place in the array of vowels is taken by Q or qof, which, being doubled K, would naturally occupy K's month, at virgo. Evidently A's replacement by Q at virgo causes Aa also to change into a consonant: the Fall and its advent of mortality caused qof's interruption of continuity at virgo, representing the womb and rebirth, and thus also by teyt at libra (span of earthly life): libra, straight down, represents physical existence, changed by *mortality* into a stop.

A key passage in the *Bahir* confirms this placement of teyt in no uncertain terms (p. 31, §84): "But R. Rahumai said that the belly is like the letter Tet. ¶ He said that it is like a Tet on the inside, while I say that it is like a Mem on the outside." For M, *muin* the vine, is the tree-month at libra, straight down—figuratively 'the belly'—and the round that teyt is the libra of is *inside* that on which mem occurs. It also means that while placement of teyt there was a closely held secret, obscured by the jumbling of the order of twelve simples in the formation of the alef-beyt, mem's placement there is 'outside', that is, revealed in *Sefer Yetzirah*, which places mem at the belly and shin at the head, one of the *things in common* between Celtic and Judaic traditions.

As I studied the roots from the Davidson *Lexicon*, I noticed at one point that it was not easy to tell the difference between teyt and mem. After some thought, I realized why: both take the form of one's legs folded beneath one when seated on the ground. They are subtly different however: mem (מ) shows them as they might be if one were just squatting there temporarily to exchange a few words; teyt (ט) shows them in half or full lotus, as in one meditating. This is because M is temporarily standing in for reysh, whereas this is teyt's proper station. The only letter in Arabic whose shape is at all useful for our purposes is this same teyt: it's shape shows the legs folded beneath one as seen from the side (ﻂ).

So the original order of twelve simples, given above, is explained. The *jumbling* of this order followed a specific logic, which I will explain in due course. For now, let us turn to the three mothers.

Sefer Yetzirah identifies alef with the torso bridging the gap between shin and mem (head and 'belly'), and sure enough its natural place in the tree-calendar, as *ailm* ("alev") the silver fir, is winter solstice (our 'Christmas tree'): this is even with the center of the third Wheel, the Egg, which it represents. The letter shin, near the head—and indeed letter-order in ogham was shifted to put S *at*, rather than *near*, aries the head (B-L-F-S-N as opposed to B-L-N-F-S)—is the center of the Cauldron-circle or Throne world (second Wheel), which it represents. What is mem, then, doing down there at Cauldron's libra if by process of elimination it should mark the center of the *first* Wheel?

There are two forms of mem. Intermediate mem (מ), which from another perspective (the side) shows a bowing supplicant, is the M of the calendar, at libra. But its final form, mem sofit (ם), whose shape is like that of the box in which the Ark of the Covenant was kept, stands for the first Wheel, at whose hub it resides. This places it atop the head of Adam Qadmon: the Jewish custom of strapping *tefillin* to the top of the head is to remind us of this. And since the Monad is omnipresent (M being the sound of the closed mouth as a whole), when R decides (for reasons we shall explore below) to desert its proper station at the gullet (as guttural R) to become the R rolled on tongue's tip—calendar R, up at the level of the winter solstice—it leaves a void that is *automatically* filled by omnipresent M, thus necessitating mem's two distinct forms. Both (you will note) are on the central vertical axis, so mem is not pushed off balance by this.

Mem sofit represents the first Wheel, being its hub. Shin, shaped like a crown perched atop the head of seated Adam, represents the second Wheel. And alef, perched at the heart—the center of the torso—stands for the third Wheel, the zodiac of the human form. What might these three signify, then, that lifts them above the other letters of the alef-beyt to the status of mothers?

Consider the Tibetan mantra OM or AUM: this latter spelling can be traced across the globe in various forms. In Masonic ritual, there are the ruffians Jubel*a*, Jubel*o*, and Jubel*um*. In the Egyptian hieroglyphic alphabet (yes, they had one), only three single-sound hieroglyphs had the form of birds (though bird signs are otherwise common): ' (equivalent to alef), the eagle-like *Egyptian vulture*; *w*, the *quail chick*; and *m*, the *owl*. And in the Huna tradition of Hawaii,[10] the High Self (of three distinct selves, High, Middle, and Low) is called Aumakua: as Au-makua it means 'utterly trustworthy parental pair';[11] but as Aum-akua—an analytical shift intrinsic to the structure of the Hawaiian language[12]—it translates as 'AUM-being' or 'AUM-god'.

Then there is the Chinese term *miaou*, which means something like 'mystical', origin of the term *myo* in the mantra 'nam myo-ho renge kyo'. This last (with *m* shifted from last to first) points to the proper pronunciation of the Logos by humans, which is as if spelled IAUM, initial I standing for the upright body in which one dwells. (I would suggest it is omission of this initial I that caused the Tibetan Buddhists to become dispossessed of their 'body' or homeland, Tibet.) I describe the proper pronunciation like this: smile; intone this and it comes out as a sort of nasal "ee" (vowel I); continue on through the whole vowel spectrum ("ee-ah-oh-oom") in a smooth gradation till the mouth closes on the final M. Pronounced with a nasal tone, it reveals a sort of *phase shift* from high to low, from cycles of brief duration to those of longer duration, and in this resides part of its power as a word, or rather *the* Word (the Logos).

What it stands for is the three parts of a Triune Self: the doer, A, united with its thinker, properly Ω (omega), and knower, M (mem sofit), in an upright body, I. It must be fairly obvious that the Monad (as Unmoved Mover) represents the eternal, the purview of the knower; that the Cauldron represents one's field of thought, things of finite duration (immediate surroundings); and that the zodiac of the human form represents that through which the doer acts (in the present instant) to *create* the things of finite duration (namely thoughts). And of course the fourth Wheel or womb represents how we enter the physical world itself. This fourth Wheel must correspond to the I of the extended Logos for us humans.

When the Intelligence (by whose Light the conscious self thinks) utters the Logos, this initial I is replaced by BR: this form has left its residue in the term Brahm (presumably from an original BRAOM). For the Trimurti, Brahma-Vishnu-Shiva, evolved (according to Harold W. Percival,[13] of whom more later) from an original Brahm*a*-Vishn*u*-Brah*m*. My own speculation as to what the initial BR signifies is not particularly relevant to this study. What is relevant is the relationship of the Hindu Trimurti to what the Logos stands for. Brahma the Creator corresponds to the doer itself: this would explain why there is so little worship of him, since he is *us*. Vishnu the preserver corresponds to the thinker, that part of self that deals with things of finite duration; and Shiva the Destroyer to the knower, since the eternal outlives the destruction of *anything* of finite duration. If that last seems tenuous, this correspondence is made clear by the dynamics of Indian alchemy: followers of Vishnu seek *longevity*; but followers of Shiva seek *immortality*.[14]

The Logos was more or less intact in ancient Egyptian hieroglyphics (vowels expressed as near-equivalent consonants). But when the Hebrew alef-beyt was formed, the middle term, Ω or omega (Egyptian *w*), was evidently replaced by shin, meaning that the secret of the Logos was *shushed*. This has its parallel in that aspect of Gnosticism wherein the Holy Spirit, feminized as Sophia or Wisdom, is also spoken of as *Prunikos*, Whore—the *lesser* Sophia—to distinguish the quality of thinking in man from that of Adam Qadmon I guess; for in man the thinker, although not affected by the Fall, still must maintain the thoughts created by its estranged doer, who seeks its guidance from *sensation* rather than from its higher self. Appropriately enough, *miniscule* omega (ω) in Greek is shaped much like the hieratic form of Egyptian *w* (a rounded *w*, like two breasts dangling in front of us). The general consensus is that omega was a late addition to the Greek alphabet, which after all also contains S (Sh), the letter that replaced it in Semitic. Yet miniscule omega's likeness to hieratic *w* confirms the opinion of Martin Bernal that in its *shape* it was an archaic holdover.[15]

Let us take a moment to look at what comes to light once the bardic numbering of letters is applied to them as we have them arranged. Samekh has taken the place of bardic F, which was numbered *eight*, the atomic number of oxygen: indeed the trump so numbered, VIII Justice, has her head prominently outlined in radiant yellow. So, even if the bards and the designers of tarot were themselves ignorant of the fact, the system of knowledge the letters embody is consistent with the undisputable fact that *eight* or oxygen is the one atom-type without which there *is* no up. The next simple, tzaddi, is *straif* the blackthorn, numbered *twenty*: this is the atomic number of calcium, whose concentration in the blood is controlled from taurus the throat (tzaddi's station) by the parathyroid glands surrounding the thyroid (which also has a role related to calcium).

The horizontal diameter of the Egg—the Egg here representing the individual cell—links potassium (19) at capricorn (Ii or yod) to chlorine (17) at cancer (U or vav): potassium-chloride is the salt that marshals the fluids *within* the cell. And the extension of that diameter out onto the Cauldron—out into the intercellular fluid—links chlorine at cancer to sodium (11) at the leo of the Cauldron (T or tav), sodium-chloride (common salt) being the salt that marshals the fluids outside the cell. By careful analysis of what organs the seven doubles stand for, it is apparent that D (at its original station) and T are at the level of the thoracic cavity (airy level), the active, conscious focus there being the lungs, the passive or subconscious focus there being the heart (active or voiced meaning behind, passive or unvoiced meaning ahead). Thus sodium (11) is the letter symbolizing the heart, tav, to whose health sodium intake is linked (it tends to raise blood pressure).

The atom-type with the largest nucleus (of the twenty-one atom-types represented by the numbered trumps or tree-letters) is, predictably, at the bottom: teyt, as Aa, is first from the end, *twenty-one*, identifying it as the first 'rare earth' metal, scandium. Rare earth metals are so rare they are often (as in the case of scandium) named for where they are actually found. Just so, the direction straight down—libra the scales (our weight)—represents one's *physical location*.

The most interesting number pattern to me is the one I call the *fundamental polarity*. For *straight down* from the two poles of the horizontal diameter, potassium and chlorine—yod and vav, the letters that begin the two halves of the Name—are (respectively) *ten* and *nine*, neon and fluorine, the latter's interaction with hydrogen in trying to *emulate* neon (i.e. seeking to complete its neon 'shell') being the strongest chemical reaction known. And these two numbers have a very interesting polarity. To understand it, first one must know a little something about number itself, and about valence.

Number has an infinitely repeating intrinsic pattern to it, as revealed by digital sums: in reducing a number to a single digit by summing its digits (however many times that is necessary) an added *nine* acts as zero, leaving digital sums unchanged; *eight* acts as a minus-one, reducing sums by *one*; *seven* acts as minus-two; *six* as minus-three; *five* as minus-four. This projects onto the entirety of number (so to speak, there being no limit to it) the repeated pattern of +1, +2, +3, +4, -4, -3, -2, -1, ±0, +1, +2, and so on. It turns out valence *also* consists mainly of the values +1, +2, +3, ±4, -3, -2, -1, ±0, the ±0 representing an inert gas, the other numbers how many more or less electrons than the nearest stable shell form its 'atmosphere'. The only difference is that in the case of valence, +4 and -4 reside in the same atom-type, which is what allows carbon, ±4, to easily join with others of its kind to form the carbon chains on which all organic matter is based. More on this later.

What interests us here is that 10 and 9 (let me use numerals to make things simple) form a perfect polarity, albeit one where the two poles cannot interact directly with each other. For 10 (G), straight down from *yod*, is numerically +1 but of 0 valence (inert, being neon), whereas 9 (K), straight down from *vav*, is numerically 0 but of –1 valence (i.e. it lacks a single electron to complete its neon shell). So they are plus-one versus minus-one, but existing in two disparate worlds: that of mathematics, and that of physical reality (each is zero in the other's realm). But if you go straight up from them to yod and vav, 19 and 17, these are +1 and –1 respectively in *both* realms; hence they are the surrogates for G and K that *can* interact, forming (as we saw) the salt potassium chloride to thus keep enough fluids inside the cell to permit life. Pretty amazing. And these are the initials of the two halves of the Name.

The bardic numbers of the twelve simples are in the order: 8—20—0—17—4—18—21—2—3—19—14—13. At first this seemed a hodgepodge, yet you have seen a measure of its consistency with physical reality, and we have barely scratched the surface. The sequence of numbers applied to the seven doubles, or rather the seven tree-months (with M at libra)—is by contrast *quite* coherent. It is 12—11—9—6—10—7—5. The sequence of differences runs 1-2-3-4-3-2. Complete the sequence with the only other letter *on* the Cauldron-circle, mem sofit at its apex, and it runs 12—11—9—6—10—7—5—6, the differences 1—2—3—4—3—2—1, exactly the same as valence. More important, it identifies the Cauldron's four *levels*—cancer-capricorn, leo-sagittary, virgo-scorpio, and libra—as elements fire-air-water-earth. This identity between the only four numbers there are (in a sense) and the elements is confirmed by geometry: it takes *two* points to determine a line, *three* not on a line to determine an angle or plane figure, *four* not on one plane to determine a solid surface. Since solid surfaces represent earth and the natural order is fire-air-water-earth, it is clear that points correspond to fire, lines to air, angles to water (form), and solid surfaces to earth. This is why Euclid called his geometry tome *Elements*.

Indeed the slope of the Cauldron at cancer is vertical or active—like fire—that at libra horizontal or passive—like earth—while at leo it is more-active-than-passive—like air—and at virgo more-passive-than-active—like water. These slopes are mirrored on the active or voiced side. Taking cancer of the Cauldron as the horizon before us, we identify it as the limit of *sight*, the fiery sense. The sign leo thereon is a descent from that, meaning what approaches within (easy) earshot, limit of *hearing*, the airy sense (primarily, though sound travels through water even better, but that is not where our ears normally *are*). Sign virgo, being further descent from *that*, represents what is gathered within reach, to be *tasted*. Sign libra, then, where we touch the earth, corresponds to the earthy sense, *touch*, but also to that same sense of surface contact on a molecular scale, which is *smell*. There are in fact only *four* senses, smell being the most focused aspect of what otherwise manifests as touch (surface contact).

Now we come to the real crux of these matters: the Grail. Taking the Cauldron as we have defined it, its two rims or lips—originally P and B—are the horizon before and the horizon behind. But what *is* the horizon behind? If one turns to look at it, it is no longer behind us but before us (that is, in the direction we are looking). Even using a mirror, what is seen is on the mirror itself (the proof being to let your breathing fog it up) and thus before us. So the horizon before represents the direction *towards other*, meaning it is the *outer* horizon, the limit of *physical* sight, whereas *straight back* from it is *back towards self*, the limit of *inner* sight.

Thus what to a druid may have seemed to represent active and passive sides of the four elements—a Cauldron of nature magic—to British Gnostic followers of Ambrosius Avrelianus—which must have mutated into Amrelianus from Welsh confusion of Latin V with M, and from that to Merlinus—the Cauldron of seven doubles was definitely something more profound: it was the Grail, which is 'seen' only when the horizon behind is recognized as the horizon within and thus *not of this world* (so to speak).

The three signs after libra on the Cauldron correspond to the three parts of the self: the doer, or what does the reaching when something is 'within reach'; thinker, or what stands behind speech; and knower, or what registers to *inner* sight, what is seen *within*. More accurately, they represent the thinker's differentiation of these three parts in its atmosphere, the Throne world. The three corresponding signs of the Monad (the knower's atmosphere) mark the three parts themselves: capricorn is on a level with the center of the Monad; sagittary is on a level with the center of the Throne world; and scorpio is linked by its *radius* to sagittary of the Throne world, which is on a level with the center of the doer's atmosphere (the Egg). Perhaps the indirectness of this last helps explain the doer's more precarious state.

The doer has an active aspect, desire, and a passive aspect, feeling, ultimately represented by signs scorpio and virgo of the Monad; these same signs on the Cauldron, G, 10, and K, 9, are the fundamental polarity mentioned earlier and represent the thinker's desire and feeling *minds*, thinking's ability to distinguish them being their ability to think—*of* the thinker, yet constituting, along with body-mind R (libra), the three minds the doer has use of. In us humans, the desire and feeling minds are enslaved by the body-mind (the senses), as pictured vividly in R's trump, XV The Devil, who looks suspiciously like that 'little devil' that keeps new parents awake all night with its demands. And well it should, as 15 is the atomic number of phosphorus, the key atom-type in chromosomes: DNA is a series of nucleotides, a nucleotide being "the phosphate derivative of a nucleoside."[16] Indeed its Hebrew shape (ר) shows the erect male organ and the duct conveying seed to it. It is the seat of the body-mind because it is the source of new bodies. (Needless to say the counterpart of the gonads would constitute reysh in the female.)

Desire, the doer's active side, is concerned with trying to shape the immediate (or not-so-immediate) future; feeling, its passive side, is concerned with trying to interpret what has just (or not-so-just) happened. In humans, the doer is off balance, so desire dominates for about a half-dozen lifetimes (I gather), then feeling dominates for a half-dozen or so, and so on. When desire is stronger, the body is male; when feeling is in the ascendancy, it is female; both are present in each, merely out of balance. Desire's concern, the near future, is still within, towards self, while feeling's concern, the recent past, has already happened and is thus *without*, already a part of our external surroundings. So a male is more concerned with what is still within, a female with what is by now without. Again, neither is exclusive, it is merely a leaning one way or the other.

Desire fully expressed is power. Feeling fully expressed is beauty. Thus what the male seeks in the female is beauty, and what the female seeks in the male is power. Plato's triplicity Truth, Goodness, and Beauty refer to the passive sides of knower, thinker, and doer respectively, the thinker's passive side being what registers right and wrong in its doer, namely conscience.

The reason for the shift of D and P should now be apparent: if D originated in sagittary or thought—what leads to self-knowledge, capricorn—then its swing over to the outer horizon must mean thinking hypnotized by the senses into desiring objects of nature. The Cauldron's outer half shows the course of such a thought as it builds itself into concreteness, starting at the outer rim and finally arriving at libra, the present. The remaining three signs show our reaction to it: scorpio, the doer's experience of it; sagittary, thought, meaning learning from experience; and capricorn, self-knowledge, meaning knowledge from learning.

These three are on the microcosmic side—within—the four elements on the macrocosmic side—without. Hence of the two hexads (groups of six signs), the one with four layers is the macrocosmic one, the one with three layers the microcosmic one: this is because the former is based on the vertical axis, which extends forever in both directions; the latter on the horizontal axis, which earth's curvature renders no longer horizontal in either direction, rendering it without real extent. The letter occupying the one sign of the self that is on the macrocosmic *hexad*, D, is the one that moves over to the macrocosmic *side* of things and trades places with P.

Now consider the layout of the Elder Futhark, the earliest sequence of Germanic runes:

<u>ᚠ</u>	ᚢ	ᚦ	ᚨ	<u>ᚱ</u>	ᚲ	ᚷ	ᚹ
<u>ᚺ</u>	ᚾ	ᛁ	ᛃ	<u>ᛇ</u>	ᛈ	ᛉ	ᛊ
<u>ᛏ</u>	ᛒ	ᛖ	ᛗ	<u>ᛚ</u>	ᛜ	ᛞ	ᛟ

I underlined every fourth rune (starting with the first), since they indicate the six signs of the macrocosmic hexad: ᚠ and ᚱ are F aries and R libra, R's original station before its delusions of grandeur, marking the vertical axis; ᚺ and ᛇ, H gemini and I sagittary, mark the second axis of the macrocosmic hexad; and ᛏ and ᛚ, T leo and L aquarius, mark its third axis. The early Chi Rho symbol of Christianity consisted of these three axes plus a loop identifying the vertical as rho, and indeed here R is used to identify the vertical axis—strong hint runes originated with Gnostics, not pagans (Gnostics would have preferred the Chi Rho to the cross symbol).

The three mothers are enlarged in bold: ᚠ and ᛗ are A (alef) and M (mem), for doer and knower—scorpio and capricorn are on the *micro*cosmic hexad, so these two are placed just *four* places out from the start of their respective *ætt*s or groups of eight—while ᛋ is S (shin), standing for the thinker—sagittary is on the *macro*cosmic hexad, so it is placed *eight* out from the start of its *ætt* (at the end). The last axis-marking rune *before* ᛋ is ᛁ, the Egg's sagittary. The runes that mark the axes jump back and forth between Egg and Cauldron, but the pattern is clear.

Interwoven with (reinforcing) this pattern are two carefully placed sequences whose Hebrew/Greek numbers foretell the following runes' bardic numbers. Rune ᛋ, mother letter shin, marks off the whole length of the second *ætt*, in the middle of which is the sequence ᛁᛄᛁᛢ or Ii-G-I-P: listing bardic numbers first, 19-10, 10-3, 3-7, and 7-80. And rune ᛗ, mother letter mem, marks off the first half of the third *ætt*, in the middle of which appears the sequence ᛒᛗ or B-E: 5-2 and 2-5. Note that both sequences involve the three-sign span of self, the first ending with sagittary twice, the second omitting it. The mothers are in the order of the Logos, the two that have these sequences being those of thinker and knower, which did not undergo the Fall (why Gilgamesh is twice said to be two-thirds divine and one-third mortal[17]).

I find the above pattern to be quite interesting, considering runes are usually considered pagan in origin. Of course the Gnostic viewpoint is as foreign to standard Christianity as is the pagan; plus, Gnostics tolerate the gods and their lore—for its knowledge—while refraining from their worship; but nor do they worship the Cross and what it stands for (the Great Scapegoat), like Christians. To a Gnostic, the cross symbolizes the body, and the crucifixion symbolizes the doer's imprisonment *in* it. (The tradition in the Middle Ages was that Christ *perfected* the body.)

2

The Two Columns

Invocation

Children of Adam, climb to where the demons
Jump in abrupt obedience to gleemen
    Who sing in the night.

Gods of Olympus, shiver in my wake
And I will show you where whole worlds do quake
    For fear of your might.

The god Phanes of Orphic cosmogony, born of the Word Egg, is described as female in front and male behind.[18] Just so, in the human, there is a front column, broken off at the sternum so that a womb may become enlarged, the female column; and a back column, the spine or male column (though both are present in both). In Masonry the twin doorposts of Solomon's temple, Boaz and Jachin, stand for these two columns: Masonic ritual shows a woman weeping next to a broken pillar.[19] The tradition of these columns is so pervasive that the Gnostics who devised the Elder Futhark kept only two tree-names when transcribing the bardic alphabet for German use, the two representing these two columns: their initials B, *bairkana-*, 'birch twig', and the bardic I, *eihwaz*, 'yew tree'.

Indeed these columns are traditionally seen as being to north and south as one looked out the east door of the Temple. Just so, B and I are the first and last letters in both ogham and the tree-alphabet and thus face each other over winter solstice, capricorn (east or rising quarter): B to the left; I to the right. Thus the tradition of these two pillars appears bound up directly with the tradition of the tree-calendar. (Since the majority of us live in the northern hemisphere, up or aries means north, down, libra, means south; capricorn, where the round rises, means east, and cancer, where it descends, west.)

If we take each sign's month as the arc leading on from it (as implied in *Sefer Yetzirah*) and divide the Egg into columns by vertical lines connecting signs, three out of the six columns thus delineated—half, far more than Chance would dictate—have floor and ceiling of matching valence. The two columns within that have matching valence are the innermost and outermost. The innermost has zayin, I—3—as floor, *idho* the yew itself; and yod, Ii—19—as ceiling, both

+1 in valence. The outermost has teyt, Aa—21—as floor and nun—13—as ceiling, both +3 in valence, this ceiling swept by the Cauldron's radius as it approaches beyt the birch—5—also +3 in valence.

The reason this iteration of Jachin-Boaz finds *both* on the male or inner side is that Jachin is still intact (and on its proper side) while Boaz, the female column's once intact form (they being *twin* doorposts), is no longer expressed on its own female side but only in potentia as it were, as the male column or spine *in* the female. This in part is why it takes two, a man and a woman, to invoke the Great Name יהוה, which stands for the original Adam Qadmon type and Its *two-columned* divine creative power, which in us has fallen to the loins to become *pro*creative. That the sexes were preceded by an undivided (sexless) type is deducible from the simple fact that *one* comes before *two* (being what *two* counts).

Think about it: if the front column was originally intact, then Adam Qadmon must not have needed—or need, assuming some have even now attained to that Ideal—replacement of Its body. This means that type was (is) immortal—divine—and only changed into a mortal type at the Fall. The two-columned nature of the human form and the implications of a once intact front column refute the whole Darwinian paradigm if you ask me, had the fossil record not done so.

I the yew is numbered 3 and B the birch 5, numbers associated with Saturn and Mars, respectively, in the Christian Kabbalah of the Rennaissance, which had the planetary cycles of the Tree of Coins (fourth Wheel) figured correctly. In astrology the signs *ruled* by Saturn and Mars occur just after the round has progressed through their respective columns: Saturn rules capricorn and aquarius, arcs approaching which are the Saturn column's floor and ceiling, zayin and yod; Mars rules scorpio and aries, arcs approaching which are the Mars column's floor and ceiling, teyt and nun.

In fact *seven* pillars of wisdom, the six described above plus the vertical diameter itself, are linked to numbers 3-4-5-6-7-8-9, starting within and working out, and to the planetary metals Saturn (lead), Jupiter (tin), Mars (iron), the year (carbon, *not* a metal), Venus (copper), Mercury (quicksilver), and Luna (silver). All the signs but leo are ruled by the column the round has just passed through to get there; leo is a special case (explained below).

Every column is identified, and the method is quite subtle; for it alternates between the valence of the column's *number* and the valence of the column's *metal*. The I and B columns are identified by the valence of their numbers, 3 and 5. The column in between is identified by the valence of its metal tin, ±4: its roof (aquarius) is L the rowan or 14, in the same column of the periodic table (as originally displayed) as tin, while its floor, inert gas helium, is swept by the Cauldron radius departing libra, M the vine or 6, also ±4, in the second half of its swing.

On the passive or nature side, taking P and R at their original stations cancer and libra of the Cauldron, the radius as it departs the one and approaches the other sweeps the roof and floor of the Venus column, P and R being 7 and 15, both the -3 valence of the column's number, 7. The next column has matching valence in roof and floor: tzaddi, *straif* the blackthorn or 20, and ayin, *onn* the furze or 4, both +2 valence, that of its metal, quicksilver. The outermost column on the passive or nature side, then, has vav, *ura* the heather or 17, as floor, roof and floor both swept by the Cauldron-radius as it approaches K or 9 itself, both being 9's -1 valence.

In expressing valence-by-height (part of the core of all this), the three inert gases are all within one arc of libra, zero height, to reflect ±0 valence—whose height could not be expressed for *three* inert gases by positioning them *at* libra because only two letters are stationed there at a time, one on Egg and one on Cauldron (mem itself is not *stationed* there). As we shall see, our model effectively expresses all valence heights, taking alef's (hydrogen's) ±1 at Egg's hub as the unit measure.

So how does Sol rule leo? In order to explain this, I must first explain alchemy's Greene Lyon, which is what sets up the situation. It is how *onn* the furze, spring's vowel, rules spring. The mercury column, the middle column without, is marked by the valence of the metal mercury, the columns to each side of it by that of their numbers. Yet Mercury's number, 8, is associated directly with the roof of the Venus column, samekh or 8, and that of the Luna column, cheyt, 8 in *Hebrew* (being no-number by bardic reckoning).

The floor of the mercury column, leo, is the hottest month of the year. And what happens to mercury when heated? It flies up into the air as poisonous vapor, requiring that the alchemical vessel be hermetically sealed.

What this means is that when mercury's column is heated at leo, its vapors fly up into the upper half of the outer vessel, taking over the upper halves of the adjacent columns as well as its own. Indeed an Æsop's Fable references this very thing, The Lion and Three Bulls: lion cannot kill three bulls because together they are too strong, so he sows dissent amongst them and after they have each gone their separate ways kills them one by one. As taurus the bull forms the roof of mercury's column, its vapor capturing the upper halves of the two adjacent columns multiplies this into three bulls, all now the roof of mercury's column, rooted in leo the lion.

Since O's takeover of the upper half of the outer vessel also symbolizes spring's filling out trees' foliage, this must be the meaning of alchemy's much touted 'Greene Lyon', sought by Newton and others.[20] By flying up into the signs of spring, *onn* the furze, vowel of spring, takes possession of it, being the *warmth* that draws spring out from under the blanket of winter. And it shows the intimate interplay between bardic lore and alchemy going back who knows how far— and by *bardic lore* I mean the tradition common to inventors of several alphabets in antiquity, not just Celtic, that to include of course the Semitic.

By growing to include all of spring, mercury's column attains its valence height of +2 at aries, where the two -2s are already perched: samekh's oxygen (8) and shin's sulfur (16). The remaining +2, dalet's magnesium (12), is the Cauldron's outer rim (on a level with aries), the Cauldron-radius in departing which sweeps the first two months of spring, reinforcing spring's identification with mercury (whose valence D shares) and the mercurial. But it is also key to note that the two forms of peh in the *bethluisnion* are P, 7, which by its radius-sweep marks 7's roof, and F, 8, which converts that roof into vapors of mercury; the latter role is transferred to the Hebrew simple letter samekh.

Sefer Yetzirah correlates (albeit in jumbled fashion) the seven doubles with the seven planets, which seems to be true symbolically even though the actual place of the planets in the

Kabbalistic world-view (as embodied in Tarot of Marseilles) is the Tree of Coins, where the suit symbol shows it is the Tree of planetary *cycles*. It must be understood that the sun, associated in modern Kabbalah (at least by occultists) with the number 6, the year, is more properly assigned the number 2, the Great Year or precession of the equinoxes. For the Great Year is actually the relationship *between* ecliptic (6, the year) and equator (10, the day). Proof of this is astrology's stipulations of which signs planets are 'exalted' in: those corresponding to the male-female pairs on the Tree of Sefirot as usually displayed—2-3, 4-5, and 7-8—are exalted opposite each other, taking 2 as the sun: sun and Saturn in aries and libra (gold up, lead down); Jupiter and Mars in cancer and capricorn, where waxing and waning year (respectively) end (Graves associates these planets with waxing and waning year); Venus and Mercury in pisces and virgo. This will surely raise the question in the reader as to how Venus managed to be a male Sefirah in that Tree while Mars managed to be a female one: I look forward to answering this, but it should wait till we get to the subject of the Sefirot.

In correlating planets with doubles, T bears the number 11, the only double with digital sum 2: it occupies a key position, being the central trump, the fulcrum or pivot halfway between 1 and 21. A *very* interesting artifact of this will surface in the context of the Sefirot, but for now all I want to do is explain how Sol rules leo.

The takeover of the outer vessel's upper half reduces the height of the Venus and Luna columns to half the round, ±1 valence, which happens to be that of their metals copper and silver (-1) and of Sol's gold as well. This squeezes Luna out of the vessel's upper half (as in the dark of the moon). What ensues is what alchemists characterize as *hierosgamos*: the sacred marriage of sun and moon, of king and queen.

Tav, height of and nearest point on the Cauldron to, Egg's cancer—to which it is linked by common salt or sodium chloride, the Hebrew feminine plural ending (ות)—comes charging in as Sol to reclaim Luna's upper half for her by the sweep of his radius, being the valence of the *metals* silver and gold. It is the same radius sweep that originally claimed the whole column for the *number* 9 (kaf) but this time claiming it for the valence of its *metals*. And Luna, grateful to be restored to her upper half, cedes her lower half to tav. It is Luna who brings to the union the realm they jointly rule: symbolically, he rules the lower half—the land—she the upper half—the heavens. Just so, the line from the archaic Greek hymn Graves reconstructs from Boibel Loth letter-names (connected with ogham) has for *ura* the heather (at cancer)—whose Boibel Loth name also happens to be *ura*—Urania, Queen of Heaven; and *tinne* the holly represents the holly king who rules the waning year (bottom half of the round) and as it turns out corresponds to *SY's* depth *below* (as we shall see).

A further link between bardic lore and alchemy can be seen in the colors associated with the first three letters of the Logos, using U, *ura* the heather, in place of omega. Poets associated the color black with the death or winter vowel I, the color white with the birth or Yule vowel A (birth of the year), and the color red with the vowel U of summer and the consummation of love. The three main stages of the Great Work are Nigredo or blackening, Albedo or whitening, and Rubedo or reddening. Often there is a yellow stage between white and red, which would be the yellow-flowered furze or gorse O (as in the term *miaou*). Moreover this link between alchemy and bardic tradition is embodied in a divine name common to Gnosticism and Orphism: IAΩ, an epithet of Dionysus.

The trumps all reference their atom-types. For instance, P is 7, which is nitrogen—four-fifths of the air—and peh, whose shape is that of the open mouth and tongue, is the active end of the airy level (of speech and thought): VII The Chariot is the only trump showing someone with wind in his face (from the Chariot's forward motion). Chlorine, XVII The Star, shows a naked woman pouring some in her pool. Neon is X The Wheel of Fortune. Oxygen's VIII Justice has a pair of scales, representing the uprightness or balance possible only with oxygen's presence. Carbon's VI The Lover (*not* LovERS) expresses carbon's ability to bond with others of its kind to form the chains and rings on which all organic matter is based. Boron's V The Pope evokes the fact that its chief ore is borax, a cleansing agent (like the pontiff). Beryllium's trump IIII The Emperor wears a beryl on his chest. Helium's II La Papesse (The Female Pope) pretty much *has* to be a Pope whose voice was made higher by having imbibed some helium. I could go on (the above are some of the more obvious ones).

Now that some of the chemistry has been elucidated, let us move on to the elementary particles. Around the year I was born (1950), science had confirmed the four elements, though no physicist would have dared admit this publicly. For 'science' had spent two centuries pooh-poohing the whole *idea* of the four elements. Nature, however, disagreed. There is the photon, or quantum of light: alchemical fire. Then there is the electron, which forms the atmospheres of atoms and molecules and is classified as a lepton (along with the elusive neutrino): alchemical air. Then there are the nucleons (proton and neutron), which form the mass of the nucleus and are classed as baryons: alchemical earth. Finally, around the time I was born, the pi meson was discovered, quantum of the strong nuclear force binding nucleons together (against repulsion of like charges): its mass had been more or less predicted by the range of that force coupled with the Heisenberg uncertainty principle. The pi meson is cohesion or form: alchemical water.

Physics was embarrassed to have stumbled on proof of what they had been belittling, so they scrambled to find a way to cover up the fact, and quark theory was born. The problem is that they did not think things through logically; for 'quarks' do not behave as particles but rather as articulations *within* particles; they were originally called *partons*, which is what they are. And since no quark can ever be extracted from the particle of which it is a part or parton, physics has had to postulate a force that *cannot be overcome by a greater force*, one that is *not attenuated by distance*: the force of 'quark confinement' (aka *color* confinement). To a *sane* physicist, this cannot be a real force. Seeing them as partons of course abrogates necessity for such a force, as they are held together by what one might call local (as opposed to global) interconnectedness—perhaps something as simple as mean separation.

Anyway, we need not be concerned, for this model of reality we are investigating lays out very clearly the more sophisticated view of those who devised it; and this is how it reveals itself. The horizontal line extending from samekh at aries to dalet at the Cauldron's outer rim suggests a line of sight; for magnesium (D or 12) burns with highly actinic (chemically active) light, used in signal lamps to cut through dense fog. By *burns*, one means rapid oxidation, oxygen, 8, being the other end of that horizontal. And what does combustion result in? Photons. The photon is *spin one* and electrically neutral, so its suggested station at aries marks the height of one round (*spin one*) and is in the middle (electrically neutral). One unit of spin is thus in two-to-one ratio to a unit of valence (±1 alef).

Scandium, at libra (opposite aries), has the largest nucleus of the twenty-one atom-types and therefore stands for that which makes such a nucleus possible: the pi meson or quantum of the strong nuclear force binding the nucleons together. Physicists speak of this force as *residual* because they are obsessed with their magic force that binds 'quarks' together, presumed quanta of which they call *gluons*. But we can dismiss this as so much hooey. The pi meson is *spin zero* and on average neutral, as it comes in all three varieties, positive, negative, and neutral. Hence it is at libra, height zero (spin), and in the middle (electrically neutral on average).

These two 'particle' types are both *bosons*, quanta of force. Bosons much prefer to group together in the same energy state—what makes lasers possible.

The actual particles of *matter* are *spin one-half*, so we expect to find them halfway up the round, even with the center. And sure enough, the horizontal diameter connects an atom-type with one extra electron (over its argon shell)—potassium (19), at capricorn—to one with one too few (short of its argon shell)—chlorine (17), at cancer. The latter mimics the proton in that it too is short one electron; that is, its 'positive' charge attracts the complementary 'negative' charge of the electron. Therefore placing the lepton (which includes electrons and neutrinos) at capricorn, 'negative' on average, and the baryon (which includes protons and neutrons) at cancer, 'positive' on average, completes the model, the two *spin one-half* particle-types of matter, called *fermions*, off to each side to express their opposite average charge, at the height of half a round. For the behavior of fermions is opposite of that of bosons: each insists on its own unique energy state (in any system of which it is part), which it refuses to share; this is known as the Pauli exclusion principle. The term *hadron*, under which physicists group both the meson—a boson—and the baryon—a fermion—thus makes no sense at all, bosons and fermions being opposite in behavior.

The above scheme aligns elements with their proper cardinal signs, as specified in the *Zohar*: fire (the photon) is up or aries, up being north on average for man; water (the meson) is down or libra, down being south on average for man; air (the lepton) is at capricorn, to the right or east when looking north (towards aries); and earth (the baryon) is at cancer, to the left or west when looking north. The only adjustment we must make in our thinking is to note that the terms *positive* and *negative*, correct from a modern perspective, are actually backwards, in that modern 'direction of current' is opposite that in which the electrons are actually traveling. Our Hermetic model did *not* get it wrong however; for the electron or lepton pole is marked by the plus-one valence (and number) of potassium, the proton or baryon pole by the minus-one valence (and number) of chlorine. There need be no confusion, as the terminology is distinct; but the reader should be aware that our model, in addition to alerting us to ignore quark theory actually corrects modern physics in something as basic as *direction of current*. It is too late to correct generally accepted terminology, but not too late to correct our way of thinking about it.

There are actually three different ways to apply the four elements to the four quarters, *all three* of which figure in the reordering of the twelve simples into alef-beyt order. There is the primordial one above, confirmed by the *Zohar*, which we thus associate with the knower. Then there is that of astrology, where air through earth are rotated to the next triad (excluding fire): earth and its senses usurp control of the triad of air or thought (east), air's thought pushed down by this into the triad of water and emotions (south), and water's emotions dragged to the realm of earth and the senses (west). This method of assigning elements relates to the thinker, responsible for seeing to it one's destiny intermeshes with the destinies of other humans. Finally, there is the method of ceremonial or seasonal magic, elements assigned directions by the poetic affinity of annual and diurnal seasons: fire-summer-south-day; earth-winter-north-night; air-spring-east-morning; and water-autumn-west-evening. This last arrangement we associate with the doer, as it is brought about by the Fall: fire—divine creative force—has fallen from the head to the loins, where it has become the *pro*creative power in humans.

The jumbling of the order of the twelve simples in the alef-beyt expresses this in a quite orderly manner. The round was divided into *upper inner*, *upper outer*, and *below*. This closely echoes how Georges Dumézil's school of anthropology specified the *tripartite* division of proto-Indo-European mythology and class-structure[21] into priests or spiritual power, our *upper inner;* warriors or secular power, our *upper outer;* and commoners (artisans, farmers, laborers), our *below*, this last both economic and chthonic, representing fertility and prosperity. Just so, B at upper right (inner horizon) is trump V The Pope, the birch, used in switches to expel evil spirits; D at upper left (outer horizon) is oak, XII The Hanged Man, representing secular power; and body-mind R below, at libra, is XV The Devil, who at present controls desire, G, X The Wheel of Fortune, as well as feeling, K, VIIII The Hermit. The mothers also show this: mem sofit, the knower, is the tefillin strapped to one's head; shin, the thinker, is a crown; and alef the ox or doer raises ground water up from below for irrigation (chthonic).

In jumbling the order of the twelve simples, the four letters of the upper inner quadrant, capricorn through aries, were all moved back one on their original triads; the four letters of the upper outer quadrant, aries through cancer, were each moved to the triad their element occupies in astrology. And the *five* of the bottom half, from leo to sagittary—the first three associated with their *manifested* element, not triad—were each moved to the triad their element occupies in the seasonal magic, there being five in honor of the 'five' senses: earth is moved twice, once for touch and once for smell. Thus teyt at libra, *manifested* earth, carries earth as touch—surface contact—to the north, leo; heh at scorpio, on earth's *triad*, carries earth as *smell*—surface contact at molecular level—to the north at aries. I will let readers map out the rest for themselves.

Having thus rearranged the simples, alef-beyt order is really quite straightforward. First comes A, the doer or creative beginning of the Word. Then come the three doubles that occupy the same signs on the Cauldron as the three letters of the Name do on the Egg. Then starting at dalet's height come the six signs on the nature side of the Egg. These leave off at virgo, so there follows the virgo of the Cauldron, kaf. Then comes libra by itself, followed by the libra of the Cauldron (in the tree-calendar), mem. Then come the three signs of the conscious self: scorpio through capricorn, followed by the double closest to Egg's capricorn (the Cauldron's capricorn having already been used), peh, its sign sagittary being the middle sign of the self. Then come the last two signs, doubled consonants Ss and Kk (tzaddi and qof), the two doubled vowels (teyt and yod) having been the last two of the first sequence of six simples (the nature side). Then comes reysh, which means 'head' or 'beginning', here at its usurped position of command (top of Egg), but at the end, not beginning. It is crowned there by our lesser Sophia, shin a crown— one's destiny being based on one's thoughts (the Buddha's Wondrous Law)—and judged (by the greater Sophia) through the agency of tav or conscience: one's mark or word.

Thus *duty* has the final say: the quality of one's oath. And I think in giving conscience the last word the sages were trying to say what I as Gnostic have long said: if a god or religion ordered you to act in a way abhorrent to your conscience, which would you follow?

I think it time I explained the seven breaths. The sign that expresses breath or activity is cancer, manifested fire; for it points towards *other*, breath meaning interaction with other. The *movable* zodiac of a unit of nature must have its aries—representing where it is currently tuned, so to speak—pointed towards the sign of the manifested element it is in. Thus a fire unit, with the aries of its movable zodiac pointed at cancer or fire, would have its cancer or breath pointing to libra or teyt: the fire breath. An air unit, with its aries pointed at leo or air, has its cancer or breath pointed at scorpio or heh: the air breath. A water unit, with its aries pointed at virgo or water, has its cancer or breath pointed at sagittary or zayin: the water breath. And an earth unit, with its aries pointed at libra or earth, has its cancer or breath pointed at capricorn or yod: the earth breath. No inconsistency here: teyt is the palm or phoenix, first-from-the-end (21), born in fire; heh is aspen, 2 or air, whose leaves are fluttered by the slightest breeze; zayin is yew, 3 or water, linked to death; yod is mistletoe, third-from-the-end (19), which is obviously 'taking a breather' from earth in that it does not touch it. Note that these four nature breaths climb up the spine from libra, representing the taking over of the spine, originally for use of the Triune Self, by nature (elemental breaths) and the senses. Thus of the twelve functions assigned (in jumbled order) to the simples by *Sefer Yetzirah*, seeing, hearing, tasting, and smelling can confidently be assigned to teyt through yod.

But there are also the three inner breaths, those of doer, thinker, and knower. Since the doer is estranged from its thinker and knower, we only have access to those parts of the mental and noetic breaths that are in the doer's psychic atmosphere (the Egg). So while the doer's own psychic breath would be its letter of the Logos, alef, the breaths of thinker and knower must act on the passive or receptive side of the mental and noetic levels *of the Egg*, which means that ayin (O) is the mental breath (the "oh" of discovery) and vav (U, "oo") the noetic breath. And this is utterly logical if you consider that bardic O represents spring's youth, when still learning, while bardic U represents summer, love's consummation, our coming of age, thus showing the origin of the term *to know* in a biblical or carnal sense. Just so, the thinker contacts us (through lungs and heart) during youth's learning phase, the knower (through pineal and pituitary) at puberty.[22]

3

Ten Sefirot

O To Be Caught

O to be caught
       eye to eye with
          child,
See through its eyes,
       vision through them,
          feel
Something of what
       innocence makes
          reel
Whisked onto the
       guardian-spirit
          wheel.

It is time we moved on to the subject of the Sefirot. They are described in their purest form in the *Bahir*, which presents them as they are in Atzilut, the Monad, which unites things. In contrast, *Sefer Yetzirah*, though it has the name of the third world in its title, has them grouped as five pairs of opposites, the Sefirot in Beri'ah, the Throne world (second Wheel). The commonly shown Tree, Sefirot as the *Zohar* treats of them—three triads plus a tenth—deals with Sefirot of the third or form world, Yetzirah, the Egg, atmosphere of the fallen doer; this is why it involves talk of *tikkun* or 'restoration'. The fourth Tree is closely bound up with the third (with all three, really) and consists of the ten visible steps from the eternal to the fleeting present: stars' energy, which is conserved; the Great Year (Sol); Saturn; Jupiter; Mars; year (ecliptic); Venus; Mercury; month (Luna); and day, today (equator).

To thirteenth-century Kabbalists, the Sefirot represented "stages in the manifestation of the personal, individual identity of God."[23] The first Sefirah is equated with nothingness—*Ayin*, or alef-yod-nun—and "through the process of emanation 'Nothingness changes into I' (*Ayin le-Ani*)"[24]—'I' being *Ani*, alef-nun-yod, thereby transposing the yod and nun of *Ayin*. "God reaches His complete individuation through His manifestation in *Malkhut* [Kingdom, the *tenth* Sefirah in the Tree of common lore], where He is called 'I'."[25] *Tenth*, called *Keneset Yisrael*, 'community of Israel'—perfectible man—is the home of the *Shekhinah*, the divine Immanence or Presence in us. For tenth means straight back (tenth sign), the direction of responsibility: self-knowledge.

Another early doctrine was that there are thirteen *middot* or divine attributes. Thus it is apparent the Sefirot are the first ten of twelve stations on the round, the thirteenth *middah* being the return to the beginning, completing the round. In other words, the goal is to return to the start and thereby *become* the round thus traversed.

So in origin, Sefirot are the Monad's first ten signs, starting at the exalted, the direction *up*, and progressing all the way to *straight back towards self*. In the first Tree, this 'I' or self is that of the *divine Form*, Adam Qadmon, hence the model for *all* sentient beings (the state from which we fell).

The *Bahir* describes the original Sefirot with great clarity. First comes Supreme Crown. Second is Wisdom, since setting forth about the round—the origin of motion itself—entails the wisdom to return, plus motion is what requires wisdom's guidance. Third is the Storehouse of Wisdom, meaning space itself—the direction out and a bit up (what is above the horizon)—the storehouse in which motion is 'stored' or occurs. Next comes the most obvious one: fourth, the direction *towards other*, the *Bahir* labels Lovingkindness, the attitude Uprightness *has* towards other. Fifth is the Great Fire, both because it completes the first side of the fire triad (being its first manifested sign) and because it is the departure or veering-away-from from Lovingkindness: it is the origin of Severity. Sixth is called the divine Throne, for the simple reason that it is the *approach to straight down* (descent of the divine). Seventh is the Holy Palace, for it *is* straight down, pointing towards the body in which one dwells. Eighth is called Foundation: it is eighth here, rather than ninth as in common lore, because in Adam Qadmon the *doer* acts as the self's foundation; the *Bahir* links this Sefirah to circumcision being on the eighth day; this is because scorpio, one's privates, are the eighth sign. Ninth and tenth are both named Netzach, meaning Victory or Endurance; for they are thinker and knower, who have not undergone the Fall.

Moving on to the second Tree, *Sefer Yetzirah* identifies Sefirot (in order) as: depth of the first, depth of the last; depth of good, depth of evil; depth above, depth below; depth east, depth west; depth south, and depth north. We can identify this series of polarities as between the two hexads: one based on the vertical axis, and the other on the horizontal axis. The former extends upwards and downwards indefinitely, while the latter does not extend out ahead or behind really at all before the curvature of the earth renders it *no longer horizontal*. So the hexad based on the vertical axis is macrocosmic, that based on the horizontal axis microcosmic. The six signs of the macrocosmic hexad are where radii of the manifested signs of the next larger Wheel, the Monad, intersect the Throne world, the first world to *have* a 'next larger Wheel'.

The first Sefirah, or depth of the first, is the aries of the Throne world, at the center of the Monad. The second advances out into the Throne world, world of finite durations and thus the depth of the last. The third is the last Sefirah still above the limits of the Egg of the fallen doer: the depth of good. The fourth marks the upper limit of the Egg itself: the depth of evil, meaning repercussions of the Fall.

Next come the six directions of space; for the arcs leading to the fifth through tenth signs constitute the Cauldron of surroundings. Sign leo is the first *manifested* sign of the triad pointing towards the sky (macrocosmic)—the depth above—and virgo the *approach* to down or towards earth (us, the microcosmic)—the depth below. The next two begin at virgo and end at scorpio, on the triads of east and west respectively: the depth of east is where heavenly bodies rise up into the sky (macrocosmic), the depth of west where they sink back into memory (microcosmic). And the depths of south and north are thinker and knower, the first associated with the U (V) of the Logos and the triad pointing south, the second with mem sofit, which is as north as you can get. The depth of south is towards the ecliptic, where the planets are (macrocosmic); north is towards the pole, towards less people, thus representing the individual self (microcosm) at capricorn (self-knowledge).

The last six, the directions of space, are assigned (in varying ways in varying versions) to the seven doubles (to include the point of intersection of axes). It took me until very recently (as I am rather slow and have blind spots) to grasp *not only* how to assign doubles to extremities but also the fact that the method of doing so confirms *once and for all* that we are indeed concerned here with the Sefirot of the Throne world. Absent R (not always at its proper post libra anyway), the remaining doubles occur (in the calendar) along the bottom half of the Throne world (signs of the Cauldron) in the order D-T, K-G, P-B. It could not be clearer (despite my tardy grasp of it): D-T are up-down; K-G east-west; P-B south-north; and R is where the three axes intersect.

D is Zeus, the sky god: oak. T, the much shorter holly, is the sun or heart: us. K, hazel, precedes this body seated upright, as does morning. G, ivy, follows it, as does evening. P the whitten, from whose dried berries ink is made, represents the gregarious south; peh pictures a mouth speaking. B the birch, a cleansing of or complete withdrawal from other, represents the more solitary north. These last, the ink-maker's tree and the white-barked birch, also represent the darker and lighter complexions found towards or away from the equator. As I have often remarked, all that skin pigment really measures is *latitude of ancestry*.

Now let us turn to the third and fourth Trees and in the process examine how planetary cycles in the fourth Tree mesh with the structure of the commonly seen third Tree, the Sefirot of the Egg or suit of Cups. First, consider what the commonly seen pattern actually means.

A single sexless Sefirah at the top: Keter, Crown. This represents the original type: Adam Qadmon. Then there is the first male-female pair: Chokmah, Wisdom, and Binah, Understanding. These two represent division into a desire body and feeling body, the test of balance: does desire-and-feeling still perceive itself as one doer or are 'they' deceived by the senses into believing 'themselves' two distinct beings. One can look at it psychologically and think of these two as innocent (chaste) male and female modes of thought, as in young children, and the first Sefirah as the Uprightness present in both.

Then, following the quasi-Sefirah Da'at or Knowledge (whose origin I will explain in a moment), there is a second male-female pair, this time producing offspring: Chesed, Kindness, and Gevurah, Strength or Severity, together giving birth to Tiferet, Beauty. These represent a change into male and female types that have intercourse to procreate, plus their (agreed upon) issue. Or, the male and female modes of thought that seek offspring and what issues from them.

Then there is a third male-female pair, followed by their *divided* issue: Netzach, Victory or Endurance, and Hod, Splendor, from which issue Yesod, Foundation, and Malkut, Kingdom. These represent a further change of type, into male and female types that have intercourse out of *lust*, that is, in pursuit of pleasurable sensation. Inevitably they do not completely agree on issue: 9 months of gestation (Yesod), or what can be grasped by 10 fingers (Malkut). Or, the four can be taken to represent lustful male and female modes of thought and what issues from them.

This last couple represents *us*, here on this fourth 'earth', that of lust. The third 'earth' is that inhabited by those who have intercourse to procreate (replace aging bodies). In the second 'earth', they do not actually *have* intercourse. And the first 'earth' is that of undivided Adam Qadmon.

This is like the tetraktys: one, then two, then three, then four. Or, since the knower is still fully present in the first two earths, the thinker perhaps yet present in the third, but the doer pretty much on its own (from its point of view) in the fourth, this gives rise to the teaching that associates the highest aspect of self, *neshamah* (our knower?), with the first *triad*, this to include Da'at (Knowledge); the middle aspect, *ruach* (our thinker?), with the second triad; the lowest aspect, *nefesh* (our doer?), with the third triad. The last Sefirah, then, must be symbolic of the body itself, of what can be touched by ten fingers, namely one ten-fingered (being).

The holiness of the tenth Sefirah, associated as it is with the Shekhinah, arises from our capacity to *control* what our ten fingers grasp.

There are three tetrads of signs on the round. Cardinal signs are neither male nor female, like Adam Qadmon. Then there is the tetrad or cross that leans forward, the male tetrad; and the tetrad that leans back, the female tetrad. Objection to this based on a suspicion of sexism would have to ignore the normal state of affairs between the sexes; its appropriateness, if you ask me, is obvious. Astrology got this all wrong: it labeled the two *hexads* (groups of six signs) male and female, which does not account for the *third* option, the sexless. The three *tetrads* astrology has labeled *cardinal*, *fixed*, and *mutable*. Indeed one might see a bit of sexism in *this* terminology: calling the male 'fixed'—ouch!—and the female 'mutable'?

Given the three tetrads in the order cardinal-male-female, we can now explain how this third Tree came to have its form. The first three Sefirot align with their proper tetrads (second male, third female), but from the fourth on they do not. This is because in the manifested half of the Egg (4 through 9) they are affected by time and decay, causing them to drift along the arcs leading *on from* them to the next sign: now they align with their 'proper' tetrads. But since 4 was dragged by time to the fifth sign leo, which is male, it leaves the fourth sign cancer unused: this is Da'at, Knowledge, as proved by the fact that it is occupied by vav or bardic U, the noetic breath in the doer.

What Da'at represents is what results if that first male-female pair are *not* misled by the senses into thinking themselves two distinct beings: they reunite in a single body, made of the four elements. This gives rise to a kind of Tree you may have seen in some books on Kabbalah where the neutral Sefirot are 1—4—7—10 (instead of 1—6—9—10).

On the other hand, if they are misled by the senses, they still must sense they should be together, which leads to conjoining sexually. In *us*, vav represents knowing *in the biblical sense*; so perhaps Da'at is that innate sense they should be together, which at the Fall is changed into 6, Tiferet or offspring, 2 and 3 having transformed into 4 and 5.

With regard to this third Tree, we are told there was a 'breaking of the vessels', which is what necessitates the *tikkun* or 'restoration'. It does not affect the first three, only the remaining seven. This teaching points to the fact that the front column is still intact in the first three types, but upon uniting physically to procreate, it is broken to make room for the womb's enlargement.

There is a very interesting phenomenon having to do with this breaking of the vessels. If we take each Sefirah as represented by a pair of trumps—first and last (I and XXI), second and second-to-last (II and XX), and so on, the fulcrum or pivot at T the heart (XI), it turns out that only the first three pairs form, with the fulcrum, coherent sequences: 1-11-21 are one thing, one thing in relation to one ten-fingered, and one thing in relation to two ten-fingereds; 2-11-20 are all numerical +2s; 3-11-19 are all +1 in valence. After that, only 7-15, without 11, share valence.

And it would appear that by the time we reach the last three Sefirot, 8 through 10, the 'reflections' have fallen down one; for they seem to be paired thus: 10-11, 9-12, and 8-13. For 10 and 11 are ivy and holly, paired in the Christmas song 'The Holly and the Ivy'; 9 and 12 are hazel and oak, alone singled out by the east Goths as being immune from felling and at the same time said to dislike one another, unable to agree;[26] and 13 and 8 are ash and alder, from which male and female human beings were fashioned,[27] according to Norse myth. The name of the woman, Embla, is often translated 'elm', but ash and alder make better sense, as ash tends to strangle plants growing in its shade,[28] while alder is beneficial to them (nitrogen-fixing), like a mother, and its wood is softer than ash.

This last might be taken to imply that the ten numbers 1 through 10 apply more to the female, while the eleven numbers 21 through 11 apply more to the male; for the Yule custom is holly *boy* and ivy *girl*. But if so, why is qof, the womb, on the *male* side? and why is that side the side that appears broken (between 19 and 17)? I will leave it to the reader to sort out, if they wish, though I will point out that qof, 18, would be the number *skipped* to produce Da'at. And funnily enough, what the reflection of 4 falls to, vav (17), happens to represent the sign at which Da'at resides. Confusing. Yet Q represents K *before U*, so they are closely connected, as are the breasts and womb they represent, which both become enlarged in pregnancy. I lean towards the side of 1-10 being masculine and 21-11 with its break at 18 being feminine, in which case ivy girl and holly boy are intertwined, as in the harvest dance, and oak and ash (a man) are what the female *seeks*, hazel and alder (a woman) what the male seeks.

Now with regard to the fourth Tree, the order of visible cycles bridging the gap between the eternal and the fleeting present once again are: 1, the eternal (stars, or conserved energy); 2, the Great Year or relation between equator and ecliptic (the sun); 3, Saturn; 4, Jupiter; 5, Mars; 6, the year or ecliptic; 7, Venus; 8, Mercury; 9, the month (moon); and 10, the day or equator (earth). These are the *visible* planets: those *not* apparent to the naked eye have a place in the scheme as well, but one that will have to be deduced, as there is no mention of them in ancient tradition. But first things first.

We can now confront the appropriateness of the fourth Tree's planetary assignments to the third Tree's Sefirot. Obviously Adam Qadmon fits the first one: eternity. Chaste male type as the sun (gold) or Great Year and chaste female type as Saturn suggest Saturn's 'golden age' ("It was a season of everlasting spring," Ovid; ". . . miserable age rested not on them," Hesiod). Then we come to procreating male and female: the father is Jupiter, for rather obvious reasons (just look at all of Zeus's peccadilloes and their resulting offspring), and the mother Mars. This latter is most interesting. For the sages must have connected procreating female with a mother defending her young, which after all constitutes the ultimate Martial ideal in that she *will not yield* (perhaps Leonidas himself was inspired by this). Their offspring being the year suggests fertility of the earth (cycle of vegetation). Indeed Frazer's *The Golden Bough* points often to a connection between agricultural fertility and human copulation.

Now to us. The lustful male type is represented by Venus, who epitomizes what the male lusts after. The lustful female type is represented by Mercury, who epitomizes what the female lusts after: a mover and a shaker, someone with power to transmute, say, poverty into wealth, or obscurity into influence, someone who has an *in* with the gods. Their issue are also appropriate: nine months of gestation, the moon; what can be grasped in the ten fingers, earth.

It is important to understand that the 'harmony' between these last two Trees exists in *counterpoint* to the fourfold structure inherent in physical matter, imposed by the four elements. For the planetary cycles are divided into four *layers*, the limit of each determined by the square of the number associated with its element. Thus 1, the stars, constitutes the fiery or radiant layer; 2-4, the outer planets or 'gas giants', the airy layer; 5-9, the inner planets and moon, the watery or fluid layer; and 10, earth, the earthy or solid layer.

Moreover, now the functions of planets in the body of the macrocosm, as well as of their metals in alchemy, can be deduced from their numbers in our Tree. Since air is more active than passive and water more passive than active, two of the three airy planets must be active and three or more of those in the fluid layer must be passive. The sun, 2, is a receiver of electrical energy from the stars. This is based on EU (electric universe) theory, an outgrowth of plasma physics, which shows the big-bang-centered gravitational cosmology to be obsolete. One of the many indications of this is that what is seen in sunspots reveals what is beneath the sun's outer surface to be *cooler*, not warmer, than the surface, contradicting the thermonuclear model. Sol is the passive aspect of air: it is the starlight or pure energy acting through the sun that acts on moon and earth. This leaves 3 and 4 as the active aspects of the airy layer: 3 must be that aspect of air that acts on water, the third element, 4 that aspect of air that acts on earth, the fourth element.

In the fluid layer we are dealing with reflections (negative numbers): 5, being numerical -4, is water's ability to act on earth; 6, numerical -3, is water's ability to act on itself. Note air did not 'act on itself': this is explained by geometry, where an angle can 'act on' (subdivide) another angle, but a line cannot 'act on' another line, since when lines intersect it is technically the point of intersection, not the line, that subdivides the other line. Switching to water's passive side, we are now governed by valence: 7, -3 valence, is water's ability to be acted on by water; 8, -2 valence, is water's ability to be acted on by air; and 9, -1 valence, is water's ability to be acted on by fire.

Alchemy's stages are characterized as the sequence lead-mercury-silver-gold (i.e. from Saturn's black through silver's white to gold's 'red', meaning *coloration* of the white). This can now be seen to mean we start from the fact that air, the thinker, acts on water, the doer, whether it acknowledges the fact or not; the first step, then, is for water, the doer, to become *receptive* to it! followed by its becoming receptive to fire, the knower, then finally joining itself to air's (the thinker's) *own* receptivity to fire or knowledge, the self now being a fully integrated Triune Self.

It now becomes clear what the three outer planets represent. For fire is a oneness, not yet differentiated into its ability to act on air, on water, and on earth. Only once air or duality 'rears its ugly head' can fire's unified activity divide up into its three 'channels'. Through serendipity (i.e. intervention of Intelligences in human choices), the three outer planets identify *themselves*: Uranus is the channel by which fire acts on air; Neptune the channel by which fire acts on water; Pluto the channel by which fire acts on earth. By the way, these outer planets are distinguished in another way (besides not normally being visible to the naked eye): the central or privileged frame of the solar system revolves in relation to the stars about once every thirty-one years, in relation to which these outer three planets are retrograde, that is, they counterbalance the *angular momentum* of the rest. (One of the main reasons that I reject Einstein's take on relativity is his complete ignoring of the existence of a privileged frame!)

Taking planets as organs of the 'body' of the macrocosm, the sun is the heart, moon the kidneys, and other planets other organs. Those I am reasonably certain of are: Mercury-spleen, Venus-liver, Mars-pancreas, Jupiter-thyroid (its Galilean moons the parathyroids?), and Saturn-thymus—it begins shrinking in adolescence, which links it to childhood and the Golden Age. Since the main asteroid belt is between the orbits of Jupiter and Mars—between active-passive air and passive-active water—it may be the remnants of a planet corresponding to some organ having to do with balance: those remnants are probably the lymph nodes.

It is interesting to note that today's occultists have agreed on one particular pattern of applying letters to the 'paths on the Tree'. In their tradition of paths an interesting phenomenon occurs: the order in which letters feed into the central Sefirah, Tiferet, happens to be gimel-heh-zayin-yod-lamed-nun-samekh-ayin. This pattern indicates that the original order of letters about the round—which this pattern follows for the entire second (inner) half of the Egg—was known to whoever devised this scheme. It also parallels another pattern, the alef-beyt itself, which *also* climbs the inner side of the Egg (via the jumbled order of simples this time) then, once at the top, jumps to leo or tav just as here it jumps to leo on the Egg, ayin. Ayin is even more appropriate as the letter to follow samekh or aries: as the floor of mercury's column, it controls spring with its vapors, which is the top half of the outer Egg immediately *following* aries.

It should be clear by now that the way scholars have rationalized difference in treatment of Sefirot between *Bahir*, *Sefer Yetzirah*, and *Zohar*—the idea that in the first two of these the

Sefirot were listed *out of order*—is simply not the case. I mean no offence, for I realize we are talking about attempts to explain what the inner teachings have not (for centuries) been around to explain: we owe a debt to the scholars who have preserved the teachings now being elucidated, flawed interpretations and all. I know it may be difficult for those in the Jewish community with an interest in esoteric matters to take the word of a *non-Jew* concerning the deepest strata of what Judaism has painstakingly preserved. I only hope such readers might overcome their reluctance and give serious thought to what is set forth herein, the prize being a much deeper understanding of reality itself.

There is one remaining subject concerning the Sefirot that I must now bring up. There is a progression amongst the four Wheels involving the direction back along the radii or spokes towards the center or hub. The radii of the Monad are exclusively outward-pointing, as there is as yet nothing *other* than the Monad to radiate back: this corresponds to fire being purely active. Radii of the Throne world involve the beginnings of a reaction back from other, but the outward-pointing aspect is still dominant: this corresponds to air being more active than passive. The radii of the Egg involve reaction back from other that *overpowers* the outward-pointing aspect, which is still in evidence however: this corresponds to water being more passive than active. And with the radii of the fourth Wheel, this reaction back from other completely eclipses the outward-pointing aspect, which is no longer in evidence: this corresponds to earth being purely passive.

Thus the Sefirot of the *Egg* project back along their radii if it is towards the manifested half. But in the context of its determining the structure of the planetary columns, technically of the fourth Wheel, Sefirot project back along their radii across the round into the unmanifested to mark where the planetary metals' columns start in the inner Egg, the limits of their columns' extent out from the center-post in the outer Egg. This is where the columns of planetary metals in the Egg or vessel originate. The fourth Wheel, representing the unknowable present instant—the physical universe—in relation to the planetary cycles, is dark, like the womb itself (and like space), so whatever pattern is to govern the planets and metals must be *imposed on* it by the third Wheel: form imposing itself on matter.

If Sefirot are our journey from oblivion to self-hood (*ayin* to *ani*), what of the remaining three *middot* and the return to aries? It would seem that the final goal of what is moved by the Unmoved Mover is to return to the top of the round *as* the round, having traversed it and thus *become* it. For right now, we are only at its tenth station. The last three signs (or last two plus first) on the Egg happen to be the three most common atom-types in the earth's crust.

The number of Wheels may be four, but the number of 'clocks' measuring each unit's progress is actually twelve. For consider the *Emerald Tablet*'s 'as above, so below', and 'as below, so above', so familiar to occultists and alchemists (including Isaac Newton, who actually translated it). From this we can deduce that there must be twelve Wheels: above *our* four are four more like them, and below our four *another* four. Percival would call the four *above* ours the spheres of the primordial elements, *our* four the four worlds (light, life, form, and physical), and the four *below* ours the light, life, form, and physical planes of the physical world.

When progression is viewed in relation to these twelve 'clocks', the soul of the body—or *breath-form*, as Percival calls it—can be defined with precision. Imagine setting forth from the aries of the largest Wheel to become distinct from-or-in consciousness (the ultimate reality) as a fire unit at that Wheel's cancer. Once it progresses by gradual refinement (after many aeons) to the libra of that Wheel, it cannot yet cross over to the intelligent side, being a unit of *nature*, so the only course open to it is to climb the central vertical axis and issue forth at the aries of the *next smaller* Wheel (each smaller Wheel a refinement on the one before). The same thing must occur again at *that* Wheel's libra. And this situation continues until it reaches the libra of the smallest Wheel (the physical plane of the physical world), having fully refined its skills as a nature unit. Once there, it climbs the center-post again, but, there no longer being any 'next smaller Wheel' for it to issue forth upon, it gets stuck (for the nonce) *on* that center-post, as the upright bodily form itself, organizing the senses, systems, organs, and other units that constitute it (based on its own experience of having *been* all the various organs and functions), uniting all of them into a single body. [See Rupert Shelldrake's *A New Science of Life: The Hypothesis of Formative Causation* (Los Angeles: J.P. Tarcher, 1981) for a critique of biology's lack of any top-down imposition of form.]

Upon the next shift in the progression of units, once the current Triune Self has achieved a balanced state (the Fall represents *our* initial failure to do so) and then progressed to become the Intelligence by whose Light the *next* conscious self will think, the unit just behind *this* soul on 'Jacob's ladder' will climb the center-post and in *its* turn gets stuck, in the process pushing or forcing its predecessor across to the intelligent side—still that same center-post, but now in relation to *within*, rather than *without*. This unit Percival terms the *aia*: being the same center-post as the soul or subconscious, it *automatically* conveys whatever affects it from the intelligent side—the doer, A—to the soul—the I of the Logos (the center-post itself)—then conveys the soul's reaction back to the intelligent side—the doer, A. The soul and aia overcome *once and for all* the age-old problem of 'Cartesian dualism'. The recognition that the vertical axis of a human being constitutes the border *between* nature and intelligence makes this solution inevitable.

4

The Great Name

Calm Needed

[Trois-par-Huit]

go ye bards
among the sylphs and stars
to transmit the message that spirit

has essence more real than the objects that fear it
suspecting that that is what moves them when near it

the breath quickens from being heated
blandness is defeated
calm needed

It is time we turn to the Name יהוה. There is much that I myself fail to understand about it, but I can certainly take the reader deeper into its meaning than others these days seem to have penetrated. This lack of understanding is evidently a result of the purging of God's consort from the Temple (in the time of the prophets), which must have been a blow to God himself, since the Name cannot be invoked by us humans *without* her involvement.

Of the four letters of the Name, three (yod and the two hehs) are on the male side of the Egg (within) and only one (vav) on the forward or female side. This is why the courts of the Tarot of Marseilles consist each of a King, Queen, Knight, and Knave. And modern attempts to create parity by changing them to king-queen-prince-and-princess (or in Crowley's case, knight-queen-prince-and-princess) render such decks mere art, not tarot. Most decks today do follow the original, though they call the Knave *Page* (the trumps are where they fall hopelessly short).

Yod is King and vav is Queen: each begins its half of the Name. Each member of the courts has its home in one of the suits. There are very clear clues. King and Queen hearken from Clubs and Swords, respectively. Their thrones tell the tale: that of the King of Clubs has one back-post, on our right—Jachin—while that of the Queen of Swords has both—in other words, she brings Boaz to join it. (In the courts, theirs are the only thrones with backs.) There is a fragment preserved by Philo that says the two first inventors of the human race consecrated two pillars, to fire and wind;[29] we shall see below why these pillars correspond to Jachin and Boaz. Moreover, although swords abound in the courts, in the most reliable deck, the Grimaud, hers is the only bright *red* one, in other words, recently used.

The Knight that stands out most is the Knight of Cups: he is the Grail Knight. He holds his great chalice out as if he would make a gift of it. And the only Knave that is at all inspiring is that of Money: he appears prosperous and refined, and in addition to the coin he holds up to his face is another one at his feet—which identifies him as the *second* heh. (The Knave of *Cups* is an obvious *thief!*) Thus each letter of the Name appears to act in its own world, the remaining court cards in each suit being more or less actors filling roles.

Prevailing occult tradition associates letters of the Name with elements in the order fire-water-air-earth, which is in agreement with the suits these four members of the court hail from. Jewish tradition, however, appears to assign letters to worlds in their natural order: I believe this has to do with the radii of the four elements of the Cauldron (cancer through libra) intersecting the Egg at unmanifested fire and water, and manifested air and earth—signs of the macrocosmic hexad. In other words, we ascribe the natural order to the perspective of the Throne world or thinker, the fire-water-air-earth order to that of the doer. But it is the doer—Brahma, Creator—who actually invokes the Name.

Percival says the Name is divided into a male half and a female half, the male half containing the female, the female half containing the male.[30] Since heh's Hebrew number is *five*, we picture it as the hand given in wedlock: the first heh is in the male half of the Name, the presence of the female therein making him her Knight. The second heh is in the female half of the Name, the presence of the male therein making him her Knave. Both hehs represent male roles, but seen from opposite perspectives. I will let the reader work out the further implications of this, saying only that I see poetic truth in it.

As to why Jachin and Boaz should correspond to fire and wind, let us consider what I probably should have explained earlier, namely how desire and feeling, having turned their back on the higher self, must therefore try to fulfill the roles of knower and thinker themselves (since the present instant is dark). This is in fact what determines the physiological significance of the mothers: in humans, desire *poses* as 'knowledge', feeling *poses* as 'thought'.

Desire, whose *seat* is the adrenals (ג, gimel), lives in the blood, as evidenced by the male erection. According to *Sefer Yetzirah*, mem rules over water (being close to the word *mayim*, 'seas'). Traditionally, Torah is likened to water in that it flows from above to below (evidently the Talmud likens intermediate mem to revealed Torah, closed or final mem to Torah's secrets). So mem represents the blood: its intermediate form stands for blood drawn to the sexual organ (being at libra); its final form represents the blood circulating clear to the top of the head when standing.

Feeling, whose seat is the kidneys (כ, kaf), lives in the cerebrospinal nerves. According to *Sefer Yetzirah*, shin rules over fire (אש in Hebrew). *Shin* means 'tooth' and originally pictured a molar, which does suggest the cerebrospinal nerves. Shin crowns the head of the one seated in meditation, one of the purposes of meditation being to *calm* the nerves, another to isolate feeling in the extremities as a *tingling glow* as I like to call it then gradually trace this all the way to the head. The importance of isolating feeling from sensation is one reason kaf is VIIII The Hermit.

This implies that alef, the third mother letter, represents the body-mind as stand-in for the doer: it is the sympathetic nerves. Its meaning, 'ox', and its position at the heart or hub of the Egg confirm this: it is what keeps the heart beating without the doer having to think about it.

Now it can easily be seen how Jachin and Boaz, the male and female pillars, signify fire and wind (air), the worlds of knower and thinker. This echoes division of the Egg into within, without, and below (for knower, thinker, and doer) in the original jumbling of the order of twelve simples, and the reversal of D and P. Moreover, it raises the issue of the precise significance of vav in the Name.

Let me introduce the subject by pointing out that modern Kabbalah, at least since the time of Isaac Luria, has specified the *Partzufim* or faces (*façades*, I would argue) of the Name as yod the father, first heh the mother, vav the son, the second heh 'his female'. Now the doctrine that accompanies this says that yod corresponds to the first two Sefirot, heh to the third, vav to the fourth-through-ninth, heh to the tenth: this appears backed up by certain aspects of the alef-beyt. For one thing, the second, third, and fourth letters of the alef-beyt represent on the Cauldron the signs yod, heh, and vav occupy on the Egg, thus linking yod to *two*, heh to *three*, and vav to *four* (Hebrew numbers of beyt-gimel-dalet).

Even more expositive is a pattern that reveals itself by shifting from bardic to Hebrew numbering only for *three* and *four*, which in the Throne world are the depths of good and evil. It is part of the general indication of valence-by-height that permeates this entire model. And the scenario the first ten numbers map out by following this detour is instructive. The best way to introduce it is with the method by which a medieval sage might hypothesize the structure of the early part of the periodic table without any knowledge of modern chemistry. It goes like this.

Originally, *two* was *part* of One or number itself. But in the thinking of fallen Adam, duality (fruit of the tree of good and evil) rebels from unity (he eats the apple). What this means is that now instead of adding itself to *one*, duality or *two* pulls against *one*, canceling it out and making *two* equivalent to no-thing or zero. That is exactly what happens in the periodic table: helium, *two*, is inert—zero valence. This creates tension between number (mind) and valence (nature), because the number *three* is only +1 in valence, the number *four* +2 in valence, and so on. This tension cannot affect number; so it puts all its pressure on nature—valence—to correct the situation, which nature does by crunching together +4 and –4 valence into a single number, *six* or carbon, which therefore likes to join with others of its kind to form carbon chains, basis of the organic matter of which our bodies are made.

Number and valence are still one apart, so said pressure once again crunches together +4 and –4 valence, this time into *fourteen*, silicon. At this point number and valence are brought into sync for *fifteen* through *twenty-one*, the third and final sequence of seven trumps. Beyond that, things get a bit more complicated, but that is as far as we need take it here.

By the time we reach the third Wheel, the centripetal has overpowered the centrifugal or radiative so that the 'arrow' made by 2-11-20 points 2 in the opposite direction (from the second sign). Alef still points up (being the fire triad), but on departing aries the arrow flips itself about, throwing *two* down to within one arc of libra or zero height, *two* being inert helium, at the same time throwing *two*'s tail, *twenty*, up to within one arc of *its* valence height (two alefs) at aries.

So we start with alef, hub of the doer's Wheel (aries of the fourth Wheel or womb). Then heh comes along and the arrow flips about (as soon as it is 'unplugged' from unity). In reaction, we 'convert to Judaism', switching to gimel for *three*, dalet for *four*: each marks valence height by the arc leading to the next sign (taking dalet at its original station sagittary). Then, switching back to bardic numbering, *five* continues on up, marking its valence height by the arc leading on from it to the following sign (Throne world's aquarius). Then *six*, the hub of the Monad, is *at* its valence height. Then we begin descent with *seven*, peh, which marks its valence height by the arc *approaching* it from the previous sign (Throne world's gemini). For *eight* we take samekh (or *fearn* the alder), at its valence height—or else mercury's vapors, which compass both bardic and Hebrew *eight*—followed by *nine* at K and *ten* at G, each again marking its valence height by the arc approaching from the previous sign (Throne world's leo and libra, respectively).

Now notice what has happened: we have used gimel, heh's counterpart on the Cauldron, *twice*: at *three*, by Hebrew numbering, and at *ten*, by bardic numbering. Just so, the first heh of the Name is assigned by Lurianic Kabbalah to the third Sefirah and the second heh to the tenth: this is why I accept that part of the teaching *even though* I reject Luria's characterization of the Partzufim, based on the obviously feminine nature of vav.

Taking vav as the root of the female half, what is there about Sefirot *four* through *nine* that might make them represent the female? I finally figured out the way the sages must have looked at it: since Boaz is broken in the human, the feminine part of the Name *can only resonate* as high as the third 'earth', Boaz in the second and first earths being still intact; whereas since the male column *is* still intact in us, the male part of the Name does resonate in the second and first earths. Now before you jump to the conclusion that this is sexist, let me explain that the Name, being the divine creative power, can only be invoked by a man *and* a woman, since in us it has become the procreative power. So though her *half* of the Name may not resonate clear to the top of the Tree, the Name itself—at least its male half—*does*, and her part is *as essential* to that process as his is. (The sexism was in banishing God's consort from the Temple.)

Consider the parallel between vav and dalet. Dalet originates at Cauldron's sagittary, the sign in between yod and heh on the Egg, which suggests it represents the creation of a thought in the intervening macrocosmic sign by desire attaching Light of the Intelligence (whose source in *us* is capricorn, the knower) to an object of nature (being under the spell of the senses). Thus the vav of the Name, at *cancer*, represents the Light trapped in nature by the thought (to use Gnostic terminology). Ultimately, the object of the Great Work or alchemical *opus* is the freeing of that Light. But I dare say the object of invoking the Name is to make the thought posited at cancer a worthy one, involving conception of offspring worthy of use of the Name in its inception.

If Catholicism admonishes us that the main purpose of sex is procreation, I cannot think otherwise than that this was true also of Judaism, properly understood. For what other meaning can the commandment *not to invoke the Lord's Name in vain* possibly have? There is a tradition that a child conceived after an absence in which the man remains 'male and female' (bearing the feminine about within him as Shekhinah, rather than conjoining with another) is a very holy and special one.[31] Percival stipulates that a year of abstinence is necessary for conception of a child that is fully immune to disease.[32]

Which leads me to the final bit I have to say on the subject of offspring (a subject I am unworthy to speak of except theoretically anyway, having none of my own). I believe I may have just now solved a puzzle that has bothered me ever since I started calling the third Wheel the Egg. For Orphism describes the Egg as 'upper half sky, lower half earth', which would seem to describe the Throne world, rather than what is here termed the Egg. Yet it has always seemed more natural to call the third Wheel the Egg, since it sits in the nest-shaped Cauldron—just as the 'serpent's egg' of druid lore is something placed in a cauldron. At any rate, I believe I now see the solution.

Both traditions, Judaic and bardic, had to have—by their very nature—put childbearing on a high moral pedestal, from much the same spiritual motivation as in Catholicism. Orphism really just means bardic tradition amongst Thracians and Greeks in the period beginning at the time of Orpheus (in the Greek 'dark ages'). Given this, I hypothesize that this Orphic doctrine, *properly understood*, means the following: parent, meditate on the toddler in your lap such that you *become*, to the child's smaller version of zodiac or Egg, *as if* you (the *actual* Egg) were to it as the Cauldron is to you (the Egg). This would surely be a powerful meditation, transforming you, the Egg of *your* universe, into that which is 'upper half sky, lower half earth' *to the child*. This surely will lead to a more precise understanding of the relationship you have to your child.

Return for a moment to that up-and-over trip where we used gimel twice. This assures us the parallel between yod-heh-vav on the Egg and beyt-gimel-dalet on the Cauldron was known to Hebrew sages. Add to this that the title *Da'at* or 'knowledge', that quasi-Sefirah associated with the fourth sign, begins with dalet. Now consider how the *Zohar* says[33] that when the second heh of the Name is missing, there is only *dalet*, poverty: this is because it now ends with vav, which corresponds to dalet (adding weight to the notion the Hebrew sages knew this stuff).

The thinker's macrocosmic sign is what enables her to be the part of self that manages the interweaving of our thoughts with those of others around us, which is to say she manages destiny (physical reality being essentially built out from thoughts). This forms the crux of the Buddha's Wondrous Law: he taught that between thought, word, and deed, *thought* was key, in opposition to the Jains, to whom *deed* was key (they were evidently behaviorists).

Judaic tradition likens vav, Hebrew *six*, to the six directions of space, and indeed what is characteristic of the feminine is that she has space within her *for* the male—both physically and emotionally. And yod's Hebrew number, *ten*, seems to indicate that it represents the male's ideal or wish that their two hands *be* joined (and the two hehs exchanged).

I believe that is all I have to say on the matter that is of any great consequence, so I will leave it at that.

Part Two:

Individual Letter Histories

Suggested names of early (Nordic) Tifinag characters are all from Barry Fell, *Bronze Age America* (Boston: Little, Brown & Company, 1982), table 2, p. 103.

That Great Whore Babylon

child of the great river
city of marvels
luxuriant growth mocking the have-nots
    in their barrenness
as it spills from terraces
like the boughs of the willows whereon we hang our harps
    to hear the wind weeping

what business
might the gods have in preserving opulence
save for feeding sacrifice
    and divine appetites

child of the great river
city of marvels
luxuriant growth mocking the have-nots
    in their barrenness

The Three Mothers

אשמ(ם)

א

Alef

Alef corresponds to the tree-letter *ailm* ('alev'), the silver fir. This tree curtails its lateral growth to put all its effort into growing tall. The letter is also linked in bardic tradition to pine, another tree distinguished for height, and for spiral growth of its branches, needles, and cones. Shakespeare, for example, used pine not fir to symbolize what is exalted. The tree-letter unifies the other symbols that have been used for alef, whose bardic and Hebrew number are both *one*.

Jews in servitude in Egypt (Goshen) would have learned Egyptian hieratic *group-writing* in recording their own non-Egyptian (Semitic) names and speech; and the view of scholars in the nineteenth century was that old Hebrew letters arose as permutations of this. There is evidence (in the coherent sequence of images) that the Egyptians themselves were party to the basic bardic corpus of knowledge underlying many ancient alphabets, belonging to peoples scattered over a wide area—from Scandinavia near the Arctic Circle to North Africa, from the British Isles to faraway Sheba.

Egyptian *alef (')* was ☥ the ***Egyptian vulture***, a tool-using bird which, eagle-like, soars to great height spiraling up thermals. It symbolizes the exalted, upraised, what is *on high*, and at the same time *us*, the tool-using human doer. It is the first of three single-sound bird signs that together spelled the Logos (*'*, ***w***, ***m***).

Its hieratic form was ⟨ which evolved (on paper) into old Hebrew ⟨ and eventually ⟨ , having acquired the name *alef*, 'ox'. So far, the predominant direction of writing has been right-to-left.

At roughly the same era, possibly slightly earlier (circa 1700 BCE), a trading prince named Woden-Lithi left a colony near modern-day Peterborough, Canada, armed with rock-inscriptions in two distinct scripts:[34] Tifinag, and *ogam consaine*, the bronze age consonants-only form of ogham writing—one-to-five strokes right of, left of, or across a line. Both scripts were current in that era in southern Scandinavia. *Ogam consaine* had the fifteen consonants but no vowels, hence no alef. But Tifinag, though it did not have all the vowels (or their consonant-equivalents), did have an *alef* ○ in the form of a dot.

This means by the mid-second millennium BCE, taking the exodus from Egypt as having occurred thereabouts (perhaps just after the reign of Akhnaten, or else in the time of Thutmose II, the princess adopting Moses being Hatshepsut? or even earlier, at the end of the Hyksos period), there were three discernible strands to the bardic corpus: Egyptian hieroglyphics; old Hebrew; and Nordic Tifinag (alongside *ogam consaine*). Since my specialty is alphabets, made of single-sound signs, the various forms of cuneiform—other than Ugaritic, which is an alphabet—are a blind spot for me. (My apologies: I can probably recall more about Chinese characters, from the book on them that I lost in a fire.) Nor have I found any actual link to the bardic current in early syllabaries, although the early Iberian semi-syllabaries do show clear connections to Phoenician, Greek, and even ogham.

What I can say with confidence is that it is likely Phoenician traders got letters from their Semitic cousins the Egyptianized Jews, not the other way around. It was Phoenicians, of course, who spread its use—even the term *Tifinag*, though referring to a distinct alphabet itself at least as old as the Semitic, is derived from *Phoenician*, as is our word *phonetics*. Perhaps it was when agreeing to profane use of the alef-beyt by such traders that Jews jumbled the order of the twelve simples.

There was gradual spreading of the Semitic alef-beyt. There was also a second, *expanded* version of alef-beyt—with very different letter-order, showing they did not hold alef-beyt order sacred—the south Semitic. I take Sabean as the standard, because all of its shapes can easily be explained, whereas Thamudic has a half-dozen shapes I do not fully grasp, plus two (M and N) that seem to show the influence of Tifinag from North Africa (where Tifinag ended up).

There was a north Semitic version of expanded alef-beyt that was once thought to long precede the south Semitic set, namely Ugaritic long order, which was in alef-beyt order—with the exception of shin, moved from next-to-last (in Hebrew) to near the middle (other side of lamedh from mem)—but with extra letters inserted here and there. The Ugaritic long order was in existence by or before 1300 BCE. The Sabean version was thought to have arisen around 800 BCE. But discovery of a Beth Shemesh short abecedarium dating to the fourteenth or thirteenth century BCE has changed that assessment: it is a shortened alef-beyt of twenty-two letters using Ugaritic cuneiform characters but arranged in south Semitic letter-order! Evidence shows both expanded sets of letters were part of the bardic corpus, that is, invented by people initiated into the tradition of letters, that is, into poetic tradition (e.g. Orphic).

In Ugaritic, alef was ⤝. Since it was written left-to-right, the two arrows must mean motion's *continuation*: the doer, the A of the Logos.

In Sabean (linked to Sheba), alef was 𐩳, which shows a flat-roofed dwelling with smoke curling up from it, signifying the spirit within it. The first consonant, beyt, was also a flat-roofed dwelling, but without the smoke curling up. Thamudic had 𐪗, which looks to me as if it was influenced by the meaning 'ox', but with its square head it does not make as clear a symbol as smoke rising from a dwelling (unless that is a satellite dish on top, rather than horns).

Meanwhile, the Tifinag of the Scandinavians had been transported to North Africa by the end of the second millennium; for these northern tribesmen were among the confederated tribes of Sea Peoples who attacked Egypt (and the rest of the eastern Mediterranean) around 1200 BCE and upon defeat by Egypt settled in nearby Libya, later to man Egypt's navy (and even found a dynasty).

Over time, a schism occurred amongst the colonists who used Tifinag, a split involving rejection of the heretical F of the Corn Spirit. The result was an offshoot *similar* to Tifinag but distinct in certain particulars, and it is this offshoot alphabet that is found wherever those hearty

Libyan sailors roamed: they reached the Polynesian islands, as well as both coasts of North America, actually founding a colony on the southwestern plateau of North America (the Zuñi language shows traces of Libyo-Egyptian[35]).

In both these last—Berber Tifinag, and Numidian aka Libyan aka *Maurian*, as in *Moor* (and *Maori?*)—the ogham version of the first four vowels and a cross stroke (as if tallying) for the fifth was adopted for the vowel-equivalent consonants we know from Semitic and Egyptian: one-to-four dots in a vertical row (in Numidian, they became stacked lines) and (in the fifth spot) an old-Hebrew zayin on its side.   Alef stayed the same but now was part of a complete scheme of the 'vowels' (as it may have been before, only with two of them secret or seldom used).

According to Herodotus, the Lycians were a decidedly matriarchal culture. This letter in the Lycian alphabet seems to have branched into several signs. The form ⊢ is roughly the same as the Chalcidic Λ ; then there is also ↑, evidently a more forward vowel: could this possibly be a division of alef into *pine* and *fir*, both of which are associated with A in bardic lore? The second form *could* have been influenced by Thamudic ⋀ , heh, but I am inclined to think its shape represented fir, and the other pine; of course both could be true, the form gotten from the Thamudic then reinterpreted and slightly redrawn. What reinforces my hypothesis is that there are also two other letters in Lycian that appear relevant, which are Ψ or ↓, and ⋁⋏ or Υ or Υ, and I cannot help but see these forms as attempts to picture the *tops* of pine and fir, for their phonetic values are also *a* and *e*, I presume with subtle phonetic difference from the previous two shapes. If they are connected to Aa, it is only obliquely, as teyt is also present in Lycian. And bardic E is distinct: the epsilon shape has a phonetic value of *i*, the iota shape *y*. I should note Anatolia has both pine and fir, being mountainous and enclosed on three sides by ocean. Lycian letters are supposed to date from around 500 BCE; and matriarchal culture tends to point towards the heart of bardic tradition, according to Robert Graves (one of the major themes of *The White Goddess*).

The next offshoot of interest is from the Ptolemaic era (last quarter of first millennium BCE), when hieroglyphs were being used to spell Greek names. Around that time developed the Meroitic alphabet used in Nubia. It consisted of a hieroglyphic version and a demotic version, the hieroglyphic version yielding many a clue about the state of bardic tradition in Nubia at the time. Interestingly enough, the hieroglyph for alef, the third Wheel or zodiac of the seated torso, is a ***seated human*** 𓀀 , and this was the *vowel* A. I would guess their inclusion of vowels was a result of Greek influence, though the Meroitic is a closer fit to the bardic alphabet than classical Greek was.

Now we are getting up towards the beginning of our era. Sometime around two hundred years before or after the beginning of the modern era, Germanic runes appeared. Now those who devised the runes were not 'simple' pagan barbarians, as generally supposed, but knowledgeable Gnostics: this is proved by the order of runes in the Elder Futhark, which shows unequivocally that, unlike even *rabbis* today, they knew which letters occupied which signs. They knew the three mothers, and which of them (shin) stood for the part of self occupying a macrocosmic sign.

The runes are closest of all to the Celtic tree-alphabet, and indeed two runes retain their tree-names: birch and yew. But it runs much deeper than that: for instance, the rune for alef, named **ansuz*, 'god' ᚨ, pictures *ailm* the silver fir. This stands for the upright vertical axis of the seated human, or the direction smoke goes in Sabean alef, spiraling up as does the **Egyptian vulture**. Where does alef the ox fit into all this? It took me a while to figure this out: in the arid Middle East, the most important task of the ox was to power the pumps bringing water up from the water table to the surface (and of course plowing, to bring plants up).

The square-Hebrew alef is a whirlwind or 'pillar of fire' (there being strong electrical impulses in twisters), which also, of course, spirals upward. *All* of these symbols, moreover, have in common that the very power of lift they represent exists only because outward extent is limited: the eagle's sustained lift comes from staying within the confines of the thermal; the power of the ox to pump water depends on its being yoked to a given radius; a human is upright only so long as blood and tissue remain within the confines of the torso; the silver fir limits the outward thrust of its limbs to concentrate on height. Also, whirlwinds (like subatomic particles) have more power the more confined their winds.

Alef bears the atomic number of hydrogen (*one*), whose sleight-of-hand way of shifting from one compound to another instills into matter the liveliness that makes life (and occurrence in general) possible. The corresponding trump is I The Magician, which pictures a mountebank. This also implies the idea of levitation (one of the mountebanks tricks), as when hydrogen was used in dirigibles for lift. Indeed hydrogen is the most common atom-type in the universe (albeit not in earth's crust), making it the common strand unifying things on a cosmic scale.

The image on this trump is male because of the pagan tradition that a boy-child should be weaned during a new or waxing moon:[36] bardic A is the new moon.

We have Greeks to thank for turning the ox so that we *become* it. I am convinced that our A came about in honor of Cretan athletes who vaulted over the horns of bulls in the arena: we see the head of the bull beneath us (A) as we pass over. Perhaps it faces the same direction the reader is facing in order to convey the idea of shamanic possession by (or of) the spirit of the bull. Such Mithra-like possession might then bleed over (pun intended) from the first vowel to the first consonant, which would explain both Meroitic B (see below, under beyt) and the archaic Greek hymn that has for B *boibalion*, 'I the roebuck-fawn or antelope bull-calf' (according to Graves).

Alef is you, the doer—the creator (in some present instant) of thoughts of finite duration, cycling about (often for many lifetimes) awaiting the Light in them being freed. Typically, alef represents the body-mind: what the doer identifies with. In this context, shin and mem represent the other minds a doer has use of, the feeling and desire minds (imitating thinker and knower), which is the source of the mothers' physiological significance. Alef stands for the sympathetic nerves (what makes your heart keep beating).

A's Boibel Loth name is *Acab*, which Graves links to the Greek term *Achaiva*, Spinner, an epithet of Demeter. Indeed the doer is the spinner of the threads of destiny; its thinker is the one (or one-third) that weaves these threads into the tapestry of life.

It is this last that points us to which of the closing six questions following the *I am* lines of the Song of Amairgin refers to *ailm*, namely the last one: *6. Who shapes weapons from hill to hill*, glossed *'wave to wave, letter to letter, point to point'*. Think of the spider spinning its web, and perhaps also the tips of the myriad firs of a mountain forest. (This poem, the oldest in the Gaelic tongue, has thirteen *I am* lines standing for the thirteen tree-months, followed by six questions I take to stand for the six runic vowels, that is, all the vowels except Aa, teyt.)

One last bit about silver fir. Consider someone a heroic six-and-a-quarter feet tall: the Monad would then be twelve-and-a-half feet in diameter. The four Wheels *above* it, then, would measure (in ascending order) 25, 50, 100, and 200 feet (in diameter). This last *happens to be* the height of the tallest (dead) silver fir ever measured. So these larger Wheels do belong to giants in a sense, by giving shape to the Greene Lyon of the surrounding, majestic trees, as envisioned by a druid or alchemist (or druid alchemist) as the ramifications of his-or-her power or *medicine*.

Alef is the hub of the Egg. In a geodetic application of the Egyptian version of alef-beyt, with its teyt or libra at Giza—since Egypt symbolized the material(istic) world to Gnostics—alef stands for the center of Anatolia, which (as I said above) sports both fir and pine.

ש

Shin

Shin corresponds to tree-letter *saille* ('sal-yuh'), the willow, summit of spring—the final number in the sequence of spring's increase 4-8-16—its drooping boughs the symbol of spring's fount of plenty. As the month encompassing taurus, it is follow by cheyt or *no-thing*, just as a fount of water ends up reflecting space in a pool at its feet.

The place of omega in the Logos was held, in Egyptian, by *quail chick* (*w*). But the Hebrew sages decided to *shush* this profound truth, replacing it with the sign from group writing for the *š* (*sh*) sound *lotus pond* or *š'*—the bottom could also be rectangular, like the sign *pond* for *š* that it abrogated the need for, perhaps related in the same way calendar-month *saille* is to mother letter shin. Hieratic for *lotus pond* led to old Hebrew shin. (The old Hebrew character often took some prominent feature of the hieratic and singled it out, in this case the *w* at the top.) This pictures a molar but can also be seen as a pair of breasts like mem but *without* the beckoning arm. To make up for subtracting a bird sign from the mix, Hebrew replaced two *non*-bird signs with two-sound bird signs from group writing, namely the two doubles marking the limits (B and T) of the minds of the knower and thinker, the parts of self that did not undergo the Fall.

As if in echo of the above, shin itself split in two in the longer sequences (Ugaritic and south Semitic). Ugaritic looks a bit *like* Hebrew shin; it can also be seen as a bow and two arrows, to go with dalet's bow and one arrow (see below under dalet), in both cases invoking the connection to sagittary. The other form is a bit like the second of the two forms and in Sabean, the latter being two of the former back to back, or else interwoven strands, symbolic of willow's use in wickerwork.

The far north Tifinag had the sign probably called *sol*, 'sun', because early spring was when the sun *appeared* in the far north. This remained the letter in Berber Tifinag, but in the Numidian the sun symbol was moved to the beginning of the year (B) and letter S reverted to the form as in the Greek. Numidian also had the sibilant, which I interpret as an echo of *sol* in spring holding the place of samekh at aries, Numidian having ditched, like Hebrew, the worship of the alder god or Corn Spirit (it had no F, only the P at sagittary).

Lycian had which at first I thought seemed Latin, but this form (mixed in with sigmas) is actually common: Etruscan (or), Messapic or S (or), Latin or S, Chalcidic or (or), Attic or . These all strongly reinforce what that archaic Greek 'hymn' Graves retrieved from Boibel Loth letter names had for S, *Salia*, namely *saloömai*, 'I lurch to and fro'.

The runic form is or *sōwilō*, 'sun' (same word as Latin *sol*), and since it represents a stroke of lightning, I wonder if these Gnostics were aware that the sun is powered by electrical current (flowing from the stars) rather than a bunch of hydrogen bombs (as obsolete gravitational cosmology still seems to believe). The first shape can also be seen as the hanging bough of the willow, which has alternate leaves.

The Meroitic simply reverts to ⫼⫼ , what started it all.

Its bardic number, *sixteen*, completes spring's increase: 4-8-16 or O-F-S or ayin-samekh-shin. So its trump is XVI La Maison Dieu, which shows a cannonball headed for an unsettled crown (upset by violence obviously) atop a tower from which the twin gods of the year topple. For this is sulfur, one of the main ingredients of gunpowder. Perhaps this tells us it is spring, not summer, we should celebrate with fireworks? The generals of the past certainly seemed to think so.

I am inclined to disagree with Graves as to which line from the Song of Amairgin refers to shin. For no other letter so fits the line: *I am a sound of the sea*, glossed *for horror*. Perhaps it is apropos that *ss* is the dominant sound we hear when spectators of melodrama *hiss* the villain (*Sefer Yetzirah* calls mem and shin 'pan of merit' versus 'pan of liability'). But *sound of the sea* fits both *s* and *sh* (ש and שׁ).

Indeed its geodetic placement reinforces this, as it is in the midst of the sea of grain of the Dnieper bend, which makes a similar sound when the wind plays upon it.

מם

Mem

Mem corresponds to tree-letter *muin* the vine, whose month encompasses libra, the vine harvest season. It is rich in symbolism: "Heard it through the grapevine" embodies some of it, our interconnectedness. Vine also stood for blood vessels, since mem is the blood, where desire lives. Wine symbolized love in Sufi poetry. Intermediate mem is at its tree-calendar position (as stand-in for R at libra), but mem sofit is the hub of the Monad, at the height of a person standing: this is the height at which the grapes hang in Æsop's the Fox and the Grapes (whence comes the expression *sour grapes*). Its bardic number, *six*, is the number of directions in space, another way of expressing interconnectedness.

You can still see a bit of the *owl* in our letter M: the hieroglyph was , one of three bird signs spelling out the Logos: *'*, *w*, and *m*. From a hieratic form something like 3 or more likely a partial outline of the owl's head came old Hebrew mem, showing a mother reaching out to draw us to her bosom.

The Ugaritic , though roughly similar, is puzzling. But I can see a way of reading its shape that touches on both mem and mem sofit: the horizontal wedge points to the top of the upright, just as mem sofit is atop the standing Adam Qadmon; alternatively one might read it as picturing the male erection, gamma-like, symbolizing that desire lives in the blood.

Tifinag expressed the shin-mem polarity as sun and moon: M was)) probably named *mán*, 'moon'. In North Africa it took on the shapes ⨅ and), or turned on its side, as many of the letters were, always right side up ⌣, being the moon (at libra, the bottom of the round).

It is interesting, then, to note that while Sabean M was 𐩣, the closed lips (Ethiopian 𐩣), Thamudic, essentially the script of desert graffiti back then, whose version of this may have been the source of Greek beta, also seems to have imported the form)) from beyond Egypt.

Lycian had ᴧ but then it had another letter X transliterated *m̃*. This second character happens to be ogham M, a bit tilted, this in an alphabet that also has *ogam consaine* Ng for the sound *ñ*.

Meroitic reverts to *owl* as in Egyptian. Do we begin to see where the 'wise old owl' gets its reputation?

Runic expresses the sound 'mm' the best: ᛗ, called **mannaz*, 'man, human', shows two **wunjōs* or 'joys' (ᚹ,ᚹ) kissing. (One is turned around: that must be the male.)

This last helps confirm the choice Graves made for *muin* among the lines of the Song of Amairgin: *I am a hill of poetry*, glossed *'and knowledge'*. The gloss certainly applies to the M of the Logos and also obviously references the idea of knowing 'in the biblical sense'.

And the corresponding trump is VI The Lover, a reference to carbon's love of its own kind, with which it easily joins to form the carbon chains that are the basis of all life. And the sixth Sefirah, in the Tree of Coins (i.e. rounds or cycles), is the year, which is the periodicity of the carbon cycle (that of vegetation separating the carbon from the CO_2 we breathe out).

In that archaic Greek 'hymn' Graves reconstructs from Boibel Loth letter names, M or *Moiria* is *moiraō*, 'I distribute'. You can see how this relates to the expression 'heard it through the grapevine'.

Moreover consider its geodetic significance; for it is the most far-flung letter—all the way up where Lake Ladoga is (near St. Petersburg, who by the way was no saint)—at the same time as it pulses away at the Great Pyramid. Mem is all-encompassing: *mm*, the Monad; the knower.

The Seven Doubles

דתכרגפב

ד

Dalet

Dalet corresponds to tree-letter *duir* the oak, whose month straddles the summer solstice; hence it is the sign cancer on the Cauldron and represents our outer horizon. This *duir* is surely cognate with the syllable *dur-* of *durable*, as well as our word *door—stout guardian of the door* Taliesin calls oak, wood of doors—after which D is named in at least two alphabets: Hebrew; and early Tifinag. As the first sign of the manifested half of the Throne world (beginning of the Cauldron), it is the doorway into manifestation.

Graves connects its bardic number, *twelve*, with the oak hero's 'twelve merry men'; but on a deeper level it stands for the zodiac and its twelve signs: cancer is manifested fire, thus it stands for the stars. The outer horizon is linked to us via sight; stars mark the *limit* of sight. For this is the month when the oak king, god of the waxing year or increasing day-length, ends his reign—is sacrificed—giving way to the holly king or god of the waning year.

The Egyptian hieroglyph for D was a gesturing **hand** ⬭ , pointing out something on the horizon no doubt, its current station. It is the first of four horizontal signs descending the outer Cauldron: **hand, tongs, basket with handle, mouth**. Since this sequence is eminently coherent, we surmise that the tradition assigning D-T-K-R to these four signs of the Cauldron was extant in ancient Egypt. And that R occupies libra is evidence Egyptian knowledge went beyond mere familiarity with the tree-calendar, for R's thirteenth *month* was an entire season removed from libra (or nearly so).

The hieratic form of this hieroglyph was ⌒ , which evolved into ◁ , the old Hebrew dalet, which seemingly pictures a jib—which makes sense, since a jib swings like a door (or a 'page', dalet's other meaning). Considering its trump is XII The Hanged Man and it symbolizes the horizon's reach (oak's breadth), this seems appropriate, and it serves as indication that jibs were actually used in ancient times (in case there was doubt). The trump shows the inverted image on the back of the eye (of a man dancing a jig). Dalet seems to signify that which swings, or swings about; horizons, of course, *compass*.

The two forms in Ugaritic cuneiform were ⚏ and ⟨⟋ , the first of these the extension of beyt (⚏) to include the outer temple (the only explanation that accounts for the shapes of these two in Ugaritic), the second, almost a caricature of our D, pictures bow and ready arrow, which points to sagittary the archer, D's origin.

Sabean also had two forms of dalet. The closer to Hebrew was ⧄ or ⧄ , the first an axe, the second a bow and arrowhead. An axe swings (like doors and jibs) and symbolizes the giant-slayer in that it can fell the tallest of trees; the bow points to dalet's origin, Cauldron's sagittary, the archer (and his reach). Thamudic had ⟨ which looks like it has softened into a mere mallet yet is actually closer to the rune and to our D.

The other was ⊟, the bier of the hero (god of the waxing year), sacrificed at the summer solstice. Thamudic has ╫, which appears to picture the same thing.

In Ugaritic and Sabean both, one D stands for the summer solstice sacrifice, and one for sagittary the archer, though phonetically the pairs are reversed.

Tifinag has ∏, probably called *dyrr*, 'door'; it stayed the same in Numidian, though in North Africa (and even in Scandinavia) it often got turned on its side. Considering the Hebrew name for this letter also means 'door', this shows surprising geographical continuity. The shape in Tifinag also conveys the notion of a dolmen, two stone uprights supporting a lintel, doorway into the Otherworld (heroic status), as the grave or monument commemorating the hero.

The Lycian alphabet had △, same as Greek delta: the door of a tent? Or it could be a fulcrum, to extend one's 'reach': the Sabean shape turned on its side ◩ is suggestive.

The Meroitic D ⬮, the ***djed eye*** (of Horus)—whence it probably acquired its phonetic significance—is a surprisingly vivid rendition of an *eye on the horizon*, the curve under the eye representing the curvature of the Cauldron beneath its outer lip. Since our connection with the outer horizon is through the sense of sight, this is an eminently appropriate picture for this letter. (The next sign on the Cauldron, T, in Meroitic has a shape that appears to reference hearing.)

The rune was ▷, named *þurisaz*, 'giant', and shows the giant's girth, but *also* perhaps a bow. (Later it became pointed and was nicknamed 'thorn' from its shape.) For this is the giant-slayer: Donar or Thor (Gaulish Taranis), or David. In the archaic Greek 'hymn' that Graves reconstructs from Boibel Loth letter names, D, *Daibhaith* (*David* in Taliesin's riddle), becomes *davizō* '(I) cleave wood'. Hence the axe in Sabean.

Based on axe as giant-slayer, I just solved a problem that has long troubled me: do the four greater Wheels *within* which Ezekiel's four rest relate to giants? Yes: the filling out of giant *trees* in spring—the Greene Lyon, mercury's vapor taking over the upper half of the outer Egg or vessel, translated to the spheres of the four elements. For the largest of these Wheels is roughly 200 feet tall, matching the tallest silver fir ever measured (A, alef).

D's trump, XII The Hanged Man, illustrates just *how* D functions as giant-slayer. For it is the inverted image on the back of the eye, as shown by the fact that he dances a jig, something a man hanged-by-the-foot would not be doing. Thus D magically upends whoever stands before him, however tall. (I love poetic symbolism!)

Twelve corresponds to atom-type magnesium, used in signal lamps to penetrate heavy fog because it burns with highly actinic light. Since 'burns' means combines with oxygen, the line from horizon without to one's brow (where oxygen resides) symbolizes a line of sight. The deep fog being penetrated is that in which the doer finds itself when led by the senses rather than by thinker and knower.

This line of sight is what identifies Egg's aries, up on a level with dalet, with the photon of light, that is, with fire, as does the *Zohar* (which sends fire north). This height stands for the height of *spin one*, that of the photon. And this is equivalent to magnesium's (D's) +2 *valence*, a unit of spin being in ratio two-to-one to a unit of valence (since the electron is *spin one-half*).

The line from the Song of Amairgin that Graves and I both assign this letter is: *I am a god who forms fire for a head* [*i.e. 'gives inspiration':* Macalister], or *I am a god who forms smoke from sacred fire for a head*, glossed *'to slay therewith'*. For dalet is on the outer rim of the Cauldron, even with the head, linked to us by sight, or manifested *fire*: oak attracts lightning. The above quote from the Song of Amairgin reminds me of the practice of the Sarmatians (who by being stationed in Britatin became the prototype of Arthur's 'knights') of finding inspiration in vapors of cannabis—though *'to slay therewith'* seems a bit out of character for that drug, but then they *were* warriors (and the gloss would have been much later than either the original poem *or* the Sarmatians). Yet in support of *'to slay therewith'*, of the seven pairs of opposites list in *Sefer Yetzirah*, the one proper to dalet is **life and death**, as depicted in its trump.

Geodetically, dalet stands at the source of Rhine and Danube, the north slope of the Alps, where Thunder (Thor) and his goat totem (his cart being drawn thereby) seem quite at home.

ת

Tav

Tav corresponds to tree-letter *tinne* ('tin-yuh'), holly, Cauldron's leo—what approaches within earshot. It is the holly-king, who rules the waning year, which immediately follows the sacrifice of the oak-king at the summer solstice. Holly represents the law of the phalanx: many little points (spiny leaf corners) that by cohesion mount up to one big point. Tav represents one's obligation to one's fellows: conscience. Conscience resides in the heart; and the sun is the heart of the macrocosm, being the passive aspect of air (the receptor of stars' energy), leo being on the passive end of the air level of the Cauldron. T's bardic number is *eleven,* D's preceding *twelve* signs *minus* the one the sun obscures.

The Egyptian system had ⊂⊃ the ***tongs*** at Cauldron's leo, preceded by the ***hand*** that wields them and followed by the ***basket*** it can pluck things out of, which is across the way from the ***alchemical oven*** the ***tongs*** were made for. (Gardiner calls this hieroglyph 'loop of rope', but I cannot agree with him, and the great Isaac Taylor called it ***tongs.***)

The Hebrew sages substituted 🦆 the ***duckling*** or *t'* from group writing, which conveys the idea that conscience (tav) is that whereby the thinker sort of mothers us (corrects, as a mother does her young). Hieratic ⌇ led to **+** or **✕** old Hebrew tav, the latter form one's X or mark—taking on of obligation—the former a crossroads—the judgment of the community that enforces or backs up conscience.

This tav is found in south Semitic as well (Sabean **✕**, Thamudic **+**). But there tav has split into two letters, the other being **⚯** which is clearly an image of the chain (of two links) that binds the individual to one with whom he or she has made an agreement. Since the heart is the crossroads of the body, one could say the cross is the inner aspect of duty, the chain the outer.

And backtracking, the Ugaritic had two tavs as well: ⊢, corresponding phonetically to the cross, and ⟨, corresponding phonetically to the chain. The first of these must simply mean an arrow, since there is just the one.   The other illustrates just why it is an arrow: the purpose of an arrow is to pierce the heart.

For far north Tifinag had **↓** or **→** , which was probably called *tagg*, 'barbed arrow'. Now why would a letter that signifies the heart be such a thing? It is what the arrow aims for. In Berber Tifinag it was changed to **✝**, probably from influence of other alphabets in the region. But in Numidian we find **✕** and **+** but also **➤** which (unless it was a clairvoyant picturing of a B-52) can only be a holdover from far north Tifinag. Note T is the arrow without the bow D.

Given these last two paragraphs, it seems appropriate that in the archaic Greek 'hymn' that Graves made from the Boibel Loth letter names, T, *Teilmon,* yields *telamōn* or *tlāmōn*, 'I, the suffering one'. This also fits tav as *conscience.*

In Meroitic, we find ⟱ or ⟱ , a permutation of the original Egyptian T. This figure is extremely interesting: what it pictures (seen from above) is a shaman or ***priest in bird mask***, with lines connecting his ears to a sound's source, reconfirming it is leo, manifested air or what approaches within earshot. Yet the original meaning, ***tongs***, is still apparent, leading me to think the two meanings were blended in this symbol: hearing taking hold of something from the surroundings.

Finally, runic ↑ *tīwaz*, the god Tiw or Tyr (the German Mars), calls to mind the line from the Song of Amairgin which Graves and I both attribute to T: *I am a battle-waging spear.* Another version of the line (embedded in the *Romance of Taliesin*) reads: *I fled as a spear-head of woe to such as wish for woe.* I have also seen the name of this rune translated 'divine honor', which is essentially what the god Tyr stands for: he was the only one of the Aesir who had the courage to put his right hand in the mouth of the wolf Fenris (one of Loki's brood) so the other gods could chain him, whereupon of course he lost the hand, thereafter surely symbolizing need for warriors to practice with the weaker hand, to make it worthy to fight beside the stronger.

This trump is the pivot or fulcrum, the middle trump: XI Force. It is unique in that it fits into three different triplets: I-XI-XXI, II-XI-XX, and II-XI-XVIIII. The first are: one thing; one thing in relation to one ten-fingered; and one thing in relation to two ten-fingereds. The second are all numerical twos. The third are all +1 valence. Tav represents sodium; and the feminine plural ending ות corresponds to common salt (used to bind oaths).

It would appear that tav, being the heart, was originally associated with the sun, the sun being the macrocosmic projection of all individual hearts beating at any given moment: it is the heart of the macrocosm (at the *very* least this is true symbolically) just as it is the heart of the trumps. Its bardic number, *eleven*, makes it the only double whose digital sum is *two*, which Kabbalah originally associated with the sun, this because the numbers *one* through *ten* stand for cycles connecting eternity—*one* itself—to *now, today*—*ten* (what is held in the ten fingers)—and *two* corresponds to the Great Year (precession of equinoxes), which is the shifting relationship between ecliptic—*six*, the year—and equator—*ten*, the day (today)—both of which have to do *with* the sun; but the Great Year represents the sun proper, while the year is the Egg of the doer and day the rotation of earth. What has survived of Hermetic Kabbalah mistakenly identifies the sun with *six*, but proof otherwise is provided by the pattern of which signs planets are 'exalted' in in astrology. Planets associated with Sefirot that form male-female pairs (2-3, and 4-5, and 7-8) are exalted in signs opposite one another: Venus opposite Mercury (pisces-virgo), Jupiter opposite Mars (cancer-capricorn), and Sol (2) opposite Saturn (3), at aries and libra, straight up (sun at zenith) and straight down (lead as plumb).

T's geodetic position is the Tyrrhennian Sea, named for the earlier term for Etruscans, a term that meant 'non-Greek sea pirates'. The rune's namesake Tyr was a war god, and that sea certainly saw its share of war! Obviously of the seven pairs of opposites listed in *Sefer Yetzirah*, tav is **peace and strife**.

כ ך

Kaf

Kaf corresponds to tree-letter *coll* the hazel, whose nuts feed the Salmon of Wisdom. It is the nut harvest (late summer), the month encompassing virgo, the virgo of the Cauldron: what is gathered within reach. And *coll* bore the number *nine*: the Nine Hazels of Poetic Art. As this was the number of Muses and the virgo symbol looks like a harp, this letter would seem to relate especially to poets. Two well-known fables reference this letter, one handed us by Epictetus, the Boy and the Filberts, involving narrow-necked jar and cupped hand, one from Æsop, the Fox and the Crane (or Stork), shallow dish versus narrow-necked jar—Egyptian kaf versus Meroitic kaf (see below).

The Egyptian hieroglyph was ⌒ *basket with handle*, symbolizing what is gathered close, within reach (to be tasted). Æsop's Fox and the Crane contrasts a shallow dish of this shape to the narrow necked jar below (Meroitic kaf). All four signs of the outer Cauldron are relatively flat, horizontal signs and fit perfectly in sequence: *hand*, *tongs*, *basket*, *mouth*. The hieratic form was ⌁ and this evolved into ⌐ the old Hebrew kaf.

The Ugaritic character was ⊢ , which is distinguishable from vav the breast in that it lacks the extra wedge that formed the nipple of the latter. This shape is like square Hebrew כ, thought to picture a cupped hand, *kaf*'s meaning, namely that of the Boy and the Filberts (cupped around a filbert, making it irretrievable from the narrow-necked jar). The Meroitic character was a *narrow-necked jar* ⍥ standing, like Egyptian *basket with handle*, for what is gathered close.

Tifinag expressed what is gathered close as a heap of stones (or nuts) ⁛ , most likely called *kuml*, 'cairn, heap'. It retained this shape in Berber Tifinag but became ⇐ in Numidian, and the only explanation I can offer is that it may have been the map symbol for *passage grave*; for one use of a cairn was to designate a point on the horizon where the rising of a particular star (or the sun) marked advent of a holiday; in cold climes (such as desert at night?), subterranean shafts were dug for use in sighting stars. What these two symbols have in common is a relation to form: the calendar.

The Sabean and Thamudic shape ⋂ symbolizes what is *under one roof* (gathered close).

The Lycian form was **K** , much like the Greek. I find it difficult to explain Greek kappa, unless it was shaped to express rays of light from a torch or lantern. In the archaic Greek 'hymn' Graves reconstructed from Boibel Loth letter-names, K, *Caoi*, yields *caiomai*, 'am consumed by fire', while in kaf's trump, VIIII The Hermit, he holds up a lantern.

Indeed the rune ‹ was named *kenaz*, 'torch', or *kanō*, 'skiff': it pictures the mouth of the poet, who was as a torch or lantern to his people. Why this rune pictures an opened mouth has to do with the lore of this letter in Celtic bardic tradition, where it is associated with salmon fed on the Nine Hazels of Poetic Art, whence hero Fionn Mac Cumhail gains inspiration: having been tasked with minding a cauldron's contents, his thumb gets splattered, and on licking it he imbibes what was meant for another. In bardic lore the hazel symbolized wisdom in a nutshell (as opposed to a long boring lecture), and the rune probably pictures the mouth of the salmon, the actual consumer of nuts in the tale.

One more thing about kaf: bardic *nine* is the feminine side of the ultimate polarity, that between 10 and 9 (numerical +1 versus -1 valence) that projects itself onto yod and vav, which are +1 and -1 in number *and* valence. *Nine* is atom-type fluorine—in the form of hydrofluoric acid it had *better* be hermit-like (not around people). The chemical reaction between fluorine and hydrogen—9, feeling, striving *towards* or trying to *be* 10, desire—is the strongest known. It is interesting that bards associated *coll*, the feminine side of this polarity, with wisdom, much like the Sophia (Wisdom) of the Gnostics. The male side, on the other hand, is ivy, symbol of the Dionysian revels. Go figure. Anyway, it follows that of the seven pairs of opposites listed in *Sefer Yetzirah*, the one proper to kaf is **wisdom and folly**.

The line from the Song of Amairgin referring to hazel is of course: *I am a salmon in a pool*, glossed *'the pools of knowledge'*. Its geodetic placement is the far coast of Libya, which I associate with Libyan seafarers (on Egyptian ships) catching sight of home, thus relating *what is gathered close* to what is brought back in trade—in ***narrow-necked jars***, or shallow baskets, or even heaps of fruits or nuts.

ר

Reysh

Reysh corresponds to tree-letter *ruis* the elder, last month of the dying year, a medicinal tree as suits late autumn. Being the thirteenth tree-month, it owns no sign (all twelve having been taken), yet it *has* a station; for intermediate mem is filling in for it at the Cauldron's libra. That this is its proper station is apparent from its Hebrew pronunciation as guttural *r* (rolled in the throat), placing it between K and G down at the bottom of the Cauldron or mouth: the gullet. Its bardic number *fifteen* suggests the theme of cheating (as in reysh deserting its proper station) in that while *twenty* represents fair combat—ten-fingered versus ten-fingered—*fifteen* implies that one combatant has one hand tied behind his back.

This was ⟨⟩ the ***mouth*** hieroglyph standing in the geodetic model for the population of Upper Egypt that were consumers of *t* the ***loaf*** of Lower Egypt (the delta). The hieratic form was ⟨⟩ which led to ⟨⟩ old Hebrew reysh, a stick horse.

The Ugaritic ⟨⟩ is most comprehensible alongside the south Semitic ⟩ or ⟨, which represented the open mouth seen from the side; this is what the Ugaritic shows, except the teeth are added, just to make it clear what it is. The teeth identify it as a consuming mouth, as opposed to square-Hebrew peh's opened-mouth-with-tongue, symbolizing speech. For at libra, reysh is manifested earth.

The far north Tifinag had O most likely called *hringr*, 'ring', symbolizing that the year has come full circle and is in need of a new central dot, in Numidian, or a new boss, in Tifinag, where the year starts with a shield. For this form remained the same in both alphabets, and since it signifies the year having come full circle, it must represent R's calendar position, the *r* rolled on tongue's tip, or perhaps liquid *r*, but at any rate up on a level with the winter solstice.

Lycian just had P, the Greek rho.

Meroitic had ⟨⟩ or ⟨⟩, the former in Egyptian signifying an ***aquifer*** or ***pond***, water being symbolic of death (this being the month the year dies). It could also be seen as a ***coffin.*** In the archaic Greek 'hymn' Graves reconstructs from Boibel Loth letter names, R or *Riuben* yields *rymbonaō*, 'I swing about again'; but this is a Gnostic replacement (referring to reincarnation), as earlier it had been *rheō*, 'I flow away', the answer to Gwion's riddle for R being (the goddess) *Rhea*.[37] 'I flow away' fits both ***aquifer*** and ***coffin.***

The runic character ⟨⟩ *raiðō*, 'ride, journey', hints of Latin influence, and yet there is a difference: it does not quite touch the vertical line in the middle. This is because it was intended to picture the animal headdress of the shaman, whose 'journey' this is. For reysh, at libra—and that is definitely where runes placed it, judging by macrocosmic signs being every fourth rune— is pointing down into the earth, towards the shamanic Lowerworld, to which he or she journeys to retrieve power, or the 'soul' of someone ailing. Being the fifth rune, R completes the vertical diameter (F, aries, being the first rune), identifying it with rho: the pattern *strongly* suggests the chi-rho symbol for Christ, which to Gnostics would have been far preferable to the cross, symbol of suffering and death and the doubtful notion (foreign to Gnostics such as myself) that someone else, however divine, could become the scapegoat for others' sins.

The beauty of this symbol is that it is so clear. As phosphorus, *fifteen*, it is the mainstay of chromosomes; and square-Hebrew reysh pictures the male organ and the duct through which seed enters it; trump XV The Devil pictures a horned and winged 'little devil', and a couple of lesser hominids with tree-like horns leashed to the red anvil on which he stands, thus picturing the enslavement of new parents by their offspring. Phosphorus and Lucifer are names for the same thing: Venus as Morning Star (phosphorus glows in the dark).

There are microorganisms that at times cause the sea to glow where it spends itself on the shore, which reinforces the choice Graves made for R among the lines of the Song of Amairgin: *I am a wave of the sea*, glossed *for weight*.

Of the seven pairs of opposites listed in *Sefer Yetzirah*, the one proper to reysh is, fairly obviously, **fruitfulness and sterility**, also sometimes translated **seed and desolation**.

ג

Gimel

Gimel corresponds to tree-letter *gort* the ivy, the month encompassing the sign or point scorpio, time of year of Dionysian revels, which ivy symbolizes. In the archaic Greek 'hymn' Graves reconstructed from the Boibel Loth letter names, G, *Gath*, becomes *gātheō*, 'I rejoice'.

This letter, and *muin* the vine of the preceding month (libra), represent *kundalini*, yoga's serpent power coiled up at the base of the spine. Since one of G's two runes is shaped like Greek chi, I connect the term *gort* with our word *cord*, ostensibly from Greek *khorde*, 'string' or 'cord'. The deeper meaning of ivy is *desire*, based on its clinging nature. Its bardic number, *ten*, means the ten grasping fingers, but also of course our governance of them.

The Egyptian hieroglyph ⟨△⟩ pictures the **alchemical oven**. Sir Alan Gardiner calls it 'stand with jar', but the triangle in it surely stands for fire and is housed by what looks like the oven later used in European alchemy (tapered and roofed). Alchemy is a tradition handed down from—or through—Alexandria, Egypt, yet of much greater antiquity.[38] Gimel is the sign where the choice must be made to follow the closed zodiac up the spine to the head or the broken-and-extended one down the legs to the feet.

I also connect the **serpent** hieroglyph, a *dj* sound originally,[39] with G. Thus there are two hieroglyphs for G, as with runes.

At any rate, the hieratic form of **alchemical oven** was evidently the source of the old Hebrew gimel ⋀ , which Greek and Sabean 'rectified' to ⅂ , a gibbet, or the male erection seen from the side. Desire's seat is the adrenals; and Abraham's covenant assigns heh, not gimel, to the male organ; but scorpio *is* scorpio (in the tree-calendar), so it is easy to see how this came about. Seemingly the same thing happened in Ugaritic, as ⊺ fits the bill (seen straight on, or as phallic pillar); yet this more likely represented an upright human (ten-fingered one, see tzaddi). (Thamudic had a square or circle ☐ ◯ , for which I can offer no explanation, unless the latter was referencing its trump, still a couple of millenniums in the future.)

The same thing *definitely* happened in Tifinag. In the far north, it had been *ghomr*, 'roof beams' ° ° ° , but in Berber Tifinag it got turned on end ∴ , its meaning obvious. Then in the Numidian, it became ⌐ , same as Greek gamma.

But old Hebrew gimel pictures either a camel's hump or a pyramid half buried in sand. As the former, and as **alchemical oven**, gimel *geodetically* stands for the desert approaches to Mesopotamia.

The Lycian form Γ or Υ is obviously related to the Greek. The form of gamma used on Samos ⅂ shows an intermediate form.

The Meroitic hieroglyphic alphabet has the Geb *goose* ,[40] Geb being the Egyptian earth god, father of serpents, the father of Osiris, Isis, Set, and Nephthys. Its sound has shifted to *k*, but it was often unvoiced even in Egyptian, especially in the Ptolemaic era. I dare say this is the goose that laid the golden egg (in Æsop's fable); for scorpio (desire) operates the earth triad.

As for the runic division of G, there is *gebō,* X 'gift', and *jēra,* ⟨ 'year, harvest'. The latter is obviously the linked arms of the harvest dance. The former is perhaps a tripod of sacrifice? or, both it and Greek chi may refer to the obliquity of ecliptic and equator. At any rate, these obviously stand for the two *modes* of G or desire: desire to *give*; and (thus) desire to *have, acquire, harvest,* or *make*, so that we *can* give. It is interesting to me—knowing as I do that the runes were devised by Gnostics—that the first of these has the shape of chi, the initial of *Christ*. When we consider the fact that the macrocosmic hexad is marked out by the order of runes in the Elder Futhark (by every fourth rune, starting with the first), it is not at all hard to see the Elder Futhark as housing hidden reference to the Chi Rho symbol of Christ: six spokes for signs of the macrocosmic hexad (four of them chi), plus a loop on top identifying the vertical staff as rho; and indeed the fifth rune is the R at libra, straight down—the staff itself.

Gimel poses a complication in the history of alphabets *after Latin*. For in Latin, the third letter lost its voicing and became our C. Amongst the Celts, this C is always hard; but in English it usually sounds as *s* before *e* or *i*, and Italian and church Latin pronounce it *ch*. It is kappa, *not* gimel—Latin C—that corresponds to *coll* the hazel; so I use K to transliterate it. When using G to transliterate gimel, we must acknowledge that its place in *our* alphabet is no longer third. Its bardic number is *ten* anyway, so no harm done. These Latin letters we use are still marginally adequate for transliterating tree-letters and the Hebrew alef-beyt, and for this I remain thankful.

The tarot trump is X The Wheel of Fortune, which, in addition to expressing desire, is an obvious reference to its atom-type, neon (think Las Vegas strip). Indeed *ten* represents the last Sefirah, which in Coins is the day or diurnal cycle, which indeed is the cycle neon is on (being turned on each night). As to how devisors of the Tarot of Marseilles were able to see into the future and make this reference, your guess is as good as mine. But since virtually every trump strongly references its atom-type, there is no question that that is part of its meaning. At any rate, of the seven pairs of opposites listed in *Sefer Yetzirah*, the one proper to gimel is **wealth and poverty**, obviously.

Again to differ with Graves as to what line of the Song of Amairgin corresponds to ivy, I suspect it is: *I am a griffon on a cliff*, or *I am a hawk on a cliff*, glossed *for deftness*. The reason is that this is scorpio, variously associated with scorpion, serpent, or eagle, and the griffon is half eagle. Plus, ivy clings to walls and cliffs.

פֵּף

Peh

Ah, now we come to the letter that accounts for two spots in the bethluisnion: this flaw, which edged *ngetal* the reed out of a job (amongst P-Celts anyway), balances the fact that ogham (the Boibel Loth) is flawed because of its juggling letters N-F-S into the order F-S-N, which put mother letter shin at the center of its proper Wheel yet displaced N over to the unvoiced passive side, where it obviously does not belong. Indeed in the New World, ogham Ng—three strokes— was used *in place* of N—as if in recognition of the fact that N's correct placement in the calendar would have allotted it three strokes, or else (as Barry Fell suggests) because it was less work.

At any rate, peh corresponds to two tree-letters: *peith*, the whitten or guelder rose (from whose dried berries ink is made); and *fearn*, the alder. The number *eight* was given to *fearn* but would have been held by *samekh* in Hebrew, which occupies *fearn*'s place (aries). The number *seven* was given to *peith*, yet peh still retains its connection to *eight* through its Hebrew number, *eighty*, while *eight hundred* is feh sofit (ף), which even resembles our F.

The Egyptian sequence does not even contain an Ng: instead, it has the prototype of samekh at aries. So the hieroglyph for P □ ***reed stool*** is geared to the Cauldron's sagittary in relation to the broken-and-extended zodiac, being on a level with capricorn, the knees (followed by B, ***foot-and-ankle***).

From the hieratic form ⼿ came ⊃ the old Hebrew peh, also written ⊃, in other words the bottom half of ⅁ (beyt). The reference to the ear stems ultimately from its number, *seven*, being the atomic number of nitrogen, which is fourt-fifths of the air.

Now *since* there is reference to the ear (by shape), I interpret the Sabean versions of the letter peh ◊ ◊ ◊ as picturing an earring. My first reaction, though, upon seeing these as well as the Thamudic versions Ω ⊓ (whence upper-case omega?) was a reference to the female organ. But now that I see the Thamudic versions sort of back the camera off to the whole head and how it is draped on each side with earrings, I demur.

Let us not forget Ugaritic ⊨ , which could be either a flattened version of ***reed stool*** or, oddly enough, the *p* of *Scandinavian* Tifinag ⊏ , *par*, 'pair', though I lean to the former, as the latter I think may hold Q's place—based on Greek influence I surmise, it being the interrogatory consonant in later Greek (and far north Tifinag having no *q*). The Ugaritic form *could* picture the fact that speech—what peh stands for—is something that progresses on two levels: that of sound, and that of thought.

Meroitic P ⊞ or ⊞ reverts to ***reed stool***.

Far north Tifinag had both F, *fearn* the alder, and Ng, *ngetal* the reed, but no Q (and pi was the Greek interrogative consonant). So Tifinag peh was ⋃ *far*, 'ferry', because in the far north it would have been ships that were made from alder, *the* moisture-resistant wood. In North Africa, this was changed to ⊟ or][, map symbol for a bridge, alder being the premier wood for bridge pilings. Interestingly enough, there is also a 'stray' *z* ⨝ which looks to me an awful lot like the 'ferry' and its reflection—in the calmer waters of the sunny Mediterranean perhaps? I am thinking it may have occupied the place of the voiced samekh or return to aries.

In the archaic Greek 'hymn' Graves reconstructs from the Boibel Loth letter names, F, *Forann*, becomes *forāmenon*, 'ferried'! And if the Nordic 'feh sofit' was the alder from which woman was created, we can see an echo of this in Sabean and Thamudic peh picturing a woman wearing earrings.

Runic has both F *and* P. The Elder Futhark starts with ᚠ **fehu*, 'cattle (wealth)', the Corn Spirit (alder). Then, at the end of the sequence of the four central runes—whose Hebrew numbers each presage the following rune's bardic number—comes ᛒ or ᛕ **perþ-*, the meaning of which is not known. But it can be seen from the shape that it represents the rune-cup having just disgorged its contents, a method of divination. This is consistent with square-Hebrew peh's opened-mouth-and-tongue of prophecy; and in the bethluisnion, P is *peith* the whitten or guelder rose, from whose dried berries ink is made; plus this suggests the archaic Welsh term *peithynen*, which means divination by a wheel on whose spokes maxims were carved.[41]

If we take *eight* as samekh (oxygen or *up*), then the trump for peh was VII The Chariot. This makes complete sense, as it is the only trump suggesting wind in one's face (the driver's), *seven* being the atomic number of nitrogen: four-fifths of the air, and thus four-fifths of speech. It also illustrates which of the seven pairs of opposites listed in *Sefer Yetzirah* is proper to peh, namely **dominion and servitude**—think Plato's parable of the chariot drawn by a well-behaved horse and an ill-behaved horse. (Associating speech with this pair makes one think of magic.)

Here is the best place to address the rather sticky problem of finalizing which lines of the Song of Amairgin go with which tree-months. I have associated *I am a boar*, glossed *for valor*, with F, and *I am a sound of the sea*, glossed *for horror*, with S. Yet this creates a problem, in that we are left with the line *I am an ox of seven fights*, or *I am a stag of seven tines*, glossed *for strength*. I have linked this to P, whose bardic number is *seven*. Yet ox and stag both explicitly refer to sign taurus the bull, which was linked to elk in northern Europe. But as we shall see, it is *tzaddi* (Ss) whose runic equivalent is 'elk', not shin or S (*I am a sound of the sea*), so we must be content to meditate on a connection between peh and tzaddi: the best I can suggest so far is that peh is closely linked to yod (the tongue in its mouth), which is on the same triad as tzaddi.

In Greek, vav's place in the alef-beyt was usurped by F, one of two letters stemming from peh. Vav's 'revenge' was to generate U, V, W, and Y (though it still did not get the last word).

While F geodetically corresponds to the grasslands of the Dnieper bend, appropriate for the Corn Spirit, P as *peith* corresponds to where the east coast of the Caspian is pinched off by a noticeable feature resembling P's Cauldron radius (emanating from its hub, F alias samekh) and consisting mainly of the Caucasus range—and thus obviously passing through L, our ***recumbent lion***, the point where that mountain range meets the Black Sea.

ב

Beyt

Beyt corresponds to tree-letter *beth* the birch, which stands for the first month of the year (beginning the day after the winter solstice), hence for birth or inception. Its white bark stood for the 'clean slate' of childhood. Its station, capricorn, is the Cauldron's *horizon within* (straight back or in), purged of all outward things, symbolizing holiness. Its bardic number is *five*, which reflects that at birth the first thing we do is count the digits of hands and feet. Yet this letter also has a decidedly martial overtone, as we shall see.

The Egyptian hieroglyphic *b* was *foot-and-ankle* . This and the preceding P-month *reed stool* follow the broken-and-extended zodiac down to the floor when standing (or seated on a stool). But the Habiru chose instead the hieratic sign used for B in group writing, a two-sound sign (its second sound being alef): the sign for the *b'* or *ba*, the *bird-soul*. The hieratic for this was a simplified , whence arose old Hebrew . This represents the high priest's mitre, or a conical helmet. Perhaps this conjunction of holiness with feet (in Egyptian) has something to do with Christ's washing of feet; remember, the family fled to Egypt when Iesus was a child.

The Ugaritic character, , pictures the interior half of the temple or manifested Throne world (Cauldron)—in relation to dalet's character , which adds the outer half of the temple *to* it. Or beyt can be interpreted as a shelter erected over alef's two arrows. Sabean has which shows a flat-roofed domicile (*beyt* means 'house'): note that it lacks the smoke rising from it, as in alef, this to make clear it is the shelter itself that is being referenced, not the spirit animating it.

In Scandinavian Tifinag, it was , apparently called *buckla*, 'shield, buckler'. This is because when the Spirit of the Year is newborn, it needs shielding. Then in the later offshoot, Numidian, it was altered to the alchemical symbol for the sun . This was to 'correct' the far-north Tifinag's placement of it at S, the willow month of early spring, when the sun first appears in the *far* north.

Meroitic has for B , a bull-like figure. I have not rendered it here, but the version of it in *The World's Writing Systems*[42] looks very like the *boibalion*—the Roebuck fawn, or Antelope-bull calf—Graves recovers from the letter-name *Boibel* of the Boibel Loth (ogham letter-names) in his reconstructed archaic Greek 'hymn'. Does this suggest survival of this hymn in Ptolemaic-era Nubia?

Thus we arrive at the era of runes, and runic B is just like ours: , profile of a pregnant torso. Its name was **bairkana-*, 'birch twig'. This obviously stands for the female pillar, Boaz, since the womb's swelling is *why* it is broken off at the sternum, and birch sumbolizes birth.

The rune surely comes from Greek beta; but where does Greek beta come from? It is fairly clear it did not come from the north Semitic beyt, above. Oddly enough, the most probable source for this shape is south Semitic mem, which has the same shape (ᖰ in Ethiopean). There is good linguistic and phonetic justification for this.[43]

Lycian had Β or β, and I wondered if the latter could be the source of our miniscule *b*? But in addition to these, there is another letter, ᗯ, transliterated β, and since this is obviously related to mem, it adds weight to what was just said about the shape of Greek beta coming from south Semitic M. But as for miniscule *b*, the betas of Thera, Crete, and Tiryns show signs of being the Semitic beyt turned upside down, and they resemble miniscule *b* almost as much.

Both the old Hebrew shape and the Greek shape express beyt symbolically, as does the square-Hebrew בּ, a dwelling or temple. Beyt's trump is V The Pope; he wears a mitre headdress like the Hebrew high priest and the old Hebrew beyt. Its bardic number, *five*, in addition to the counting of digits at birth happens to represent the Sefirah Mars in the suit Money, identifying the martial ideal as a mother defending her young—because she will not yield. This is why old Hebrew beyt can also be seen as the helm of a warrior. Hebrew בּ as *house of, temple of*, points to the sacred purity of one's home and creed; and old Hebrew beyt, the mitre or helm, points to that of one's chosen side in conflict. Is this not an injunction to be careful whose side you pick?

Since this tarot trump is often misunderstood, let me point out that the definitive feature of V The Pope is the *mother's arm* entering the card from the right *presenting* her twin sons (the waxing and waning year) to the Pope to be blessed. This is not only *not* a pointedly male symbol but in fact stands for Boaz, the female or front column of the body, and for motherhood. Perhaps the way to read old Hebrew beyt is to recognize that in a *civilized* society, both warrior and priest serve the institution of motherhood: warriors through strength, priests through their sagacity.

The atom-type that this corresponds to, boron, expresses both motherhood—the purity or 'clean slate' of the infant—and the cleansing or purification represented by the mitre of the high priest or Pope: its best known ore is borax cleanser. Based on this and its trump, of the seven pairs of opposites listed in *Sefer Yetzirah*, the one proper to beyt can only be **grace and sin**, also translated **beauty and ugliness**, but the first translation is clearly nearer to how the designers of Tarot of Marseilles saw it.

I differ from Graves with regard to B's line from the Song of Amairgin. I attribute to the birch month the line: *I am a tear of the sun*, glossed *'a dewdrop'—for clearness*. It must refer to sap of the birch, drops of which may appear on its bark (from which a refreshing drink is made). In Irish lore, Deorgreine, 'tear of the sun', daughter of Fiachna, in Magh Mell, the Otherworld (land of eternal youth), was given as wife to Laegaire for championing her father and winning, and he ruled there (first he visited Ireland but stayed mounted lest he touch the earth and die, as Ossian did in the tale of Niamh of the Golden Hair.)

Geodetically, beyt is perched in the Kirghiz-Kazakh steppe, which the Georges Dumézil school of comparative mythology identified as the birthplace of the Indo-European culture.

The Twelve Simples

סצחועקטהזילנ

ס

Samekh

Here we confront the zodiac sign involved in the Corn Spirit heresy. Since aries is the top (tip) of the Egg (tongue), Hebrew has for it a sound actually *on* the tongue, rather than the F that sprouts out *beyond* it. For in the tree-calendar, aries was F, *fearn* the alder, tree of Bran or Vran, whose severed head continued chatting for years. Since *Vran* apparently derives from the same root as Scandinavian *Fro* or *Freyr*, whose totem was the boar, I differ with Graves and assign to alder the following line from the Song of Amairgin: *I am a boar*, glossed *for valor*. For man reputedly learned to plow from observing the boar root up the ground with his snout. I used to wear a (pewter) boar pendent round my neck, in honor of the Corn Spirit: I guess this makes me something of a heretic (as if I were not already so from being Gnostic). I also use a boar-bristle brush on my hair.

One can see how the Jewish sages might have considered the alder god or Corn Spirit a pagan abomination in their monotheistic fervor, whereas I rather revere it as being not only the spirit of vegetation (surely a good thing) but the spirit of civilized *cultivation*, in place of raiding and looting, or hunting and gathering. Interestingly, Bran, the Celtic Kronos, provides evidence that the Greek *Kronos* was originally identical to *Krishna* by metathesis, *krns* versus *kršn: fearn* the alder is associated with *flutes*[44] and with the number *eight;* Krishna, who seduced using a flute, was the eighth avatar of Vishnu; and both Krishna and Kronos were apparently associated with the darkness of storm clouds.

Samekh is, obviously, the head and thus bears the (bardic) number associated with aries, *eight*, even though its actual letter-antecedent is *ngetal* the reed, whose tree-calendar station was (Cauldron's) sagittary, where it was replaced (in the bethluisnion) by P (numbered *seven*). But P and F both come from peh, F being its softer pronunciation—indeed feh sofit (ף) looks a bit like F. Since peh by this logic has two numbers associated with it, *seven* and *eight* (atomic numbers of the two main ingredients of air, nitrogen and oxygen), when samekh replaces *fearn* the alder at aries it adopts the number already assigned aries, *eight*, as confirmed by the fact that the head is spectacularly outlined in yellow (the color of ripened grain) in the trump VIII Justice (at least in the only reliable version, the Grimaud). Greek Phoroneus, whom Graves links to *fearn*,[45] was the Argive *lawgiver*.

There is a very good reason to retain *eight*'s assignment to the top: oxygen is the one atom-type without which there *is* no up; it is what we head upwards in water to find. And who is to say it was not samekh that first occupied aries, and *fearn* that was the usurper: this would seem the case, since the Greek alphabet added vau-digamma when it 'sprouted' from Semitic.

Yet Kronos was dethroned by Zeus: in Thera, xi (samekh) was only used as the initial of

Zeus.[46] So looking at it from a purely Gnostic point of view, the old way—nature worship—is represented by the Corn Spirit; but to prepare the way for the new dispensation (knowledge of the Triune Self, aka the Trinity), the alder god was unseated by the god of the oak D (sometime during the first millennium BCE, perhaps even earlier in Egypt), which, being on the Cauldron's outer rim, is on the same level as *fearn* the alder's station atop the Egg, to represent the metal mercury's +2 valence and toxic vapors by its swing across from Cauldron's sagittary, Mercury being Jupiter's (D the oak's) messenger.

The number bards gave aries (in the guise of *fearn*) fit into a number sequence expressing spring's increase: 4-8-16 are O-F-S, the vowel of spring followed by its first two tree-months. As the third spring month is H, *zero*, it would seem to mean plants' prolific flowering followed by wilting disappearance of same, source, I gather, of the motif of the oak king being sacrificed at the summer solstice (yes, oaks bear flowers).

At any rate, to begin at the (presumed) beginning, the sign for aries in the Egyptian model was ⚱ , which Gardiner calls **wick of twisted flax**, standing for the flame at the tip of the candle. It sounded as emphatic *h* (*h* with a dot under it), which, although unvoiced, occurs in the mouth where the sound Ng is, what samekh became in Tifinag, Lycian, runic, and ogham (the Boibel Loth).

The hieratic ⌐ evolved into ⊤ old Hebrew samekh. But samekh is an *s* sound, so what gives? The Greek letter stemming from this was xi, an *x* or *ks* sound; this combines a palatal (*k* from Egyptian emphatic *h*) with an unvoiced dental on tongue's tip (*s*), as does Ng (*n* + *g*), albeit in the latter case voiced. Samekh is on the cusp between voiced inner and unvoiced outer and is found in voiced and unvoiced form in the expanded south Semitic sequence, samekh's equivalent by shape that is, with my apologies to phoneticists for the slight phonetic shift (see below).

It is interesting that Graves[47] puts the adoption of xi and psi in Athens (i.e. adoption of Ionian over Attic) at the very time (403 BCE) that the Dorians finally dropped vau digamma: in other words, the Corn Spirit 'heresy' was being overthrown or downgraded, xi taking F's place, as does samekh in Hebrew. Indeed the *s* of xi better expresses aries than the *n* of *ng*.

In Ugaritic the unvoiced Ⴛ obviously pictures the head (or perhaps a budding flower). The voiced ⊨ is more problematical, yet as we are about to see the corresponding Sabean form suggests an animal, so we can interpret this character as horned prey felled. Since it is the voiced version, it would signify aries as approached from the voiced side, that is, as the thirteenth step (the return) and thus the *end of the round* (for the prey). This may indicate that the Egyptians' sign **animal belly with teats** (also a carcass), which sounded 'perhaps like *ch* in German *ich*' according to Gardiner (i.e. not far from *sh*), was also associated in some way with the end of the cycle. Yet phonetically the Egyptian counterpart of voiced samekh would have been the flat sign **bolt**, or *z*, which also poetically fits the end of the cycle (sealing things up). Perhaps the sign **animal belly with teats** was an alternate (less fortunate) ending, akin to mother letter shin, but this is a mystery I have yet to solve (if there *is* a solution).

To identify samekh's equivalent in Sabean, we must take into account two symmetrical pairs of sounds that were reversed in terms of letter-shape (heh-cheyt and samekh-tzaddi) and assign ⚲ as unvoiced equivalent, since it obviously pictures head-and-shoulders. The voiced version is ⚲, which can either be a person seated in a chair or a four-footed beast of some sort. When more curved ⚲ it could almost be a flower (apropos of spring). The Thamudic version of the unvoiced sound was curved ⚲ ; it does not appear to have had the voiced one.

Ethiopian has for the unvoiced sound the shapes ⛢ and ⚲ , the latter being again the head and shoulders, the former suggesting a cauldron; for samekh is at the center of the Wheel of which the Cauldron is the bottom half. There is evidence also in Tifinag and Numidian of the use of the cauldron symbol, namely for a *g* sound that must have taken the place of Nordic Tifinag's ⌠ , Ng, which was probably called *gneipa*, 'bent', eminently appropriate for the reed (which in the fable survives the oak *because* it bends). The Berber Tifinag no longer has this character but does have ✗ for a *g* sound different from the one cited under gimel, whereas in Numidian this same figure had the phonetic value of P: does this not smack of the cauldron shape being used for sagittary (Ng's station in the Boibel Loth)—this being the sign of the thinker, to whom the Cauldron belongs—and that it simply shifted to P when the latter was substituted for it as in the bethluisnion? The Numidian letter sometimes has the shape ☿ , the bag of winds from the *Odyssey* no doubt, sagittary being the active side of air. Numidian also had the sibilant ⊙ which I take as an echo of the (now moved) sun symbol of spring, possibly a stand-in for samekh at aries.

The old Hebrew character for samekh ⵊ , which is *ogam consaine* for Ng, represented Lycian *ñ*. This does not fit aries quite as well phonetically as *s*, but then neither does Egyptian emphatic *h*, nor the *k* part of Greek *ks* (xi).

Meroitic, while it has the hard P rather than soft F, since it does not have *both* of these *does* have Ng: ⚘⚘ , which in Egyptian (unpaired) represented a plant (probably sedge) standing for upper Egypt and the south;[48] yet unlike *ngetal* the reed in ogham, it would appear to occupy the sign samekh occupies, aries. For Meroitic P is **reed stool** from the Egyptian, which follows the broken-and-extended zodiac down the legs to the feet as Cauldron's sagittary: thus it stands in the place of *peith* the whitten.

As I see it, there are two possibilities. Either the Meroitic letter was meant to compass both ends of the broken-and-extended zodiac—which begins and ends at aries—or else it was the Egyptian sign for **rushes**, which, in Egyptian, showed *two* plants with only one pair of branches each. In fact, the latter is more probable, since it represented **nn** phonetically.[49] The single plant with two pairs of branches is *śwt* in Egyptian—cognate with our word *south?*—and it was used in group-writing with **quail chick** to represent *s*. Is it not interesting that these two hieroglyphs parallel the *ng* versus *s* dynamic of old Hebrew samekh? [Note that the unpaired two-branch-per-side version was also rendered growing from **mouth** (*r*) to represent phonetic **rśw** in the word **rśwt**, 'South',[50] thus linking **mouth** to its correct geodetic station (see above, under reysh).]

In ogham, Ng comes right after G, which makes sense since in Greek Ng was written as doubled gamma. The dynamics of all this I think can be described thus: the Corn Spirit heresy placed F at aries *whether or not* it also had P at sagittary, but wherever this heresy was absent (in Hebrew, Numidian, and Meroitic, there will only be found the version of peh at sagittary, where the bethluisnion places P. Thus the reason ogham (the Boibel Loth) still has its version of soft P (F) at aries is because they kept the Corn Spirit heresy but corrected the bethluisnion's doubling of peh by replacing it with samekh-equivalent Ng—unless ogham came first, which I doubt. For the order was slightly skewed in ogham—BLNFS became BLFSN—a sure sign in my estimation of which was the original and which was the version of it exported to the profane with its order skewed to conceal the secret. It is the bethluisnion order of letter-months that yields the amazing chemical and particle physics content (part of the oldest strata, if such knowledge dates from the last civilization, as it surely must).

The runic has two peh-equivalents *and* Ng; for it incorporates both Boibel Loth (ogham letters) *and* bethluisnion. Its Ng is ◊, which since it became ✗ in the Anglo-Saxon version of runes can be seen to picture a knot, the latter showing interwoven strands of reed, provocatively reminiscent of the hieroglyphic from which samekh itself evolved. The rune is named *inguz*, 'the god or hero Ing' (Inguis, as in Inguifreyr), and sure enough in the archaic Greek 'hymn' that Graves reconstructs from the Boibel Loth letter names, Ng, *Ngoimar*, yields *gnōrimos*, 'I, the famous one'.

The trump for aries—whether as samekh or as F—is VIII Justice, which corresponds to atom-type oxygen, without which there *is* no up, as expressed by the scales she wields (sense of balance). In its best rendition (the Grimaud version), the head is strikingly outlined in yellow (that it is *not* outlined in yellow in the Jodorovski version makes the latter an inferior rendition, in spite of its attractiveness). For this is the prophesying head of Bran or Orpheus, and stands, here at the top of the round, for the chief or lawgiver (which oxygen *is* for the diver). Thus its proper function (of the twelve listed in *Sefer Yetzirah*) is *speech*.

Samekh's geodetic placement is the grasslands of the Dnieper bend.

צץ

Tzaddi

Tzaddi corresponds to tree-letter *straif*, the blackthorn, bardic Ss or St, which, since it doubles S, occupies the latter's calendar month taurus, so S itself can be mother letter shin at the hub of the second Wheel. Since taurus is the neck or throat, intermediate tzaddi must picture the throat when breathing, tzaddi sofit the throat in swallowing. Its bardic number was secret, but it is easily seen to be *twenty*, as it represents strife, conflict between two ten-fingered beings. This stands for spring being campaigning season.

Its place in the Egyptian sequence was held by ⌐ *folded cloth*, an *s*, which is the cloth draped over the forearm in wall-paintings, presumably there for clearing one's nasal passage or throat (being taurus). Hieroglyphs on the Egg are: tall-tall-compressed, flat-flat-compressed, compressed, medium-tall-tall(x2), flat-flat (or flat-flat-flat). The pattern is an eminently coherent one.

Hieratic ⌐ led to ⌐ a banner waved in battle (occasionally it looks like an upset chair), the old Hebrew tzaddi.

The Ugaritic ⊤⊤ can only be understood in relation to bardic numbering: gimel, bardic *ten*, is ⊤ and tzaddi, bardic *twenty*, is ⊤⊤. These numbers represent *one* ten-fingered and *two* ten-fingereds, respectively: the first symbolizes individual *desire*, the second *strife* or *fair contest*. (Thus while Ugaritic G *can* be a pillar of Hermes or phallus, its primary meaning is one upright ten-fingered being's desire.)

I honestly cannot say for sure if far north Tifinag had a letter corresponding to *straif* the blackthorn, but they did have a second *r*, and since the other *r* is an *hr*, *hringr*, a classic initial sound, and since later Germanic had a final *z* sound that is often transliterated *R* (sound it tended towards), I should point out the possibility (for the study of those better qualified than I) that the Nordic Tifinag ⌐, probably called *rifa*, 'to split', represented *straif*. There is certainly resonance between the two—as well as consonance (agreement of more than one sound). This might pass for a symbol of what blackthorn *does* as La Mère du Bois: it splits earth with new growth.

But once this alphabet arrived in North Africa, there is no doubt what letter stood for tzaddi the throat: ⊃ phonetically *š*, which obviously pictures a torc, worn at the throat. There is another form of it that reminds me what a woman-friend of Irish background told me once. She said a proper torc would *strangle* the liar, which (from above) is precisely what ⌐ looks like (grabbing throat). Perhaps this latter form led to Numidian ✕ (*s*): my explanation is that an hourglass suggests time whose passage opens up once-tilled fields to La Mère du Bois.

This being the neck or throat, it is clear which letter-shape fills the bill in Sabean: ⌐, which is like samekh without the head. This and the preceding simple, samekh, are one of the two symmetrical pairs we reverse from their actual phonetic counterparts: fifth- and eighth-from-the-end in Hebrew, sixth- and ninth-from-the-end in Ugaritic.

The rune for taurus is the letter mentioned above that used to be transliterated with an *R*, a *z* sound found at the ends of words: Υ *algiz*, 'defense, protection', or *alhiz*, 'elk'. You can see that it is a bird's eye view of one. What better symbol both of a strong neck (like taurus the bull) and strife (rutting)! In fact, in the far north taurus was not the bull but the stag.[51]

I do not find any trace of tzaddi in Lycian. Indeed in classical Greek san M (sigma on its side?) was dropped completely from the sequence, having merged phonetically with sigma, a mere echo called sampi ϡ holding down *number* 900 (the number given tzaddi sofit in Hebrew). The makers of runes chose the form of Greek psi to stand for bardic Ss, and frankly, since they lived much closer in time to the Greeks *and* were Gnostics, I am inclined to take their word for it that psi stood for bardic Ss in Greek bardic tradition.

Trump XX Judgment pictures Judgment Day: angel surrounded by *spikes* holds trumpet up to *throat*, couple and child emerge from ground below (child from a coffin). This represents judgment by *fair* combat, whereas XV The Devil represents unfair combat, one side having one hand tied behind its back. I would remind the reader sometimes unfair combat is needed, say as military commander against superior numbers: the prime object in war is not to kill the foe but to so demoralize his command structure that you do not *have* to kill him.

It is the atomic number of calcium, main constituent of bone, referenced in the trump by the quasi-poetic notion that bone is all that will be left of one come Judgment Day, and of course by reference to the throat, blood calcium being regulated by the parathyroids, located in taurus the throat. The skeleton was used to symbolize aluminum's lightness-combined-with-strength, *that* trump's nickname being more suitable for the *last* sign than the *second* sign, which being straight back *from* the second sign represents an abstraction *of* that quality of bone. In fact you can look at it as: going on from aries, Judgment is with you; going back from it, against (Death).

As a sidelight of this, it is the male (taurus) tetrad that leans forward, the female (pisces) tetrad that leans back. So the trump nick-named Death is atop the female tetrad: why? It just came to me: the base of this tetrad is qof, the womb—life—and nun is its opposite. Similarly, the low end of the male tetrad is heh, the organ of pleasure, and Judgment is often spoken of as *its* opposite.

Bardic Ss is not named in the Boibel Loth, its place seemingly taken by *Idra* (see under yod). (Could this be why Lycian has no Ss?)

Its geodetic placement is the mouths or throats of the Danube. And the proper function to assign to tzaddi (of the twelve listed in *Sefer Yetzirah*) is *laughter—tz-tz-tz*—though this laughter is pictured in the barking dogs (or laughing hyenas) in the sign straight down from it, XVIII La Lune, which depicts *sleep*'s refuge *from* it.

ח

Cheyt

Cheyt corresponds to *huath*, hawthorn, whose month encompasses sign gemini, and we can see it pictures the shoulders-and-arms. This is the sign just prior to (just above) cancer or straight ahead and thus represents what is above the horizon: space itself (what arms reach out into). This explains its bardic designation as *no number*, since space represents no-thing, to us humans. It is what separates things; thus hawthorn is a hedge, and our letter H shows a section of fence. Indeed in the archaic Greek 'hymn' Graves reconstructs from the Boibel Loth letter names, H, *Uiria*, yields *ūrios*, 'I, the guardian of boundaries (or the benignant one).' And the line from the Song of Amairgin referring to hawthorn is of course: *I am fair among flowers.*

The corresponding hieroglyph ⊖ Sir Alan Gardiner calls **sieve**. The symbolic meaning is that shoulders-and-arms gemini can be used to block the way, filter who gets past. Its hieratic form ⊘ ended up squared off ⊟ in old Hebrew cheyt.

Ugaritic had ⊀, which can only be understood in relation to its version of teyt, ⊀, in that if we take the first as the shoulders and the second as the loins, then the extra *little* arrow pointing left at the bottom of the first one is to indicate there is more to come below (i.e. the loins), which is not true for the loins themselves. They are the only two letters that are crosses, which I interpret as cross-pieces (beams that cross the central vertical axis), as are shoulders and pelvis.

The Tifinag had ⠒ probably called *Hestemerki*, the constellation Pegasus: it certainly gives an impression of space, which is the meaning of this sign. Later, in Numidian it became half an H ⊢ which pictures blocking the way with one's shield, seen from the side, its probable source southern Italy (Heracleia, Tarentum), where this same sign was used to distinguish the consonantal H from the vowel eta. Other letters in Numidian that show Greek influence are the gamma and tau. Unless inscriptions in Numidian are found that are older than 400 BCE (which is doubtful), it can be surmised that the branching-off of Numidian from Tifinag must have taken place sometime after that, since the half-H sign dates from about then.

Sabean cheyt raises, again, the issue of the symmetrical shift of shapes from what would be strict phonetic equivalents, between heh and cheyt and between samekh and tzaddi. What was closer to cheyt phonetically was a comb, like old Hebrew heh (see below), and here what is closer to heh in sound is plausibly a glyph of a person with arms raised ⵖ and indeed it has been doubled in Sabean by a shape ⵗ that obviously represents the same thing only when seated. It turns out the letters that Sabean chose to double (divide into two letters), to bring its total up to twenty-nine, are the four macrocosmic signs on the nature side of the Egg, plus dalet, tav, and shin—the mother linked to the sign of the self on the macrocosmic hexad, plus her two minds (reason and rightness). The Thamudic has ⵉ for the standing one but ✕ for the seated one, perhaps to indicate that the one seated is a woman (with a skirt), the standing one a man (this is just my guess).

Interestingly, the Lycian alphabet does not really have a cheyt, but it has both the eastern and western versions of Greek chi: ✚ (Attica had both ✕ and ✚), transliterated *h*; and ⴸ (as in Etruscan), transliterated *k*. This suggests a rather eclectic Lycian perspective. Perhaps Lycian saw eta as a mismatch (as bardic H) and so used one of the above forms of chi for H instead, to avoid confusion with Greek eta; for the Greek it was exposed to is Ionian, which lost its *h* sound early on. That Lycian has both eastern and western chi suggests to me that one—I would opt for the cross in this case—stood for bardic H and one—Poseidon's trident?—for a second G (here unvoiced): desire to bestow (as opposed to acquire, see under gimel), albeit switched about from the eastern Greek (where desire to bestow was X-shaped chi, as in Christ).

For a long time I had a difficult time understanding what Greek tradition thought vowel eta symbolized, till it dawned on me it may have been meant to replace the 'missing' I—a vowel between *e* and *y*—that had originally been zeta, zeta having been promoted to Zeus's initial.

In Meroitic, H was ⬮ which seems to picture an open mouth: hot air, poof! Nothing. No-thing. Space.

The rune ᚺ merely adds a second crossbar to the H and slants them so they will not be horizontal and dig into the grain of the wood. It is named **hagalaz*, 'hail', which blocks the way forward for the farmer at least (turns his crops into empty space).

H's trump is The Fool, the one unnumbered trump, which pictures a vagabond walking through the countryside with a dog nipping at his pouch: he is the one *excluded* by hawthorn's hedge. His entire being is engaged in traversing space (H's 'atom-type'). The image on this card actually confirms that it is gemini: his mantle has five tassels ending in large dots (balls?), plus two white dots (or balls) where the staff with his belongings crosses the shoulders, these in all arrayed in a semicircle representing the seven manifested signs (the white ones are cancer-capricorn), which makes the one remaining dot, *bright red*, at the upper left—out on the tip of whatever that is on his head (coiffure? hat of some sort?)—the sign gemini. It could hardly be clearer.

The proper function assigned to cheyt (of the twelve listed in *Sefer Yetzirah*) is *walking* or *motion* (traversal of space) and what blocks it—***sieve*** or fence or hedge—the latter represented by its geodetic counterpart, the mountains of Thrace that blocked incursions of steppe horsemen that menaced from the northeast (which otherwise would have been a recurring *nor'easter*).

ו

Vav

Vav corresponds to tree-letter *ura*, heather, vowel of summer, the full moon, and love's consummation, occupying Egg's cancer (summer solstice). It is the bed of summer trysts; small wonder vav means 'and' in Hebrew. Its bardic number, *seventeen*, was the age of consent in ancient Ireland;[52] in the context of Irish mythology the "seventeenth birthday was the *aimsir togu*, the age of consent, when boys became men."[53] In piecing all this back together, I arrived at U being this number because V (Roman numeral *five*) was seemingly displaced from *five* (A-E-I-O being 1-2-3-4) to *seventeen* or fifth-from-the-end by B just as vav's Greek counterpart upsilon was displaced from sixth in Semitic to fifth-(or-sixth-)from-the-end by F.

Corresponding to vav is hieroglyph ⟿, **horned viper** (*f*), what stretches out ahead (forward on the Egg). The hieratic form ⟋ became Y old Hebrew vav: not a chalice, since it lacks a stand, it can only be a breast pouring forth milk. The Ugaritic ⊳⊢ makes this more than clear, even providing it with a nipple. South Semitic had ⊕, which is either cleavage (it is also found as a lazy-8) or a melon halved, either way symbolic of breasts and of the female.

It can be seen from the above that the doctrine of *Partzufim* in Lurianic Kabbalah has to be a blind: far from representing 'the Son' of a complete family (since *two* and *three* are the one male-female pair that do *not* bear offspring), the vav in the Name is the root of its female half. Apparently God's consort was expelled from the Temple in the time of the prophets, and I dare say the Ari (Luria) and his gang simply went along with a cover-up dating from those times—but only in part, since the Ari's 'unifications' of God with his Shekhinah are said to be between the YaH (yod-heh) and the WeH (vav-heh) of the Name.[54] It is hard to hear language like that and think the secret was unknown at the time; but their obsessive secrecy was even then precipitating decay's forgetfulness.

Tifinag *w* was ⁝ or ⊜ and most likely called *waettir*, 'weights' (Numidian was ⹀). This creates a quandary, in that its form corresponds to ogham O yet its sound corresponds to vav or bardic U. The sound in Berber Tifinag occupying the ogham U spot is transliterated *g̣* (*y?*), which seems to point more towards ayin than vav (though I could be wrong), and *w* points more towards vav than ayin. I am tentatively of the opinion that this branch of bardic tradition may have *reversed* O and U in the ogham sequence, for the same reason I would be tempted to myself: the simples U and O are on the Egg's fiery and airy level, respectively, and fire and air more naturally flow through index and fool's finger, respectively, so a simple switch and they are now on the proper fingers. As upsetting as this possible reversal may be, it is still remarkable to find vowel-equivalents represented in their later ogham guise in this era a millennium or more before ogham vowels appeared in Ireland and Britain.

The Meroitic vowel U was ⟨lasso symbol⟩ the ***lasso*** that limits (phonetically) how far ***bull's head*** O can stray from ***seated human*** A (*ah*)—just as summer's adulthood limits how far spring's youth and schooling extend outward from yuletide alef (year's birth).

The transmission into Greek resulted in a strange fate for our original vav—whether any of it can be attributed to de-feminization of vav I will let the reader judge. In Lycian (mid-first millennium BCE), F represented *w*, from Greek vau-digamma (our F), which took vav's place and name. Vav itself, Greek upsilon (our U *and* Y) was displaced to (or near) the end in Greek. Western Greek (whence our Latin) kept both; but in the east vau-digamma became a mere cipher for the number *six*, no longer a letter. The vowel (upsilon) was placed after tav at the end; in fact it took tav's number (400), pushing tau-through-qoppa back to 300-90.

In spite of F occupying vav's place in the sequence, I instead classify it as the soft version of peh and trace its provenance to the Corn Spirit (spirit of vegetation), the heresy of the alder-god. This would mean the suppression of vau-digamma in Greek was similar to Hebrew having at F's station of the Egg a sound (samekh) actually *on* the tongue, rather than a duplicate of peh.

Oddly enough the runes offer corroborative evidence: if you turn runes F and P on their sides thus ⟨runes⟩ they resemble Greek pi and omega, numbered 80 and 800, where Hebrew places peh and feh sofit. So if you do not mind, I will defer discussing F till we get to peh, its proper context.

The rune for U is ⟨rune⟩ *ūruz*, 'aurochs', and represents the upended drinking horn that made a youth a warrior (back before the aurochs was hunted to extinction), this because the meaning of *ura* the heather is youth's coming of age (full moon).

The vowel U shapes the mouth as if it were suckling, vav being a breast. Its trump, XVII The Star, the only trump with realistic breasts (those of XXI The World look pasted on), shows a nude woman pouring some chlorine (atomic number *seventeen*) in her pool from two amphorae. That she pours from two amphorae also symbolizes the mingling of fluids in *coition*, this being the function properly assigned the simple letter vav (of the twelve functions jumbled in various versions of *Sefer Yetzirah*). For bardic U is the noetic breath; the knower contacts us at puberty. The trump sports a female figure because of the pagan tradition that a girl-child is to be weaned during a full (U) or waning (Aa-E-I) moon.[55]

In that archaic Greek 'hymn' Graves constructed from Boibel Loth letter names, U, *Ura*, leads to *Urania*, Queen of Heaven. This suggests that of the six questions following the thirteen *I am* lines of the Song of Amairgin, the line for U is: *5. On whom do the cattle of Tethra smile?* the 'cattle of Tethra glossed (when first mentioned) [*i.e.* '*the fish*', Macalister, *i.e.* '*the stars*', MacNeill].

Geodetically, vav represents the west coast of Greece (the region of Ithaca, Odysseus's home). And indeed the Greeks as they moved west (to colonize southern Italy, for example) did represent a ***horned viper*** in that they were *the* formidable warriors of their time—at least till the Roman maniples managed to out-flex the phalanx on rougher ground, which is perhaps why this ***viper***, like all Egyptian signs, faces back towards us as we progress from right to left on the page.

ע

Ayin

Ayin corresponds to tree-letter *onn*, the furze or gorse, vowel of spring, symbolized by its bright yellow blossoms: in spring, the old prickles are burned away so that tender new ones will sprout, which sheep love to eat (spring equinox being the sign of the ram). Its bardic number, *four*, identifies spring as the flourishing of nature's four elements. Its station on the Egg, leo, would seem at first out of place, but being the hottest month of the year, it represents where the alchemical vessel is heated, and being the base of mercury's column, the latter's toxic vapors then leap up into the top half of the outer vessel to *compass* spring, this being the only way any vowel, all of which are confined to the bottom half of the Egg, *could* rule it. This is the famed Greene Lyon of Newton's alchemy, as it implies also the filling out of foliage in spring: O is the hermetically sealed vessel necessitated by mercury's vapors; of operations, the *circulatio*.

Just as O's station, leo, is the summer warmth that attracts spring, its shape is what draws the waxing moon to it, what the moon *grows towards*, thus symbolizing teleological causation in a sense, educating youth *so* it might become educat*ed*, or cultured. This leads me to associate with O the question (of the six questions following the thirteen *I am* statements of the Song of Amairgin): *3. Who foretells the ages of the moon.* As spring and as waxing moon, O signifies youth, when discovery makes us say, "Oh!" It is the mental breath (that part of the thinker's breath or activity that is in the doer's atmosphere, the Egg); hence its proper function (of the twelve listed in jumbled order in *Sefer Yetzirah*) is *thought*.

The Egyptian hieroglyph was ▭—◦ *forearm*, man's rough approximation of the cubit. I take this to mean *measurement*—the cubit was a round fraction of a degree of latitude—but also an arm *extended in greeting*, in addition signifying *elbow-grease*. In the geodetic model, it is the straits between Crete and mainland Greece, where one can imagine the typical crew might have found it prudent to row vigorously, to get past it quickly and safely.

The hieratic was ↪ , which led to a bit of horseplay on the part of the Hebrew sages who were adapting Egyptian hieratic and group writing to their own tongue (letters taken with them in the Exodus). It looked like a stick with a feather tied to each end *spinning . . .* so they *spun* it O to produce ayin. You can see in old Hebrew how Egg's leo or air, ayin, is the wheel *spinning*, while its libra or earth, ⊗ teyt, is the wheel *stopped*.

The Ugaritic split ayin into two letters (it being on the nature side of the macrocosmic hexad): ‹, and ↗. The first, I finally figured out, expresses circularity in its own way, as an arrow pointing back the way we came (Ugaritic being written left-to-right). I deduced this from this and another letter in which it is used, namely qof, where it would also have stood for an orb (see qof). The second form above points to leo's being one thirty-degree angle beneath straight out. It also suggests looking at a thing from two different angles (triangulation); or two paths crossing; or perhaps the more esoteric meaning of *where two thoughts intersect*, this being what precipitates the *exteriorization* of a thought: it is the exteriorizations of thoughts that constitute physical reality. (The two crossed lines in old Hebrew *teyt* show these intersecting thoughts *in the act* of precipitating the concrete.)

Sabean and Thamudic both have the O , while the other ayin, usually transliterated *ğ*, is in Sabean ⊓, which would appear to me to be a ligature of B ⊓ and L ⌐ , the consonants in the god-name Ba'al. I would guess that this second ayin was distinguished from the first as the one in the name Ba'al (spelled with ayin in Hebrew), storm and fertility god: this ligature letter may perhaps have stood for *Ba'al*; it was a word that meant 'lord' originally, then was later used as a divine title. In its simpler form BL (first two tree-months), it is seen inscribed in Phoenician and *ogam consaine* across Old World and New, indeed wherever Phoenicians and their Celtic allies roamed (including North America). (After the downfall of Carthage, its fleet was replaced by that of the Veneti, Gauls' maritime-and-navy-in-one, till *they* were ground under by Caesar; both managed to keep it secret from Rome, thus excluding its iron boot from the New World, though a few individual Romans made it here.)

The Thamudic second ayin was ⅃ , which would seem to be two pairs of arms pushing a crank of some sort—oxen-like, powering a pump? Perhaps the 'arms' are harness connected up to oxen. This latter interpretation appears to be corroborated by Meroitic O ⵣ , the head of one of them. The Thamudic, at any rate, does reinforce my *spin* theory of O's origin.

Meanwhile, in Tifinag (as pointed out earlier) it seems that O and U got turned around in terms of their ogham representation, the *ġ* there being ⦂ or ☰ (⦂ or ☷ was *w* or vav).

Runic has ᛜ *ōþila,-ala*, 'heritage, inheritance', which pictures either the hood of one's teacher or that of a child being sent to class; for this is the vowel of spring, of youth when one is still learning one's way in the world—Little Red Riding Hood? What has made its mark on the past is what is taught the young: in that archaic Greek 'hymn' Graves reconstructs out of the Boibel Loth letter names, O, *Ose*, becomes *ossa*, 'fame'.

Ayin's atom-type, beryllium, shares mercury's valence (+2), and that is a beryl (emerald or aquamarine) on the chest of trump IIII The Emperor, who, since this is spring-into-summer, is enthroned out in the countryside, no doubt campaigning. It is a male figure because of the pagan tradition that a boy-child should be weaned during a new or waxing moon,[56] O being the waxing.

One last consideration. While *onn* the furze as symbol of spring is yellow-flowered, O's station is summer's heat; so yellow O is part of the red U (coloration) phase of alchemy, or the Rubedo, a preliminary type of gold perhaps; perhaps some such consideration led to Little *Red* Riding Hood.

ק

Qof

Qof corresponds to tree-letter *quert* the apple (probably originally the crab apple, which is a thorn tree), glossed 'shelter of a hind' in *The Scholar's Primer*. Since this is Kk, it occupies K's sign, but on the Egg: virgo the womb, which the modern Hebrew letter is a cross-section of (with its two openings, navel and birth canal). Its number, also, doubles K's (*nine*): *eighteen*, being nine months' gestation for the mother *plus* nine for the child in her womb.

The hieroglyph was 𓈋 ***hillslope***—the pregnant belly, in a sense. This is about the time of year in ancient Egypt when the Nile was flooded and high ground was one's refuge, 'refuge of a hind' you might say. Hieratic 𓈋 gave rise in time to ♀ old Hebrew qof.

The Ugaritic 𐎖 shows that this large shaft-less left-pointing arrow on the right, when used in this letter and ayin, expresses what old Hebrew expressed with an orb, the rationale being it points so as to 'circle back' the way we came (writing left-to-right). The difference from ayin is that here it has a stem attached.

In the south Semitic alphabets it took the form ቀ , the fruit on its branch.

The place of qof in far north Tifinag is obscure, but in addition to F *and* Ng, there was a *p* sound ⊏ , probably called *par*, 'pair': I suggest this might have held the place of interrogative consonant Q—which later became pi in Greek. In Mycenaean Linear B, roughly contemporary with these Scandinavians, it was still *q*, but who knows if in some branch or other of Greeks the change had not already occurred; these seafarers from the north perhaps *associated* questioning with Greeks. It is like a pi on its side, or perhaps a simplified ***reed stool***, the Egyptian ***p***.

At any rate, once Tifinag arrives in North Africa, there is ∘∘∘ a clear Q showing fallen apples strewn about before they are picked up and stacked in a ⵂ (K). This Q was then turned into ||| in Numidian.

Q being doubled K, in Lycian K is K like Greek kappa, and Q is Ж , two of them back-to-back. Eastern or classical Greek, which discarded qoppa (except as numeral 90), had the letter phi Φ , which is virtually the same letter, albeit after the interrogative sound-shift from *kw* to *p* or *ph*.

Meroitic reverts to the Egyptian 𓈋 ***hillslope***, sometimes crudely rendered Δ thus.

Runic has ᚹ, half the fruit on the end of a knife. This is *w*, the interrogative consonant in German: **wunjō*, 'joy'.

Qof is XVIII The Moon, in which a face seeks refuge in the moon's dark orb to evade the barking of dogs (or laughing of hyenas) between two towers, while a crustacean lurks in a pool. This represents argon, through the reflex by which we often mistake an argon-filled street lamp *for* the moon. Appropriately enough, in the archaic Greek 'hymn' Graves reconstructs from the

Boibel Loth letter names, Q, *Cailep*, yields *calyptomai*, 'I vanish' (as does the moon, which in this trump is dark), confirming that the figure in the moon is trying to hide. Appropriately, qof's proper function (of the twelve jumbled about in *Sefer Yetzirah*) is *sleep*, since this is what the child in the womb spends the bulk of its time doing.

Geodetically Q is the near shore of Libya, in the vicinity of Kyrene (whence *Cyrenaica*). They phonetically match as well: Q = K before U, upsilon in Greek, our *y*.

ט

Teyt

Teyt corresponds to bardic Aa, which Graves identifies with *ailm* ('alev') and the palm (a second meaning). This perfectly fits the symbolism of palm as *phoenix* (reborn in flame), since as bardic Aa it is the fire breath: the aries of a fire unit's movable zodiac is at cancer (manifested fire), so its cancer or *breath* points to libra (teyt); hence of the twelve functions listed (in jumbled order) in *Sefer Yetzirah*, the one proper to teyt is *sight*. A is *one*, hence Aa is first-from-the-end, or *twenty-one*. This makes it the heaviest atom-type, which suits the direction *straight down*.

The Egyptian hieroglyph ⌓ or *t* Gardiner calls **loaf**. It shares libra with reysh, **mouth**: in the geodetic model, this latter stands for the masses of Upper Egypt that consume the former, meaning the bread produced in the bread-basket of the Nile delta (Lower Egypt). For libra is at Giza and marks the border between the two.

The hieratic was ⌒ and it is difficult to reconcile this shape with old Hebrew ⊗ or ⊕ until you connect the Hebrew with a different style of loaf, namely flatbread or pita, here cut into quarters: this is the oldest type of bread archeology can attest, and it *originated* in the Levant. And since teyt stands for location, location, location, there is no doubt it was influenced by the sign ⊗, ideogram for 'place', from common association with the word or prefix *t3*, 'land', as in *T3-mri* ⊗ 𓈖 𓏤 𓂋 𓄿 ⬅ 'the land of *mr*', one name for Egypt.

Perhaps this crossroads sign influenced the shape of Ugaritic teyt, ⊬; it was explained earlier (see cheyt, above) that this letter's lack of a smaller arrow pointing to the bottom of the staff meant there is *not* another 'cross-roads' beneath it, teyt thus being the loins.

Tifinag had ᚒ, probably called *thili*, 'planks, partition', which suggests to me seeing palm trees from the deck of a ship. Berber Tifinag divided it into ᚒ voiced (*d*), and ᚓ the unvoiced (*t*). In Numidian these became ꓱ and ꓱ⌐ .

A similar division of teyt occurred in Sabean: voiced (*d*) ⊟ and unvoiced (*t*) ⊓ (easy to remember if you just note that to lift up a crate to place it on top of another is accompanied by a grunt and thus is voiced). Thamudic has what Bernal calls the 'open theta' (which he traces to several peripheral alphabets), namely ⋂ and Ψ, which reinforces my idea that the Thamudic was subject more to outside influence (Tifinag), Sabean being an intact symbol system making no use of imported letter-shapes (other than the influence of north Semitic).

Meroitic is very interesting: the only two (from my perspective) syllabic signs, ⌐ *to* and ⊓ *te*, illustrate to me that there was deep understanding here; for bardic Aa is in part a symbol of the fact that vowels go off in both directions from it. And in these two is embodied a scheme I only noticed recently, by which the Meroitic characterizes the Boaz side of things (that is, towards U from A) as 'bullish'—B is a **bull-calf**, O an **ox-head**, *to* is the bull's **horn**, and U a *lasso*—and the Jachin side of things (towards I from A) as 'reedish'—Ii is **two reeds**, *te* a **reed hut**, and I a **standing person** based on association with **one reed** in Egyptian (see under zayin).

It is the last rune ⋈ or ⋈ , called **dagaz*, 'day': this is an hourglass on its side, symbol of the present instant (today). Though it was the last rune in the oldest known inscribed *futhark*, in later *futharks* the last two were switched about, an obvious ploy to avoid the accusation that they revealed the whole secret. But there is no doubt in my mind that **dagaz* was last, so that the entire sequence 'dumps' its results into the present instant, so to speak.

This is XXI The World: libra, the present. It is the last *trump* for a reason: Aa reflects alef or *one*. What I mean is that whereas alef is the A of the Logos and symbolizes the doer, who is part of the conscious self and therefore eternal in nature, Aa symbolizes the fleeting present instant in which the doer must act, which is dark. The midpoint between the two, or XI Force, is T, rightness, the thinker, and thus concerned with what has finite duration. These three are one mother (alef), one double (tav), and one simple (teyt), and they form a sort of framework for the trumps. Because libra is the point the four Wheels have in common (the present instant being present also in any finite or non-finite duration), XXI Le Monde pictures (outside the wreath) the four signs Ezekiel mentions that identify the Wheels as zodiacs. The dancer within the wreath shows that the function properly assigned teyt is *sight*.

The chief figure in the trump is female because in pagan tradition a girl-child was to be weaned during a full or waning moon,[57] and Aa represents a return to the middle of the vowel spectrum (after full moon U) to progress in the other direction as moon wanes (E-I).

The atom-type is scandium, first of those rare earth metals whose rarity has led to many of them being named for *where they are found* (location, location, location), as with scandium itself. Indeed an early variant of the trump shows a hamlet seen through the porthole of a low-flying jet.

As for teyt or theta in the Song of Amairgin, the questions twice mention Tethra, king of the Fomorians (*Fo-* being 'under' and *mor* being 'great'). *Tethra* comes close, as does possible cognate Tethys or Thetis (the latter the mother of Achilles), to *teth* (as sometimes written) and *theta*. But I am inclined to associate it with the first of the six questions following the thirteen *I am* statements: *1. Who makes clear the ruggedness of the mountains?* or *Who but myself knows the assemblies of the dolmen-house on the mountain of Slieve Mis?* glossed *'Who but myself will resolve every question?'* For this question makes me think of reading a map to identify one's location. Yet teyt is the one bardic vowel that is not a vowel anywhere else, so it probably does not merit one of the six questions (which I assign to the six runic vowels).

ה

Heh

Heh corresponds to tree-letter *eadhe*, quivering aspen, vowel of autumn and the waning moon. The aspen's leaves shimmer in the slightest breeze; for E is the air breath, which means that of the twelve functions listed (jumbled) in *Sefer Yetzirah*, the one proper to heh is *hearing*.

Its place on the Egg is sign scorpio (mid-autumn), attributed in old almanacs to 'secrets' (meaning one's 'privates'); for it corresponds to the male organ (clitoris in females). This is why it was added to Abram to make Abraham, commemorating the covenant of circumcision. And indeed circumcision is on the eighth day *because* heh is the eighth sign. Its bardic number is *two*, since air (whose breath this is) is the second element: as the vowel of autumn, it stands for maturity and thus for 'second thoughts'.

First of the concious self's three signs on the Egg, in Egyptian it is ***reed hut*** 𓉔, such as was put up in the field for workers. Since its hieratic shape was , it is easy to see how this became old Hebrew 𐤄 a comb. Ugaritic 𐎅 had virtually the same form. The Sabean character corresponding to this—even though phonetically closer to cheyt (see below)—was 𐩢, a slightly different kind of comb (which in Thamudic lost its handle). That compresses quite a few centuries into one short paragraph.

The interesting thing about a comb is that in the Eleusinian Mysteries, this according to Clement of Alexandria,[58] a woman's comb symbolized the female organ. This combined with its being the letter added to Abram to make Abraham confirms it is scorpio, which is where bardic E falls in the distribution of vowels across the floor of the Egg.

Unexpressed in Scandinavia, the heh in Berber Tifinag was ⵓ or basically the ogham E of a later era; in Numidian this was usually written ≣. That the ogham vowels of a later era were used in early-to-mid first millennium BCE for vowel-equivalent consonants like those of Semitic is powerful evidence in favor of the labeling of certain Hebrew letters *bardic vowels*. I see the Celtic and Judaic traditions as two serpents entwined on the *caduceus* of truth (balancing two waveforms or snakes).

The Lycian form E was the same as the Greek. So in the north—including Ugaritic long order—the comb form had the sound associated with heh's place in the alef-beyt, while in the south it was closer *phonetically* to the sound of cheyt in north Semitic. Heh and cheyt are fifth and eighth in the alef-beyt, sixth and ninth in Ugaritic long order (akin to alef-beyt order). And by *shape* one can say the same of the south Semitic phonetic equivalents of samekh and tzaddi, eighth- and fifth-from-the-end, ninth- and sixth-from-the-end in Ugaritic. So I hypothesize the only thing that makes sense: that Sabian reversed each pair of sounds in terms of the shapes used to express them: perhaps they heard them differently. At any rate the sounds that were switched were very close, so no upset occurs to the bardic view. Letter-order in Sabean was very different anyway.

One gathers from Sabean letter-order that heh by *shape*, which was third, was correctly coupled with alef, third *in the second half* (the first half consisting of fourteen, the second half of fifteen, just as L and R are bardic 14 and 15). Only when the last two letters, the two variants of samekh, are compressed into a single place (to make the halves equal, like the two *l*s in Apollo) does yod then become third-to-last and thus couple with alef (third in the second half), allowing heh, third, to be coupled with mem, fourth (next to it), by juxtaposition—vav, sixth, is coupled with shin, seventh, by juxtaposition in either case. It is clear that this way of reckoning expresses a heretical viewpoint (one that was current then) and that the correct coupling is yod with mem, and heh with alef.

The Meroitic E was ꓐ, Egyptian hieroglyph of a feather, since it is the air breath. This links it to its counterpart on the Cauldron, where scorpio is the Geb goose (see under gimel). The only other bird in Meroitic was the *owl*, M, one of the original three bird-signs constituting the Logos in Egyptian.

Then we come to the rune: runic E was ᛗ, *ehwaz* or 'horse', and pictures (this being scorpio the privates) a horse's underside or belly, suspended between its two pairs of legs. This smacks of horse-breeding of course. One version of Latin E (according to the Britannica of the early fifties) was ‖ (to go with ‖ for F), which could have inspired the rune; yet the runes seem more closely linked to the eastern Greek (as opposed to western Greek) alphabet (as evidenced by psi's having been adopted as runic Ss).

Heh's trump is a very interesting one: it took me decades to realize it, but II La Papesse can only be meant to portray the Pope after he has imbibed a quantity of its atom-type, helium, causing his voice to rise up into the female register. Considering all the trumps reference their atom-types, this is the obvious explanation of why this trump exists. And yet another interesting characteristic of this trump is that there is a quite risqué love scene in the air above La Papesse so to speak, since what passes across 'her' chest to fasten 'her' cloak is shaped like an erect phallus extending from the draperies on the left to those on the right that resemble a woman's skirt. So the very picture identifies this trump as the privates.

Judaism or druidism *either one* might be described as a *religion of second thoughts*. In the Great Name, יהוה, the two hehs symbolize by their *Hebrew* number, *five*, that each half of the Name has given the other its hand in troth. And consistent with the function *hearing*, La Papesse is reading to us out of a book.

We moderns may be aware that La Papesse only *seems* female, from having inhaled some helium. But it is still ostensibly a feminine figure (and title), this because pagan lore stipulated that a girl-child be weaned during the (full or) waning moon.[59] And in the archaic Greek 'hymn' Graves reconstructs from Boibel Loth letter names, E, *Esu*, becomes *(h)esuchia*, 'repose', which is appropriate for one's mature years (and the time just after the harvest). It also calls to mind the modern expression *slept with*, meaning 'had intercourse with'.

Given the season represented, it probably follows that of the six questions following the thirteen *I am* statements in the Song of Amairgin, the one refering to E is: *2. Who but myself knows where the sun shall set?*

The geodetic significance of heh is Moab, where Moses remained when the Jews entered the promised land after their exodus from Egypt.

ז

Zayin

Zayin corresponds to tree-letter *idho*, yew, the vowel of winter, the old moon, old age, death, and rebirth. It is one of the longest lived of trees and possesses the ability to regenerate itself (extend new roots) and survive damage. Its leaves are poisonous, its botanical name *taxus* being cognate with our word *toxin* (both borrowed from the Scythian). And it stands for Jachin (toxic masculinity?), the male column (spine), originally for use of the Triune Self. Hence its number, *three*, which identifies it as the third member of the sequence new moon, full moon, old moon (the Goddess's three faces). It also identifies this letter as the water breath: its station on the Egg is sagittary, where the cancer or breath of a water unit (with aries at virgo) points—next sign after Samhain (Halloween), the start of winter in Celtic tradition. So of the twelve functions jumbled up in *Sefer Yetzirah*, the one proper to zayin is *taste*.

In Greek, zeta is the initial of Zeus (genitive *Dios*) and represents corruption of D by I (they occupy the same sign): like our letter J, it is an I that has solidified into a consonant. This stands in part for the corruption (takeover) of the lower spine by the elemental breaths. In that archaic Greek 'hymn' Graves reconstructs from Boibel Loth letter names, I, *Jaichim* (close to *Jachin*, the version from Gwion's riddle), yielded *iachema*, 'shrieking' or 'hissing', the natural human reaction to death.

Of the questions following the thirteen *I am* lines of the Song of Amairgin, by process of elimination bardic I would be: *4. Who brings the cattle from the House of Tethra and segregates them?* [*i.e. 'the fish'*, Macalister, *i.e. 'the stars'*, MacNeill]. The best argument I can make for this is that taking them *as* cattle (or fish), some are apparently being separated out for slaughter, being winter and death.

The Egyptian hieroglyph corresponding to zayin is ∤ *one reed*, the second of the three signs of the self, all involving reeds. It is sagittary the archer, so we view this reed as a potential arrow. The sequence *one reed*, *two reeds*, or sagittary-capricorn, echo *Bahir*'s calling ninth and tenth two Netzachs or Victories, this because they represent thinker and knower, the two parts of self that did not undergo the Fall. The hieroglyph represents a guttural sound transliterated *ỉ*, and indeed this is the bardic letter I. Its geodetic position is upper Mesopotamia; this goes well with the following sign, *two reeds*, which marks the source of its two rivers, near Mount Ararat.

The hieratic was ⅃ which evolved into old Hebrew zayin's various versions: sword-handle or pillar-like I (what Bernal would call a 'bobbin'), swan-like ⲍ (swans winter in the Middle East), and the one we still use (though it has been kicked to the very end of our alphabet), namely Z , which I finally realized pictures—better than the rune (see below)—a cold front, that is, cold air moving in under warmer air (my father was a weather observer during WWII).

The Ugaritic character was , which is obviously a sword: *zayin* means something like 'sword' or 'weapon'. Sabean had  or , an hourglass. (I see this as evidence they had them.) The reference must be to the yew's extreme longevity. Thamudic had T or ˥, the former a sword-handle perhaps, the latter *possibly* referring to zayin's being on the Cauldron-radius of gimel (gamma).

Meroitic had , which is found in the Egyptian word 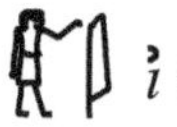 *ỉ* (an expression of distress, like our 'o' or 'woe is me') and thus came to replace ***one reed*** in meaning winter, old moon, and death. It is the only other human besides alef in Meroitic and thus reinforces prefacing the Logos with I, which (as here) stands for the upright human form.

The rune proved to be crucial to identifying zayin as bardic I. It is clear from Meroitic that there is a distinction between this bardic I and bardic Ii the mistletoe, for they also have the hieroglyph ***two reeds*** standing for the consonantal *y* sound, corresponding to yod. And in runes the same two vowels are ᛇ **eihwaz*, 'yew tree', a sound between *e* and *i*, and ᛁ **īsa*, 'ice'. The former is obviously bardic I, the latter bardic Ii. It is easy to see that the shape of the former is precisely what zeta would look like carved across the grain of wood, eliminating horizontals (by slanting them). This is what confirmed for me that zayin was indeed bardic I.

The trump for this letter manages to express its atom-type, lithium, in a subtle way: the eagle on the shield at the feet of III The Empress extends its tail feathers out beyond its shield to *embrace her about the middle*, obviously to comfort her, just as lithium comforts those who are bipolar. This is actually the biggest stretch of any of the trumps with regard to expressing their atom-types. The main image on its trump is female because pagan custom prescribed weaning a girl-child during a (full or) waning moon, and this is the old moon.[60] Yet it is the letter standing for the male pillar Jachin; hence we identify with the eagle on the shield reaching out to comfort her, just as with B's trump we identify with the mother whose arm enters the card from the right. The trump reminds us that in the traditional family structure (of which a few vestiges still exist), the wife is Empress in her own kitchen.

י

Yod

Yod corresponds to the (perhaps grafted) oak-mistletoe sacred to Gauls, or the loranthus, *ixias* in Greek, which grows on oaks naturally: mistletoe is a part of our Yule custom and thus occupies sign capricorn on the Egg. It is the only tree-letter not rooted in the ground, just as yod is the one letter that in square Hebrew does not come down to the line on which one writes.

Since it is bardic Ii, and bardic I is *three*, I make it third-from-the-end, or *nineteen*. This is a number associated with reconciling solar and lunar time, and mistletoe is Virgil's 'Golden Bough', so it is trump XVIIII The Sun. Moreover, it is the earth breath, since capricorn is where the cancer (breath) of the movable zodiac of an earth unit (with its aries at libra) points. Thus Ii continues a theme of earth being a mere adjunct or result of water, the element preceding it, just as *Sefer Yetzirah* 1:11 of the Gra version says, regarding the third Sefirah:

> And He poured snow over them
> and it became dust
> as it is written
> "For to snow He said, 'Become earth' " (Job, 37:6).[61]

This means earth, the physical, is a result or solidification out of water or form, the third Sefirah ('Water from Spirit').

The hieroglyph was ◖◗ *two reeds* (or // *two strokes*); and just as mistletoe or loranthus does not grow in the soil but on other trees, this sign only occurred at the ends of words. The hieratic was ⑪ which somehow got twisted about into ⟍ the old Hebrew yod. This last is a striking picture of someone drawing a line in the dirt with a stick—the old method of teaching *secret* letters, right here before our eyes, a secrecy maintained by then rubbing it out with the foot. This must have been a method of teaching letters in cultures like that of the Celts (with whom the Phoenicians of Carthage were allied against Rome) where the public inscription of letters was taboo. This yod can also be seen as someone plowing, and the tiny square-Hebrew yod of a later era (י) the seed that gets sown. Since this is the sign signifying knowledge, we should interpret **one reed**, the I or zayin preceding it (at sagittary), as *making a record of*, and **two reeds**, Ii, as *confirming the record of*—the former *thought*, the latter *knowledge*.

There is an echo of this all the way over in ancient Mexico, "where Quetzalcouatl is also called 'Ce acatl' = 1-Reed, and Tezcatlipoca 'Omacatl['] (Ome acatl) = 2-Reed."[62] For these two mark the levels of thinker and knower within the doer or Egg. All this may well point to Ii being linked to the first question after the six *I am* statements of the Song of Amairgin, namely:

1. Who makes clear the ruggedness of the mountains? or *Who but myself knows the assemblies of the dolmen-house on the mountain of Slieve Mis?* for it is glossed *'Who but myself will resolve every question?'*

The Ugaritic letter is ⌗, which pictures treetops, and indeed that is where one looks for mistletoe or loranthus. Somewhat in the same spirit is ↑ the Sabean (and Thamudic) yod, which also hints at the teaching that identifies the Name with the human form and yod therefore with the head—of one's offspring, being even with the aries of the fourth Wheel. If the tail were a bit wavy, it could represent the individual sperm.

The Tifinag character is extremely interesting. In the far north, it was ⌇ and probably called *Yorsa*, name of the constellation Cassiopeia, judging by its shape and phonetic value. This shape was also found in Berber Tifinag, where it appeared also in the form ⌇, which is as vivid a confirmation as one could wish; for it pictures the golden sickle with which druids reputedly harvested their oak-mistletoe! This was one of those jaw-dropping discoveries for me, telling me I was on the right track. Numidian had **Z**, as if altered to be a scythe instead, still a cutting off, since yod is the end of manifestation on the Egg. It may also hint of Ii's connection to zeta or I.

The transmission into Greek shows something interesting. Early on in some places, iota took the form ↄ, which shows, not someone drawing a line in the dirt, but someone drawing a line on a chalkboard. But it eventually became everywhere just the line itself. Lycian and runic both had **|**; the rune was named **isa*, 'ice', identifying it as an icicle, which is like mistletoe in that it hangs from the eaves of a roof (next sign, lamedh), thus hovering in air so to speak.

Interesting how our expression *jot* (which comes from *iota*) is especially well illustrated by both old Hebrew yod and early Greek iota.

The Meroitic is no surprise: it is just the hieroglyph **two reeds** 𓏭 as in Egyptian.

Trump XVIIII The Sun shows the twins of V The Pope out in the open air (next to a wall) wrestling, with drops of sweat flying everywhere. The sign of the winter solstice is when waxing year's oak king overcomes waning year's holly king, to reign until 'slain' at the summer solstice. The drops of sweat refer to the death of the satiric antihero and to the function (of those listed in jumbled order in *Sefer Yetzirah*) proper to yod as the earth breath, namely *smelling*. The trump's two male youths match its being the hieroglyph **two reeds**; the card features male figures because pagan tradition stipulates a boy-child is to be weaned during a waxing moon, and included in that was the dark of the moon leading to it,[63] which is what little yod signifies—the dark of the moon when all that is *left* is the sun.

This little yod is ideal to represent the earth breath, active aspect of the element whose active aspect is no longer in evidence. *Being* the earth breath, it rather suits what Graves makes in archaic Greek out of the Boibel Loth letter-name associated with 'Y', *Idra*, namely *idryomai*, 'I establish'. Its geodetic placement is near the source of Tigris and Euphrates (two reeds?), so it establishes Mesopotamia in a very real sense.

ל

Lamedh

Lamedh corresponds to tree-letter *luis* the rowan. It is the second month, encompassing sign aquarius, the spine opposite the shoulders: the modern letter pictures a child swinging its arms learning to walk, seen from above. It follows B, the *birth* of the Spirit of the Year, and thus signifies his schooling: rowan tends to shelter other species that in the end displace it. This fits *lamedh*'s supposed meaning 'ox-goad' (*lemedh* means 'learning'). Its bardic number, *fourteen*, signifies half a month (two weeks) in the calendar-name Apollⲱn.

Egyptian did not have the L sound. But it did have to transliterate that sound in other languages. The one chosen in Ptolemaic Egypt was ⌂ *recumbent lion*. It represented *rw* in Egyptian, but was used as a substitute for L in group writing. The nineteenth-century scholars thought its hieratic form ⌐ the *source* of old Hebrew ∠ or ∠ lamedh. That the curved form was a degeneration of the angular one is reinforced by south Semitic, where Sabean has ⌐ and Thamudic ⌐ (two strokes reduced to one). Lamedh simplified the hieratic, adopting only its most prominent feature. (How much time this took, I could not say.) The hieroglyph references the opposite sign, leo, where the full moon is when the sun is in aquarius.

The Ugaritic ⵊ is mysterious. It is the upper part of ⵊ, the inner-plus-outer temple (D). Since Sabean had eaves-of-a-roof, perhaps this L is a colonnade connecting inner to outer; indeed lamedh *is* a reaching out, as is obvious from its square-Hebrew shape. And lamedh is linked to dalet in being on the Cauldron-radius of D's original station, before it shifted over to the outer horizon.

Tifinag L was •• or ⑴⑴ two strokes (⑴⑴ in Numidian), probably called *liki*, 'like', for this was the second month, in which the Spirit of the Year is educated, taught to classify like things.

The Lycian had ∧ the classical Greek lambda. Early Greek had ⌐ and ∠, ⌐ in Samos, Etruscan ⌐, Latin ∠, L . It just occurred to me (I can be *extremely* slow) that the classical Greek lambda pictures a drawing compass: after all, Euclid is all about what can be constructed with compass and straight-edge, and he was from Megara, where lambda took this shape. Halleluiah! this was one of the gaps in my grasp of letter-shapes. The compass defines learning or teaching as a process of marking limits.

Meroitic had ⌂ *recumbent lion*, no surprise there.

The rune is ⌐ **lagu*, 'water' (Eng. *lake*), and obviously pictures eaves. The notion of sheltering is at the heart of this symbol. The line from the Song of Amairgin corresponding to this letter is: *I am a lake on a plain*, glossed *for extent*. And in the archaic Greek 'hymn' Graves reconstructs from Boibel Loth letter names, L and F, *Loth* and *Forann*, yield *lōto-forāmenon*, 'lotus-ferried', the lotus a symbol of the opening mind becoming aware, in the learning process, of circles of greater and greater radius.

An interesting question is what would have been the *Egyptian* letter for aquarius, since they had no L and ***recumbent lion*** was a two-sound sign. I have a theory concerning this. The hieroglyph for N at pisces is a flat sign (***surface of water***); two other flat signs have not figured in this narrative because they did not seem to have a place; yet I now bring them up. One is the hieroglyph ⬭ , which Gardiner calls ***animal's belly with teats***, "perhaps like the *ch* in German *ich*," and the other is ⬩ ***bolt***, originally a voiced *z* but later used for *s*. My guess is that the latter represented the last sign, pisces, completing the round—voiced equivalent of the *s* that is at taurus—while the *n* we have for pisces stood for aquarius to the Egyptians; perhaps it sounded closer to *ñ* originally, that is, a little farther back in the mouth. The remaining flat sign, ***animal's belly with teats***, *may* have indicated a return to aries, marking the end of the cycle, symbolized by an animal's carcass: it is close to emphatic *h* (samekh's Egyptian prototype)—speculation on my part, but it might help explain Ugaritic voiced samekh and relate it to Sabean voiced samekh (see above under samekh).

L's corresponding trump is XIIII Temperance—the purpose of education—in which a woman dressed up as an angel (in a morality play?) pours the aquarius symbol from one vessel to another. This is atom-type silicon, main ingredient (besides oxygen) of quartz and glass. Since it is straight across from gemini, or space itself, it represent an abstraction *of* space, a section of space set apart. The functions proper to the two signs reflect this, for cheyt is *walking* or *motion* (traversing space), while lamedh is *working*, the *application* of motion (of the functions listed in jumbled order in *Sefer Yetzirah*.

Lamedh's geodetic placement is where Caucusus meets Black Sea, a gigantic reclining lion lapping up its waters (so to speak).

נן

Nun

Nun corresponds to tree-letter *nion* the ash, whose month encompasses pisces, the last sign, representing the spine opposite the cervical vertebrae (back of the neck). As this is the axis of shaking one's head, one of its meanings is negation, as in Indo-European *as well as* ancient Egyptian, where the commonest word conveying negation is spelled either ***nn*** or ***n***.[64] Ash is the world tree in Scandinavian mythology, and it is obvious why: as the wood of tool handles, oars, and spear shafts, it is where man grasps the world as he sets about changing it. For the actual center of the universe is where nature and mind meet: in upright sentient beings. Its bardic number, *thirteen*, points to its being the approach to aries, the *return* to which constitutes the thirteenth station of the round. And indeed in that archaic Greek 'hymn' Graves reconstructs from the Boibel Loth letter names, N, *Neiagadon*, yields *ne-āgaton*, 'new-born'.

The Egyptian sign from which nun evoved was ∿∿ *surface of water*, nearer tongue's tip than L. The hieratic form was ⸜ and evolved into ⸝ or ⸍ in old Hebrew, which pictures a hand raised in greeting or farewell.

The Ugaritic ⸖ shows signs of hearkening back to *surface of water*, but there is another possibility: this sign forms the floor of D's ⊞, of which L's colonnade ⊞ is the superstructure, L and N being adjacent to each other in the calendar. In a way this makes sense, as nun is pisces, the feet in astrology.

Tifinag N was ❙, most likely called *naddr*, 'nail', which in North Africa became ❘. For after learning to classify like things (in L or ‖), the ash month signified the Spirit of the Year setting off on his own.

The Sabean was ⸝ or ⸜ , essentially the same as Hebrew. The second of these *could* be interpreted as kaf (ⴼ) without its left wall, which signals the fact that nun and kaf are opposite signs in the calendar (nun on the upper right). Thamudic again shows signs of influence from across the Red Sea, for it had ❘ for N, which is the Tifinag character.

The Lycian had *N*, the Greek *nu*.

Meroitic ∾∾ essentially reverts to *surface of water*. It looks like they decided one zigzag was not as tall as *recumbent lion*, so they doubled it.

The runic character ⟩ is rather interesting. Since ash was the wood of oars, this clearly pictures an oar through the side of a ship. But it can also be taken as the stick plus the rope or string used to twirl it in kindling the Needfire (slanted in the rune to avoid digging into the grain of wood across which it is carved). For the name of the rune is **nauðiz*, 'need, necessity'. I take the oar as its primary signification: Old English termed a Danish Viking warship an *asc* (ash) or a *ceol* (keel). (Oars, after all, were used only in *need*, that is, when becalmed.)

As the oar of a vessel, ash certainly fits the line Graves picked for it from the Song of Amairgin: *I am a wind of the sea*, glossed *for depth.* And indeed N approaches the sound the wind makes in the rigging. Rowing is man making his *own* wind (so to speak).

The trump for N was XIII (Death), picturing the grim reaper, thus linking it to the fable where man asks the ash for its wood, which it agrees only to then find as the handle of the axe it has become the grim reaper of its own kind. This is the one unnamed trump (Death being but a nickname), and he holds his scythe like an oar.

This trump points to the main quality of ash that makes it such useful wood: lightness combined with strength. For the corresponding atom-type is aluminum: lightness combined with strength. Moreover, it is an abstraction—a separating off—in that it must be separated from its natural compounds in order to exhibit said quality. In fact it is the abstracted version of what the atom-type straight across from it at taurus, calcium, is naturally, in the form of bone. This connection is implied in the trump, which has the skeletal grim reaper to *symbolize* aluminum's lightness-combined-with-strength. Of the twelve functions listed in jumbled order in the *Sefer Yetzirah*, the one proper to nun is *anger*, which is consistent with its representing negation.

As befits this letter descended from the hieroglyph **surface of water**, its geodetic position is the Sea of Azov.

ϜΦΧΨΩ Τ
Added Greek Letters

In the interest of the history of alphabets, here is what I have been able to surmise about the letters of the Greek alphabet that were seemingly added onto the Semitic template, and why. Omega is of special interest, as the middle letter of the Logos (as in Egyptian), for which mother letter shin was substituted in Hebrew. And vau-digamma offers some insight into the state of the Corn Spirit heresy when the Greek alphabet was formed. The remaining three (other than sampi) would appear to be replacements for bardic letters that had fallen out of use (phi for Q-qoppa, chi for H-heta, and psi for Ss-san), except I have had to rethink the case of chi, based on runic.

In vav's place, as if it came from Semitic vav, Greek had vau-digamma, which became Latin F. The Greek letter whose shape *actually* descended from vav was upsilon. It is amusing to read attempts to trace F's shape from vav (sorry, but breasts just are not square). It is apparent that the Semitic letter-shapes were first adopted by a Greek culture that included worshipers of the Corn Spirit, Celtic Bran or Vran, Scandinavian Fro or Freyr, Greek Orpheus, or Phoroneus, the spirit of *fearn* the alder. They were probably initiates of the (archaic) Orphic Mysteries, or something comparable. And where they repositioned upsilon in the sequence shows familiarity with bardic numbering, where vowels A-E-I-O were 1-2-3-4 but U shifts all the way over to 17, fifth-from-the-end: taking omega as last, upsilon ended up fifth-from-the-end alphabetically, or sixth-from-the-end if we count sampi. F's link to vav is that 17's digital sum is 8; plus F is soft peh, and peh's original station on the Cauldron was the same as vav's is on the Egg.

I am tempted to attribute F's shape to runic—even though its advent predates any known inscription therein—for the simple reason that its runic shape, ᚠ, is a perfect expression of the Corn Spirit, whereas the earliest attested form of F (with branches slanted downward) is not, or else should be viewed upside down. Perhaps even before the Elder Futhark had taken shape it had been a magic symbol—perhaps the letter-shape (taboo in public) the Mysteries associated with F the alder—that Greek turned upside down to conceal its secret. The runes adopted its original shape; indeed runes demonstrate deep arcane knowledge on the part of their creators.

A clue to runic is that Ϝ and Ϲ turned sideways (ᴨ, ꜱꜱ) suggest Greek pi and omega. It seems to indicate that runic is most closely related to eastern Greek, not western, and that it has built on knowledge of not old Hebrew but square Hebrew *numbering*, since pi and omega occupy the same numbers as Hebrew peh and feh sofit, or Ϝ and Ϲ in reverse so to speak. Reinforcing kinship to eastern Greek letters, rune **gebō* (X) is closer in sound to eastern chi than western xi.

Omega entered Greek in the eastern Ionian region (seventh century BCE). Its shape, Ω, may have originally had the opening on the lower left, suggesting it pictured lips in the process of *saying* Ω (as O does lips saying omicron)—perhaps *akin* to runic Ϲ. Or was omega's shape adopted from Ω, Thamudic P, which I interpret as picturing a woman wearing earings (since the Sabean version is variously ◊ ◊ ◊, which appear to picture the earrings themselves). This would seem to point to omega having originated as a labial consonant, which one could classify Egyptian *w* as. (Bernal makes the case for the shape of the usual Greek beta having come from south Semitic mem.) It was Thamudic whose area of use included more northern reaches of the desert, where Greeks could easily have had contact with it. The shape symbolized the feminine (woman wearing earrings), so it is appropriate as the Gnostic symbol for Sophia, the feminized Holy Spirit. Her other guises, ayin/omicron and vav/upsilon, are mere Prunikos, the Whore, in a sense, what our mostly materialistic lifestyle has turned the mental and noetic breaths into for us—same radio station, but full of static. Was it to ensure we remain acutely aware of this static that Hebrew kept bardic vowels hidden behind their consonant disguises and shin as substitute for omega?

To add weight to the possibility of omega being descended from a south Semitic P, the letter P's *original* station does mark the upper limit of the thinker's minds on 'her' macrocosmic side of the Cauldron.

The Egyptian hieroglyph corresponding to the omega of the Logos was 𓆴 *quail chick*. Well it turns out that its hieratic form was ⌮, close to miniscule omega (ω), which entered the picture during the third century BCE, that is, after Egypt had been incorporated into the Greek world by Alexander the Great.

Once it had omega (several centuries before that), Greek kept both it *and* the shin or sigma that had replaced it; although having jettisoned san (tzaddi), one could perhaps see sigma as bardic Ss were there not a better candidate in psi. Yet Egyptian hieroglyphics had themselves both **quail chick, w, and pool, š**, replaced in Hebrew by the hieratic of **lotus pool**.

The tradition of alchemical colors associated with bardic IA(O)U points to the alternate spelling (I)AUM, and thus in Hebrew יאום (or perhaps יהום); the Tetragrammaton itself has been taken as a form of the divine name IAΩ. So I would suggest one does not need to abandon the alef-beyt to invoke the Logos. For myself, since it is the Gospel of John that actually speaks of it, I prefer the Greek spelling. What relevance this all has for Jewish theology I cannot say: I am Gnostic and cannot see the world quite as rabbis do, though I have immense respect for them and what they have managed to preserve—first and foremost the alef-beyt itself.

Runic obviously took psi (Ψ) to be the bardic Ss (ᛦ); and since runes' creation was closer in time to the Greek Mysteries than we are, I tend to take its interpretation as definitive. After all, the Ionian alphabet that included psi lacked san (tzaddi), which was even purged from letters' number sequence. That psi has the form of Poseidon's trident is interesting: note that the place of Ss is straight across from nion the ash, Poseidon's tree, so taking N as Poseidon's active side, Ss might be construed as his effect on nature, on the outer vessel (or Egg). That this same shape stood for chi in western Greek is a bit odd. Western Greek had its H, so chi would not have been a substitute for missing H, as it might be construed in the east, where H was eta. I am inclined to conclude that chi was not a substitute for H but rather a second G, like runic X (albeit unvoiced). This implies that ', the diacritical mark for a rough breathing, itself stood for bardic H, since this could be justified by the fact that it was the bardic letter to which no number was attached.

This leads me to reinterpret the Greek as more of a conglomeration: I think I now see it *not* as just the bardic alphabet with a few replacements, but as more of a 'catch-all' like the runic, which has both Ng and P plus two Gs (a trend the Northumbrian runes, centuries later, would carry to extremes). This has the advantage of explaining why for instance many Greek alphabets had both xi (*ogam consaine* Ng) and vau-digamma (F the alder) in addition to pi; or both qoppa and phi, Q's obvious replacement in eastern *and* western Greek (shift of the Greek interrogative consonant to pi or phi); or both omega and sigma (Sophia and Prunikos): Greeks surely grasped the significance of the three mothers; runes' creators certainly did.

I take runic X to picture a tripod of poles on which a sacrifice—a *gift* to a god or gods—was placed. The tripod of Greek religion had parallel legs; but one can imagine a cruder form of tripod being used in the countryside and especially in more wooded northern realms. Greeks might have added to chi the meaning: obliquity of equator and ecliptic.

The earliest Etruscan abcedaria (Masiliana Tablet, circa 700 BCE) had *all* of the Semitic letters, with vau-digamma displacing vav (as upsilon) to after tau, followed by western xi (X), phi (Φ), and western chi (Ψ). This would take numbering (if they were *used* for numbers) up to 800 without omega. It would seem xi (X) in Etruscan was an *s* sound (like Hebrew samekh), suggesting that the *characters* for bardic Ss and for chi might simply have switched places from what they were in the east. Our Latin alphabet is thought to be descended from the Etruscan.

The eastern Greek alphabet is what stayed behind in the Aegean area, as epitomized by the Ionian or classical Greek alphabet, which was adopted officially in Athens after the end of the Peloponnesian War (403 BCE). Changes thus imposed on its Attic precursor are attributed by Graves to religious changes: suppression of H (its replacement by ') and of vau-digamma, and the addition of xi (samekh, not used in Attic), along with psi and omega. We see here that Attic had *fearn* the alder for aries; it was now replaced there by xi (samekh). Since heta had morphed into eta, it would appear Ionians did not realize the bardic vowel between iota and epsilon had been zeta, so eta filled that role, with zeta delegated to its special role as Zeus's initial—in other words, they did not realize that his real name was Juice (only half joking). (Of course the fact that eta and zeta rhyme may mean they did know and were simply messing with things: they occupy opposite signs, whereas in Hebrew it is zayin and ayin, base of the fire triad, that rhyme.)

Digamma was no doubt dropped as heretical: did this perhaps signal a diminution in the status of the Mysteries? Hebrew had samekh at aries, a sound *on* tongue's tip, whereas F is out beyond the tongue or seed (Egg), to symbolize a sprouting-forth from it. Perhaps this is why the samekh character, which is the *ogam consaine* Ng and has the value *ñ* in Lycian, was used for an *x* sound in Greek: it was reinstating samekh at tongue's tip, so to speak, by including the sibilant sound (*s*) in xi The *k* part derived from its original Egyptian value, an emphatic *h*, but was also perhaps meant to point to its affinity with bardic Ng (similarly placed in the mouth)—specially in Ionia, which would likely have had contact with Lycians.

The problem with this is that most of the alphabets with *western* chi (the trident) had both xi (X) and vau-digamma. One could hypothesize that Laconia, Arcadia, Achaea, Thessaly, and Euboea fostered freedom of religion by tolerating both the heretical and the non-heretical, thus catering to both in their alphabet (perhaps they were the 'hippies' of their age). *Or*, this western xi may have fulfilled a different role altogether, that of bardic Ss suggested above.

Sampi's shape (T) may well have originated from some Greek form of battle standard, since Semitic tzaddi was shaped like a banner blowing in the wind (to glimpse which necks must strain in the course of battle). Psi and runic Y as bardic Ss could also picture a standard of some sort. That sampi occupied the position not of intermediate tzaddi (90) but of tzaddi sofit (900) suggests kinship with square Hebrew numbering. Since sampi and omega are both attested as early as the seventh century BCE, this would suggest Hebrew's post-exilic extension to twenty-seven characters—the original twenty-two plus five final forms—may actually have occurred under Greek influence. We know that the original Hebrew numbering (probably secret) must have been bardic, so the modern sequence—1-9, 10-90 by 10s, and 100-900 by 100s—was an innovation.

Let us briefly consider the correlations. Phi is 500, which is kaf sofit: I take this as more evidence (besides shape) linking phi to qof, here obliquely through kaf (Q = Kk). Chi is 600, as is mem sofit: as blood that reaches the crown of the head when standing, it links chi to desire, being G ('gift') in runes. Psi is 700, which is nun sofit: here is the link between trident and nion the ash of Poseidon. Omega is 800, feh sofit, and sampi 900, tzaddi sofit, as remarked on earlier.

Just a side-note: while studying the Wikipedia article on Greek alphabets, I noticed that the one from Tiryns—where Heracles resided during his labors—which is a Mycenaean site and therefore quite old, had no omega but did have the 8-shaped *f*-sound found also in Etruscan and Lydian. The Etruscans were first known as Tyrrhenians, or Tyrsenians—Tiryns merely reverses the *n* and the *s*—Greek for 'non-Greek pirate', no doubt the *Teresh* of the Sea Peoples who had attacked Egypt. These Teresh migrated to Italy; Tiryns remained in the east and so ended up with eastern chi (X) and xi (samekh).

The above discussion of the Greek alphabet accompanies a presumption that the Greeks had their own alphabet tradition—with a taboo on letters' public use—long predating adoption of Phoenician letter-shapes. Their bardic tradition almost certainly centered around that greatest of all poets—since he was even able to enchant wild beasts—Master Orpheus. This is, as far as I know, the oldest of the Greek Mysteries.

Part Three:

Parsing

Roots

In the following, each letter's concluding SUMMARY section was assembled over a decade ago, and the notes on which it was based were destroyed in a fire. The study had to be redone, and this second, more recent study of the roots, then, is given in the initial PARSED ROOTS section. *In* the SUMMARY section at the end, the meanings are summarized in single quotes, within which parentheses show side meanings not present in all roots counted by the preceding number (of roots starting with that letter than mean roughly that). The numbers may be taken as slightly inflated, as not all roots similar enough to be essentially the same root had been weeded out, the numbers in *italics* showing where I had already found possible equivalents lurking and reduced the count. Normal brackets [-] enclose my labels and comments, when *not* within quotes; otherwise, meanings that seem to go off on tangents. Fancy brackets {-} enclose meanings found only in proper names. Note that the PARSED ROOTS section uses both types of bracket differently (for which see Abbreviations and Symbols).

I apologize for the unevenness in the study: going back over it, I realized my notes early on were somewhat less inclusive than later, so you might notice, for example, two identically spelled roots that in Davidson were numbered that I have failed to number, or less variants of meaning in a root than Davidson listed. My indication of which roots were not used except in derivatives is nowhere near complete either. And I omit vowel markings, mainly since otherwise this study would have taken a prohibitively long time to complete. And of course my apologies for errors, as they will mostly be mine, not my sources'.

The Blind Truth

I see it (but it can't see me)
and grasp it (gently, tentatively)
for guidance (what a fool I be)

the one it leads (a fool for sure)
hangs on words (the only cure)
whose hidden light (of praise or censure)
beckons sweetly (its path my stature)

I quell the stark (with truth's cold stroke)
as trumpets sound (yet who awoke)
no light just warmth (this fire I stoke)

The Twelve Simples

סצחועקטהזילנ

Sight Blinds
[Inverted Hexaduad]

Sight blinds
the most perceptive minds
as they struggle to make some sense
of present tense.

For they've been told the air
is all that's there.
Yet the mind's light
is not a *thing* of sight.

No gag muzzles
the shout of time: it still puzzles
the most perceptive minds
sight blinds.

ס

Samekh

PARSED ROOTS

This is the letter originally at the top of the round, sign aries. As you can see, it is shaped like the head, which is what aries signifies. Its pronunciation is on the tongue's tip, for the round of the twelve simples (the Egg) *represents* the tongue in relation to the Cauldron or mouth it is seated in.

The Irish tree-letter here at aries was *fearn* the alder or F, symbolizing by its sound that which sprouts out *beyond* the tongue or seed. The alder is the tree of the Corn Spirit, the god Bran or Vran (cognate Fro or Freyr), the Celtic equivalent of Kronos or Saturn. There is a very good reason for this: alder fixes nitrogen in the soil, which greatly benefits vegetation. And F's position at the vernal equinox reinforces this.

Further complicating samekh (the rest of the simples are much more straightforward) is the fact that the actual 'tree' samekh corresponds to in bardic lore is the reed. The old Hebrew samekh, which pictures the spine (what holds the head up), is identical in form to the letter Ng in *ogam consaine*, the early (bronze age) form of ogham lettering (better known from its use in Ireland and Britain much later, in the age of Patrick). The same letter-shape in Lycian (from southern Anatolia) has the sound value ñ. But Reed Ng occupied a different sign in the tree-calendar: it is the month encompassing sign sagittary (late autumn). In its place in the P-Celt (Brittonic) version of tree-calendar (the bethluisnion) is P, the whitten or guelder rose; P and F both derive from Hebrew peh, being the hard and soft pronunciations thereof.

There is evidence of an ancient 'heresy' surrounding worship of the alder god, or Corn Spirit, which was suppressed in certain alphabets, including the Hebrew. Yet we will find some of the roots starting with samekh do resonate with the meaning of F simply because of samekh's place in the calendar being the vernal equinox. Let us start with these.

Some signify *plenty* (F's rune is called **fehu*, 'wealth'): סאה, 'seah (dry measure)'; סגל, 'treasure' (Ch. 'gain/acquire'); סלת, 'flour'. Then there is סמדר, 'vine blossom', which has mem in it, M being *muin* the vine. Then there are: שׂ\סעף, '*branch, bough*, fissure' (A. שׂאב, 'divide'?); and סחיש, 'what grows of itself the third year after sowing'. There are five that (appropriately enough) begin with ‒סס, namely: סאב, 'provender/fodder' (A. 'satiate', Ch. 'feed'); ספח, 'admit, join, be gathered or scattered, *an overflowing, self-sown (i.e. spilt) grain*, quilt or coverlet (from *spreading*)'; ספל, 'dish/bowl'; ספף, '(stand at) threshold (as doorkeeper), *dish*' (Ethiop. '*extend, expand*'); and ספק, '*abundance, sufficiency*' (Syr. '*suffice*'), which can also mean 'strike, smite, clap, chastise, waver, doubt'—also 'throw oneself about' (as a drunken man), thus shading into the meaning of root סבא, 'drink to excess', linked to a son of Cush and the Sabeans (ים—)—in whose alphabet, by the way, samekh also pictures the head (but with shoulders attached).

Three roots using reysh call to mind spring's quickening, perhaps drawing on the rolled guttural R sounding like a boiling or bubbling up: סיר, 'pot/vessel, thorn, (fish-)hook', which Gesenius compares with Arabic root שאר, '*spring/boil up*, rage (a fever)'; סער, 'be tempestuous, agitated, rage, *scatter*, storm, tempest'; and סרח, '*be stretched out, spread forth* (luxuriant vine), hang over, loose, be redundant, *be poured out/spilt*, superfluous part/remainder'. This last sort of shades into סדן, 'wide linen undergarment' (A. '*loosen* [garment]'), which sort of shades into סחב, 'draw/drag along ground, old torn clothes', which links to the idea of sweeping: סחה, 'sweep away', and the closely related סוה, whence 'sweepings/filth' (can you say *spring cleaning*?), and סחף, 'sweeping/driving (rain), be swept away' (*Whan that Aprille with his shoures soote*).

I relate this last (both *sweeping* and *waters*) to *ngetal* the reed: סוף, 'seaweed/sedge (—ים, 'sea of weeds [Re[e]d Sea]), *reed*/rush/bulrush'. Reed's ability to bend but not break—as in the Æsop fable—leads to סבך, '*interweave/entwine/fold together*, thicket', which hearkens back to the hieroglyph whose hieratic form spawned samekh, **wick of twisted flax**, showing interwoven strands. Hence סיון, name of the third month (from סיו\ז, '*bright*/splendid'?); סרפד 'brier? nettle?' (from שׂרף\ז, '*burn*'); סס, 'moth'; סנור, Ch. 'blind/dazzle'; סדם, 'Sodom' ['dew/plentiful waters? *conflagration*?']; סלד, 'be hard, Ch. burn' (A. 'leap'); סוך, 'anoint, oil flask'; and perhaps סמם, 'sweet spices, aromatics' (A. 'smell'); and סמל, 'figure/image' (as in our word *similar*?); and of course (since one needs light to read) the root ספר, 'write, number/count, recount/tell, talk, book, letter/epistle' (>ספיר, 'sapphire'?).

Some roots reflect the fact that samekh is at the top of the round. First: סלל, 'raise/cast *up* (heap), prepare (way), basket' (A. '*knit/link together*'), relating back to **wick of twisted flax**. Continuing on: סלק, 'go/come *up*'; סמך, 'lean/lay (hand על upon), *support*, advance, refresh, trust' (whence the name *samekh*); סעד, '*support/uphold*, aid, refresh (heart)'; סבל, 'bear/carry', Ch. 'lift *up*/erect'; and סלא, 'be weighed', cognate with סלה, 'lift *up*/carry off, reject, *be weighed*'. Indeed prominent in the Tarot of Marseilles trump VIII Justice—fearn's and samekh's trump—is the balance scale. Plus: סגד, 'fall down/worship (idols)'; סגן, 'chiefs/prefects' (Babyl. and Pers.); סנחרב, Sennacherib (king of Assyria); סרך, Ch. 'superintendents'; סרן, 'axles, princes/lords'; and סרס, 'castrate, eunuch, courtier/chamberlain/*chief officer*'. The last three build on -סר, and reysh means 'head, beginning'.

Furthermore, there is ספה, 'take off (beard)/-away (life)/destroy, perish, *add/increase*, heap *up*/accumulate', forging a link between 'heap up' and spring's 'increase'. And related perhaps to 'heap up' is סכן, 'sit/dwell, become familiar, *profit*, poor' (note again the concept of *plenty* in 'profit'). Also perhaps related to *up* are סמר, 'shudder/bristle up (hair)'; סנפיר, 'fin (of fish)'; סנא\ה, 'thorn-bush/prickly' (Syr. 'hate', hence סנבל, a name ['hatred in secret']); and סיני, Sinai ['mire? thorn-bush?']; and maybe סנן ['palm branches? full of thorns?']. Closely related (I think) to the meaning 'thorn' are: סלע, 'rock/Petra' (ם— is a species of locust); and ספל, 'stone, be stoned, clear of stones'.

The largest cluster of meanings pivots on samekh being both the first and last sign of the *round*: סבב, '(re-)turn/surround, a change'; סגר, '*shut/close*, precious (fine gold), locksmith'; סדד, 'stocks/fetters' (A. '*shut/stop up*') - שׂהר\סהר (Sam. סחר, '*surround/be round*), roundness, prison'; 2. סוג, 'fence/hedge about'; צפה\סוה\ז/ה, '*cover*(-ing)/veil, garment'; סור, '*turn aside/depart, approach*, remove' (samekh as both first and last sign); סחר, 'go/travel about/*go round*, trade, market, profit'; שׂכך\סכ, 'cover, conceal oneself, defend, *hedge in*, crowd, booth/tent, porch'; סכר, '*be shut*/stopped, deliver up'; ספן, '*cover* (w/ boards)/hide/preserve, *ceiling*, ship'; סרבל, 'trousers' (Ch. '*cover*/clothe'); סתם, '*stop up*/obstruct, *shut up*/conceal, *close*/repair (breach)'; and סתר, '*hide/conceal oneself*, be hid/lie hidden, secret things, protect/defend, *destroy*/put out of sight, shelter/protection, ambush'; and perhaps סכת, 'be silent'. Also (as first and last) סמן, '*be marked off*/appointed'. Being the last sign: סוף, '*cease/perish, destroy*, Ch. be filled' (—ה, '*whirlwind*'); 1. סוג, 'backslide/*depart*, dross, retirement'; סלף, 'subvert/*overthrow*, pervert'. And from being the first sign and also the head: סות, 'urge/excite/induce/persuade' (note that tav, the heart, is involved).

Remaining roots are connected in more subtle ways (if at all) to aries. Several seem to relate back to the last three ('urge/induce/persuade', 'subvert, pervert', and 'backslide, dross'): סכל, 'act wickedly, frustrate' (Syr. '*be foolish*'); סעה, 'run/rush'; סער, 'be tempestuous/tossed (at sea), be agitated/disquieted, *scatter*'; סרב, 'rebellious'; סרר, 'be refractory/rebellious/perverse, sad/sullen/angry' (A. 'bad/evil'). Perhaps these also relate back to the drunkenness encountered earlier. 'Tossed (at sea)' calls to mind that F in its Scandinavian Tifinag form (from the Bronze Age) was a semi-circle with vertical radius probably named *far*, low German for 'ferry'—rather appropriate for the letter that remains on top while the round (read *sea*) turns beneath it.

Being the top of the round has its psychological ramifications: סבר, Ch. 'hope/purpose'; and סלה, 'forgive/pardon'. And perhaps ספד, 'mourn/lament/bewail' (and סרד ['fear']?). Since aries marks the end of winter, סתה, 'winter' (A. שׁתא, 'to winter'). Perhaps related to this last, or else to the idea of *to close*, as in *to close up*, or most likely to the idea 'be marked off/appointed', are: סדר, (Syr./Ch. 'set in) order, row of soldiers, porch/portico'; and סיסרא ['battle array'] Sisera (a general). Finally here we can bring in the only two remaining roots we have not mentioned: סאן, 'shod (or fitted with greaves)' (Syr. 'to shoe')—which ends with nun, nun being pisces the feet (sign before aries)—and סוס, 'horse, swallow', a root with two heads (samekhs), suggesting a mounted rider. Could the secondary meaning, *swallow*, have to do with samekh being on top, ready to flit away at a moment's notice?

SUMMARY

Samekh as aries: [*ram:*] 'run, rush' ['urge'] 'strike, suffice', 'go about, trader, mart, profit'; [*spring:*] 'profit, be prosperous, stores', 'to winter' [*endure till spring*], 'to hope', 'come up', 'what springs up the 3rd year out', 'vine blossom', 'spread luxuriantly, be spilt', 'extend, threshold, dish' ['dish, bowl'], 'join, overflow, split [*self-sown*]', 'divide, branch', '{plentiful*?* [*Sodom*]} conflagration'. **Top of round:** 'anoint, oil flask' [*cf.* **wick***, below*], 'palm tops', 'fin', 'chiefs, prefects [*Babyl., Pers.*]' [*Assyr. kings* 'Sennacherib' and 'Sargon'] 'superintendents', 'eunuch, chief officer', 'princes, lords, axles'. **13**[th] **sign closes ring:** 2 'surround (-ings, circuit, return, turn, turn of events) (be round)', 'fence, hedge about' ['treasure'] 3 '(precious) shut up ((conceal) stop up (stocks [*or* fetters]))', 2 '(shelter, hiding place, protection) hide (preserve, cover, ceiling)' [*cf.* **top***, above*]. ***Wick of twisted flax***: [*woven:*] 2 'interweave, thicket (hedge in, protect, cover)' ['be silent'] 2 '(veil, garment) cover (clothe)', 'moth [*insect that eats cloth*]'; [*candle:*] 2 'burn' {'bright*? [3rd month]*'} 'blind, dazzle'. **Old Semitic shape:** [*strings+fret:*] 'a type of stringed instrument'; [*support for vertebrae:*] 'provender, fodder', 3 '(bear (laden [*with young*], erect)) raise, lift up (ladder, knit together, basket, thorn)', 'bristle up, bristly' [*like Fro's boar*] ['brier*?* nettle*?*'] {'Sinai [*miry? thorn-bush?*]'} 'thorn, hook, pot' [{'thorny'} 'thorn-bush {[*name of a rock*]}'] 'a rock', 2 '(lean) support, refresh'. **Rune *Inguz:** [*nasal:*] 'aromatics'; [*the hero:*] 'figure, image' [*=SML, cognate with Eng.* similitude*?*], 'shod with greaves, warrior' {'battle array'} 'horse, -man' {'fear'} 2 'perish (come to end)' [*cf.* **13**[th] **sign***, above*], 'mourn, bewail'. **Ngetal** [*reed or broom*]: 'symphonia [*bagpipe?*]', 'reed, bulrush, sedge', 'sweeping [*rain*], be swept away' ['be tossed, tempest', 'type of locust'] 2 'sweep away, sweepings', 'drag along ground, old torn clothes'; [*bends to survive in Æsop:*] 'let garment hang loose, loosen', 'fall down [*before idols*]', 'turn aside, degenerate [*vine-shoots*]' ['drink to excess, strong drink, drunkard', 'be foolish'] 2 'be refractory, rebellious (perverse)', 'pervert, overthrow, subvert', 'be turned, driven back', 'a turning, departing, apostasy'. **VIII Justice** [*with scales*]: 'be weighed', 'fine meal, flour', 'extend, [*dry measure*]'; 'pardon', 'to stone, clear of stones', 'set in order, row', 'be marked off, appointed', 'number, recount, book, scribe, sapphire'.

צץ

Tzaddi

PARSED ROOTS

The next sign, throat or neck taurus, is tzaddi. Indeed there is the root צוּר, 'bind up, *besiege/press (forward), beset/assail, stir (city)*, form/shape, *neck*, rock, *sword edge*, distress, *bulwark, fortress, entrenchment*', which also incorporates the essence of this letter, *motion* and *strife*. You can see that the shape of intermediate tzaddi is that of the throat when breathing, the shape of tzaddi sofit that of the throat when swallowing. Tzaddi's sound is sometimes described as a sort of whistling sound, which I place a little farther back on the tongue than (or down on the Egg from) samekh: it is the sign that initiates motion on the round *towards* the gullet—down where Egg's tongue is joined to Cauldron's mouth. First and foremost, it is motion itself: the departure from aries. It connects the head to its 'vehicle'.

Now think carefully: other than when you need to (because of buildup of phlegm), when do you clear your throat? It is when you 'beg to differ', either to politely introduce a new subject or voice to a conversation, or to indicate you wish to voice a dissenting view. Just so, the tree-letter corresponding to tzaddi is *straif* the blackthorn, wood of the shillelagh, which is close to (most likely cognate with) the word *strife* in English. Its number in bardic tradition, *twenty*— kept secret but easily ferreted out—signifies *fair* combat: two ten-fingereds. Its trump, XX Judgment, pictures Judgment Day. Reysh's trump XV The Devil, on the other hand, signifies *un*fair combat, that is, where one contestant has one hand tied behind his back. Hence the root: צדק, 'be just/(in the) right(-eous)/equitable, have just cause, be right/correct, be vindicated, blameless'.

Signifying strife or fair combat, then, are: צבא, 'go forth *to war*/service (e.g. in temple), *army, warfare, struggle*'; צדד, 'side, *adversary*'; צדה, *lie in wait for*, be destroyed/desolated'; צהל, 'neigh, shout (for joy/fear)'; צוּד, 'hunt, *pursue*, lay(en-)snare(s), game/provision/food, prey, *fortress/citadel*'; צוח, 'cry/shout for joy/sorrow'; צוּק, 'straiten/distress, *(op-)press(-er)*/urge, trouble, narrow/scanty'; צחק, 'laugh, play/sport/jest, *mock/insult, ridicule*' (whence the name Isaac); צלף ['fracture/*wound*, rupture']; צלק ['fissure'] (one of David's *military* chiefs); צמם, 'veil, noose/snare (fig. *destruction*)' (A. טמם 'braid/plait/bind')—and of course, since tzaddi is the *second* sign, צעף, 'veil' (A. 'to *double*')—צמת, '*(be) cut off*/destroy(-ed), perish, extinction'; צרע '[leprous] wasps [smiting/defeat]'; and צרר, 'tie/bind up (fig. of wind), shut up, *be hostile to/adversary*, (be) straiten(-ed)/distress(-ed), stone/flint, anguish, rival(n.), bundle, bag/purse, small stone/grain/kernel'. And of course צפע, 'basilisk', which reputedly kills with its eyes.

Moreover, צות, 'set on fire/kindle', is used but once (Isaiah 27:4), but in this sense: the complete sentence is, "I would march against them in battle; I would set them all on fire." And similar is צרב, 'be scorched, burning, inflammation'. Then there are: צפה, 'look about/keep watch, *lie in wait*, select, expect (help), *watchtower*'; and צרח,'cry aloud/shout, (watch-)tower'.

Old Semitic tzaddi pictured a banner waving in battle, no doubt causing much turning of heads on necks. In that spirit, we have roots צבט, 'reach/hold out'; צוה, '*set over*/appoint, decree, charge, *command*(-ment), precept, pillar/monument, way, mark' (Syr. 'set up/erect'); צעק, '*cry out* (esp. for help), (come/)*call together*/convoke'; צפד, 'adhere/cleave'. Suggesting a standard such as might top a banner's pole: צפה, 'cover/overlay (as w/ wood/metal), *capital* (of column)'; צפת, 'chapiter' (Syr. צפתא, 'ornament'); and perhaps צוג, '(to form/design) carved work'.

French for blackthorn is *La Mère du Bois*, because in vegetation's reclaiming of land previously tilled, it leads the attack, it is the vanguard. Since forest is what it is the vanguard of, roots express this mostly as *cool* and *shade*, namely: צנן (prob. = שנן 'be sharp', Ch. צנן, '*be cold*') 'thorn(s), fig. (fish-)hooks, *a cooling/refreshing*, shield' (A. צאן, 'keep'); צרד ['cooling' (pl.)] (A. 'to cool'); צלל, 'tingle (of ears, fig. lips)/quiver, roll/tumble down, *(be) shade(d/dark), shadow*, rattling/rustling, cymbals, death (fig. thick darkness)'; צלם, '*shade/shadow* (illusion), image/likeness, Ch. idol, *gloom/darkness*' (A. 'be obscure/*dark*', Syr. 'figure/delineate'); צפן, 'hide/conceal, (lay) treasure (up), restrain, lurk, the north (prop. hidden/*dark* quarter)'; and the similar meaning, צבר, 'heap/lay/treasure up' (spring's increase); צול, '(the) deep (place/depth)'; and צבב, 'covering, sp. of lizard'. Referencing vegetation directly are צמר, 'wool, foliage'; and צאלים, 'lotus bushes (?)'.

The sign taurus is the heart of spring. In the tree-calendar its tree-month is S, *saille* the willow, but this corresponds to mother letter shin: tzaddi corresponds to the bardic Ss (or St), which 'holds down' S's taurus while she's off being a mother. Hence the letter strongly reflects what willow itself symbolizes: the fount of spring, an overflowing abundance. Chiefly: צוף, '(an) *overflow*(-ing)/overwhelm, *willow*, honeycomb'. Then: צבע, 'Ch. *wet/moisten*, dyed garments, (fore-)*finger, toe, digit*', linking moisture to the digits referenced in *straif*'s number, *twenty*, utilizing beyt—B's number, *five*, stands for the counting of digits at birth—as does צבת, 'bundle/sheaf? *handful?*' (A. 'bind, *take in hand*'); צוק, '*pour out*, pillar/column (precipitous rock)'; צנר > 'waterfall/cataract'; צפע, 'excrement/dung, *shoots*' (A. 'emit/thrust out'); צרה, 'balsam [fragrant]' (A. '*flow*'). Since spring means youth: צער, 'be small (fig. brought low), *young*, few, short time'. Spring's increase: צבה, '*swell*(-ing), gazelle, splendor/beauty/glory'; צמח, '*shoot/spring/grow up* (fig. arise/begin), grow (hair), *shoot/plant/branch*'; צפח, 'flask, flat cake' (A. '*be spread out*'); צוץ, '*flower/flourish, blossom*, glitter/shine, shining plate (of gold on forehead of high priest), plumage/wing, lock (hair), fringe'. Which brings up spring's increased light (over winter): צהב, '(*shining* like) gold(-colored)/yellow'; צהר (= זהר, '*shine*') 'press out oil, *light*/window, noon (fig. great prosperity), moon? splendor?'; צחר, 'whiteness'; and צחח, '*be bright/white*, serene, clear/plain, *dry/parched*'.

This last leads to other roots expressing a dry throat, so to speak: צחה, 'Ch. thirst/be dry'; ציה 'a ship, drought, *dry/parched* land' (A. צוה Ch. & Syr. צוא '*dry up*'); צמא, '*thirst*(y)/desire earnestly'; צמק, '*be dried up*, dried grapes/raisins'; צנם, 'be hard/*dry?*'; צפף, 'pip/chirp(/whisper)'; and צפרדע, 'frogs' (who *croak*). One might add to these (as *vaguely* similar): צום, 'to fast'; and צלה, 'roast'.

Now we come to the last major category, referencing motion itself, with a bit of 'strife' in the mix as well: צבא, Ch. 'will/please/choose, *determination*/resolution/purpose'; ציר, (A. '*go*') 'prepare for *journey*, messenger, (*go round*/revolve) hinge, writhings/pains/pangs' (cf. A. צאר, 'writhe w/ pain'); צעד, '*step/walk/advance* (fig. shoot), *pass through, make march/chase, a stepping/going, pace (fig. conduct)*, ankle chains, bracelet'; צעה, '*step/stride, wander/emigrate, exile, wanderer*/stranger'; and צען, '*wander*/remove'—three that start with tzaddi-ayin and mean virtually the same thing—perhaps צרך, 'need/necessity'; and of course צמד, 'be bound/joined (to), be fastened, contrive/frame, band/bracelet, lid/cover, pair/couple/*yoke* (*oxen*/mules/horsemen), acre (land plowed by *yoke of oxen* in one day)', invoking taurus the bull or ox. To these we could add: צנע, 'be bowed down/humble/lowly' (as the ox); and its cogn. צנח, 'alight (from mount), go down/penetrate (earth)'—as alighting from a mount is what sign taurus *does* in beginning to slip out-and-down from aries (where the saddle is, i.e. on top).

And since taurus's motion is motion *about the round*, there are: צנף, 'wind/wrap *around*, turban, a ball?'; and צנק, 'fetters' (Sam. 'shut up'). And that about does it.

Unaccounted for are: צפנת פענח, 'Savior of the Age'? (Egyptian title Pharaoh gave Joseph in Gen. 41:45); צלא, 'pray' (perhaps connected with the humility of the ox?); and as *afflicting* motion (since the letter-meanings tend to include their opposite), צלע, 'rib, side, lean on one side (halt/limp), a halting/a falling'. Finally, there is צרף, 'refine (metals), fig. purity, try/prove, gold-(silver-)smith': I have not yet figured out the connection here, but then taurus *is* departure about the round, which represents the Great Work.

SUMMARY

Tzaddi as blackthorn [*straif*]**, strife:** 'thorn, hooks, shield', 'leprous, wasps {smiting? defeat? place of hornets?}', 'basilisk', 'laugh, Isaac, jest, mock, insult', 'roast', 'be scorched', 'set on fire', 'go forth to war, warfare, struggle, army', 'stench [*of an army*]' {'fracture, wound', 'fissure [*one of David's military chiefs*]'} 'cut off, destroy', 2 '(oppress) straiten, distress (shut up, be hostile to, adversary)', 2 '(adversary, turn away) side (rib)', 'hunt, pursue, ensnare, capture, provisions, fortress, citadel', 'shut up, fetters? prison?'. **Old Semitic shape** [*standard in battle*]**:** 'bind, take in the hand', 'reach or hold out, hand to', 'erect, set over, command, pillar, monument', 'ornament, capital [*of column*]', 'cry aloud, shout, watchtower', 'cry out, exclaim, convoke', 'neigh, shout for joy or fear, cause to shine', 'cry, shout for joy, a cry [*for joy or sorrow*]'. **'Mother of the Wood':** [*wood's encroachment:*] 'foliage, wool, to stand out or bristle up?', 'shades [*i.e. shady trees*]?' {'to cool'} 'be obscure or dark, shade, shadow, illusion, delineate, image, likeness, idol' ['to form, design, carved work'], 2 'to cover (overlay [*as with wood, metal*])', 'be spread out, flat cake, flask'; [*spring's fount of growth:*] 'pour out', 'to flow, balsam', 'overflow, honeycomb, willow' [*what Ss doubles*], 'shoot, spring, or grow up, arise, begin, grow [*of hair*], a shoot, plant, or branch', 'emit, thrust out, excrement, shoots, lower offspring', 'swell, be prominent? glory'. **2nd sign** [*Nordic Tifinag rifa, 'to split' (table 5)*]: 'be bound, joined to, pair, yoke [*e.g. of oxen; also, land plowed by same in a day*]', 2 '(to double) a veil (braid, plait, bind, snare, destruction, noose)'. **As taurus:** [*the neck:*] '[*TzUR*] the neck, bind up, press, besiege, assail, thrust forward [*as troops against a city*], sharp stone [*used as knife*], edge [*of sword*], strait-ness, distress, bulwark, fortress'; [*motion about round:*] 'wind or wrap around', 'roll or tumble down, be shaded, shelter, protection, defense' [*cf. rune's name (table 8)*], 'pass over, cross [*river*], come or descend upon, advance, flourish, prosper' [*being mid-spring*], 'go, go round, hinge, writhings, messenger' ['traveling bag'] 3 [*all start tzaddi-ayin*] 'to step or wander'; [*departure from aries:*] 'small cattle, sheep and goats, flock'; [*spring sunshine:*] 2 '(flower, flourish, blossom, plumage, shining plate [*of gold on forehead of high priest*]) shine (make or press out oil, light, window, noon, the moon)', 'gold colored', 'whiteness', 'be bright, white, dry, parched'. **Square-Hebrew:** [*throat:*] 2 '(be dry, dry [*from thirst*]) thirst (desire earnestly)', 'be dried up, raisins', 'dry up, parched land, Zion', 'be hard, dry', 2 '([*TzPR*] turn, return, circle, a turn [*Eng. vers.* morning], dance, spring, leap, scratch) chirp ([*TzPP*] whisper)', '[*TzPRDO (O=ayin)*] frog'; [*bowed shape:*] 'be bowed down, humble', 'pray', 'need, necessity', 'be small, be brought low, youth'; [*swallowing (tzaddi-sofit):*] 'go down [*i.e. penetrate*]', 'pipes, tubes, waterfall', 'to sink, a death, the deep'. **XX LeJugement:** [*twenty digits:*] 'dip in, dye, digits, wet, moisten'; [*fair combat:*] 'be equitable, have just cause'. **Libyan shape** [*hourglass (table 4), time's passage for wood's encroachment*]: 2 '(heap up) lay treasure up (conceal, keep back, restrain, lie hid, lurk [*in ambush*], be laid up or destined, north)', 'refine [*metals*], purify, try, prove', 2 '(determination, to will) purpose (intention, lie in wait for, be destroyed)', 'lie in wait, expect, look out for, keep watch, watchtower, await', 'cling [*skin to bone*]', 'to fast'.

ח

Cheyt

PARSED ROOTS

Cheyt is the next sign, gemini the shoulders, which cheyt obviously pictures. The tree-letter corresponding to cheyt is *huath* the hawthorn, a flowering hedge. Graves says, "In Welsh mythology the hawthorn appears as the malevolent Chief of the Giants, Yspaddaden Penkawr" (*tWG* p. 175)—and one can see how the shoulders might epitomize the brute (I mean poetically, not necessarily astrologically). The form(s) this letter takes in various alphabets would appear to be a section of fence. The old Hebrew version is perhaps stacked crates, suggestive of the labor of lifting one up to stack on another. And in south Semitic (Sabean), its two forms show arms raised while standing and while seated (the former of these linked by linguists to the sound heh, but there heh's and cheyt's sounds' letter shapes were reversed, as per the symmetrical pattern mentioned earlier that also involved samekh and tzaddi).

The roots starting with cheyt convey a plethora of meanings. One of these is 'to hedge in': חבש, 'bind/*bind round/about*/up (as wound), to saddle, restrain/govern/stop'; חגר, '*bind about*/gird(/on/up/oneself), be straitened, girdle, apron, cincture'; חדר, '*enclose*/besiege/beset, chamber'; חוג, 'draw circle/*circumscribe*, circle/sphere, *compass*'; חוץ, '*surroundings, wall,* outer/civil (vs. sacred)' (Syr. '*surround*'); חמה, '*wall* [fortress]' (A. 'guard/*surround w/ wall*'); חצר, '*enclosure*/area/court, village/hamlet, trumpet' (A. 'be present, convoke'); חרך, (perh. = כרך 'wrap around') '*enclose*/catch in net/toil, lattices, Ch. be singed'; חרצב '*tight bonds*, pangs/pains' (coll. w/ A. 'bind fast a cord'); and חתל, '(be) bandage(d/swaddled)'; חתם, '*seal (/up)*, finish, signet'.

In *The White Goddess*, Graves reconstructs an early Greek 'hymn' from letter-names of the Boibel Loth (linked to ogham): H is *uiria*, which he interprets as *ūrios*, which in context translates "I, Guardian of Boundaries (or Benignant One)." Roots suggest we interpret this as relating to the Mysteries, to sacred spaces and taboos. In terms of action: חבא\ה, 'conceal/hide, covering/veil [hidden]'; חוד, '(propose) riddle/enigma, proverb/parable'; and three starting with cheyt-peh, to wit חפא, (= חפה) 'act secretly/clandestinely'; חפה, '*cover/veil*, overlay (as gold)'; and חפף, (= חפה '*cover*') clean/*pure*/faultless, covering/defense, bridal chamber, coast/shore' (A. 'scrape/wipe/wash off'). And then there is the converse, namely חלט, 'declare/confirm'. More concretely: 1. חבל, 'twist/*bind*/- *by pledge*, writhe (as in labor), cord/rope, *measuring line, district*, company/band, mast, sailor, deposit, guidance, wise counsel, cunning devices'; חמט, 'kind of lizard (unclean)' (a taboo); חנך, 'instruct/initiate[d (s. of Cain)], *consecrate/dedicate (house/temple)*'; חרם, 'flat-nosed, net, allurement, *devote* to destruction/*to God (consecrate)*' (A. 'cut/tear off, *shut up/prohibit*'); plus *its* converse, חנף, 'be(-come) profane/pollute(d/defiled)'.

Watch how that last meaning, *to profane*, shades into aspects of the hawthorn itself: חלל, '(be) *pierce*(-ed)/wound(-ed), *profane/pollute/defile*, violate, play pipe/flute, open/begin'; חרץ, 'cut in/wound/*lacerate*, decide/determine, *be sharp*/quick, ditch/trench, sharpened/*pointed*, gold'; and חדד, '*(be) sharp*/-en(-ed), be fierce'; חדק, '(sting/be *sharp*) sp. of thorn'; חוח, '*thorn*/-*bush*, (fish-)hook/ring (for fastening prisoners or in nose of man or beast)'. For hawthorn has thorns, and its white flowers are reputed to have a smell reminiscent of female sexuality: חבצלת, 'sp. of flower (lily? narcissus?)' (חמץ=חבץ '*have pungent fragrance*', or 'be bright/splendid'?) ; חור, 'become *white*/pale, white linen/bread [free-born]'; 2. חלה, '*adorn*, ornament/necklace' (Syr. חלי, 'be sweet/pleasant'); חשן, 'ornament (spoken of breast-plate of high priest)' (A. 'be beautiful, adorn'), this last looping back to the sacred.

And then there is the meaning 'block the way', as expressed in the shape of H: חדל, '*cease/leave off*/fail, forebear/decline/omit, frailty (transitoriness), forsaken'; חטם, (prop. 'to muzzle') '*restrain oneself*'; חכה, 'wait'; חנק, 'strangle/*hang oneself*, suffocation/*death*'; חסם, '*stop*/bind up, muzzle'; and חשׂך, '*hold back/restrain*, save/preserve/deliver, withhold, spare'.

There are two clusters of meanings that gather around two further stipulations by Robert Graves concerning the hawthorn. One, he sees it as the tree of Sunday, that is to say, of the sun. And two, he calls it the *unlucky* hawthorn month: hawthorn is called *sceith* in the Irish Brehon Laws, which Graves connects to our word *scathe* (through Indo-European root *sceath* or *sceth*). "In ancient Greece, as in Britain, this was the month in which people went about in old clothes," says Graves (*tWG*, p. 174). "They also abstained from sexual intercourse—a custom which explains May as an unlucky month for marriage."

As for the first: חזה, '*see*/behold (vision/prophecy, revelation), *look*/gaze, choose/select, perceive, breast (of beast), agreement, *appearance/view, window*'; חזז, '*lightning*' (A. '*pierce through*')—rune *sowila* ('sun') is vertical zigzag, and 'pierce through' refers back to thorns— חכל, 'red? bright? cheerful? *glowing*/ fiery? refreshed?'; חמם, '*be/grow warm*, burning/inflamed, to warm/hatch, *warm/hot* (Ham, fig. Egypt), heat/glow/*the sun*'; חרב, '(be) dry(-ness)/dried up, desolate, rain(s), cutting instr., *drought, heat*'; חרה, 'burn/be kindled, become hot/angry/wroth, ardent/zealous, emulate/rival, *heat/glow*'; חרל (= חרר '*burn*'?) 'nettles'; חרס, (= חרה? חרר?) '*the sun*, pottery' (A. 'scratch, be rough'); חרר, '*burn/glow*, be dried up/scorched, kindle (contention), lamentation, nobles/free-born'—note the cluster here of five that start with cheyt-reysh, reysh being the initial of Re or Ra, the Egyptian sun-god—חשׁשׁ, 'dried grass/hay'; and perhaps חתה, 'take/lay hold of/seize (fire/coals), censer, fire-pan/shovel', since in ceremonial magic, the south is identified with fire, which is where the divine creative power has fallen, namely to loins libra to become the procreative power, cheyt being on the triad of the south. And last but not least, חגלה ['partridge'], which Graves points out was sacred to the sun (*tWG*, pp. 327*ff*).

As for the second, the wearing of old clothes brings to mind this letter's trump, The Fool (Le Mat), since H was associated with *no number* and The Fool is the only unnumbered trump. It pictures a vagabond, a vagrant: חלך, '*wretched/poor*' (A. 'be black, fig. sad/*wretched*'); חסר,

'*want/lack/be without*, be diminished, fail, *poverty*'; חרף, '(pass) autumn/winter, reproach/scorn'. He hoists his few belongings over his shoulder with a stick: חטר, 'stick/rod'. And from his waist hangs a חמת, 'skin-bottle'. He walks at a crisp pace, so: חוּש, '*(make) haste(n)*, be incited/ardent, feel/enjoy, be excited/confused/confounded'; חלף, '*pass by/on*/away/through/beyond (law, i.e. transgress), rush upon/assail, revive/flourish (plant/spirit), *change (garment)*'—putting on old clothes?—חמק, 'turn oneself/withdraw/*depart, wander about*, circuits?'; חפז, '*start up* (esp. in *haste* and alarm)/take to flight, *haste/hurry*'; חצף, Ch. 'urge/hasten'; חרד, '*hasten*, tremble/be fearful, care/be concerned for'—these relate to cheyt's proper function of the twelve the *Sefer Yetzirah* assigns to the simples, which is *walking* or *motion*. And since the terrain is constantly new to him, and it is spring: חדש, '*(make/re-/be re-)new(-ed)*/restore, *recent/fresh/new*, new moon'; and חדת, Ch. 'new', which are no doubt related.

As for unlucky (sceith): 2. חבל, 'corrupt/destroy, hurt, damage, fault/crime'; חתף\חטף, 'catch/seize'; 1. חלה, 'be weak(-en)/feeble, diseased, pained, grieved, wearied, wounded, afflict, sick, sore, calamity (מחלת, name of mus. instr.)' ; חלש, 'overthrow/discomfit, be weak/feeble, defeat'; חמס, 'injure/wrong/oppress/do violence to, shake off (as tree fruit), sp. of unclean bird, ill-gotten wealth'; חרג, 'be straitened/troubled? tremble/fear?'; חשך, 'be/-come obscure/dark, calamity, ignorance'. Finally, just to put a fine point on it: חגב, 'locust'; חסל, 'crop off/devour, sp. of locust'; חנמל, 'host (ants? locusts?)', their effect much like the rune, *hagalaz, 'hail'.

Another term for hawthorn is may, after the month that used to coincide with hawthorn; and although since the reform of the calendar it usually has not yet bloomed by then, it is still traditionally associated with Mayday celebrations, hence: חגג, (= Syr./Ch. חוג '*move in circle*') '*dance, keep/celebrate feast, reel/be giddy, festival*, commotion/tremor/fear [*festive*]'; חדה, 'rejoice/make glad'; and חוּל, '*dance*, be hurled/fall upon, writhe (in pain), bear/bring forth, *whirl*/precipitate itself, tremble, be strong/firm/durable, might, army, virtue/integrity, (= יחל) *wait/stay/delay*, sand, riches', that last with a little of what blocks the way thrown in for good measure.

Returning to cheyt's placement on the round, as the sign before cancer or *straight ahead*, it stands for what is above the horizon, *space*, also signified by its being 'numbered' zero (nothing) in Irish tradition. And space—like a hedge—is *that which divides*. Hence: חגה (= חקה 'cut/hew'?) '*chinks/clefts* (of rocks) or refuges' (A. חגא 'take refuge'); חום, 'black' (space being dark); חוּר (prob. = כוּר, 'dig/bore') 'hole'; חטב, 'cut (wood)/*(be) hew(n out)*, striped/variegated'; חטיטא ['a digging' (Aram. חטט 'dig')]; חלד, 'lifetime, world, mole' (Syr. '*dig*', A. 'endure'); חלק, '*be smooth*/fig. flattering, *divide*/apportion, bald, slippery/false'; חפר, '*dig (pit/well), digger of holes* (mole or rat), search out/*explore/investigate*/espy', and חפש, '*explore/investigate*, disguise oneself, device/purpose'; חקר, '*search/- out/explore*/examine/try, deliberation, secret/inmost part'; חצב, '*cut/hew/- out* (stone/wood), kill/destroy, *be engraved*', and חצה, '*divide*/halve, arrow, middle/midst, half/part/portion', with the second letter, tzaddi, adding its tinge of strife; חקה\ק, '*engrave*/carve/inscribe, *furrow*, portray'; חרט, 'pocket/purse, *graving tool*, writing stylus, sacred writers (wise men/magicians)'; חשה, 'be/make *silent/still/quiet*' (there is no sound in space, plus this hearkens back to secrecy, to the Guardian of Boundaries).

Next, the pairing of the shoulders, plus their labors: חבט, 'beat off (fruit from tree), beat out/thresh'; חבק, '*embrace*, fold hands (in sloth)'; חבר, '*bound/joined together*, charm/bind w/ spell, company, *companion*, beam/brace, bruise [alliance]'; חוט, '*fasten/join together*, thread, cord/line'; חזק, 'be(-come) *strong*/firm/fast/confirmed, harden (heart), heal/restore, help, adhere, *hold*/retain/contain, an urging on, *force*/vehemence'; חטיל ['waving']; חסן, (Syr./Ch. 'be strong') '*strong*, might, possess, riches'; חפן, 'hollow hands/fists [fighter]'. Shoulders represent one's bulk, how far one extends out *into* space: חלב, (prob. 'be fat') '*fat(-ness)*, milk [fat/fertile (pl.)]'; חלם, '*be fat/stout*(/make)*strong*/restore health, (cause to) dream, hard stone/flint, amethyst? emerald?'; חשם, 'opulent/noble' (A. '*be fat*/rich'); חמש, 'brave/*ready (for battle)*, belly/abdomen' (A. '*be fat*, courageous')—H in Numidian is a hefted shield seen from the side—so perhaps also חלץ, 'draw out/off (shoe), withdraw, (get) *ready/prepared/armed*, (be) deliver(-ed), strip/spoil, make easy/pliant/flexible (or strong), loins, booty, costly dress/mantle'.

This is the first sign of the triad that points down, the water triad (astrological air): חזז, '*decline*/recede, haven'; חנה, '*decline* (day), let oneself *down*/encamp, dwell, vaults/cells (or *wells*?), spear/lance, camp, troop/host, swarm *(locusts)*, droves (cattle)'—'locusts' again—and ; perhaps חפש, 'be set free(-dom), a spreading (couch? bed?) or *prostrate* (among the dead)' [Ps. 88:6] (A. 'stretch out/*prostrate, lie*'); and of course חשר, '*collection of waters*, nave of wheel' (A. 'collect'). And perhaps this is where to mention חרא, 'excrement/dung, sink/privy' (A. 'ease oneself/nature').

Some roots seem to reference cheyt's being the sign leading to vav's breasts, the sign cheyt was *moved* to in the jumbling of the order. Hence: חבב, 'love/cherish, *bosom*/lap'; חוק (prob. from חבק 'embrace', ב being softened into ו) '*the bosom*, feelings/affections, *hollow* place' (A. חאג '*surround*')—with a couple of earlier meanings thrown in (space, and hedging about)— חצן, 'bosom/folds of garment covering breast'; חתן, '*marry/give in marriage, bridegroom/spouse*, relative by marriage', vav being *ura*, heather, bed of trysts, vowel of summer's 'coming of age'.

It would seem that because in this one case the 'jumbling' was to the very next sign, a cluster of meanings attach to it that invoke the direction *straight ahead* (cancer, the breasts), representing desire's object: חמד, '*(object of) desire*/delight in, covet, *desirable*/precious/costly things'; חפץ, 'head/incline(/towards), will/*desire*/be pleased to do a thing, delight/pleasure, wish/will, business/concern/affair'; חשב, 'think/*purpose/intend*/devise/plan, impute/compute, intelligence/understanding, Ch. regard/count, warlike engines, artifices/devices'; חשח, Ch. '(be) *need*(-ed/necessary), have need/occasion'; חשק, '*be attached/cleave, desire*/be pleased, delight, spokes, curtain rods (of tabernacle court)', the last three all starting with חש, which makes sense since moving cheyt to cancer celebrates the arrangement of triads in astrology, relating thus to the thinker (shin).

The remaining categories are perhaps more subtle. For one, the origin of the letter cheyt in old Hebrew can be traced to the hieratic form of the Egyptian hieroglyph **sieve**, to which the following all loosely relate: חבת, 'cakes/pastry? or pans' (A. חבז 'bake bread'); חטה, '(grains of) wheat'; חסף, 'scaled off, shards/earthenware'; חרז, 'strings of pearls/corals' (Syr. '*put in order, dispose regularly*'); חרק, '*grind*/gnash (teeth)'; and חשל, 'enfeebled, Ch. *beat small*/pound'.

The triad of signs that points down towards libra is that of water. Astrology calls it that of air, but tradition associates the triangle pointing down in the Star of David with water (likened to Torah, since it flows from high to low), and that pointing up to fire. Likewise, the *Zohar* puts the quarter assigned to water (the south) opposite that assigned to fire (the north). Cheyt is its first sign and in fact stands for the top of said triad, the gemini-aquarius line, in the symmetrical pattern of letters brought about by associating each of its signs with the side of the water triad that feeds into it (as opposed to the side emanating from it): H marks the top; R the outer side (being the original libra of the Cauldron); and L the inner side—L and R being the only two non-nasal liquid consonants and initials of *left* and *right* in this, the most spoken language in history.

And the top of the water triad suggests *evaporation*, as well as the *scum* on the surface of a pond. This aspect of cheyt or H seems directly relevant to the following roots: חלא, 'be sick, rust? *scum/froth?*'; חמא, '*curdled* milk, cheese, milky (sweet) words' (A. '*curdle/coagulate*'); חמץ, '(be) sour/*leavened*, soured/embittered, what is *leavened/fermented*, violent man/oppressor, salted/seasoned, vinegar'; חמר, '*rise/ferment* (fig. be agitated), daub/cover w/ bitumen, become excited/troubled, become red/inflamed, turbid *effervescence* (sources of bitumen or asphaltus), wine, a *fermenting/foaming (of waters)*, clay/cement/mire/mud, a heap, an ass, sp. of goat or gazelle'; and perhaps חנט, 'embalm, *ripen* (fruit)'. Three of these start with חמ (*hmm*).

Our final category took a bit of thought on my part but is not particularly complicated: sign gemini on the Egg, where cheyt is, happens to be on the Cauldron-radius of tav, Cauldron's leo. We have already associated H with the sun (based on Graves), and indeed tav represents the sun amongst doubles (see its history), being the heart (its microcosmic counterpart), seat of conscience. Related roots in cheyt are: חוב, '*render guilty*/forfeit, debt'; חוס, '*pity/spare*/grieve for'; חטא, 'miss one's (aim/)step (stumble), forfeit, (induce) *sin(-ner)/sin offering*/failure'; חכם, '*be(/-come) wise*, teach, *wisdom*/skill, Ch. magician/wise (adj.)'; חמל, 'pity/have compassion, spare/save, mercy/clemency'; חנן, '*be merciful/compassionate to*, give graciously, find favor, *supplication*, gratis/for nothing, in vain, *grace*'; חסד, '(show oneself) kind/merciful, reproach, pious/holy, grace'; חסה, '*trust/confide in*, confidence, shelter/refuge (cogn. חוש flee for same)'; חפר, '*blush/be ashamed*/confounded, *put to shame/cause disgrace*'; and חתת, 'be broken(/in pieces)/terrified/dismayed/confounded, fear, *dread*, destruction/ruin'—complete with a bit more of that *sceith* we encountered earlier. Might I add, at least half seriously, חם, 'parent-in-law'.

And tav, as the leo of the Cauldron, also signifies life, hence: חוה, (cogn. חיה, 'breathe') '*breathe* out/declare/show [*life* (Eve)] villages, Ch. explanation'; and חייה\ה, '*live, revive*, living creature'.

SUMMARY

Cheyt as gemini: [*twins:*] 'marry', 'need', 'love, bosom, lap', 'be bound together'; [*shoulders and arms:*] {'waving'} 'embrace', *2* 'seize', *4* '(take hold of, seize) be strong (stout)', 'disengage, make pliant or strong*?* ready for war, loins' ['loins'], 'fists'. **Hawthorn:** 2 'be sharp (species of thorn)', 'thorn, -bush, hook'; [*its white, pungent flower:*] 'become white, pale', 2 'adorn', 'lily or narcissus or saffron [*from 'pungent' or 'bright'*]'. **Hedge in:** 3 '(bosom) surround (wall)', 2 'enclose', 'enclose in net', 4 '(twist) bind (-round) (-about, gird)', 'tight bonds', 'fasten', 'collars, necklaces, strings of pearls [*etc.*], put in order', 'strangle', 'bind up, muzzle', 'bring back, hog', 2 'collect (decline, haven)'. *Sieve*: 'hold back, restrain', 2 'shard', 'beat small, pound', 'beat out, thresh', 'wheat'. **Where radius of tav [*conscience*] intersects Egg:** 'five' [*tav = 5th sign, cheyt = 5th (i.e. last) unmanifested sign*]; 2 'pity, spare', 2 'gracious, merciful (pious, reproach)', 'be or make wise', 'instruct', 'rod', 'be straitened', 'muzzle, restrain oneself', 'parent in law', 'blush, be ashamed', 'gnash [*teeth*]', 'tremble', 2 '(render guilty) forfeit (miss, stumble)', 'pass beyond, transgress', 'be profaned, defiled', 'corrupt, harm, fault'. **Top of water triad:** [*ferment:*] 'curdle, coagulate, cheese', 'be sour, what is leavened, fermented', 'ferment, wine, a foaming [*of waters*]'; [*evaporate:*] 'skin bottle', 'hay, dried grass', 2 'be dry (dried up) (hot)'. **Moved to sign cancer:** [*fire:*] 3 '(be dried up, glow) burn (become hot)', 'heat', 'fiery, bright, glowing' ['polished brass*?* elektron*?*'] 'see, behold', 'pierce through, lightning', 'seize coals, fire-pan', 'baking or frying pan, be low or flat' ['a kind of lizard'] [*where the Egg descends:*] 'decline, encamp, vaults' {'decline'} 'ease oneself, excrement'; [*desire's object:*] 3 '(cleave to) desire (bend)' {'bent'} 'intend, reckon, devise', 'pluck', 'snatch up'; [*breast:*] 2 'breast', 'bosom, breast [*of garment*]', 'milk, fat {fertile}', 'be fat, opulent'; [*breath:*] 2 'live (breathe)'. **'Guardian of Boundaries'** [*in 'Orphic' hymn*]: 'be silent', 'riddle', 'seal up', 'embalm, ripen', 'bandage', 3 '(hide, conceal) cover (protect, act secretly)'. **Space:** [*dark:*] 'be dark', 2 'be black'; [*what separates, hollows out; no-thing:*] 3 'divide (apportion, disperse, be smooth) (cut)', 'cut or hew wood', 'cut in, wound, be sharp, trench', 4 '({trench} limit) engrave (cut in) (plough)', 2 '(engrave) cut, hew (-out, be engraven)' {'a digging'} 2 'dig ([*as pit*], mole, explore) (bore, cavern)', 'cave, be pierced, open', 'lack', 'strip, make bare', 'tear away with violence, shake off [*fruit*]', 'pluck or gather fruit' [*yet assoc. w/ autumn*], 'cut or tear off, devote to destruction, devote to God' ['sickle'] 'crop off, locust'. **That which blocks the way:** 2 'locust' [*rune = 'hail'*] 'host [*ants? locusts?*]', 2 '(overthrow) be weak (sickness)', 'turn oneself, withdraw, depart', 'cease, fail', 'wait'. **LeMat** [*vagabond*]: 2 'explore', 'spreading, free', 'trust, shelter, flee', 'take flight, haste', 2 'hasten (enjoy)'. **May Day:** 2 '(whirl) dance (festival, move in circle)', 'circle', 2 '(renew) new', 'rejoice', 'partridge' [*WG, pp. 327-9, 330*].

ו

Vav

PARSED ROOTS

The letter vav by itself means 'and'. For this is the sign cancer, or *towards other*. And contrary to the stipulations of modern-day Kabbalah, it is the root of the female half of the Great Name (יהוה). That is why it is extremely interesting to me that there are *very few* roots that begin with vav. There are also a few roots in yod whose Arabic equivalents begin with vav. Since yod is the root of the male half of the Name—and is still recognized as male—I am led to speculate that these roots may have been appropriated by yod at roughly the same time as the expulsion of God's consort from the Temple, in the time of the prophets. (This last must have had a negative effect on God Himself, since it requires a male and female *together* to *invoke* the Name.)

Consider root וו, 'hook/pin (used for suspending the curtain in the tabernacle)'. Hmm. There are only two other roots in vav, plus two others that appear only in proper names of places, collated with the Arabic, one of which reinforces the meaning 'and', namely ודן [A. 'two rivers']; plus two more that appear only in names of persons and are collated with Persian. And they tend to reinforce the feminine character of this letter.

But let us take these together with roots in yod (and one in qof) whose Arabic equivalents start with vav and consider the picture they give us of the significance of this letter. I realize by doing so we veer slightly away from just considering Hebrew and Chaldee (Aramaic) roots used in the Bible, but as it turns out it is rather interesting.

The bardic letter is *ura*, heather, vowel of summer; hence vav's station, summer solstice. It symbolizes coming of age, consummation of love. Thus the root ולד (= ילד 'bear/bring forth'), 'child/offspring'; as well as perhaps {ישח (Gesenius coll. w/ A. וחש '*be empty*'), 'emptiness of stomach/hunger'}. Closely linked is the Greek term Graves extrapolated from the Boibel Loth name of U, *ura*, namely *Urania*, whom he identifies as 'Queen of Heaven'—and indeed the corresponding tarot trump is XVII The Star, showing a nude woman pouring chlorine (atomic number 17) in her pool under the stars. Hence: {יפת (A. ופת '*be entire/perfect*') 'arrive?' > מופת, 'sign/wonder, mark/portent'}; {ירם [(A. ורם '*be high*') 'height']}; ויזתא ['*pure*' coll. w/ the Pers.]; and ושתי ['*beauty*' coll. w/ the Pers.]. One way to think of this letter is as the consort—Ashera perhaps—reached by the heroic oak king, the king of the waxing year, at summer solstice: she is both his death and his apotheosis (symbolically).

Three roots reflect that cancer is *towards other*: והב [A. '*gift*']; {יזיאל [(A. וזח 'assemble') 'assembly of God']}; and {ישה (A. ושה '*to help*'), 'be/exist/subsist, be firm, help/deliverance, wealth, counsel/wisdom'}. And three roots reflect that this sign is where the round progresses straight down: וזר (A. '*be loaded*, commit crime') > 'laden w/ guilt/guilty'; {יקר (A. וקר '*be heavy*'), 'be dear/precious/esteemed/prized/honored/respected, make rare, splendid/beautiful, dear/beloved, honor/glory, value/price, Ch. hard/difficult/noble'}—with a bit of God's consort thrown in as well—and from a slightly different perspective, {יעף (A. ועף '*run swiftly*'), 'be wearied/fatigued, flying/swift course'}. And finally, one, maybe two, roots reflect that cancer is the passive pole of the round: {יקה (A. וקה '*obey*') > יקהה, 'obedience'}; and {קוּע (= קוּר '*dig*' cogn. A. וקע 'wound, mark, brand'), 'mark cut into skin, prince'}.

So while our data base is limited with this letter, it is clear that what there is reinforces placement of vav at the outer limit of the round, on the feminine side of the Egg—as if it needed such reinforcement, considering the old Hebrew letter is shaped like a breast pouring forth milk.

SUMMARY

Vav = 'and' [*in keeping with U-heather being love's consummation (SY's 'coition')*]. Arabic roots mentioned include VZH [H=*heh*] 'assemble', VPTh [Th=*tav*] 'be entire, perfect', VRM 'be high' [*Urania, Queen of Heaven (table 6)*], VQR 'be heavy' [*sign of round's descent*], VOP [O=*ayin*] 'run swiftly' [*velocity of descent?*], VQH 'obey' [*being Egg's passive side*], and VQO 'wound, mark, brand' [*ditto*].

ע

Ayin

PARSED ROOTS

This is an interesting letter, for it reflects a rich mix of meanings. However, it is rather complicated to explain. Of the seven *bardic* vowels (only six of which are vowels in the runic Elder Futhark), ayin is the only one whose position on the Egg seems out of place: it is the vowel of spring—O-F-S (O + the first two spring months) are 4-8-16, signifying increase—yet O resides down at leo, *summer's peak*. The phonetics placing it there precluded *any* vowel ending up at aries or any other spring month, as they are arrayed across the bottom half of the Egg, from cancer (U) to capricorn (Ii), with A, alef, being replaced at virgo by Q so that it might occupy the center of the Egg as the mother letter whose round that is.

The resolution of this quandary is that the Egg represents the alchemical vessel, and ayin, being leo, is the hottest month and thus represents where fire is applied to the vessel. Moreover, ayin's month (the arc extending on from leo) forms the base of the mercury column in the vessel; and once heated, the metal flies into the upper vessel as toxic mercury vapor—what necessitates it be a hermetically sealed vessel—taking over not only its upper half but the upper halves of the two adjacent columns (Venus, and the Luna half of Luna-Sol), *at which point* it has risen all the way up to aries and commands the *whole* of spring. Proof of this involves atomic numbers, the pattern of rulership in astrology, and placement of bardic and Hebrew *eight*—Mercury's number (of the ten)—as explained in the introduction to this tome: briefly, aries (as F or as samekh) is bardic *eight*, while gemini (as H, cheyt) is Hebrew *eight*, *eight* thus gaining possession of the two adjacent columns' upper halves to compass the entire upper half of the part of the Egg that is in nature. Further proof of this is Æsop's fable of a lion and three bulls: three bulls cluster together for protection, so lion sows distrust and dissension till they separate, at which point he slays them one at a time. This clearly references the base of mercury's column, leo the lion, taking over the roof of its column, the arc or month of taurus the bull, *plus* the tops of the two adjacent columns, two more 'bulls', since they turn into the *expanded* roof of the column whose roof is taurus.

Mercury's vapors filling the upper outer vessel has its counterpart in nature's filling out trees with foliage: the Greene Lyon. So, to start with: עתני-(אל) ['*lion* of God']. As for the heating itself: עוג, '*bake* (bread/cakes)'; עיר, '*heat* (oven), anger/terror, enemy' (A. 'be ardent'). Add to this the flying-up of mercury's vapors (or seen as the filling out of what provides shade): עתם, '*be burned*/consumed/*darkened*?'; עשׁן, 'smoke, fig anger/*cloud*'; ערף, 'drop/distil, clouds, gloom'; 2. ערב, '*become dark*/evening, raven, *osiers/willows*, —מ the west' (A. 'be black'); ענן,

'cloud'; עלט, 'thick darkness' (A. 'be dense' עטל 'be dark'); עוב, 'darken, thick(-et/cloud)', and cogn. עוף, '*cover with wings/darkness, fly*, vanish, birds/fowls'. I italicized 'osiers/willows' as well, because it connects directly to spring, specifically to the vernal equinox, where shin the willow is.

Then there is the outward sign of the clouded Egg, the abundance of spring itself: עבת, '(be twisted/interwoven?) perplex/complicate (sc. oppression), *interwoven/bushy/thick*'; עדן, 'live *luxuriously*, delicate, delight/pleasure/[*Eden*]' (A. 'be soft/lax/pliant'); עדף, 'be overabundant'; עור, Ch. 'chaff'; עלה, 'ascend/arise/*spring up*/be exalted, *leaf/foliage*, ascent, H. & Ch. Most High/Exalted, Ch. burnt offering'; ענף, '(full of) branch(-es)'; עפה, Ch. 'branch/bough' (Syr. 'flourish'); עפל, '*be swollen*/proud, tumor/hill'; עצן ['his spear'? (A. '*branch*')]; ערג, 'low/bleat, desire/long for, raise bed (of *garden*)' (A. '*rise/ascend*'); ערש [in ־יה 'whom the Lord fattens' (Syr. 'fatten')]; עשׂב, 'green herbs'; עשׂו ['hairy' (Esau)]; עשׁר, '*be/-come/make/*act *rich*, arrogant'; 2. עתר, 'be rich/abundant/multiply'. And touching on rising up to become a constellation (as per the myth): ע(י)שׁ [Arcturus, the Great Bear?]. Note that four involve (soft) peh, *fearn* the alder, conveyor of mercury's *eight* to aries.

There are a few meanings in direct negation of this last: עבל [(A. 'be leafless')]; עקר, '*root out*/up/hamstring(horse), *barren/sterile*, root(stock), Ch. *stump*/trunk'; 3. ערב (= חרב 'arid/sterile') '[Arabia] desert, open country (fig. heavens)'; עשׁשׁ, '*waste away/become old*, moth'. Note that none of these involve peh.

Many more roots touch on the mercurial or volatile: עבר, '*pass over/by/away/overflow/-whelm*, remove, *passage*, ford, ferryboat, conceive, be proud/angry [Hebrew] because'; עבשׁ, 'dry up'; עגב, '*love overly*, flute?'; עוז\עוּז, 'flee for refuge'; 1. עור, '*(be) awake(ned/roused)/arise, stir up/excite, - (a cry), raise/lift up* (sword/scourge), city/town (prop. a watching, pl. fortified and watched) [watch] [-ful/waking] [-man/citizen]'; עושׁ, 'hasten'; עזאזל, 'scapegoat (lit. goat of *departure*)'; עזב, '*leave*/forsake, *set free/loose*, market'; עזניה, 'sea-eagle/osprey'; עטשׁ > 'a sneezing' (A. 'sneeze'); עוט\עיט, '*be angry w/*, rush/fall upon *w/ fury*, birds of prey'; עים, '*ardor*/violence or drought?'; ערד, '*flee*, wild ass' (Syr. '*be wild*'); ערף, '*neck* (in expressions meaning *to flee*), break (animal's) *neck*, fig. throw down/destroy (altar)'; ערק, '*flee*, gnaw [Arkite]'; עשׂק, 'strive/contend'; and עתק, '*(be) remove(d)/transfer(ed), transcribe*, grow old, beautiful/shining, neat/elegant/splendid, bold/insolent/wicked, removed (from mother's breast, i.e. weaned), ancient'; plus 2. עמד, 'make tremble', which also touches on IIII The Emperor (see below). And perhaps עכבישׁ, 'spider', Mercury's number being *eight*. The first three above have ayin & beyt (4 & 5); three or four build on ayin vav (4, 5ᵗʰ-to-last); three, including two five-letter roots, build on ayin zayin (4, 3); and the three built on ayin reysh (4, 15) all mean 'flee'.

Further reference to neck taurus, the roof of mercury's column (as in ערף above): עוג ['long-*necked*/gigantic']; ענק, 'necklace/neck chain [long-necked' Anak(im)]'; and perhaps עלע, 'sip/suck up'. Four in the last two paragraphs involve qof: Q the apple is glossed 'refuge of a hind' in the *Book of Ballymote*, is 4ᵗʰ-from-the-end (18), and follows ayin on the Egg (at virgo).

The shape of ayin in old Hebrew is the same as our letter O—the hieratic of **forearm** was like a horizontal stick with a feather tied to each end spinning, so they spun it—and from this come roots that signify *revolving, enclosing, hollowing out*. To start with the first of these: עגל, '*round*, calf, cart/war chariot, way' (Syr. '*roll/revolve*'); עגר, 'crane (Ethiop. גער cry out) or swallow (*turn about/fly in circle*)'; עוד, '*(say) again (and again)/surround*/testify, proof, Ch. while'; עוה, 'sin/*be bent*/pervert, ruin, *overthrow*'; and עול, 'decline/*turn aside*, deal unjustly (עול wicked)'; עטר, 'surround/encompass, crown'; עלל (= גלל 'roll') '*repeat*/do habitually/effectually, roll (thing in dust)/glean/act as child, Ch. enter'. Three use lamedh (a reaching beyond oneself).

Then regarding the second, an *enclosing*: עבב, 'cover/hide'; עגן, '*be shut up*/prevented (from marrying)'; עטה, '*cover/wrap/roll up*/faint, garment'; עטן, 'skin-bottle (for milk or water)' (A. 'dress skins'); עטף, '*cover/close*, weak/faint'; עכס, 'wear anklets, *fetter*' (A. '*bind*'); עלם, '*hide/conceal, secret*, youth', indefinite time (antiquity/eternity) (A. 'come of age'); עלף, '*be covered over*/languid/faint/*veiled*'; עמם, '*hide/conceal*, people/nation (esp. Israel), w/at/by/near (union/connection)' (A. 'be (in) common'); עמר, '*bind*, wool, sheaf/Omer [Gomorrah]'; ענב, Ch. '*bind together* [cluster]s of grapes'; ענד, 'bind on, bands'; עקד, 'bind, striped/ring-streaked'; עקה, 'parapet/railing/battlement' (A. 're-/detain'). Three of these build on ayin teyt: wheel revolving, wheel stopped.

And as for the third, a *hollowing out*: עוט, '*style/graver*, pen' (A. '*impress/dig in*'); עור, '*dig/- out*/blind, cave'; עזק, '*dig, engraved ring*/seal (Ch.)'; ערה, 'make bare/uncover/*empty/pour out*/spread oneself abroad, bare places/pastures, need/destitution, nakedness (unfortified)/nudity, shamefulness/disgrace, Ch. damage/detriment, scabbard/sheath, razor/knife'. And on a tangent related to this last: 2. עור, '*be made bare*, skin'; and ערר, 'be/*make naked*/demolish (foundation), solitary/forsaken/childless, destitute'. Four involve reysh, three of which mean *make bare* (since reysh pictures the male member and the duct conveying seed to it).

Ayin's trump is IIII The Emperor (cf. 'crown' above), and a couple here relate also to *enclosing*: עות, 'make crooked/pervert/subvert/wrest (judgment)/*bow down, oppression*'; ענש, 'to tax/fine'; עצם, '*close* (bind) eyes/*be/-come strong/mighty/great*, bone/body/self'; עצר, '*shut/close up*/restrain/retain(strength)/*rule/reign*/be assembled, *oppression*'; ערץ, 'terrify/tremble w/ fear, *strong/mighty*/violent/fierce/*tyrant*'; עשק, '*oppress*/treat unjustly/defraud, *oppression*/injury, distress/pressure/anguish'; and 1. עתר, 'entreat/*supplicate*, false'. (Two involve reysh, which means 'head'; two involve shin, which is a crown.)

Somewhat similar to this are meanings related to the hieroglyph **forearm**, from whose hieratic character ayin probably stems (by rotation); at the very least it is the Egyptian equivalent of ayin. Thus: עבד, 'work/till, serve/bondage'; עוק, 'press down, oppression'; עות, 'aid/help'; עזר, '*assist/ally*, court (of temple)'; עיף, 'weary'; עמל, '*toil/travail, weary*/wretched'; עמס\ש, 'take/lift up/bear/carry/load/burden [Amos]'; 2. ענה, '*labor upon/oppress*/humble, intent/purpose, furrow'; עצב, '*travail*/pain/grieve/worship, idols, earthen vessels'; and finally עשה, '*work/labor/fabricate*, yield/acquire/prepare/dress/execute/perform'. It is easy to see how עות gets its meaning of *help*: it is 'heart-chakra' ayin the emerald relating to the salt of the earth, waw-tav (based on atomic numbers, which I often use as *symbolic shorthand*). Before that, עוק is straightforward: leo *up*, then *down*—ayin as *four* paired with its reflection *after* the breaking of the vessels, *seventeen*, and the effect this ends up having on its reflection *before* said breaking, 'lowly' qof at *eighteen*

(Q as Da'at, Knowledge, in that it naturally pairs with U, the noetic breath, next to it in number).

There are roots which express the opposite of industry. The number bards gave O is *four*, for as you can see it covers all four quarters. *Four* means the fourth element, earth. (Even as Jupiter among the ten, it represents that aspect of air wherein it acts on earth.) Quite a few roots appear to express earth's 'sluggishness': עבה, '*be thick/gross*, compactness'; עון, '*dwell*, (co-)habitation/dwelling, refuge/*den*'; עסס, '*tread down*, must/new wine'; עפר, '*dust/earth/clay/clods*, fawn, lead(weight)'; עצל, '*be sluggish*/slothful'; ערל, 'uncircumcised/*dull of speech*(/ear/heart), foreskin'—utilizing reysh, which pictures the male organ—2. ערם, 'become heaped up, heap (rubbish/grain)'; ערש, 'couch/bed'. And three earth-dwellers: עכבר, 'mouse'; עכשוב, 'asp'; and עקרב, '*scorpion*/scourge' (scorpio again). For its sluggishness: עלק, 'leech' (A. 'adhere'). Plus: 1. עמד, '*stand/- by*/for/endure/*stop/arise/set/place*, column', with a little of earth's sluggishness but also a bit of the industrious *and* of spring's volatility (*arise*).

One of the larger groups clusters around ayin's core meaning in the deepest Kabbalah: the mental breath. It is that part of the mental breath that is within the psychic atmosphere of the doer (the Egg). In fact, this is the aspect of ayin that explains its square Hebrew shape, in two ways. On one level, it can be seen as that part of the face that contains the eyes and the bridge of the nose, which is where one focuses when trying to read another's thoughts. On another level, it expresses what Harold W. Percival says of the mental breath: that it has one center in the heart (the stroke at the lower left, mimicking that of tav, the heart) and two in the mental atmosphere of the doer, which is the part of the thinker's atmosphere (Cauldron or Throne world) that is in the doer's atmosphere, the Egg (this explains O's round shape). These last two centers are the two yods at the top.

The thinker is concerned with finite durations. Thus: עבט, '*pledge*/borrow/lend/alter (course)'; עדד, Ch. '*time*' (A. 'number/*compute*'); עדה, 'pass by/remove, adorn, *while/until*, eternity, *time*'; עדל [A. 'be just']; עדר, '*set in order*/arrange/omit, flock'—four built on ayin dalet, two of which mean *time*—עוץ, 'consult/take counsel'; עמק, 'be/make deep, *profound*, vale'; 1. ענה, 'answer/testify/declare'; 1. ערב, 'exchange/barter/*pledge*/intermix/interfere/have intercourse w/, mix, agreeable, gadfly, woof/foreigners, surety, wares, hostages'; ערך, '*set in order*/arrange, place together/dispose/*compare/estimate*/value, disposition/row/pile/heap/array'—another *set in order* involving ayin and reysh—1. ערם, '*be cunning/subtle/act prudently/wisely, crafty/cautious*, plane tree, *naked*/stripped' (A. '*make bare*')—a tangent run across a bit earlier—and עשת, 'be made smooth/bright/polished, *think of/remember, intend/purpose, thought/opinion*, something wrought, eleven(th)'—*eleven* being the bardic number of the letter it ends with.

The effect of finite durations on a doer is: עגם, 'be sad/grieve for'; and עזה [A. 'console']. The effect of conscience on a doer would be: עכן ['troubler']; and עכר, 'trouble/cause sorrow/be irritated/excited, confusion'. On the other hand, if one's conscience happens to be clear: עלז\ס\ץ, 'exult/rejoice'; and ענג, 'be delicate/*delight in*'.

A final category references, as with cheyt, the sign to which it was moved when the order was jumbled: ayin was moved to the tenth sign (opposite where cheyt was moved to), capricorn the goat (in Babylonia, a sea-goat), the mid-spine (straight back). Thus: עזז, 'strengthen/make bold, might, fierce/harsh/fortified, refuge, *goat*'; עצה, 'close (eyes), *backbone/spine*, tree/wood' (A. 'be hard/firm'); עשׂר, '*ten*, tithe'; and עתד, 'prepare/be destined, things acquired (riches), *he-goat*/(leader/prince)'.

Then there is the root עקב '[Jacob] take by the heel/*supplant*, defraud/*circum*vent/*retard*, heel/(horse)hoof/*rear*(of army)/track(s) [insidious] (to the)end/reward/because', referencing the direction *back*, the idea of overturning, and even a bit of earth's sluggishness.

Three roots remain. One references youth, the spring of life (O, vowel of spring): עיר, '(*young*) ass'. The other two may relate to feminization of the Holy Spirit or thinker (this being the mental breath): עלע Ch. 'rib'; and עשׁתרת [Astarte/Ashtaroth].

SUMMARY

Ayin as leo: 'lion' [*and from Æsop*, 'mouse']; [*hottest month:*] 'bake, cake', 'to heat [*an oven*]', 'be burned, be darkened'. **Clouding of vessel** [*mercury's vapors = spring's foliage*]: 'smoke [*of* anger *or* cloud]', 'to cloud', 'become dark, willows, raven, the west', 'cover with wings, fly away, darkness', 'be thick, gross, density', 'be dense, thick darkness', 'distil, thick clouds, darkness, gloom', 'darken, thick cloud, thicket', 'interwoven, thick, bushy [*of trees*]' {'hairy [*Esau*]'} 'bat' [*anyone who has seen the cloud of bats exit Carlsbad Caverns at dusk will understand*], 2 '(cover) hide (conceal, grow ripe of age and desirous of marriage)'. **O's shape surrounds:** 2 'cover, clothe', 'to dress skins, skin-bottle', 2 '(ring-streaked) bind (fetter, anklet)' {'bind together, cluster'} 'bind around', 'be shut up, prevented [*from marrying*]', 2 'detain (shut or close up, rule, reign)'. **IIII L'Empereur:** 'surround, encompass, crown', 'tax, fine', 'tread down', 'entreat, supplicate', 'Great Bear, Arcturus', 'wax strong, show oneself powerful', 'strong in number, become mighty, close or bind up [*eyes*], break [*bones*], strength', 'oppress, press upon'. *Forearm:* 'press down, oppression', 'bind [*sheaves*], treat as slave', 'bestow labor upon', 'be weary', 4 'weary (depressed) (travail)', 4 '((toil) travail) labor (work (serve, make weary))', 'lift up, carry, load' ['ass'] 2 'aid, help (assist)', 'strive, contend', 'break, pound, mix', 'cut with axe'. **As furze** [*old growth burnt off so sheep can nibble spring's shoots*]: {'stripped of foliage'} 3 '(expose, uncover) make bare (crafty, cunning, prudent, subtle)' [*the converse, respectively, of 'bushy' and 'cover, hide', above*], 'root out, stock, stump, barren'. **Volatility** [*quicksilver*]: 'dry up' ['chaff'], 'arid, Arab, desert, heavens', 'sneeze', 'to trouble, be excited', 'stammerers', 'excite, awaken, stir up', 'terrify, fierce, violent', 'violence, ardor', 'rush upon with fury, birds of prey', 'osprey, sea eagle', 'crane, cry out?', 'hasten', 'flee for refuge', 2 'flee (be wild)', 'leave, forsake, set free, market, commit to' [*cf.* **'heritage'** *below*], 'exult, rejoice', 'inordinate love', 2 '(bleat, long for) ascend (arise [*of the dawn*], spring up, foliage, increase)'. **Spring's increase:** 'eye, surface, appearance, sparkle, spring, fountain', 'green herb', 2 'branch, bough (flourish)', 'exceed, be superabundant', 2 '(be abundant, multiply) be rich (become rich, enrich)', 'be soft, pliant, live luxuriously', 'be dainty, delight in, indulge in luxuries', 'fatten', 'become heaped up', 'be swollen', 'being with young' ['ass colt']. **Moved to capricorn** [*mid-*

spine]: 'be ready, he-goat', 'ten' [numeral *ten is yod*]; 2 'scorpion, scourge' [*tail goes up the round behind, as move grabs scorpio and joins it* to *capricorn (mental breath when a thought is created)*]. **Circulatio** [*to progress about the round*]: 2 '(round, revolve) roll (repeat an action)', 2 '(again and again) while (during, pass by, spoil [*from idea of rushing upon*])', 'pass through-over-or-along, drop [*as a liquid*], overflow, a Hebrew', 2 '(be bent [*in pain*], overturn, invert) be perverse (false, deceitful)', 'take by the heal, supplant, circumvent, defraud', 'turn aside, deal unjustly', 2 '(be removed, transfer) grow old (waste away)'. **Rune 'heritage':** 'console', 'be sad, grieve for', 'society, fellowship', 'hide, conceal, be in common, swarm, flock, people, nation [*frequently Israel, opp. to Goyim*])', 'entangle, load [*of debt*], give a pledge', 'pledge, exchange, barter, be agreeable, intermix, have intercourse', 'uncircumcised [*of speech,* dull; *used also of ear, heart*]'. **Bardic number** [*four=earth, volatility's converse*]: 'sluggish, slothful', 'stay, dwell, cohabitation', 'couch, bed', 'adhere, leech' ['asp'], 'dust, the earth, clods, lead' [*i.e. a weight*]. **Base of pillar of Hermes:** 'endure, stand, stand up, arise, erect, pillar, column, stage, scaffold', 'tree, spine, be firm, close [*eyes*], counsel, plan'. **Square-Hebrew** [*eyes and bridge of nose, as mental breath*]: 'think, make bright, Astarte', 'deep, profound', 'to number, compute [*esp. time*]', 2 'arrange, set in order (flock)', 'answer, testify', 'be just', 'consult, take counsel'. **O's column's number** [*eight*] **and roof** [*taurus*]: 'spider'; 'neck', 'necklace {long-necked}'. **O as hollowed out:** 'impress, dig in, style, graver', 2 '(seal, engraved ring) dig (-out, make blind)'.

ק

Qof

PARSED ROOTS

Qof is virgo, the virgin, and pictures a cross-section of the womb, the two openings being the navel and birth canal. This is the reason for the customary substitution of *qof* for *heh* in the Name outside of Bible-reading and prayers: it is the gap waiting for the child in the Great Name (the one sign of the microcosmic hexad in the manifested half that is missing in it). The bardic letter is *quert* the apple—doubled K—and stands for the *k* sound when followed by *w* or *u*, and this and its counterpart in English, *wh* (Old English *hw*), the interrogative consonant (initials of *question* and *why*, respectively), reproduce the sound of *biting into* one. Its connection in Celtic lore to Avalon, the Otherworld, and immortality stems from its inherent idea of rebirth; poetic meaning, *fruitfulness*, ultimately fruitful *inquiry*.

In the Hebrew, at least scripturally (*our* study), qof begins roots for many things *related* to this meaning, but seems to shy away from explicitly expressing this. Might the sages have missed here an opportunity to reinforce the emphasis in Judaism on questioning and study (as opposed to blind acceptance)? After all, does *Israel* not mean 'who wrestles with God'? The chief question of course is the character of the child-to-be *in* the womb. The bards numbered Q *eighteen* (kept secret yet easily ferreted out), because the nine months in the womb for the child is *also* nine months for the mother.

What I learned from these roots is how central is the meaning *to cut* or *cut off*. The best illustration of this meaning is the rune **wunjō*, joy—*w* being the interrogative consonant in High German—which pictures half of a fruit on one's knife-edge (like our letter P). Let us start with the various roots that prove that this is indeed *quert* the apple (or whatever fruit most epitomized fruitfulness to Jews in ancient Israel). First, consider the seven involving qof and tzaddi, Hebrew equivalents of doubled K and doubled S (*quert* and *straif*): 3. קוץ (= קצץ '*cut/- off*'?) thorn/-bush, locks of hair, *fruit harvest/summer fruit,* pass the summer'; קצב, '*cut off/down* (wood/tree), shear sheep, *form/shape*, end/extremity'—I italicized 'form/shape' because virgo represents form— קצה, '*cut off*/destroy, *scrape off*, end/limit, whole/sum, judge/leader/prince'; קצע (= קצה\ץ '*cut*') '*scrape off*, angle(s)/corner(s)/plane, cassia'; קצץ, '*cut off/up*, end/limit/after, last'; קצר, '*cut down*/reap, shorten(ed)/impatient, deficient, *fruits cut down/harvest/time of same*/branch/bough'; קרץ 'close/press together? (lips/eyes) or *cut/bite*? (lips), *be cut out*, Ch. *pieces*'. Other similar meanings: קטב, 'destruction' (A.&Ch. 'cut/- off'); קטט, 'be cut off' (A. transl); קסס, 'cut off'; קפד, Ch. 'cut off, destruction, hedgehog' (A. קנפד); קרש, 'board/plank/bench (of ship)' (A. '*cut*');

קְשֹׁט > 'truth' (A. '*divide out equally*, be right'); קְשֹׁט > 'something weighed' (A. '*divide*, pair of scales')—three involving shin or sin—and קרדם, 'axe'. Furthermore, there are: קטף, 'pluck off'; קמט, 'to seize firmly (cogn. קפץ, קבץ, קמץ), be taken away'—four so far involving teyt, two that mean *cut* and two that mean *pluck/seize*—קיקיון, 'gourd'; קמץ, 'grasp, handful/s (abundance)'—another one with tzaddi—קרע, '*tear/off/away, rend/in pieces/cut out*, rags'; and קשא (= קשׁה 'be hard'?) > '*cucumber/melon*'; and not too far away in meaning, (Syr. קדי '*possess*') > [יקדעם 'possessed of the people'].

Relating to harvest: קבץ, '*collect(ion/heap)/gather/-* together/to oneself, company/troop'; קמה ['assembly'] (A. '*heap together/collect*'); קמשׁ, 'nettles' (A. '*heap together*')—three with labials (beyt, mem) that mean *heap*—and קשׁשׁ, 'collect/assemble together, *collect/gather* (as stubble/wood), stubble/chaff'.

Since virgo is manifested water, some few roots signify things tasted: קדה, 'cassia'; קמח, 'flour'; קנמון, 'cinnamon'; קצח, 'black cumin'; 1. קלה, '*roast/parch(corn)*/burn(-ing disease)'; and required for this last, קדח, '(be)*kindle*(d), fever, carbuncle'.

Manifested water means form (what precedes the physical or earthly); all three of these involve nun, qof's opposite, or what pushes in against it, like form or cohesion (overpoweringly so within the third and fourth Wheels): 2. קון, 'lance/spear [(Cain)]' (A. קאן '*form/forge*'); קנה, '*form/create*/get/buy/own, wealth(cattle)'; קנה, '*(measuring) reed*/stalk (of wheat)/beam (of balance), branch (candlestick), arm-bone above elbow *[reeds]*', brushing up against water itself. Hence: קור, '*dig well*/undermine/destroy, *spring/fountain*'; קלח, 'pot/kettle' (Talm. 'flow'); קער, 'dish/charger' (A. 'be deep' cogn. קור); קפא, 'congeal/*become condensed*'; קרקע, 'floor/*bottom (of sea)*'; קרר, '*cold/cool*/quiet, a *cooling/ refreshing*' (Syr. 'be cold', A. 'be cool/quiet'); קשׂה, '*dish/bowl*, inkhorn, scales (fish/armor)', four of which make use of reysh's gurgling, gargling sound (rolled guttural R).

Form logically precedes the physical, as virgo immediately precedes libra or straight down: קבל, '*be before/infant*, receive (someone/instruction)/(under-)take, fig. battering ram, over against/before (in presence of), *because of*' (A. 'meet'?); קדם, '*precede/-vent/anticipate*, front, east, ancient, *origin*'; קוה, '*hope in*/bind/be strong/*gather together*, cord/string/line/rule/might, *expectation/confidence*/collection (of waters/beasts/men)'; קול, 'voice/noise/thunder/*rumor*/cry (beasts)/report'; קסם, '*divin*(e)-*ination*'; 1. קרא, 'cry/call out/shout, *call upon/invoke*, convoke, proclaim/publish/praise, to name/*nominate*, partridge'; 2. קרא, '*meet/befall, towards*/against'; קרה, '*meet/befall*/fall in with, *happen*/chance, join/lay beams/rafter/*frame/build, let occur, make suitable/convenient*, accident, *event/result*, beam/roof, bldg., city/town'—three that actually use reysh to point at libra—קוף (= קף 'go round') > 'ape, *circuit(of sun)*'; 1. קוץ, '*loathe/abhor/(put in)fear*'; and the similar קוט, '*loathe/abhor*/be grieved w/'; and to go with *divination*, 1. קטר, 'burn incense/fat/sacrifices, incense, smoke/vapor, censer'—three built on qof waw, plus reysh again (pointing to libra).

Along these lines, let us now look at roots touching on qof being the womb: קבב, 'curse, cab(dry measure), *alcove*/tent' (A. '*hollow out*/arch/*vault*'); קנן, '(build) *nest, a nest* (fig. young birds therein), *dwelling* (fig. family), *cells/chambers*'; קושׁ, 'lay snares, bow/rainbow/archer [winding]' (A. '*be curved/bent*')—how one is when *in* a womb—קרס, '*bend/stoop*, hook/tack [weaver's comb] ankles'. And roots suggestive of the birth process itself: קדד, 'bow head, *crown of head*'; קרח, 'make bald (smooth), ice/cold/crystal, *bald on crown* (from Ch.)'; plus קלע, 'sling/throw/*cast out*/reject/cut out/carve, sculpture, curtain/hanging'; קפז, 'arrow-snake' (A. '*leap/spring*'); the perhaps related קפץ, '*contract*/close/shut(mouth/hand)/die/leap/*spring*'; and קשה, 'be hard/severe/harden(heart/etc.)/*have hard labor*, strong/depressed, wreathing/plaiting (of hair)'; and the *obviously* related קשח, 'harden(heart)/treat harshly'. In addition, there is: קוא, '*spew out/vomit*/fig. reject, pelican (the bird)'—as in morning sickness. Finally, form and womb must both bind us about: 2. קטר, 'bind/bound/joined [knotty] Ch. joints/ligatures/knots/difficult questions'. Bingo!

There are two roots which I can only relate to qof's sign standing (apropos of its being the womb) for feeling, the passive side of the doer: קצף, '*be/make angry/wroth*, chip/splinter, strife'; and קנא, '*be*(provoke)*jealous(y)*/emulate, *zeal/anger*'. In fact, anger is the function in *Sefer Yetzirah* that rightfully belongs to the sign *opposite* qof: nun at pisces.

The tree-letter *quert* the apple is glossed (in the *Book of Ballymote*) 'refuge of a hind' (as the womb is a refuge), and Q's trump, XVIII The Moon, suggests it is refuge from laughter or satire: קדש, 'be holy/consecrate, prostitute (m. or f.), Holy of Holies, *sanctuary/asylum*'; קלט, 'contracted/dwarfish, *refuge/asylum*' (A. קלץ 'contract'); קרם, 'cover'; קבע, 'defraud/rob, helmet, cup' (A. '*cover/hide*'); and perhaps קיר, '*wall* (of city/house)/side (of altar/heart)'. And relating obliquely to the moon: קרן, 'horn/strength/mtn. peak/*beams/rays (of light), shine/have horns*'.

A close kin to the concept *refuge* is the hieroglyph from whose hieratic form qof evolved, **hill-slope**, since this is the season when Egyptians sought refuge on high ground from the Nile's flooding: קום, '(a-)*rise(up)/appear*/flourish/*stand*/remain/confirm/fulfill/raise/restore, standing corn, stature/height, erect, adversary, a being, statute, place/room/ abode/home/town'; and 2. קוץ (= יקץ) 'awake (from sleep/death)/*arise*'—this hillslope projects onto the sign opposite, and thus evokes the last three angles or arcs, which *form* our hillslope and lead to the three most common atom-types *in earth's crust*, silicon-aluminum-oxygen (lamedh-nun-samekh). And in fact both these roots build on qof-waw, bardic U *defining* Kk as the Q that precedes U.

Perhaps obliquely related to this last is the term for Q in Graves's reconstruction of the early Greek 'hymn' from Boibel Loth names, in this case Cailep: Calyptomai, '(I) vanish'. For *when* the Nile floods, most of the land *vanishes*. Roots possibly linked to *vanish* are: קבר, 'bury, sepulchre'; קדר, 'be turbid/*dark/mourning*'; 1. קון, '(utter) *lament*(-ation)'; קמל, 'wither'; and loosely, קטל, 'kill/slay, slaughter'. One root has *vanish* in it but also what precedes the present: קרב, '*draw near/approach*/advance/offer/*remove (oneself)*, near/kindred/(for a) short (time)/(-ly), encounter/battle/war, *offering/oblation/sacrifice*'—that last linked to the *divination* encountered earlier (in what precedes the physical) and again pointing at libra via reysh.

Then there is the fact that Q in ogham is on the little finger: קטן, '*be little/small*/of no account/unworthy, *little finger*, young'; 2. קלה (= קלל), '*be made light of*/despise/d, shame, pudenda'; קלל, '*be* light/swift/lessened/despised/*mean*, be slight/cursed, lighten/remove (burden), *shake together (arrows in divination)*, polish/sharpen, be shaken'—touching upon *divination* again—and perhaps קוּר, '*thin* thread (of spider web)'; and קלס, 'mock/scorn, derision', as this lower half of the year represents the tanist or holly king and the satirical mode (as opposed to the upper half's heroic mode)—what apple is our refuge from. And that about does it.

SUMMARY

Qof as *hillslope* [*refuge from Nile flood*], **'shelter of hind'** [Book of Ballymote*'s gloss on Q-apple*]**, and XVIII LaLune** [*refuge from barking scorn*]: 'mock, scorn' ['loathe, abhor']; 2 'cover (hide, defraud, cup, goblet)', 2 '(holy, set apart) asylum, refuge (to contract)'. **Form** [*virgo*] **as cohesion:** 'contract, close, shut [*as mouth, hand*], leap, spring', 'become condensed, congeal', 'close, press together [*lips, eyes (in cunning, fraud, etc.)*]', 'thin thread [*of spider's web*]', 2 '(create, creature, obtain) form (forge, spear, Cain)', [*doubles **K**, Tifinag's 'cairn, heap' (see table 4):*] 2 'heap together (collect)', 3 '((a heap) collect, gather) assemble (come or call together)' {'assembly'} '[*Arab.* twist, wind, bind] collection [*of water, men, animals*], reservoir, gather themselves together, cord, [*also:*] wait for, hope in, expectation'. **Womb in square Hebrew:** 2 '(awake [*from sleep, death*]) arise (rise, appear [*e.g. light*], endure, keep, fulfill, restore, raise up, upright [*adv.*], living being, place, room, space, habitation, abode)', 'hollow out, to arch or vault', 'be curved, a bow, rainbow', 'circuit, orbit, ape', 'to bend, stoop {weaver's comb} ankles', 'bow head, crown of head' [*what comes out first*], 'one bald [*on crown of head*], bareness, ice, crystal', 'be cool, quiet', 'be black, dark, turbid', 'inward or inner part, bowels, heart, middle, midst, within [*of time*]', 'spew out, vomit, pelican', 'throw with a sling, reject, carve out, sculpture', 'to nest, chambers', 'be jealous, ardor', 'be hard, harsh, difficult, have hard labor [*in childbirth*]'; [*womb's converse:*] 'bury'. **Manifested water:** 'dig a well, let spring up, a spring, fountain', 'floor, bottom [*of sea*]', 'to flow, pot, kettle', 2 '(be deep) dish (bowl, vessel for ink, scales [*of fish*])'; [*3ʳᵈ element:*] '3-pronged pitchfork' [*trident?*]. **Quert the apple** [*fruit on branch*]**:** 'gourd [*in Septuagint*]', 'cucumber or melon', 'pluck off'. **Old Semitic** [*fruit being cut*]**:** 'tear, tear off, cut out or in pieces', 'cut down, reap, fruits cut down, harvest, -time, bough', 6 '(summer fruit, fruit harvest, pass the summer) (cut down [*as wood, tree*], a form or shape) cut off ((cut in pieces) destruction (a limit))', 'be cut off', 'cut, board, plank, bench [*of ship*]' ['axe', 'be angry, a breaking, a chip, a splinter']; [*bisects:*] 'side [*of altar, heart*]', 'divide, pair of scales, something weighed', 'divide out equally, be equal, right, truth' [*last two same root?*], 'beam of balance, branch [*of candlestick*], stalk [*of wheat*], measuring reed, sweet cane'. **Water's sense** [*taste*]**:** 'cinnamon', 'black cumin', 'flour [*Talm.* to grind]'. **Sign virgo:** [*leads to present instant:*] 3 '(go before, precede, be beforehand, anticipate, east, beginning) (be before, in front, receive) meet (befall, happen, towards)', 'be blunt, set [*teeth*] on edge', 'approach, advance, shortly, soon', 'to divine' [*what is coming*], 'attend, listen, hearken', 'to cry, invoke, proclaim, call for', 'a voice, a cry [*of animals*], thunder, rumor'; [*angle matter:*] 'angle, corner', 'horn, rays'; [*shape of symbol:*] 'harp, lyre, cithara'. **'Vanish'** [*in 'Orphic' hymn*]**:** 'utter lamentation', 'vapor, smoke, burn incense', 2 '(fever) burn (burning disease)', 'wither', 'kill, be slain'. **Q in**

Ogham [*on 5th finger*]: 2 '(be light, lessened, diminished, shame, pudenda) be small (the little finger)', 'handful, grasp'; [*curls next finger with it:*] 3 '(seize firmly) bind (joints) (be joined)'.

ט

Teyt

PARSED ROOTS

There are not a whole lot of roots in teyt, and none seem to reinforce my contention that, as bardic Aa, it represents the fire breath, except perhaps in the sense of *taking a breather from*. For what is indicated is that it is the bottom sign of the water triad: astrology calls it air, but it points down, and the triad pointing down in the Star of David is traditionally linked to water (and Torah): teyt is the material reality Torah, the water triad (form), is to govern. Geodetically, libra is at Giza, and in the *Hymn of the Pearl* the corrupting material world is symbolized by Egypt, to which the protagonist arrives from the east (the direction of self, capricorn). Embodying this last are the following: טול, '(be) throw(n)/cast/out/forth/down'; טמא, 'be unclean/defiled'; טמה, 'be unclean/defiled/despised'; טנף, 'soil/pollute'; and טעה, 'cause to err/seduce'.

While intermediate mem at libra shows the legs crossed beneath one while squatting on the ground *temporarily*, teyt represents the legs crossed beneath one when seated in meditation. The old Hebrew (and Greek) crossed circle is the same as the Egyptian hieroglyphic ideogram for **location**, which is close to the core meaning of this letter: it is the alchemical symbol for earth (as planet). Indeed libra is manifested earth, being where the water triad manifests *as* earth.

Being the lowest point on the water triad (manifesting in earth) spawns the largest group: טבל, 'dip/immerse/stain [purified]' (A. 'dye'); טבע, 'sink (in water/mud)/ be immersed/settled, seal/ring'; טבת [Tebeth (10th month)] (Assyr. tebituv, 'rain')—three built on teyt beyt, beyt being bardic *five* thus corresponding (in Olam ha-Asiyah) to Mars, water's capacity to act on earth— טוא (prob. '(be) remove(d)' cogn. זוע) 'remove dirt/mire/sweep away, besom, mire/mud'; טוח, 'besmear/daub/plaster/cover over/(eyes), inward parts/reins'; טין, 'potter's clay'; טלא, 'patchy, patched/clouted'; טלל, 'to cover/to roof, dew' (A. 'moisten/shade'); טפל, 'smear/plaster/impute, add/join/attach'—making four with the liquid lamedh in the second or third spot (or both)—טרד, 'beating/tempestuous (of rain)/continually dripping, Ch. drive out'. To which I would add: טהר, 'be/-come/pronounce clean/pure/(be) cleanse(d)/purify (oneself), brightness/clearness/splendor'.

Its tree, the palm (though Tamar, 'palm tree', begins with tav, not teyt), links it to the phoenix, born from fire and representing renewal: libra, the constantly renewing present instant (one's location). Hence: טלה, 'young lamb' (Syr. 'be fresh/young'); טרה, 'fresh/moist' (A. 'be fresh/new'); טרם, 'not yet'; and perhaps טוש, 'fly swiftly'. Ans as for physical location: טבר, 'high, eminent place'; טור, 'series/order/range/row, castle/palace/range or row of bldgs.'; טור, Ch. 'mountain' (in Targ. cogn. טבור); טמן, 'hide/conceal (esp. in earth)/reserve, store/treasure'—five pointing at libra also with reysh, one also with intermediate mem. And from being the direction *straight down*: טפף, 'trip/mince, little ones'.

The celebratory nature of the palm can be seen in the following: טאב, Ch. 'be glad'; טבת ['celebrated']; טוֹב, 'be (do) good/well/agreeable/joyful/make fair/glad/wealth/beauty', all three involving beyt. With celebration come victuals, reminding us that the Egyptian hieroglyphic equivalent was **loaf**, a semicircle on its base, the old Hebrew shape likely coming about because the style of 'loaf' used in Palestine changed to (quartered) pita or flatbread: טבח, 'slaughter (esp. beasts)/slay, cook/executioner/guard, meat'; טוא > Ch. 'a fasting' (Syr. 'to fast'); טנא, 'basket'; טעם, 'taste/perceive/discriminate, feed, discernment/judgment/decree/edict, dainty meat'; and טרף, 'tear in pieces/rend/feed/provide for, fresh/new, prey/food/leaf', this last touching on the present instant. And teyt being the loins: טחר, 'hemorrhoids' (Syr. 'pant/strain to eliminate').

As manifested earth, it stands for the sense of touch: טפח, 'spread out/extend/stroke w/ palm/caress, swaddle? palm/hand breadth, nursing of children, upper garment/mantle/cloak', to which טחה, '(bow) extenders (i.e. archers)' may be distantly related; and טפר, 'nail/claw'.

Several have to do in other ways with being the direction *down*: טחן, 'bruise/grind w/ hand-mill/the face of the poor'; טלם [A. 'oppress']; טען, 'load (as beasts of burden)/be pierced'; טפש, 'be gross/dull/stupid'; טרח, 'load/burden/trouble'.

Two roots relate to the wheel-like crossed circle of the old Hebrew teyt: טוה, '*spin*, yarn'; and (sanctifying one's location), טוּף, 'frontlets/phylacteries' (A. '*surround*/bind/- *round*')—teyt and vav form two of its four spokes (the opposite direction on them being the other two).

SUMMARY

Teyt as palm: 'be glad', 'be pleasant' {'celebrated'}. **Rune** [*hourglass on side, fleeting present instant*]: 'not yet, when', 'fly swiftly', 'devise, contrive, forge, sew on', 2 'be fresh (moist)'. **Bottom:** [*of water triad:*] 'moisten, shade, dew', 'dip, immerse, stain, dye', 'sink [*as in water, mud*], be immersed, seal ring', 'mud, remove dirt' ['cleanse'], 'clay', 'daub, plaster over' ['patchy, spotted']; [*of round:*] {'oppression'} 'be cast down or forth', 'beating [*rain*]', 'trip, little ones'. **Loins:** 'seduce, cause to err'. **Crossed circle:** 'bind round', 'spin, yarn', 'hand mill, grind with same'. *Loaf* [*victuals*]: 'to fast', 'meat, slaughter' ['nail, claw'] 2 '(tear in pieces) feed (taste)', 'be fat', 'basket'. **Digestive tract:** 2 'to load, burden', 'strain to eliminate, hemorrhoids', 'soil, pollute', 'be unclean, despised', 'hide [*esp. in earth*]' . **Location:** 'spread out', 'expand', 'mountain', 'high, eminent place' ['general, chief'] 'castle, row of buildings'.

ה

Heh

PARSED ROOTS

Now we come to the letter that was added to *Abram* to make *Abraham*, signifying the Covenant: circumcision is on the eighth day because scorpio, the privates (called 'secrets' in old almanacs), is the eighth sign. So it shows that at that time the original order of simples about the round was known. And by the way since the jumbling of their order was done systematically, rather than haphazardly—based on esoteric knowledge—it makes a strong argument for the *Hebrew* being the original Semitic alef-beyt, *not* Phoenician. This would certainly fit my own model, namely that the Jews when they came out of Egypt in Moses's day brought with them letters based on the Egyptian hieratic characters used in transliterating non-Egyptian words. There is much more evidence for this scenario than for the later idea that letters originated in some proto-Sinaitic scratchings (brainchild of the otherwise level-headed Sir Alan Gardiner).

This letter's shape is a remarkable example of shall we say *symbolic shorthand* (every poet's goal): it reflects the twin doorposts Jachin (on the right) and Boaz (broken front-column), and the horizontal at the top is the male erection reaching across to the opening on the left there to receive it. This dual interpretation of its shape is reinforced by the fact that when the Great Name is taken to represent the human body, the first heh represents the shoulders and arms (up where the front column is broken), and the second heh the legs.

Let us see if any of the roots here might help confirm this: הלךְ, 'go/proceed, *(w/* את\ם*)* *accompany/have intercourse with*, depart/continue, lead/conduct/flow (of wine), stream, Ch. toll, way/caravan, procession'—to which I would attach the probably related הוךְ, Ch. 'go'—and הרה, '*conceive/become pregnant/devise*'. This last one utilizes *two* hehs with reysh, representing the gonads—bardic number *fifteen*, atomic number of phosphorus, key ingredient of chromosomes—so what other meaning could it possibly have. And in addition there are: הדה, '*thrust*/put forth (hand)' (A. 'lead/direct'); and הדף, '*push/thrust/repulse*'—as if dalet wanted us to think it also represents the male organ, or is it the battering ram beating down an oak door?

Since 'slept with' is one way of saying 'had intercourse with', it is not surprising that the early Greek 'hymn' Graves reconstructed from Boibel Loth letter-names (its vowels a series of titles) has, for *esu, (h)esuchia,* 'repose'. Thus: הזה, '(talk in one's) dream? *nod/doze*?', to which might be added two meditative roots (cognates to each other), הגג, 'musing/meditation/prayer' (Syr. 'imagine'), and 1. הגה, 'murmur (coo/lament/growl)/utter/meditate(/tion/thought/muttering thunder)', fitting for the letter of the Covenant and both touching on the audial (heh as air breath, see below); plus הדו ['Hindustan'].

The reason this is the key sign of the entire round is that it is that of desire, of the doer (us), and moreover the sign in which the choice is made whether to climb back up the spine to the head (closed zodiac) or continue on down the legs to the feet (broken-and-extended zodiac). It is a sign of crisis, but also the sign *following* libra, the present (physical existence): הה, 'Ah! (in grief)'; 2. הגה, 'separate/take away'; הגר [(Hagar) 'flight' (coll. w/ A.)]; הדך, 'cast down/tread upon'; הדם, '(foot-)stool, Ch. piece' (Syr./Ch. *cut in pieces*, A. *to level w/ ground*'); 1. הדר (= Ch. *turn*') 'uneven/crooked places'; הוי, 'ho! (exhort.)/wo! (threat)/alas (grief)'; היך, Ch. = (H.) איך, 'how?'; הלם, '*strike/beat (in pieces)*, hither, *hammer [blow]s*, sp. of gem'; המם, 'put in motion/drive, *rout/disperse/defeat, destroy*'; הפך, '*(over)turn/-* back/*ruin*/change/pervert, roll/tumble, *reverse/contrary*, crooked, stocks/imprisonment'; הצן, 'armament/force'; הרג, 'kill/slay (any living thing)'; הרס, 'break/pull down/destroy, a ruin'; התת, 'break in upon? attack unjustly?' (cogn. חתת). (Three are built on heh dalet, so I guess it *was* a battering ram.)

Then there is the complete converse (celebrating the covenant?): הגן, 'be worthy/suitable, -/corresponding'; 2. הדר, 'adorn/honor/respect/show oneself glorious, glory/splendor/beauty'; הוד, 'glory/majesty/beauty/brightness' (name of the eighth Sefirah)—with these last two the door has obviously withstood the ram—הלל, '*shine/boast/glory/praise, shame/make foolish*, morning star, *hymn/Psalms, folly/sin*'—a root reflecting the necessity that the doer make its choice—and המן ['magnificent'? (Pers.)].

Heh's tree is *eadhe*, aspen. Like the privates, it is highly sensitive: the slightest breeze causes its leaves, dark on one side, light on the other, to flutter: הום, 'move/confound/*perturbate, be moved/excited/*be tumultuous, confusion/consternation, wave, ocean/the deep'. Its letter, E, is the air breath, mostly expressed in sound, from noise to breathing, thus: הבל, '*breath/vapor/*mist, vanity/foolishness (idols) [Abel]'; הדד, 'a shouting [a Syr. idol]' (A. 'break/give forth a heavy sound'); הוה, 'exist/be [יהוה] *desire/lust, fall/calamity*' (A. *'breathe'*)—this, containing a bit of the previous category (the calamitous) *and* the reason for it, is echoed by היה, 'be/exist, happen, become, be-/*fall, calamity*'—then המה, '*(make) humming (noise) (i.e. growl, coo, etc.) bustle/*be turbulent/agitated/*disquieted*, multitude of riches/wealth, *noise/disquietude, sound (of harp)*'; המל, '*noise/bustle/turmoil*' (A. 'rain continually'); המה = המן, '*make a noise/*rage'; הרם, 'be high'; הרר, 'mountain[-ous/-eer]'; and (appropriately) spelled the same, הרר, Ch. 'think, thought'; הכר, 'amaze/stun'; הבר, 'cut/divide (the heavens, i.e. astrol.)', this last referencing the sky but also the number given *eadhe* by the bards, *two (cut/divide)*. Eight of these use labials, five of them mem! indicating, I guess, that we can make noise and still keep our balance. Five utilize reysh, two or three of them to elevate (reysh means 'head'), the rest to take charge (reysh means 'head').

Somewhat relevant to this last group: ה, 'this/the/a/O/who/which/whether/?'; הא, Ch. 'lo/behold'; הל (particle of interrogation); and הן, 'behold! lo! whether/surely, hither/here/there'.

Further leftovers I am unable to categorize: הם, 'they (m.)'; הן, 'they (f.)'; and המס > 'melting? or brushwood?'.

SUMMARY

Heh as air's breath: 'breath, vapor, vanity, Abel', 2 '(breathe) be', 'a shouting', 'noise, bustle, tumult'. **Quivering aspen:** 'be moved, excited', 'amaze, stun', 'show oneself glorious', 2 'glory (shine)', 2 'lo! behold!', 'aha!', 'this, the', 'that same', '[*heh prefixed to first word signals interrogative*]', '[*particle of interrogation*]', 'ho! [*threatening, exhorting, grieving*]', 'put in motion, disperse', 'be agitated, disquieted, hum, howl, mourn'. **Scorpio** [*end physical, depart, begin ascent*]: 'ho, alas!', 'ah! [*grief*]', 2 '(beat) break (destroy)', 'throw or tread down', 'force, armament', 'attack', 'kill', 2 '(overturn) turn', 'level with ground, cut up', 'cut, divide', 'take away, separate', 'be removed, onward', 'go', 2 'flow, stream (go, depart)'; {'flight'} 'high, lofty', 'mountain'. **Male organ:** 2 '(push) thrust (stretch out [*hand*])', 'conceive, devise, become pregnant'. **'Repose'** [*as waning moon's age, in 'Orphic' hymn*]: 'think', 'dream', 'make light of', 'murmur, meditate', 'hush', 'suitable, convenient', 'counselor'. **II LaPapesse:** 'myrtle, {*orig. name of Esther* [*Christ. trad. "seeing her as prefiguring the Virgin Mary in her chastity, beauty, and ability to intercede for others"*]', 'palace, Temple [*Jerusalem*]'.

ז

Zayin

PARSED ROOTS

In Greek, this is the initial of *Zeus* (genitive *Dios*) and thus stands for the softening of *d* by *i* (or *y*) in the Indo-European root **dieus* (Sanskrit *dyaus*)—a hardened *i* like the English *j* (which started out as initial *i*). This is bardic I, the vowel of winter—1. זרר, 'sneeze'—and of the old moon: זהם, 'loathe/abhor'; זוע, 'move/shake/vex, disquiet/terror, Ch. tremble'; 2. זור, 'be loathsome/depart/be stranger/become estranged' (A. זאר, 'loathe'); זחח, 'be removed/displaced'; זחל, 'creep/crawl/fear [(stone of) the serpent]'; זעך, 'be extinguished'; זקן, 'beard/chin, *be/grow old*, *old age*, elders/chiefs'. Note here that the only two zayin roots with cheyt in second place are in keeping with the spirit of the rune 'hail'. *Continuing* with the theme of unpleasantness (though not winter): זלעפה, 'violent heat (of poisonous wind/famine/anger)'.

The rune that led me to the discovery that zayin *was* bardic I has the shape zeta would take if carved across the grain of wood, namely a vertical stroke with half an up-arrow on the right and half a down-arrow on the left. Hence: זבב (as in *Beelzebub*), 'rove up-and-down in the air, a fly'. Since it means winter, this shape, and that of zeta even more so, is to be seen as cold air moving in under warmer air—a cold front. Hence זאב, 'wolf'.

Its sign, sagittary the archer, completes the fire triad: זנק, 'leap/spring forth, (burning) arrows/(fiery) darts (sparks?)' (Syr. 'cast/dart forth'). As the active pole of the leo-sagittary horizontal (airy level), it can signify thought, and the speech that expresses it, even though these two functions would have been allocated to ayin and samekh, respectively: זהר (as in *Zohar*), '*enlighten/teach/admonish/warn*/shine, brightness/splendor'—hence זהה '[beauty (esp. flowers), name of second month, spelled זו] Ch. brightness/splendor'—זמם, '*devise/purpose/intend/think* (esp. evil), *plan*/sin'; זמר, 'cut/prune, (prop. to divide, w/ ref. to rhythmical numbers, hence) *sing hymns/praises, song/praise/music/psalm,* pruning time/instrument [pruner/singer] branch/bough'; זעם, '*be angry/indignant/insolent/sullen*/cursed'; זעף, '*be angry/enraged/sullen,* raging of sea, sad/gloomy'; זעק, '*cry/call out* (in pain/for help)/assemble/convoke/*proclaim*'—three built on zayin ayin, to complete the Egg's airy level—and זכר, 'call to mind/remember/recollect, be born male/mention/record [mindful] [renowned] male'—recalling both that zayin stands for male pillar Jachin *and* that the corresponding Egyptian hieroglyph (from whose hieratic form zayin sprang) was **reed**, which stands here for writing, making a record. And indeed this is the sign whose month was *ngetal* the reed in the Gaelic tree-calendar (as opposed to that of the P-Celts). Also, reed suggests measurement: זמן, 'appoint/determine, be determined/fixed, appointed time';

זער (= צער 'be little'), 'a little, small, -ness (time/number)'—ogham I and R (zayin, reysh) were both on the little finger—and זרב, 'become *straitened/narrow* (or warm?)' (Syr. '*compress*'). To these I would add: זן, '*sort/kind/*manner'; and זוה, '*angle/corner, garners*' (A. 'hide/conceal').

As sagittary, zayin is the terminal filament of the spine: זנב, '*tail (of beasts),* smite rear of army'. As pillar Jachin: זיז/זוז, 'abundance/wealth [motion] *doorpost* (on which it moves)' (Ch. 'move/- about')—note the two zayins side by side—זקף, '*set upright/erect/raise up,* Ch. lift/hang up (criminal)'; and זרח, 'rise (sun/light/glory/leprosy/plants), native tree/native, *(the) east(ward)*', east being the direction within (towards Jachin). Two have meanings *somewhat* related to these: זבל, 'dwell, habitation'; and זה, 'this, here/hence'.

Subtly linked to being the active side of manifested air, bardic I is the water breath (the next element beneath air on which air acts): זוב, '*flow/over-/*abound w/waste away/expire, *flux (blood)*'; זיד/זוד, '*boil/seethe/*act insolently/proudly/wickedly/pottage, *overflowing/*-whelming, proud/haughty, pride/insolence'; זול, 'shake/*pour out*'; זוק (= זוב), 'pitch [*flux*]'; 1. זור, '(be) press(ed)/squeeze out'—five with waw in the second spot, in this case standing for the triad of the west, which astrology and ceremonial magic agree represents water—זלפה ['a dropping (trickle)']; זנח, 'stink/be abominable/reject/cast off [*marshy place*]'; זרה, 'spread/scatter/disperse, winnow/sift/discern, *be* spread or *besprinkled,* span (measure), scatterer (fig. the north wind)'; זרם, '*flow/pour/- down/*overwhelm, *violent shower/*storm, effusion/emission'; זרף, 'a copious rain' (A. 'flow'); and זרק, 'scatter/*sprinkle* (dust/ashes/*water/blood), dish/basin* (used for same)'. With these I include the closely related זרע (cogn. זרה), '*spread/scatter/*sow/plant/bear/yield seed/conceive, -/issue/progeny, arm/foreleg, strength/might, legumes/vegetables, crop'. This makes five built on zayin reysh, the latter obviously here representing the outward side of the water triad (the one pointing down). Three more that surely belong with this group are: זהב, 'gold (shekels)/brightness'; זרש ['*gold*' (coll. w/ Pers., Gesenius) or 'star of Venus']; זקק, '*pour out/fuse/refine/purify (as gold), be purified (wine/metals),* bonds/fetters/chains' (Ch. 'join/bind together'). Hence: זבן, Ch. 'buy/gain [bought]'; and זבד, 'give/endow, gift/dowry'.

The following also seem to relate to the water breath: זגג, 'be pure'; זכה, 'be (morally) pure, *cleanse/purify,* Ch. innocence'; זכך, '*be clean/clear/pure (physically/*morally), upright, *glass/crystal* [innocent]'. Akin to these last three in meaning, but also relating to the water breath's corresponding originally to the function *tasting* (in *Sefer Yetzirah*): זבח, 'slaughter (beasts, *esp. sacrifice*), a slaughtering (fig. *flesh of slaughtered animals, i.e. repast/banquet*), *altar*'. Plus: זון, 'be fed/fattened/Ch. nourished, food/meat'; זית, 'olive'; and זלג, 'fork'.

And then there is: 2. זרר, 'wreath/*crown/*border, bound together/*girded*' (A. 'bind/fasten together'), which can be linked to the meaning of letter-name *zayin* according to the website Chabad.org: 'crown', 'weapon', 'sustain'. (The letter's shape is sometimes said to represent a scepter.)

Finally, sign sagittary is associated with the thighs in the broken-and-extended zodiac of the astrologers, which I might point out puts a twist on 'archer' in that *Cupid's* arrow can be seen to be a woman's thighs: זנה, 'commit whoredom/play the harlot'.

SUMMARY

Zayin as sagittary [*thought*]: 'devise, intend [*esp. evil*], think', 'recollect, memorial', 'loathe' [*cf. Shrieking or Hissing (see table 6)*] 2 'anger (raging of sea)', 'be stinking, ill-savored, reject, cast off {marshy place}'. **Bardic I, the water breath:** 3 '(sift, discern, be besprinkled) scatter (sprinkle)', 'sneeze', *4* 'flow (rain, storm)', *3* '(cleanse) be pure', 'boil, seethe' ['violent heat'], 'trickle down' ['creep, crawl'] 'press, squeeze out, be sprinkled', 2 '(be agitated) shake (pour out)'. **Water as form** [*cohesion*]: 2 '(pour out, fuse, refine [*gold*]) bind (gird)', 'be called together', 'compress', 'be little'. **Old moon** [*form as limit*]: 'prune, divide, song', 'be fixed, appointed time', 'beard, grow old, old age', 'hide, conceal', 'be removed', 'draw out, bring up, a fork' ['be fed, meat', 'wolf'] 'repast, slaughter [*of animals*], sacrifice', 'be extinguished'. **Yew** [*of longbows (sagittary=archer)*]: 'spring forth, arrows'. **Shape of rune:** 'rove up and down in the air'. **Jachin** [*base of spine; sagittary*]: 'rise, native tree, east', 'set upright, erect', 'dwell, habitation', 'tail, cut off rear of army', 'doorpost, move about, wealth'. **Contains earth** [*suit Money*] **in solution:** 'gold', 2 '(gold) brightness', 'buy, gain', 'gift, dowry'.

י

Yod

PARSED ROOTS

The tale (as opposed to tail, which is brief) of yod is an interesting one. In *The White Goddess*, Robert Graves postulated two secret doubled vowels, Aa and Ii, to complement the two doubled consonants (Ss and Kk) of ogham—to fill out the spaces on the dolman as he pictured it (where ogham turned corners, a second instance of the same letter was needed to inscribe in its place on the new edge). And his hypothesis turned out to be quite correct, leading me to suspect he had it on the authority of an intact oral tradition, perhaps through his father, a scholar of Irish literature. Even so, he failed to realize that the clearest evidence for his doubled I is the shape of Hebrew yod (he mistakenly identified it with *idho* the yew): Ii is mistletoe, or loranthus in the eastern Mediterranean, both of which grow aloft on other trees, not in or on the ground, just as yod hovers in the air and does not touch the line on which one writes. Hence: יהר (prob. '*be high*', cogn. הרר, הרה), 'elated/haughty/vain'; and {ירם [(A. ורם '*be high*') 'height']}. Both use reysh, which means 'head' or 'first'.

Its station in the year is (surprise, surprise) Yule season, the winter solstice, which fits root יעד, '*appoint (pl./time)*/betroth, meet (/by appointment), agree, arraign, be fixed/set/directed, assembly/faction/household/swarm (of bees), *a set time/season* esp. *festival days*'. It is the sign straight back, mid-spine (or knees), capricorn the goat (or in Babylonia, a sea-goat): יעל (= עלה? '*go up/ascend/arise*'), 'help/profit, *mtn. goat*/ibex, *wild she-goat*', this being where the round itself ascends—yod followed by the diameter (leo-aquarius) of the following, next higher sign.

This sign conveys two starkly contrasting meanings: if we take the round to symbolize outward things, yod marks the end of manifestation (last sign of lower half); but in context of the Grail, taking libra as the passage within, it represents self-knowledge. This reminds us that the Egyptian counterparts of zayin yod (thinker knower *in the Egg*) were **one reed**, **two reeds**: make record (thinker); confirm record (knower).

First, concerning the end of manifestation: יאש, 'despair/despond/render hopeless'; יבב, 'call aloud/cry out'; יבש, '*dry up*/(cogn. בוש) make/be ashamed, dry land'—yod in relation to beginnings, alef or beyt—then יגה, '(be) afflict(ed)/ grieve(d), affliction/grief/sorrow/vexation, remove'; יגע, 'labor/toil/*be wearied/-ying*, toil, *earnings*/wealth'; יגר, 'fear/be afraid'—three with gimel in second place—יחל, 'wait/expect/hope'; יחר, 'delay/tarry'—yod as H, barring the way—ילך (= חלך 'go') > ['journey (pl.)']; ילל, 'wail/howl/lament'—getting on with life (lamedh, the next sign) or getting stuck there (in the next sign)—ינה, 'oppress/vex (w/מן dispossess/drive out)';

יעבץ ['because I bore him in sorrow?']; יעה, 'carry/*sweep away*, shovel'; יעט, 'clothe/*cover*'; {יעף (A. ועף 'run swiftly'), '*be wearied/fatigued*, flying/swift course'}; יער, 'honeycomb/*thicket/wood/ forest*'—a rich mix of roots built on yod ayin (six altogether)—{יפת (A. ופת '*be entire/perfect*') 'arrive?' > מופת, 'sign/wonder, mark/*portent*'}; יקע, '*be dislocated*/alienated, suspend/hang'; יקש, 'lay snares/*be ensnared*, fowler'; ירא, '*fear/- for*/honor, holy/marvelous/wonderful, *to alarm, dreadful/awful*'; ירה, 'fear/be afraid'; ירח, 'moon, month'; ירע, '*be fearful/ distressed*/tremble, curtain/hanging'; ירק, 'greenness/verdure/herb/vegetable, *foliage*, yellowish livid paleness (of corn/man)'—the three that go yod reysh plus bardic vowel mean *fear*, the one ending in Q finds refuge—ישט, '*stretch out/extend* (as sceptre)'; ישם, 'desolate/laid waste, waste/desert'; ישן, '*(fall a-)sleep*/be dry/*grow old, sleep/dream*'—since this is the sign towards which the head is pointed *when* we sleep—ישש, '*old*/aged man'—the four built on yod shin show a satisfying concord in their meanings—יתח, 'a club' (A. '*beat w/ club*'); יתם, '*be lonely/bereaved* [solitary (pl.)] orphan [orphanage]'. To which I should add (as *opposite* yod's east, yet the end of manifestation for land): ים, '*sea*/great river, *the west*', yod being numbered third-from-the-end—the earth breath, but contained in water (as in *Sefer Yetzirah*).

Next, referencing capricorn as (self-)knowledge: ידע, 'know/perceive/discern/be aware of/acquainted w/recognize/acknowledge, know carnally, regard/care for/appoint (make known), knowledge/intelligence/understanding/wisdom, opinion, show/inform/teach, acquaintance/friend, thought/mind/intellect, wizard/soothsayer/spirit of divination, why?'; then יכח, 'show/prove, reproach/correct, punish/(be)chasten(ed), decide/arbitrate/appoint, punishment/chastisement, contend/reason/dispute, (re)proof/argument/admonition/correction'; יסר, 'chasten/correct/punish, admonish/exhort/instruct, learning/doctrine/warning'; יעט, Ch. (= H. יעץ 'advise/counsel') 'consult together, counsel/wisdom'; יעץ, '(take) counsel(lor)/advise/decree/direct (as eye), instruct/consult together, advice/purpose/plan/deliberation, device'; יצב (= נצב 'set/put/place'), 'set/place oneself, stand/- firm/- up (for), certify, firm/fixed/settled, certain/true'; and cogn. יצג, 'set/put/place, establish, let stay/leave, be left'; {ישה (A. ושה 'to help'), 'be/exist/subsist, be firm, help/deliverance, wealth, counsel/wisdom'}; ישע, 'deliver/save/set free, help/succor, be saved [salvation of the Lord (Isaiah)] deliverance/safety'; ישר, 'be straight/even/right/make straight the way, esteem/approve, straight/righteous/upright, -ness/integrity, the righteous (a term for Israel), plain/level country [Sharon] justice/truth, sincerely'—yod plus sibilant tzaddi or shin, five roots, show nice unity—יתן. 'perennial/constant, strong/mighty/firm [-ness (seventh month)]' (A. 'be perennial/flow constantly, hence be stable/firm'); יתר, 'remain/be left, (cause to) abound/excel, abundance/profit/pre-eminence, mere/further, too much, besides'; and thought of as uniting the self's three parts (being self-knowledge), {יזיאל [(A. וזח 'assemble') 'assembly of God']}.

Quite a few roots reflect the fact that yod occupies the same sign as beyt, letter of birth or inception (birth of the waxing year) and of purity (direction *away* from all that is external). For purity: יקה ['pious' (A. 'venerate')]; יטו, '*be*/do *well*/good/be/make cheerful, adjust/dress, *the best/- part of*'; יונה, 'dove [Jonah]'. And birth: יאל, '*begin/undertake*, be willing/foolish'; יהב, 'give/set/place, *(interj.) well come on let's*'; יהוא ['he shall exist/live']; יחש, 'lineage/family'; ילד, 'bear/bring forth/beget, deliver, be born, declare one's pedigree, lad/youth/child/young (of beasts), girl/maiden, born/offspring/son [genitor] birth/-pl./progeny/family'; ינק, 'suck/-le/-ling child, sucker/sprout/shoot'; יסד, '*found* (bldg.)/*throw up (heap)*/settle/*establish*/ordain/decree, consult together/plot, basis, *beginning*, deliberation/intimacy/secret, plot'; and ירך, '*thigh (> descendents)*/smite on same (in distress)/shank (of candlestick)/side (of tent/country)/hind(-er part)/recesses/*remotest parts* (as of earth, the north)', that last with a bit of purity sprinkled in.

Similarly, some roots recall mistletoe's berries' viscosity resembling sperm and yod's close link to gimel, desire, its Hebrew number (*ten*) being G's bardic number (they begin the four-rune sequence within the heart of shin's att): יאב, 'desire/long for'; 2. ידד (= דוד 'to love'), 'beloved/friend/lovely/pleasant/love'; יחד, '*(be) unite(d)/one/join*, only/alone/solitary/forsaken, *darling/most dear*, *union/together*/in one place, wholly/entirely, together/at one time'; יחם, '*be hot(/warm)*/w/ anger/*for sex*, conceive, heat/anger/fury/poison/venom'; ימש (= משש 'feel/grope'), 'let feel/grope'; יען, 'ostrich' (Syr. '*be greedy*/voracious'); יצר 'be straitened/distressed/anxious, *make(r)/creator/potter*, *form/fashion/devise/frame*, imagination/thought'; ירש, '*take/- possession of/seize upon/(drive out/dis-)possess*, hold, become, make poor, net, new wine/must'; to which I should perhaps add יבם, '(husband's) brother(-in-law)'. Plus two epitomizing what desire seeks, reminding us in the jumbling of the order yod was moved to virgo: יאה, 'be suitable/becoming'; and יפה, '*be fair/comely*, good/excel'. Perhaps I should add: יסף, 'add/increase/enlarge/grow/do again [he shall add (Joseph)]'.

Related to the fact that capricorn is where the round rises or lifts up: יגר, Ch. 'heap of stones'; יד, '*hand/power*/care/part/side'; יזן, 'weigh/be heavy, -/stout'; יחל, '*be able*/can/could, permitted/may/might/prevail over/endure [enabled/*strong*]'; יעז (= עזז '*be strong*/firm'?) '-/- /obstinate'; and {יקר (A. וקר '*be heavy*'), '*be dear/precious/esteemed/prized/honored/respected*, make rare, *splendid/beautiful*, *dear/beloved*, honor/glory, *value/price*, Ch. hard/difficult/noble'}, this last hearkening back also to yod's connection with gimel (desire).

In the round, capricorn's station is the east, as in the following root, which also touches on *end of manifestation* and *birth or inception* (and of course the fact that at capricorn the round is progressing upward): יצא, '*go out/come/- forth/issue*, *descend (posterity)*/escape (danger)/*rise (sun)/spring up*/forth (water)/ be issued (decree)/*end (point of time)*, lead/*cause to go/spring up*/yield (as earth plants), exact (money)/produce/make/separate, *excrement/ordure/filth*, Ch. *finish*, *offspring*, *origin*/race/breed, *a going out* (gate/fountain)/*rising (east)*/what comes out (speech)'—what a delightful root! rooted in the completion (top) of the air triad.

With this last root, the meaning *excrement* introduces another category, for Ii is the earth breath, which on its most concrete level is the digestive cycle, and more generally, the active aspect of earth (the solid), which includes human bodies: יהצה/יהץ ['place trodden down' (coll. w/ A.)]; ילע (cogn. לוע '*swallow/devour*'), 'speak rashly/utter at random (Gesen.), or *gulp*/talk wildly'; ילף, 'scab/scurf' (A. 'stick fast'); יפח, '*breathe/pant*/sigh, -ing/puffing out'; יצע, 'spread down/strew/bed/couch/floor/story'; יצק, 'pour(ed) out/cast, hence hard/firm/molten, funnel, casting'; ישב, 'sit/- down/stay/(be) dwell(t in)/set/place'; יתב (= ישב), 'sit/dwell'; and {ישח (Gesenius coll. w/ A. וחש 'be empty'), '*emptiness of stomach/hunger*'}; ישם, '(be) put/place(d)'. To these I add: יַיִן, '(heat and ferment), mire/mud, wine/fig. intoxication', and the possibly related יָוָן [Ionian Greeks]; and יָם (only in plural), prob. 'hot springs' (surely related to יָם, 'sea', albeit with a different vowel).

The old Hebrew yod, picturing two arms drawing a line in the dirt with a stick, can also be construed as two hands operating a plow (which for all I know was the original intent): יגב (= גוב 'plow/till'), 'plowman, field'. Distantly related to plowing a furrow, or perhaps to yod being a seed or source: יאר, 'river (esp. Nile), streams (canals of Nile)'; יבל, 'lead/bring (forth)/carry, *stream/river/canal*, protracted sound, *produce/increase (of earth)*, *provision*/wealth, world/earth, inundation/deluge [*propagation*]' (A. '*flow/run*')—whence the name Tubal Cain ['propagation of Cain'], who is identified in scripture as the first blacksmith—and יקב, 'wine-vat/wine-press (trough in which grapes are trodden)'—all four of these reference inception (either alef or beyt).

One final category is suggested by the trump associated with yod, XVIIII The Sun, which shows the twin gods of the year (waxing year and waning year) wrestling: 1. ידד, 'throw/cast'; ידה '*throw/cast*, confess openly/freely/give thanks/praise, hymn [praised (Yehuda)] Ch. [Judah (pl.)]/Jew'; יום, '*day/by day*, time'; יזע, '*sweat*' (A. '*flow*')—the trump shows drops of sweat flying off of the two boys—יח, 'unshod/barefoot'; ימן, 'turn right, *south* [felicity (coll. w/ A.)]'; ימר, '(ex)change (places?)/boast'; יפע, '(cause to) *shine* (forth) [splendid] [brilliancy/*beauty*]', relating back also to the connection with gimel; יקץ, 'awake'; ירד, 'go/come/*flow*/run down (as eyes with tears)/descend/decline /*(be) cast down/fall*'; ירה, '*throw/cast*/shoot/show/*teach*/lay foundation, archer/*teacher*, mode/manner, direction/precept/*law*, former rain (in Judea ~ Nov.)', linking also to (self-)knowledge; and ירט, '*cast down*/precipitate/be perverse/destructive/*hurl*'. All four that use reysh, plus the two that use dalet, relate directly to wrestling! The rest, not so much.

There are a couple of roots reminding us that yod is on the fiery level of the Egg: יצת, 'set on fire/kindle/be burned/consumed, burn (w/ anger)'; and יקד, 'burn/-ing mass (on hearth), be kindled', these perhaps pointing back to Yule (the Yule log). And one possibly related to yod's diminutive size: יתד, 'pin/peg/nail/tent-peg/(pointed) stake'.

I am left with {יקה (A. וקה 'obey') > יקהה, 'obedience'}, which does seem more suited to vav than yod; and ירק, 'spit'.

SUMMARY

Yod as capricorn: 'mountain goat, profit'. **Where Egg rises against world's weight:** 2 'be heavy (prized)', 'labor, be weary', 'pant', 'hand, power', 'be able, prevail over', 2 '(point out) throw, cast ({praised [*Judah*]} Jew)', 'set, place, burden, gift', 'heap of stones' {'height'} 'be high'. **G's** [*desire's or +1's*] **expression in Egg:** 'be suitable, becoming', 'be fair, comely', 'be good, pleasing', 'love's object', 'greed', 'hunger', 'desire, long for'. **Seed, spark:** 'fashion, devise, be anxious, creator', 2 '(beget, be born) bring forth (flow, canal, river)' ['canals, river'], 'found, establish, beginning, support, prop' [*has samekh in it*], 'begin, undertake', 'sprout, shoot, suckle', 'hot springs', 'thigh [*from which issue descendents*], side', 'lineage', 'husband's brother [*obliged to marry brother's widow if without issue*], to marry the brother's wife', 'spring forth, rise, go out, end [*period of* time]'. **Manifestation's limit or end:** 'beat with club', 2 'burn (be consumed)', 'dry up', 'be desolate, laid waste, desert', 'be dry, fall asleep, grow old', 'old, aged man', 'carry or sweep away, shovel', 'be ensnared', 'clothe, cover', 'be entire, perfect, arrive, sign, portent' [{'dove'} 'dove, Jonah'] 'locust', 'wail, lament', 'grief, sorrow', 'be bereaved, orphan', 'despair of, desist from, render hopeless', 2 'fear', 'be fearful, curtain, hanging', 'wait', 'delay, tarry', 'add, enlarge, do again', 'spread out, bed', 'stretch out, extend', 'peg, nail, tent-pin', 'be dislocated, suspend, hang', 'cast down, be destructive', 'descend, flow, be cast down, fall', 'sea, westward', 'moon, month', 'wine-press'. **Mistletoe:** [*tree-suspended:*] 'honeycomb, thicket, forest'; [*evergreen:*] 'verdure', 2 '(sit, dwell, stay, abide) remain (be left)', 'stick fast', 'be constant, firm, flow constantly'. **Self-knowledge** [*and knowledge*]**:** 'pour out, cast, molten, firm', 3 '(establish) put, place (firm, certain, true)', 2 '(be, subsist) be firm', 'be straight, even, right, true, make straight [*the way*], uprightness' [*yod=mid-spine*], 'obedience' {'pious'} 'know, discern, know carnally', 2 '(proof, reproof) to correct (instruct)', 'counsel, instruct', 'call aloud {crier}'. **XVIIII LeSoleil:** 'awake', 'shine forth', 'day, duration, period', 'barefoot', 'be hot, warm', 'wine [*signification of heat and fermentation*]', 'flow, sweat', 'right, south' {'assemble'} 'be one, unite, solitary', 'meet, appoint', 2 '(take, inherit) dispossess (vex)' [*wrestling youths*] 'change places'. **Earth breath:** 'touch'. **Old Semitic shape** [*arms with plow*]**:** 'plough, till'. **Unparsed:** 'talk wildly, gulp', 'act foolishly', 'spit [*in presence of*]' {'Ionian Greek'}.

ל

Lamedh

PARSED ROOTS

This is aquarius the water carrier, third and last sign of the water triad: לחח, *moist*/fresh, -ness/vigor' (Ch. and Ethiop. לחלח '*moisten*'); and לשד, *'moisture*/vital power, oil cake' (A. לשד '*suck*'). Also: לאב, 'thirst/drought' (A. 'to thirst'); להם, 'dainties' (A. 'swallow greedily'); לוע, 'swallow, throat'; לחך (= לקק), 'lick/- up (as ox)/lap up (as dog)'; לקק, 'lick/lap'.

The old Hebrew character showed a goad, or left nostril; but it began as the Egyptian hieratic of the hieroglyph **recumbent lion** (*rw* aka *l*) because in this Wheel the reaction back the other way outweighs the radiative, and leo is the sign opposite: לבא (onom.?), 'lion(s), lioness'; לוש, 'knead, *lion*' (A. 'be strong'). Whose organ is the heart: לבב/לב, '*heart/middle/midst/vital principle*, become wise/encourage/embolden, (pan-)cake'. It was the sign of the Great Fire in the Monad: להב, '*flame*/glitter (of sword, etc.), sword/iron spearhead [Libyans?]' (A. '*burn*'); להט, '*(burn/flame)-ing, kindle*, glittering, enchantments'; לפד ('shine?') > 'lamp/*torch/flame*'; and perhaps לבן, 'be/-come/make white/clean/make bricks, moon, brick/tile, white poplar [white (Mt. Lebanon)] brick kiln, frankincense'. Four of these involve the purity of beyt: I wonder if the one meaning *lion* might derive from the one meaning *heart* (since both are leo).

The most striking thing about this letter is the way it reaches out beyond itself, unlike any other letter. For the sign itself reaches beyond self: it represents the process of learning, and its reciprocal, teaching. That is why it is shaped like swinging arms of a toddler learning to walk. In the Tifinag alphabet, it was two parallel vertical strokes, named (prob.) *liki*, 'like', and stood for the *second* month of the sun-hero: the learning that follows birth. Thus: להג, 'study (n.)'; להן, Ch. (= H. לכן) 'therefore/nevertheless/but/except'; לוח, '*tablet* (of stone/wood)/(of heart)/leaf (of folding door)/boarding/deck (of ship)'; לטש, 'sharpen/- the eye (cast sharp penetrating look)'; למד, 'accustom (oneself)/learn/teach, trained/taught/disciple, ox-goad'—the name of the letter— לעד ['put in order' (A.)]; לקח, '*take (/- hold of/away/possession of)*/capture/receive, *captivating speech/doctrine/instruction*, spoil/booty, jaws, tongs/snuffers'; לקט, 'collect/*gather/glean*, be gathered together, bag/scrip'; and לקש, '*glean/gather* last fruits, latter grass/aftermath, latter rain (March, April)'—note how those last three use qof's meaning of *harvest*.

Subjects to be learned: לג, 'Log (liq. measure)'; לתך, '*a dry measure'; לוב > 'Libyans'; לוד > 'Lydians'; לאם, 'people/nation'; לשן, 'tongue/(of fire/sun)/speech/dialect/(to slander)'—this last may relate to the old Hebrew shape, a left nostril—לא, 'not (yet)/no/without'; לוא/לי, 'O if/O that!/would that!, if not/unless'; לוז, '*turn aside*/decline/depart/perverse, almond'; and the almost certainly related לזה > 'perverseness'; לול ('*wind/turn/move round?*'), 'winding stairs, loops/*eyes (for hooks)*'; 2. לון, '(a) complain(ing)/murmur(ing)'; ליץ, '*mock/deride/scorn, scoffer, derision, interpreter/intercessor, obscure saying/enigma*' (A. '*turn/twist*, talk in obscure sentences')—lamedh waw seems to convey turning aside, complaining, deriding. Three similar meanings start with the top of the water triad, לח: לחה, 'cheek/jawbone'; לחץ, '(op)press/squeeze/afflict'; and לחש, '(mutter/whisper)/-ers/charmers, amulet, charm/incantation'. Five start with opposites לע, the consonant *and* vowel of learning: לעב, '*mock at/deride*'; לעג, '*mock/scorn/deride/*stammer, *derision/scoffing*'; לעה, 'be rash (in speaking)'; לעז, 'speak in barbarous or foreign tongue'; לען, 'wormwood (distress)' (A. 'reject/detest/curse'). Finally: לקם ['fortress (A. stop the way)']; and לתע, 'teeth' (A. 'bite'). Wow, that paragraph took an unexpected twist, almost as if it expressed my attitude towards school! (Educating the educators by mocking them.)

In distribution of functions in *Sefer Yetzirah* to the simples, it is evident that the function rightfully belonging to lamedh is *working*: לאה, 'labor (esp. in vain)/vex/be/make weary/faint, be grieved/disliked/loathe'; and להה, 'be weary/faint, insane/mad person'. Perhaps these refer to the Great Work of alchemists—considered madmen—whence the negative connotations.

Some roots express reaching and extending beyond oneself generally: ל, 'to/unto/towards (w/ verbs of motion/longing)/(rest/delay/condition) at/on/in/into (transition)/as to/because/at (occasion), about/concerning/according to/after/as if/like'; לאך > '*messenger*/angel/perh. priest, work/business/labor, acquisition/wealth/property, *message* [messenger (Malachi)]' (Ethiop. '*send, minister*'); לכד, 'take/*catch*(*/hold*/hang together)/intercept/choose, snare (n.)'; and לפת, 'embrace/turn (- aside/round)'. Note the recurring theme of *winding* or *turning*, possibly from the *twisting* motion in swinging one's arms when walking?

Two categories remain. First, consider the form L takes in south Semitic and runic (ᚱ), eaves of a roof, in the spirit of which are: לאט, 'veil/cover (face)'; לבש, 'put on garment/be clothed/fig. -/covered (w/ flocks/worms/glory/justice/etc.), garment'; לוה, '*be joined to/adhere to/borrow/lend*, Ch. by/with [Levi/te] garland/crown, sea monster/large serpent/crocodile (Leviathon)'; לוט, '*wrap up/cover/conceal/secret(ly)/- arts, veil/covering*, ladanum?/purest myrrh? [Lot]'; 1. לין/לון, 'lodge/(let) remain/pass the night/abide [-ing] inn, hovel/hut'; ליל, 'night/(calamity/adversity), screech-owl (Lilith)'; לעט, 'give to eat'; לשך, 'chamber (esp. one joined to side of Temple)' (prob. A. לשק/לצק 'be joined/adhere to'); לתח ('spread out'? = מתח, Sam. נתח), 'wardrobe/vestry'.

And a few roots seem to echo where the jumbling of simples moved lamedh, that is, to libra, where it forms the pivot of the alef-beyt and where the water triad manifests in earth (cf. Leviathon, earlier, and esp. *swallow/throat* early on above, libra being where Egg or tongue is attached to Cauldron or mouth): לבש, 'stumble/fall'—relevant to *learning*—לחם, 'consume/eat, (make/wage)war/fight, flesh/body, food/meat/fruit/meal/feast/bread, fighting/battle'; לחן, Ch. 'concubine' (A. 'rancid/corrupt/fig. obscene'); לטא, 'sp. of poisonous snake' (A. 'adhere to the ground'); לשם, 'ligure/jacinth' (one of the stones on the High Priest's breastplate). Since libra is where the Wheels all meet: להקת (from קהל 'assemble', by transposition), 'assembly/company'.

SUMMARY

Lamedh, follows B-birch [*in calendar, in name Bel, Baal*]: [*LBN:*] 'be or make white, Mt. Lebanon'. **Aquarius** [*water-bearer*]: '[*liquid measure*]', 'moist, fresh, vigor', 'moisture, vital power', 'thirst', 'swallow greedily', 'swallow', 'lick, lap up' ['jawbone', 'eat', 'give to eat']. ***Recumbent lion*** [*full moon in leo*]: 2 '(knead) lion (roaring)', 'heart, vital principle'. **Moved to libra:** 'adhere to ground, species of poisonous lizard', *2* '(decline) perverse (-ness)', 'be rancid, corrupt, obscene, concubine'. **On triad of the south** [*'fire'*]: 3 '(lamp) flame (iron spearhead, Libyans?)'. **Square-Hebrew** [*twisting, reaching*]: 2 '(winding stairs) turn round (or towards)', 'unto, towards', 'send, minister, angel, messenger', 2 '(doctrine, jaws) take (hang together)'. **Tifinag-Libyan** [*2 spears*]: 'a people', 'assembly, company'. **Learning** [*lemedh*]: 2 '(collect, gather) glean', 'tablet', 'measure [*of capacity*]', 'put in order', 'therefore, except', 'study', 'learn, teach, ox-goad', 'stumble' [*in learning to walk? cf. square-Heb.*]. **Rune, south Semitic** [*shelter under eaves*]: 'weary, faint, mad person', 2 '(borrow) adhere to (attached chamber)', 'to spread out? wardrobe, vestry', 'clothed or covered with' ['veil, cover', 'night, screech-owl'] 'to lodge, pass the night'. **Old Semitic shape** [*haughty nose or overseer's whip*]: {'stop the way'} 'no, not', 'oppress', 'labor, make weary', 'O if! O that!', 'sharpen, cast a sharp look', 'bite' [*at bit?*], 'reject, detest', 'whisper', 'complain, murmur', 3 'mock, deride (scorn)', 'speak rashly', 'slander, tongue, dialect', 'speak in barbarous or foreign tongue' ['Lydian'].

נ

Nun

PARSED ROOTS

We have arrived at the last sign, sound of negation and newness in English (since at the end of one cycle, another is about to begi*n*). In the archaic Greek hymn Graves constructs from Boibel Loth letter-names, N's name, Neiagadon, yields ne-āgaton, 'new-born': נוב, '*put forth shoots/increase*, produce/utter, produce(n.)/*increase/fruit*'; נון, '*sprout/flourish/propagate, offspring*/posterity [fish (Syr. & Ch.)]'; נוץ, '*flourish/blossom*'; נוק (= ינק) '*give suck/-le*'; ניסן [first mo. of yr.]; נכד, 'progeny'; 1. נער, '*roar (as young lion)*'; נפג ['sprout']; נקב, '*pierce/bore/-thru, determine/specify/mark out/name, bezel, female, womb*, stomach/maw, hollow/shaft (of rock), (= קבב) execrate/curse/blaspheme, hammer'; and finally נקה, '*be pure/innocent/blameless*, free/cleared/empty/desolate, cleanse/cleanness, Ch. pure/white, acquit/pardon'—qof the womb is opposite nun, and here in the Egg, reaction back along each radius outweighs its outward thrust. Plus this meaning, similar to נקב: נבב, 'bore through/*make hollow*, fig. *empty*/stupid/foolish', perhaps linked to negation (see below).

Its old Hebrew shape shows a hand raised in greeting or goodbye, hence: נא (or נא אמון) [Egyp. city (Thebes?)]; נבזבה, 'Ch. gift (Pers. orig.?)'; נבח, 'to bark'; נבט, '*look/behold/regard* (w/pleasure) [aspect] *expectation/hope*'; נגש, '*draw/come/bring near*/be offered'; נדד, '*move (/as wing)/wander about/flee/fly away*/be agitated, heap/mound, uncleanness (menses/idols/incest)'; 2. נדה ('give'), 'gift'; נחה, '*lead/conduct/guide, lead back*'; נטה, '*stretch out/extend (hand), lead to*/incline/turn, measure/expand, decline/*depart*, branch/rod, staff/sceptre/tribe, couch/bed/bier, wrest/pervert'; נטש, '*leave/forsake/abandon, leave (in charge/fallow)/remit (debt)/allow*, draw out (sword)/*spread/scatter/be left*/forsaken, shoots (of vine)'; נסג, '*recede/depart*, remove/take away (boundary) /be turned back/perverted'; נסע, 'pull/pluck up/out (tent pins)/*break up (camp)*, put away/remove/quarry stones, *lead/guide, depart/travel, journey/march (n.)*, missile/weapon'; נסק, '*go up/ascend*, Ch. take/bring up'—nice clump of three built on nun and next sign samekh—נף [Memphis (Egyp.)]; נפץ, 'break/dash in pieces, *disperse/scatter(abroad)*, violent shower/flood, a bruising, hammer?/battleaxe?'; נפק, '*go/bring forth/out*, Ch. expense'—three built on nun and next sign *fearn* the alder (soft peh), signifying expansion beyond the seed or tongue—נצא, 'fly away'; נצה, '*fly*/be desolate/laid waste/strive/contend, quarrel, feather/pinion'; נשא, 'lift/raise up, (יד —) *lift up hand (in oath, etc.), bear/carry/take away*, endure, *lead /take/- up/bring*, lofty, *be borne off*, exalt, etc. etc., Ch. *bear/take away*/rise up (על against), chief/prince, vapors/clouds, rising of flame/smoke, elevation/dignity, *signal*/prophecy, burden, *gift*'; נשׂג, '*reach(/as hand to mouth*)/attain to/overtake/*come upon*/befall/acquire/obtain, *pass/go beyond'*—four with sibilant in the second spot that are fairly close in meaning—נתן, '*give*/grant/permit, ascribe, do/make, emit/yield/bear/render, *put forth (hand)* [giver (Nathan)]'. And waving is of course a way to נעם, '*be pleasant/agreeable/amiable*, delights/pleasures, beauty/glory/kindness/grace'. Whew!

Oh, and נוד, 'move/be agitated/shaken/driven about, *fugitive/depart/flee*, deplore/*shake (head/in derision)/bemoan*, disturb/reel, console, *wandering [Nod (whither Cain fled)]*', relating also to negation (see below). In addition: נוע/נֹעַ, 'move to and fro/be agitated/shaken/stagger, move (lips)/be changeable/*wander about*, agitate/disturb/cause to reel/tremble [a shaking (pl.)] [moving/motion] sistra (played by being shaken in cadence)'. Plus נוּף, '*sprinkle (which is done by) waving/shaking (the hand)*/lift up (instr.)/move to and fro (as sieve)/scatter, *wave/shake (hand)*, elevation, *lifting/waving (of hand)*, height, *dropping/distilling*, sieve/fan', this last also relating to water (see below). All three build on nun waw, the completion or top of the earth triad. Then there is spiritually waving the hand: נשתון, 'epistle/letter'.

Nun is *back* one from the head (where *we* point), at the back of the neck (spine opposite cervical vertebrae), axis of shaking one's head in negation: נאץ, 'deride/despise/condemn/reject, reproach/insult'; נאר, 'abhor/reject'; נדא/1. נדה, '*remove/separate*, put away/thrust out'; 2. נהג, 'sigh'; נהם, '*grumble*/murmur (as sea)/*growl/groan/moan*'; נוא, '*refuse/decline/hinder/prohibit, hindrance/opposition/hostility, restrain/dissuade/discourage*'—three with just alef, two with just heh, and one with both—נכל, '*fraudulently withhold*/act deceitfully/*plot* together *(against)*, craft/deceit, miser/niggard'; נכר, '*seem strange/alienate, mistake/reject/discriminate*, alienation, (— בן) stranger/foreigner, feign/dissemble, admire/gaze at/ regard/care for/recognize/be known, friend/acquaintance'; נסח, '*pluck/tear away, removing* (changing of guard)'; 2. נסך, '*cover*'-ing' (A. 'weave'); 2. נער, '*shake/cast* out/*off*/rouse oneself/*throw off*, tow'; נצל, '*strip off/take away, escape/strip oneself of*, deliver/rescue/(de)spoil/plunder'; נקט, 'be weary of/loathe (life, Job 10:1)'; נקם, '(be) avenge(d), vengeance/vindictiveness' (nun's proper function of the twelve *Sefer Yetzirah* lists is anger); נקע (= יקע), 'be alienated'; נרג, 'slanderer' (A. 'whisperer'); 1. נשא, '*err*/go astray/*corrupt*/seduce, deceive/come suddenly (upon על), deceit'; 1. נשה, '*forget/neglect [cause to forget* (Manasseh)]'; נשל, 'fall/drop off/draw off (shoe)/cast/drive out (nation)'—three that build on nun plus the next sign, shin (nun as shaking one's *crown* in negation).

Nun derives from hieratic for the hieroglyph **surface of water**, a horizontal zig-zag: נחש, '*serpent*, (use) enchantment/divination (by *serpents*)'. It is pisces the fishes: נאד, '(skin-)bottle' (A. 'yield water'); נבך (= Ch. נבג 'spring/gush forth?'), 'fountain'; נבע, '*gush/bubble out/up/pour forth*/utter/declare, *spring/fountain*, render putrid'; נגב [Negev] (Syr./Ch. 'be dry'); נגד, Ch. '*flow*, declare/show/announce/publish/proclaim/praise, betray, before/in front/presence of/opposite/in comparison w/, leader/chief/prefect/overseer/prince/noble thing, straight/forwards, Ch. towards' (A. '*be clear*/manifest'); נגר, '*flow/be poured/out/run (as wound)*/deliver'; נזה, '*spatter/sprinkle, expiate?/scatter?/cause to leap/exult?*'; נזל, '*sink/drop down/distil/flow*, wandering star (planet)'; נחל, '*stream/river*, brook/valley, shaft (of mine)'; נטף, '*drop/distil*/let drop (prophesy), *myrrh*, pendants/earrings'; 1. נסך, '*pour/- out/make libation, melt*/cast/found/anoint (king), mage/prince, *drink-offering*/molten'; נתך, '*flow/be poured out (water*/anger/curses)/*melt*'. And the opposite:

נשת, '*dry up (tongue)/be parched*, fail/dry up/waste away'.

In contrast, the next category derives from the shape of N's rune—ᚾ, an oar through the side of a ship (ash being the wood of oars), but also interpretable (from its name, 'need') as a stick being twirled by a string in the kindling of the *needfire*: נהר, '*flow/run, shine/be bright, current/stream/river*, light/wisdom, daylight, clefts'. Roots related just to the needfire: נגה, '*shine/give/make light/*enlighten, *brightness/*splendor, *light*'; נוּר (= A. נהר '*shine*'), Ch. '*fire, light*/lamp/fig. prosperity/happiness, candlestick/chandelier'; נפח, '*breathe/blow (a breath/a fire)/puff at/despise*, cause to pant, *bellows*, apple/- tree'—that one with a bit of negation as well—נפשׁ, '*respire/take breath/*refresh oneself, breath/odor/perfume, fig. anything that breathes (animal/person), life, *self*, *feelings*/spirit, *desire*/inclination'—you can see here that the *nefesh*, which represents the lowest of the three parts of the self (in the Kabbalah), can only be the doer, for it encapsulates both *feelings* and *desire*—נצץ, '*glitter/shine*, flourish/fly, flower/blossom, hawk, *spark*'; נצר, 'shoot/branch (n.)' (A. '*shine*/be green'); נשׁב, '(cause to) *blow*/drive away (as birds, w/ puffing)'; נשׁם, '*breathe/pant*, breath/life/*living thing*, *mind*/spirit, anger, sp. of lizard (chameleon?)/waterfowl (swan/seagull/crested purple heron?)'—not *as* appropriate for the knower, *neshamah* (highest part of self in *Kabbalah*), but *mind* is close—נשׁף, '*breathe/blow*, twilight (from refreshing breezes at that time), dawn/dusk/darkness/night, sp. of unclean bird (ibis/heron? Ch./Syr. owl?)'; נשׁק, 'kindle/set on fire'—here nun plus next sign shin and a labial means *blow* (three roots), nun plus next sign *sin*, blowing on flame. And somewhere in between water and fire: ניא, 'raw/*half-boiled*' (A. 'be raw').

Related to negation (and poetically also to water) is N's trump, XIII (Death), which pictures the grim reaper: נבל, '*wither/fade/fall off* (leaves/flowers)/away/wear/waste/be weak/act foolishly, lightly esteem/despise/condemn, foolish/wicked/impious/ungodly, (skin-)bottle (as shriveled/flaccid), vessel/jar (earthenware), mus. instr. (lute?), *corpse/carcass (men/beasts)*, shame/nakedness'; נגע, '*touch*/meddle w/affect (heart), reach/come to/upon/arrive at, *strike/smite, stroke/blow/calamity/infliction of evil/plague, spot/mark (as leprosy)*'; נגף, 'strike/smite(w/ hand/sword/disease/calamities, thrust/push/stumble against, plague/defeat'; נגל, 'sickle' (A. 'cut/wound')—three built on nun gimel, one of G's runes being named 'harvest'—2. נדר, Ch. 'threshing floor' (A. 'cut off'); נהה, 'wail/lament(ation)'; נושׁ = אנשׁ, 'be sick'; נזק, 'suffer/cause loss/damage'; נחם, Ch. '*grieve/- for/mourn*/pity/console, repent/feel regret' (as A. 'sigh', cogn. נהם); נכא (= נכה '*smite*') 'be beaten, smitten/afflicted, broken spirit, spices (prop. something *crushed*/bruised)'; נכה, '*be smitten/beaten(/smite/strike) down (w/ fist/arrow/rays/cold)/beat in pieces (as hail)*/push (w/ horn)/*kill/slay*, smitten/injured, blow/wound, *slaughter/calamity (from God)*, smiters (w/ tongue, i.e. slanderers)?/jesters?' (from נוּך i.e. A. נאך 'jest'); נמל, '*circumcise*, ant (from cutting, consuming)'; נסה, 'try/prove/(at)tempt, trial/temptation/*calamity*'; 1. נסס, 'pine/waste away'; נפל, '*(be) fall(en)/(in battle)*, cast/bear/bring forth, alight/dismount, *terminate*, fall to (inheritance), *fall sick, cast/throw down*, untimely birth, desist from, Ch. prostrate oneself/fall out/happen, giants, refuse (of corn)/flaccid parts (of flesh), *fall/ruin(s)/carcass*'; נקף, '(let feasts) go/come round?/*let them kill* (sacrifices), *destroy/cut down*, surround/compass, a beating/shaking (of olive tree), a bruising/wounding'(Ch./A. '*smite/hew*'); נקשׁ, '(lay/)en-

/snare(s)/be –d/enticed, Ch. *smite/strike*'; נתח, 'divide/cut in pieces, a piece'; נתס, 'destroy/tear up'; נתע, 'be broken out', and its cogn. נתץ, '*tear/break down/destroy/*break out (teeth)'; נתק, 'pluck off/draw away, be torn/broken (as a string), castrated, *uproot/break/*be withdrawn, a kind of *leprosy*'; and נתש, 'tear/pluck up/be expelled (from a land)/*destroy/tear down*, fail (*spoken of water*)'—six built on nun tav (contradicting conscience?).

Somewhat akin to the above are roots reminiscent of the name of N's rune, 'need': נא, 'I pray!/I pray thee!, woe now!/alas!'; נאק, 'groan/lament'; נגש, '*impel/drive/urge/exact*/-er/(be) oppress(ed/wearied/distressed)'; נדב, '*impel*/make/show oneself willing, give/offer willingly, liberality/abundance, noble/-minded/liberal'; נדח, '*(be) impel(led)/*force/thrust/- out/expel/cast down/*urge*/seduce/be chased, seduction'; 1. נהג, '*drive* (beasts/vehicle)/lead/conduct/carry away (spoil), —מ a driving of a chariot'; נוט, 'move/be shaken'; נוס, 'flee/- away/escape, proceed/ride swiftly, *impel/drive/*put to flight, -/*refuge*'; נחץ > 'urgent'; 2. נשא, 'lend/exact/creditor, usury, *debt*'; 2. נשה, 'lend/creditor/usurer/borrow, *debt*, sciatic nerve (etym. not known)'; נשך, 'bite/vex, oppress/*exact interest*, -/*usury*'—here nun plus next sign shin means continuing on around the Wheel (of Fortune) to arrive at the top.

Then there is a category I might describe as *doing one's part* to help the grim reaper do his bit: נבוכדנצר [Nebuchadnezzar, k. of Babyl.]; נגח, '(prone to) push/butt (w/ horns)/fig. of conqueror prostrating nations'; נדף, 'drive about/scatter/put to flight/rout'; נסרך ['Nisroch (a Ninevite idol)']; נקר, '*bore/dig/put/pick out (eye, as bird)/pierce*/apportion/give/distribute, portion/lot'; נשק, 'be arranged/regulate/*arm oneself*, kiss, join/touch, *battle/- array/arms/armor, armory/arsenal*, a kiss' (A. 'join/arrange'). And since pisces marks the *last* of the signs (the nd): נשׂר (= Ch. נסר 'to saw'), 'a saw'.

Consider N in Tifinag, a single vertical stroke: it follows two such strokes (L, 'like', i.e. learning) in the tree-calendar and therefore symbolizes the sun-hero as he sets off *on his own*. Hence: נאם, 'utter/speak/declare'; נבא, '*announce/prophesy*, prophet/-ess [Ch. idol (Mercury?)]'; 1. נדר, 'vow, vow (n.)'; נזר, '*restrict oneself/separate/withdraw, devote/consecrate oneself*, set apart/restrict/abstain from, *Nazarite*/unpruned vine/prince, *separation/consecration/long hair*, crown/diadem'; נטל, '*lift*/take up, lay/impose upon, burden, laden'; נכח, 'opposite/before /over against /in sight of/*straight forward*, in behalf of/as far as, *straight/(up)right(eousness)*'; 2. נסס, '*lift/raise oneself up/shine?* (= נצץ?), (rally round) a *standard/banner*, sail?/flag? (of ship), *pole, sign/token*'; נער, 'male infant/*boy/lad/youth*/servant, childhood/*youth*, girl/young woman/(hand-)maiden'. Ash being the wood of oars and tool handles: נצב (= יצב), 'set/place/erect/fix/appoint, *handle/haft*, stem/root, firmness/strength, statue/pillar/idol, officer/overseer, station/garrison'. And perhaps נבה ['height'] (A. נבא 'be high') (since the line in tifinag points straight up, and nun is the approach to straight up). And נתב, '*trodden path*' (A. 'be high/raised'?), relating back to the waving hand.

The last major category reflects the fact that pisces completes the earth triad, that is, the internal dynamics of the earthy element—stasis, the soil, wealth (suit Money or Coins). And thus: נאה (= נוה '*sit/dwell*'), 'be suitable/becoming/comely, *seats/dwellings/habitations/pastures*' (cogn. יאה); נהל, 'lead/conduct/*sustain/provide*/proceed, *pasture*'; נוה, '*sit/dwell quietly/prepare dwelling*(/adorn?), *inhabiting*/comely, *dwelling*, *fold (for cattle)/pasture*'; נוּחַ, 'rest/alight/settle down, abide/continue, cease/leave off (speaking), set/put/lay/let down/fall, give rest/repose, place/deposit, let rest/remain, permit/suffer/let alone, leave behind, be set/placed, rest/quiet, satisfaction/delight, sweet odor/incense'; נוּם, 'slumber'; נֶזֶם, '*nosering*/earring'; נָחַר, 'snorting [snorer] nostrils' (A. 'snort')—these last two relating to nun being a nasal consonant—נָחַל, 'obtain/acquire/possess/inherit'; נְחָשׁ, Ch. 'copper/brass, fetter/chain/money, brazen'; נָחַת, '*descend/penetrate* (w/ב)/*press/bend down (bow)/prostrate/level (furrows)*, Ch. *descend/bring down/deposit/place*'; נָטַע, '*plant (trees/gardens)/pitch tent/settle (a people)/fix/fasten (nail)*/set up (image)'; נָטַר, '*watch/guard/keep/retain* (anger), prison, mark/butt (target), Ch. *keep/preserve*'; נוּר/נִיר, '*break up ground/till/cultivate, fallow ground/land first broken up*, (weaver's) beam (prop. yoke)'; נֶכֶס, 'riches/treasures'; נָלָה (A. נָאַל, 'complete'), '-/accomplish, possession/wealth'; נֹפֶךְ, 'carbuncle/emerald?'; נָצַר, 'watch/guard/keep/preserve, conceal/besiege, observe/scrutinize'; נֵרְדְּ, 'spikenard (an aromatic)'. Four with reysh, two with teyt, to point to manifested earth, libra.

And one root epitomizes the fact that the month or arc of nun reaches the completion of the round, the *thirteenth* of the thirteen *middot*: נָצַח, 'excel/preside over/superintend/lead in music, overseer, chorister, *be entire/perfect, truth/uprightness/faithfulness, confidence/trust, excellence/glory, completeness/entireness, permanence/perpetuity/eternity*, Ch. conquer/surpass, juice (A. splatter)' (Syr. 'conquer', A. '*be pure/innocent/*faithful').

In the jumbling of simples, nun was sent to scorpio, and even in its correct position it is straight up from scorpio and therefore may easily be looked at as symbolizing the more exalted aspect of scorpio, namely: נֶשֶׁר, 'eagle'.

Leftovers: נָאַף, 'commit adultery (fig. apostasy)'—which does touch on negation—as does נָגַן, 'play on stringed instr., music/song, satire'. Plus: נָדָן, 'sheath of sword, Ch. fig. the body', which relates obliquely or symbolically with the earthy element, as does the following (since it focuses on the surface), נָמֵר, 'panther/leopard' (A. 'be spotted'). Speaking of earthy: נוּל, 'dunghill' (Ch. 'to dirty/soil').

SUMMARY

Nun's Semitic shape [*arm raised, extended, or waving goodbye*]: 3 '(ascend) take up (burden, lift up ([*hand, voice, etc.*], leader, gift)), 'gift', 2 'give (permit, yield [*fruit*], put forth [*hand*])', 2 'lend [*on usury*]', 2 '(extend [*hand, measure*], stretch [*tent*]) depart (be turned back)', 'go forth', 'epistle', 'leave, forsake, scatter', 'scatter, put to flight', 2 '(wave [*hand*]) sprinkle (spatter)' ['be spotted, leopard', 'speckled'], 2 '(shake) -off (loosen, spring)', 'fly away' ['eagle'] 2 'flee (fly away [*of bird*], move [*as wing*], wander about)', *3* 'be shaken, move ((-to and fro, wander about) shake [*head*] (bemoan oneself))'. **Negation** [*back of neck, axis of shaking head*]: 'grumble, growl, murmur [*as sea*], moan, groan' {'to bark'} 2 'watch, guard (conceal)', 'refuse, prohibit, dissuade, frustrate', 'bray', 'to bar, bolt, latch, footwear' [*pisces=ankles*], 2 '(abhor) reject (deride, reproach)', 'whisperer, slanderer', 'plot together against, fraudulently withhold, miser', 'snatch away, plunder, rescue, escape', 'remove', 'cover, weave' [*2ⁿᵈ letter is samekh*], 'sheath', 'forget, neglect, Manasseh', 'be weary of, loathe', 2 '(groan) lament (wail)', 'sigh'. **Runic shape** [*stick with string (kindling Needfire)*]: 'breathe out, blow [*a fire*], puff at, bellows', 2 '(puffing [*noise*], frighten away [*as birds*]) blow (breathe)' [*latter=NShP (from NPSh by metathesis?)*], NPSh='respire, take breath, refresh oneself, breath, perfume, feelings, spirit, desire, inclination, soul [*as principle of life*], self [*reflexive*])', NShM='breathe, pant, breath, life, living thing, mind, spirit, anger', 'kindle, set afire', 2 '(spark, glitter, flourish, fly, hawk) shine (light)', 2 '(fire, light, prosperity) lamp'. **Tifinag-Libyan:** [*straight line:*] 'regard, look towards with expectation', 'pole, standard, lift oneself up', 'straight, right, upright, straight forward'; [*one's own narrow path (departure from L's 'like'):*] 'vow', 'declare', 'roar [*as young lion*]', 'try, attempt, tempt', 'commit adultery, apostasy', 'fall off, cast out', 'be removed, alienated, disgusted', 'separate oneself, abstain from, consecrate oneself, Nazarite', 'estrange, alienation, reject, strange, new'. **Wave of greeting, 'New-born'** [*in 'Orphic' hymn*]: 'be pleasant, amiable, kindness, grace', 'draw near, approach, offer', 2 '(touch, arrive at) come upon, reach ([*as hand to mouth*], overtake)'; 'Nissan [*1ˢᵗ month*]', 'plant, settle, pitch [*tent*], fix [*nail*], set up', 'shoot, branch, be green', 'raw, half-boiled', 'put forth shoots, produce' {'sprout'} '(sprout, propagate {fish} offspring) flourish (blossom)', 'progeny', 'suckle', 'childhood' ['nitre, soap'] '(cleanse, cleared, empty, destroyed [*of persons*]) be pure, innocent (faithfulness, uprightness, permanency, be entire, perfect, complete)' [*cf.* **last sign**, *below*], 'circumcise'. **XIII** [*Grim Reaper*]: 'cut, wound, sickle' ['to prick, thornbush'] 'bore, dig, or put out [*an eye*], pick out [*as a bird*], pierce, cleft [*of rock*]', 2 '(hollow) bore through (pierce, bezel, womb)' [*latter root has qof*], 'to saw', 'cut off', 'cut in pieces', 4 '(hew, cut down) smite (ensnare) (slay, pestilence)', 2 'tear down, destroy (pluck up)', '(tear away) pluck (-up, -out, depart)', 'pluck off, uproot', 'suffer loss, injury', 'descend, flatten', 'break, dash in pieces', 'fall, -in battle, carcass, ruins', 'wither, fall off, corpse, wickedness', 'err, deceive, corrupt', 'to dirty, soil, dunghill', '[*species of unclean bird*]', 'be seriously ill', 'pine, waste away', 'mourn, grieve over', 'fly, be laid waste, feather', 'avenge' {Nineveh} {Nisroch [*an idol of the Ninevites*]} {Nebuchadnezzar}. **Rune's name** [*'need'*]: 3 '(give willingly) impel (force, be impelled, cast down) (drive, urge, exact)', 'urgent', 3 '(drive [*beasts, vehicle*]) lead, conduct (sustain, provide, proceed)'. **Ash:** 'till, break up the ground, cultivate', 'handle, haft, firmness, pillar, stem, root, appoint, place, erect'; [*as Yggdrasil (world-tree):*] '{interpreter of gods [*Hermes-type idol*]} prophecy', 3 '(trodden, path, -of life) be high (magnificent)', 'dwelling, habitation, fold [*for cattle*]', 'chamber [*NShKH for LShKH*]', 'I pray! [*interj. of respectful entreaty*]'. **Last sign:** [*precedes aries:*] 'butt [*with horns*]'; [*connects or binds ends of closed round (why its bardic number is 13):*] 'join, kiss, touch', 2 '(touch) reach (go beyond, acquire)', 'brass, fetter, chain, money'; [*completes earth triad (suit Money):*] 'riches, treasures', 'carbuncle? emerald?', 'obtain, possess, inherit, bequeath, apportion'; [*completes:*] 'complete, accomplish, possession, wealth', 'fully', 'slumber', 'rest, alight, abide, resting-place, acquiescence, sweet odor'. **Nasal:** 'spikenard', 'snort {snorer} nostrils', 'nose-ring, earring'. *Surface of water*: 'distil, drop, myrrh, earrings', 'libation, pour, melt' 5 '(drop down, distil) (pour out, melt) flow (straight, be clear) (shine, light, river)', 'river, torrent', 'bottle [*Arab.* yield water]', *2* '(gush forth) spring, fountain (pour forth, bubble up)'; [*its converse:*] 'be parched', 'be dry, the south'; [*wavy:*] 'serpent, use enchantment' ['play on string instrument, song'].

The
Seven
Doubles

פתכרגדב

Sorcery

I wade through seas of spirits
        Upon my dismal flight,
Dim spirits of the ocean void
        That clamor for my light.

I pick among them choosing
        The ones that seem to fit
My solitary purpose here,
        These walls around my pit.

The great celestial angels
        Look down upon travail
And form instruction out of woe,
        Whose tests we mostly fail.

Yet now come I determined
        Upon this surly scene,
Resolved to make the best of things,
        Thereby my soul to wean.

There'll be no tolerating
        Of mindset or excuse
That bar my way from conquering
        The forms of fate's abuse.

For I shall walk unbowing
        Among the demon hordes
And choose the ones that seem to fit
        And harness them with words.

פף

Peh

PARSED ROOTS

Peh originates as the outer or unvoiced rim of the Cauldron (the horizon without), its physiological station the pituitary: פ the rear half, ף the front half. The rear half is where the passive side of the knower, I-ness, contacts the body; the front half is the seat of the breath-form or living soul (not to be confused with the conscious self). The horizon represents the ability of the eye to jump a distance our haunches cannot manage, hence: פזז, '*be light/active/agile, leap, pur(e/ified, an epithet of gold)*' (A. פצץ 'purify (metals)')—source of English *pizzazz?*—and פסח, '*leap/pass over*/by/spare, halt/limp/become lame, *leap about*, Passover [passage] Paschal lamb'. Visible clear to the horizon (being the sign of manifested fire): פחם, '(burning) coal/charcoal'. And realizing that that horizon is really the rim of our Cauldron—nay the *outer* lip of the Grail itself—we thus become our own פחר, 'potter', and look forward to פעל, 'work/make/(per)form, practice, acquisition, wages, work/deed/action/thing made, work/employment/business/reward'. It is the Great Work, namely that of living well: פלא (= פלה), 'be extraordinary/great, be/appear hard/difficult'; פלה, '(be) separate(d)/distinguish(ed)/set apart/wonderfully made'; פנק, 'bring up/train delicately'.

In the regrouping after the Fall, the *letter* peh has retreated within, to the Grail's sagittary or thought. At the heart of the Kabbalah is a pattern that corresponds in detail to the Georges Dumézil school of comparative mythology's basic *tripartite* division of proto-Indo-European mythology and class-structure: the sacred—our *within;* secular power—our *without;* and the chthonic—commoners and artisans.[65] These three mirror knower, thinker, and doer, oriented as are desire-mind, feeling-mind, and body-mind (behind, before, and beneath). The way to think of P is as the external or outward-facing aspect of the sacred (our inner reality): what is preached (its doctrines). Conversely, D's move over to the outer world (in a ruling capacity, being oak) represents the secular's *inner* aspect: the power *thinking* has over matter (air acting on earth).

The tree-letter is *peith* the whitten or guelder rose, from whose dried berries ink is made. Egyptian hieroglyphics had **one reed** and **two reeds** at Egg's sagittary and capricorn, no doubt symbolizing 'make record of' (on papyrus) and 'confirm record of': P's new station at sagittary, on a level with Egg's capricorn, is **reed stool** (knee-high, for the scribe to sit on), thus following the broken-and-extended zodiac down the legs to the feet. Consistent with this: פתשגן/פרשגן, 'transcript/copy of a writing'; פתגם, 'word, sentence/decree, Ch. epistle/letter, Ch. thing/matter'; פשר Ch. (= H. פתר), 'interpret(ation)/explain'; and פתר, 'interpret(ation)/explain'—all using the conscience, tav (or thinker, shin) to ensure accuracy.

From this, and its new station being air's active side, peh's shape is an opened mouth and signifies speech. Amongst simples, the function speech was originally (I surmise) delegated to samekh, which occupies the same station as peh's 'soft side', F (in the Corn Spirit 'heresy'); for the heads of both Bran and Orpheus prophesied after being removed. P's bardic number has to be based on its new station, since nitrogen (7) constitutes four/fifths of the air (hence of speech). I cite nitrogen to show how nature confirms druid's numbering, not to suggest they had isolated nitrogen from air. And thus: פאה, 'blow away (scatter like wind), wind (quarter)/region/corner, mouth/aperture/entrance, edge (of sword)/border, side/part/portion'; פוח, 'blow/breathe/- fire, fig. inflame/rail at/utter/speak, dust/ashes' (which blow in wind); פום, 'mouth/aperture'; פעה, 'cry out [bleating (pl.)] adder/viper' (Syr. 'bleat/low', A. 'hiss (serpent)'); פער, 'open wide (mouth)/gape [gap (mtn. in Moab, idol of Moabites)]'; פצה, 'open (mouth)/(w/ על) gape upon, save/deliver/tear away'; פצר, 'press (w/ב upon)/urge, be stubborn/willful, pressed/rubbed upon (edges, i.e. file)'; פקח, 'open (esp. eyes, also ears)'; פתה, 'open wide (babbler, in context)/be open/ingenuous/(thus easily) persuade(d)/entice(d), deceive/seduce, make wide/enlarge[-ment (Japheth, son of Noah)] Ch. breadth, folly/foolish, inexperienced/ignorant'; פתח, 'open (door/window/womb/sack/roll) (/hand, i.e. act liberally ל to)/cleave (rock) , begin, loosen/untie, draw/unsheathe (sword), plough, engrave/carve/sculpture, entrance/door/gate, an opening (of the mouth), engraving/carving, key, drawn swords' (for 'cleave' and 'engrave', see below).

You will notice above and as we go on the meanings 'scatter' and 'spread' are common with peh; found in different contexts, they always relate directly back (or rather ahead) to the attraction of P's original station, the outer horizon, which is all about us.

Related to speech are meanings connecting peh/feh to *fearn* the alder and thus to trump VIII Justice (the remaining fifth of air): פדה, 'redeem/ransom/set free/let go/deliver/preserve, price/redemption/ransom, distinction?'; פדע, 'redeem/deliver'; פלל, '(ad)judge/inflict judicial punishment, suppose, intercede/pray for, justice'; פלס, 'make (a way), level/plane, weigh/ponder, balance/steelyard'; פקד, ' *observe/attend to/seek/- in vain/miss, muster/number, -ing/census, lay as charge (command), -s/precepts, overseer/chief officer, oversight/office/charge, think of/recall, visit/- upon/punish, appoint/assign, entrust/deposit, appointments/arrangements, appointed pl., custody, care/providence, visitation/punishment, store/treasure'; and פרע, 'free/exempt (from punishment)/deliver, let go loose/in state of disorder, neglect/reject (counsel), make bare (the head), become lawless, hair/locks (as growing loose and free) [free-town]'. (Three involve dalet and three involve lamedh.)

P's own trump references air directly (of which it is four-fifths): VII The Chariot, whose driver has the wind in his face. First, consider those most likely to *be* said driver: פרעה [Pharaoh (title)]; פוטיפר [Potiphar (chief of Pharaoh's guard)]; פחה, 'governor/deputy (of province)'; פלך, 'circuit/district/(di)staff' (A. 'be round'); פנן, 'battlement/parapet, red coral/chief/prince'; פרא\ה, 'wild ass [like a - - (k. of Canaan)]'; פרס, 'Persia(ns)'; פרתם, 'nobles/princes'; פַּתְרוֹס [a country in (upper?) Egypt]; and, spilling over into our next sub-category, פרז (perh. 'scatter'), 'ruler/leader, scattered place/unwalled town/village' (A. 'to separate' = פרש/פרד). And the cavalry wing such leaders command: פרשׁ, 'horseman/rider, horse for riding'. Eight of the eleven utilize reysh!

Then there is what the chariots of these elites have a tendency to do if they are ever unleashed, especially on a פדן, *field/plane*, palace': פגע, 'meet/w/light/border/*fall upon/assail* (w/ petitions), urge/entreat/supplicate, regard w/favor, occurrence/incident/event, *(object of) attack, assailant/enemy*'; פגשׁ, 'meet/fall upon/in w/'; פור, '*break (in pieces)*/violate/frustrate, winepress'; פזר, '*disperse/scatter*, distribute liberally'; פעם, '*impel/urge*, (be)move(d/disturbed), *a striking/stamping*, anvil/(foot-)step *(fig. progress of chariot)*, bell'; פצח, '*break* forth (into singing/rejoicing)/*in pieces*'; פצם, 'break/rend'; פצע, 'wound/(n.)' ; פרך (= פרק '*break*'), veil or curtain separating (holy pl. from Holy of Holies), '*oppression/rigor*'; פרץ, '*break/demolish/tear down (wall)/break asunder (disperse/scatter)*, afflict, break forth (as child from womb), (of water) burst forth, *increase/overflow*, spread abroad(/common), break away/loose, *breach (of wall), overflow/calamity, violent*/rapacious, ravenous/wild/- beast'; פרק, '*break (off)/crush (as wild beast the limbs)/tear away/rescue/deliver, tear off/rend in pieces*, Ch. *break off*/expiate, broth (from pieces), *violence*/rapine, vertebra of neck'; פרר, '*break (/in pieces?)*/violate/frustrate (counsel)/declare void (vow)/annul/abolish/*rend*, fail/come to naught, cleave/be broken/rent, *shake/agitate*, young bull/bullock/cow/heifer [swift] *violently*' (A. '*be borne swiftly/run*'); פרשׁ , '*break* bread (= פרס) stretch/*spread* (garment) out (hands), *disperse/scatter*, expansion/sail'; פתן, 'asp (= פתל?), threshold' (A. '*be strong/firm*'); פתת, '*break*, piece/crumb/morsel (of bread)' > פתבג, 'delicate food/dainties' (= בג + פת 'food'). Six use just reysh's overbearingness, three use just tzaddi's strife, and one uses both of them together.

And this sort of behavior will (it is hoped) make the enemy: פוק, '*(be) move(d)/to and fro/waver/be unsteady*, give out/furnish/supply, get/obtain, to further, stumbling block, *tottering*'; פחד, '*tremble/fear/be afraid*/agitated (w/wonder/joy), *terrify, hasten*, be very careful/solicitous'; פלט, 'slip away/escape/(be) deliver(ed)/bring forth/carry away safely, escaped-by-flight'; פלץ, 'shake/tremble'; פלשׁ, 'roll oneself/wallow (in dust) *[Philistine]*'; and פלת, 'runners/couriers [swiftness]' (A. '*escape/flee*')—four that start peh lamedh, the latter on the radius of the former *at its new position* (sagittary, where it has withdrawn from the horizon, it original station).

That middle group has interesting echoes in the next category, relating to *fearn* the alder as Corn Spirit: פוץ, '*disperse/be scattered/overflow*/shatter/confuse/*pour/spread abroad, battle hammer*/maul'; פושׁ, 'spread/thrive/grow fat/spread out/be scattered [spreading/overflowing (r. issuing from Garden of Eden)] excess?'; פטר, '*burst open (flowers)/let out (water)*, dismiss/let go/exempt from duty, slip away, *an opening/a breaking forth*'; פטשׁ, 'hammer, Ch. a tunic' (A. 'hammer, *spread out*'); פצץ (= פוץ) ['dispersion']; פקע, '*wild cucumbers?/mushrooms?* (as architectural ornament)' (Syr. '*split*' = בקע); פרא, 'be fruitful'; פרד, '*spread* (wing)/separate, -ed (singular?/dispersed?), scatter? divide? be sundered, mule, seeds scattered/corn sown*'; פרדס, 'garden/park'; פרה, '*(be/make) bear fruit(ful)*, - (and fig.), sedan/litter'; פרח, '*sprout/flourish[-ing]/blossom, -/flower/young shoot*, fly, *brood, young (birds)*, break out (ulcers/leprosy)'; plus פרשׁד > 'fecal matter' (A. 'separate/*spread out* feet'); פרשׂ, 'spread out/expand'; and פשׂה, '*spread* (as leprosy)'. Those last three all have shin, our S, in the penultimate position: taking peh here as *fearn*, F-S are the 8-16 that follow *onn* the furze's 4 to indicate spring's increase (shin is the

willow, expressive of the fount of spring). Also: פדר, 'fat/grease'; פים, 'fatness' (A. 'be fat');
and, of course, פכה, '*flow out*, flask', and פרת ['sweet water (Euphrates)']. And from the idea of
urban growth: פרור/פרבר, 'suburb'. That makes eleven that involve reysh and reference the
fount of spring! peh reysh as in *fearn* itself (and Orpheus, and Scandinavian Fro or Freyr).

Rune P shows a dice-cup on its side (having disgorged its runes in divination), hence:
פור, 'lot, lots (feast of Purim)'. And suggested by the hollowness common to dice-cup and open
mouth: 2. פאר, 'explain/declare oneself, holes (see חפר) [abounding in caverns]' (A. 'dig down'
cogn. באר); פחת, '*pit*/fig. ruin, corrosion (leprosy)' (Syr. '*dig/excavate*'); פנם, 'hide/conceal?,
interior, inner'.

Since *fearn* the alder is Bran, Celtic Kronos or Saturn: פגר, 'become weary/exhausted,
corpse/carcass (man or beast)'; פוג, 'become chilled/languid/cease to act, intermission/rest'; פוט
['afflicted (name of Libyans?)']; פול, 'beans'; פחח, '*spread* net/ensnare (denom. from פח snare)';
פיד, 'calamity' (A. 'disappear/die'); פכרת הצבים ['snaring the gazelles']; פסס, '*cease/fail/have an
end*, Ch. extremity (of hand), *abundance*'—this last referencing the Corn Spirit aspect as well!
From his confusion with Chronos we can add: פתע, 'sudden(ness)/-ly/accidently/undesignedly'.

Somewhat related to VII The Chariot are roots recalling F's Tifinag character in the far
north, which pictures the *relationship* between F's perch at Egg's aries and P's original station at
the outer horizon: a bowl-shaped (boat-shaped) half-circle (prob. named *far*, 'ferry') bisected by
its vertical radius (standing for the passenger, *us*)—as if being cut in half. Therefore: פלג, '*cut
out/form/(be) divide(d)*, brook/stream, *division*, Ch. *half*'; פלח, '*cut (/in pieces)/cleave/*let break
forth, *slice/piece/*millstone, Ch. serve/worship'; פסג, 'view/consider, prop. *divide/*distinguish,
part/piece'; פסל, '*cut/hew* (esp. stones)/carve (wood), *carved image/idol*, quarry'; פרט (prob.
'*cut/divide*' cogn. פרד), 'sing, (fallen grapes lying about) *scattered/strewed*'; פרס, 'break (bread to
anyone)/give/distribute, *cleave/divide* (hoof), Ch. *divide*, osprey, hoof'—the Tifinag letter looks
a bit like a cloven hoof—פרש '(prop. *divide*), be dispersed/scattered/made clear, decide/declare,
Ch. *distinctly/*accurately, dung, sting/*wound*, distinct declaration/specification'; פלד, 'iron/steel'
(A. 'cut up'), and פרזל (= H. ברזל), Ch. 'iron'—four with lamedh and four with reysh (left and
right). Later, in Libya, the Tifinag character, the ferry (of alder) that cuts through water, was
changed to the map symbol for a bridge (with alder pilings), which cuts a river.

Roots pointing to the *heretical* nature of the alder cult (peh's soft side): primarily פחז, 'be
wanton/rash/proud, pride/arrogance' (A. 'boil up/over'), that last relating to spring as well. And
then: פגל, 'a thing impure/abominable' (Ethiop. 'be impure'); פון, 'be perplexed/distracted'; פנה,
'*turn/- oneself, decline (time)*, remove, clear (house/road), turn (neck), face/countenance, lest
(conj., prop. *a turning to*), surface/appearance/front, person/presence, forwards/before (of time),
because of, anterior'; פשע, 'revolt/rebel, transgress/sin'; finally פתל, '*(prop. be twisted) fig. be
perverse/false/*deceitful, wrestle/struggle, -s, thread/string/cord, crooked/*perverse*'.

Related to these are roots recalling the south Semitic character for P, a diamond-shaped
earring (or a vulva): 1. פאר, '*adorn/beautify/*honor, *ornament/beauty/splendor/*honor, vaunt,
glean, green bough, pot for boiling'; פג, 'unripe fig' (A. 'be unripe') (Canticles 2:13); פוך, 'eye-
paint/stibium (prepared from antimony)'; פתח/פות '(*be spread open*? cogn. פוש, פחח), tottering,

block, *nakedness/pudendum*, hinges'; פטדד, 'topaz?'; פלֶגֶשׁ, 'concubine'; פֵּצֶל (= בֵּצֶל), '(parts) *peel*(ed/*stripped* of bark)' (Gen. 30:37-8); פרם, 'rend/tear (garment)'; פרעשׁ, 'flea'; פּשׁח, 'tear in pieces'; פּשׁט, '*strip/put off (garment)*, spread oneself out (of hostile troop), *strip (pers.)*/flay/skin, *strip*/pillage/plunder'; פּשׂע, 'step/pass thru/stride, *buttocks*'; פּשׂק, 'distend/open wide (lips/feet)'; פּשׁת (?), 'linen/flax (of tree, i.e. cotton)/wick (of lamp)', that last reminiscent of the hieroglyph **wick of twisted flax**, from whose hieratic form samekh derives (*fearn*'s alter ego)—seven that use shin or sin—plus פּא (= פּה), 'here', and פּה, 'here/hither' (for that 'come hither' look).

Also relevant to a sensual lifestyle: פְּסַנְתְּרִי/פְּסַנְטֵרִי, Ch. 'a psaltery'; פְּתִיגִיל, 'wide mantle (i.e. fine clothing)'; (from Ezekiel 27:17) פַּנַּג, 'prob. some delicate spice or gum (Vulg. balsam, Gesen. pastry/sweet cake)' (Ch. פְּנַק 'be delicate'). This last, the *Pannag* of the KJV, since its passage is a lament for Tyre, I would suggest is from Greek (through seafaring slang?) *Phoiníkē*, meaning variably 'a Phoenician', 'Tyrian purple/crimson', or 'date palm' (source, Wikipedia), and that it referred perhaps to a pastry made from dates and thus associated with that region.

SUMMARY

Peh in square-Hebrew [*open mouth with tongue*]: 'open [*door, sack, etc.*], an opening [*of the mouth*], gate', 2 'open [*mouth*], gape', 'open [*esp. eyes, also ears*], seeing, having eyes open' [*i.e. poetic initiation*], 'cry out, hiss, viper', 'blow, breathe', 2 '(blow away, side [*quarter, wind*], word, command) mouth, aperture', 'word, decree', 'transcript', 2 '(interpret) explain (dig down)'. **Runic P:** [*cavity:*] 'dig, excavate, pit, corrosion', 'interior, within', 'threshold', 'flask, flow out', 'potter'; [*dice cup on side (divining):*] 'lot(s), Purim'. **VII LeChariot:** [*battle cart:*] 2 '(carry off safely) escape (couriers {swiftness})', 2 '(shake) tremble (fear, be agitated [*with wonder, joy*], hasten)', {'afflicted [*son of Ham, and descendents (in Sept. and Vulg., Libyans)*]'}, 'wound', 4 ' (be borne swiftly) break (-asunder, overflow) (curtain separating holy of holies) (morsel)', 2 '(violate, break) -in pieces (break forth [*into singing, rejoicing*])', 2 'rend, tear (-in pieces)', 'cut up, iron, steel', 2 '(hew [*esp.* stones]) cut (cleave)'; [*divides manifestation into 7 palaces (heikhalot):*] 5 '(cut out, a brook) (corner, parapet, chief, prince) divide (hoof, break [*bread*]) (be dispersed, declare, determine, wound) (distinguish)'; [*equestrian:*] 'distinguish, set apart, be great', 'governor', 'nobles, princes' ['topaz'] 2 '(pure [*epithet of gold*], purify, be agile, active) leap (Passover)', 3 '(anvil, progress of chariot) (stride) step (urge)', 'here, hither, hence', 'horseman, horse' ['wild ass'], 'bring up, train delicately'; [*wheeled:*] 'be round, circuit', 'roll oneself', 'turn oneself [*or neck*]', 'be twisted, perverse, wrestle, thread, cord'. **Feh-sofit as Fro** [*pagan fertility principle*]: 'be impure', 'to rebel, sin', 'boil up, -over, be wanton', 'suddenly, undesignedly', 2 'meet, fall upon (attack, urge)', 'press, urge, rubbed [*on*]', 'move to and fro, be moved', 'be distracted' [*cf.* **P**'s *Semitic forms (ear, earring)*], 2 '(be seduced) open wide ([*lips, feet*])', 'eye-paint', 'adorn, beauty, green bough, pot for boiling' [*cf. Num.* **P** (*table 4*), *Ethiop. samekh (table 2)*], 2 '(visit, miss) look after (-for)', 'concubine', 'be free, make bare, hair [*loose, free*]', 'peel', 'strip [*person, garment*], flay, skin' ['flea'] 'be spread open, nakedness', 'spread feet, interstice of legs'. **F-rune** [*Corn Spirit*]: 'spread out, expand', 'suburb', 'spread, thrive, grow fat, be scattered {overflowing}', *3* '(overflow) disperse, scatter ((separate, seeds scattered, corn sown) spread ([*hands, garment*]))', 'spread a net, ensnare, plates of metal' [{'snaring'}] 'hammer, spread out, tunic', 'flax [*-Y HOTz, flax of tree=cotton*], linen, wick of lamp', 'wide mantle', 'be fat', 'fat, grease' ['delicacies', 'some delicate spice or gum*?*'], 'work, make, form', 'be fruitful' {'sweet water [*Euphrates*]'} 'burst open, let out [*water*], let go', 'break forth', 'split, mushrooms*?*', 'sprout, flourish, blossom, young shoot, brood', 'be unripe', 'garden, park', 'field, plain'. **F=VIII Justice:** 'make level, plain, weigh, ponder, balance, steelyard', 'judge, adjudge', 2 'redeem (set free)'. **F=alder-god Vran** [*Saturn*]: 'spread [*as the leprosy*]', 'become chilled, languid, intermission, rest', 'become weary, exhausted, corpse', 'disappear, die, calamity', 'cease, fail, have an end, extremity, abundance', 'beans' [*which Romans linked to souls of dead*]. **P and F both being on the fire triad:** 'charcoal, burning coal'.

ת

Tav

PARSED ROOTS

This is Cauldron's leo, a descent from the horizon: תּוֹח, *'below/beneath, under [low/-ness]* in place/stead of/return for, on account of, *lower/-est'* (A. *'descend/sink down'*); תכה, 'be laid down' (A. 'lean upon'). What approaches within earshot: תּוה, Ch. 'be astonished/amazed'; תמה, 'wonder/be astonished/amazed/look w/ surprise, Ch. wonder/miracle, consternation'; תנך > 'extremity/tip (of the ear)' (Syr. 'come to an end'); תפף, 'beat (tabret), smite upon (breast), a drum/tabret' (a tabret was like our tambourine); and תרגם, Ch. 'interpret/translate'.

In Egyptian hieroglyphics, the horizon is **hand**; next is **tongs**, a straightened version of leo's symbol (the lion's jaws); therefore: תמך, *'take hold of, obtain/acquire, hold fast/fig. retain, hold up/support,* hold together/follow each other'; תפש, 'lay hold of/seize, take/capture, handle (bow/harp/etc.)/fig. administer (law), be taken/caught/captured, held/set (in gold), take hold'. And context: תנן ('stretching out/extending'), '(huge/)great serpent(s)/sea monster, crocodile, dwelling/habitation?' (A. תנא 'abide/dwell') > אתּון *'Ch. furnace'* (Ch. תנן 'to smoke')/< תנּוּר > תנר 'oven/furnace' (from נוּר 'shine, Ch. subst. fire'?)—compare the alchemical term *athenor*.

But it was not **tongs** whose hieratic form spawned old Hebrew tav (a cross or an X), but a **duckling** skittering through the shallows. It was topped with a prominent cross, which became its shape in Hebrew. Thus its core meaning became one's *mark* or *word* (what is in one's heart). So: תאה, *'mark out,* sp. of gazelle' (A. תאי 'outrun'); תאר, *'(be drawn/)mark(ed) out/delineate,* form/personal appearance, handsome form/beauty'—in Greek, *tau* is a T-square—and 1. תוה, 'make marks/scribble, *mark/sign (tav), (set a) mark (on), signature/subscription, limit?/grieve?'* (Syr. *'repent/be grieved'*).

Tav signifies one's heart or conscience: תכן, *'(be) weigh(ed)/fig. ponder/examine(d)/try, equal/fair/just, measure/direct/fix(ed quantity),* arrangement/structure/perfect(ion of beauty/) form, proportion? costly furniture?'; תמם, '(be) complete(d/ended)/finish, be complete/whole (in number), *be(/show oneself) perfect/upright,* -/*sincere,* cease/be consumed/spent, sound/*without blemish/defect, integrity,* welfare/prosperity'; תקל, Ch. '(be) weigh(ed)'. Too often the verdict of conscience is not very positive: 2. תאב (= תעב) > 'abhorring'; תהה (Ch. תהא 'be waste/desolate'), 'desolation/desert/emptiness, *vanity/a vain/worthless thing,* in vain (adv.)' (the *tohu* of Gen. 1:2); תּוּב, 'return/give/send back'; תּוּף, 'a spitting' (A. 'spit out w/ contempt'); תעב, 'abhor, render abominable/cause to be abhorred, excite/be object of abhorrence, act abominably, be detested, abomination'; תעה, 'wander/go(be led) astray, stagger (drunk)/fig. err, perish?, error/apostasy, hurt/injury'; תפל, '*anything unseasoned/unsavory/fig insipid/foolish*, lime/mortar, *folly/impiety*'. And perhaps by contrast, symbolizing what is 'lily-white': תלג (= H. שלג), 'snow'. And what conscience judges: 1. תאב (= אוה 'desire/long for'), 'desire (n.)'.

The old Hebrew letter was sometimes a plus-sign (+), signifying the public square (a crossroads); for where conscience fails, shaming often succeeds. Hence the following: 2. תוה '(= A. תוי abide/dwell), chamber'; תוך, 'middle/midst (—ב among/etc.)'; תור, '*go round/about* (cogn. דור) *troop about (as merchant/spy), search out/explore/investigate*, think of/purpose, *go astray, lead/direct aright*, turn/order (n.), row/string of beads, *a searching out*'—looks remarkably like our English word *tour*—תלא, '*suspended/placed in suspense/uncertainty*, hanging after (i.e. bent upon/addicted to)'; תלה, '*hang/suspend/execute*, a quiver (as being suspended) [hanging/lofty (pl.)] > armory (where weapons are hung)'; תנה, 'bestow gifts to hire (anyone) [whom God bestows] praise/celebrate/hire, gift/wages (of prostitution) [giving/munificent]'; תפתיא, 'Ch. lawyers/judges'; תקן, 'be arranged/straight, make -, set in order/compose, Ch. be established'; תרע, 'Ch. door/gate (of k. for royal palace) [gate (pl.)] Ch. doorkeeper/porter, from'. Moreover, we have תור, 'turtledove', symbol (in Rome) of the goddess Fides of trust and good faith (*bona fides*)! Also on a symbolic level: תפר, 'sew/join together'.

I am going to insert here a rather important: תבה, 'prop. a chest/box/ark of Noah (built in form of chest)/ark in which Moses was exposed' (often translated 'basket'). Noah's ark marked preservation of *a* public sector, Moses's a symbolic giving up of the babe *to* the public sector, so to speak. (Moses, the great Hebrew deliverer or Hercules, appears to embody both waxing *and* waning year, oak king *and* tanist, one as Egyptian, one as Jew: the latter would be tanist, since he 'slays' the former.)

The months of D and T (oak and holly) are 'straddled' by Tammuz (June-July), the fourth Hebrew month: תמוז [Tammuz] (Ezekiel 8:14), its namesake Sumerian god Dumuzid, a shepherd god and spirit of vegetation whose death was mourned this month, thus presumably dying at the summer solstice (god of waxing year). Since D and T are the twin gods of the year: תאם, '(be double) -d/coupled, (bear) twin(s)'; תנא (= H. שנה 'repeat'), 'Ch. (a) second (time)'; תרין, 'Ch. two'; and since they are usually paired, תור (= H. שור), 'Ch. (only plural, ין—) oxen'—could this be our word *taurus*?

Associated with midsummer is the color red: תלע, 'clothed in scarlet, worm/esp. – used in dying scarlet (coccus)'. And purple is associated with royalty (king of waxing year, sacrificed at the solstice): תכל (prob. 'to peel/shell'), 'cerulean purple (color obtained from a mussel, *helix janthina*)'.

Though Dumuzid was evidently the *waxing* twin, the tree-letter of the *waning* twin— whose place tav holds in the calendar (sign *after* summer solstice)—is *tinne* the holly or *ilex* (holm-oak or evergreen oak): תרזה, 'sp. of hard tree, for which the Vulg. has *ilex*' (Isaiah 44.14). Holly, T, is three notches *above* the line in ogham, being the third letter of the second or middle group of five consonant-months: תלת, 'Ch. three, third'. Graves takes the holly king or waning year to rule satire, the poet's weapon: תלל, 'raise/heap up (as mound), raised/lofty, *mock/deride, mockings/fig. mockers*, (be) deceive(d)/delude, heap (ruins), hill/mound, waving palm branches (or clusters or hanging strings of its embryo fruits)'; תעע, '*mock/scoff, - at, mockeries*/delusions'.

Two other trees also start with tav: תאנה, 'fig/-tree (root doubtful)'; and תמר, 'palm-tree, column/pillar, - (of smoke)', plus תדמר ['city of palm trees' (Palmyra in Greek)]. The palm is the tree associated with bardic Aa, hence with teyt, but tav is phonetically similar. Interestingly, use of the fig leaf by Adam and Eve to hide their nudity also resonates with conscience (in the world of lust, at any rate); and the fig tree generally symbolizes Israel in the Bible.

T's trump is XI Force: תבר (= H. שבר 'break'), '*fragile/brittle* [quarry?/height? (Tabor)]'; תגלת פלסר [Tiglath-pileser (k. of Assyria)]; תיז, 'cut off (sprigs)'; תכך, 'violence/oppression, - s/injuries' (A. 'cut/- off', Ch. תוך 'injure'); תלח ['a breach']; תלם, 'furrow [full of –s]' (A. '*break/- open*'); תקע, 'smite/clap (hands, in joy), strike hands (in surety), cast/throw in, drive/fix in (nail), fasten w/ nails/pitch (tent), thrust in (spear), a blast w/ the trumpet'; תקף, 'overpower/prevail over/oppress, Ch. be/become great/strong/powerful/firm/obstinate, might/power/authority, Ch. strong/hard/mighty/powerful'; תרן, 'mast/banner'.

The rune is an arrow pointing up (interpreted as a spear, since it is named after Tiw or Tyr, god of warlike fortitude): תיש, 'he-goat/ram'; and תכי, 'peacocks' (for their posture?). Both involve yod, where the round progresses upward.

The only relevance of תשע, 'nine/-th', to tav that *I* can think of is that it introduces the bardic number of the next double letter, kaf.

SUMMARY

Tav as heart: 'desire, long for', 'to beat [*the tabret*], smite upon [*the breast*], drum, tabret', 'clap [*hands, as sign of joy*], strike hands [*as sign of surety*], drive [*as a nail*], thrust in [*e.g. spear*], blast [*of trumpet*]'. **As conscience, T-square shape:** 'mark [*boundary*]', 'to mark, to limit, a mark or sign', 'be drawn, mark out, delineate, handsome form, form', 'make straight, set in order', 'lawyers or judges', 2 'weigh (ponder, examine, be equal, fair, or just, measure, direct)', 'go about, think of, to purpose, go astray, lead or direct aright', 'be completed, perfect, upright, integrity, sincere, without blemish', 'come to an end, extremity'. **XI LaForce:** 2 'cut off (cut, injure, violence, oppression)', 'overpower, oppress, might, -y, be or make strong', 'he-goat, ram', 'badger', 2 '(brittle, Tabor [*a grove of oaks...*]) break (-open, furrow)' {'breach', 'Tiglath-pileser [*Assyrian king*]', 'fear'} 2 [*ThMH, ThVH*] 'be astonished'. **What conscience rejects:** 'go astray, err, seduce', 'abhor, render abominable', 'spit out with contempt, a spitting {[*place known for abominations*]}', 'unsavory thing, impiety, lime {[*place in Sinai desert*]}'. *Tongs:* 'take hold of, hold together, -up, support, follow each other' ['oxen'], 'seize, handle', '[*ThNN, sense of* stretching out, extending] great serpent, sea monster, furnace [*Chald. ThNN, to smoke*]', '[*ThNVR, ThNN(?)+NVR, shine, Chald.* fire] oven, furnace' [*whence alchemy's* athenor]. **Hottest month:** 'desert, emptiness, vain, worthless', 'straw, heap of straw'; [*inverse:*] 'snow'. **Holly:** 'species of hard tree [*Vulg.* ilex]' [*i.e. holly- or holm-oak*]; [*holly-king, satiric waning year:*] 2 '(scoff, -at) mock (deride, heap up [*as mound*], hill, deceive, delude)'. **2nd manifested**

sign [*Cauldron's leo*], **twin of oak-king:** 'second', 'two', 'sew or join together', 'be double, twin, coupled, joined'. **Crossroads:** 'middle, midst, among', 'distribute gifts to hire [*persons*], praise, celebrate, wages [*of prostitution*]', 'peacocks [*symbol of wealth of Tarshish*]', 'fig, -tree', 'palm tree [*ThMR*]' [*could it originally have been TMR?*], 'turtle-dove [*sin-offering after post-birth confinement and purification, brought to priest at doorway to tent of meeting*]', 'door, gate', 'abide, dwell, chamber', 'descend, what is below or underneath [*hence a place*], in place of, in return for', 'interpret, translate'. **'(I,) the suffering one'** [*in 'Orphic' hymn*]: 'lean upon, be laid down', 'suspend, hang, execute, in suspense, hanging upon, quiver [*hung*]' {'Tammuz'}. **Rune** [*arrow pointing up or ahead*]: 'mast, banner'; '[*Chald.*] there', 'outrun, species of gazelle [*Vulg.* oryx]'; [*O.E. rune-name* tyr, *'divine honor' (god-name* Tyr*):*] {'Tiras'}. **Ogham T** [*three strokes*]: 'three, third' ['nine, ninth']. **Unparsed:** 'clothed in scarlet, a worm', 'peel or shell? cerulean purple [*from mussel*]'.

Kaf

PARSED ROOTS

One root touches on several themes explored below and includes kaf's physiological station, the kidneys: כלה, '*be completed/finished/ended*/hence *accomplished/fulfilled/spent, waste away*/pine, waste/ruin/destroy/*cause to languish*/vanish, *wholly*, vessel/utensil, *boat/skiff*, implement/tool, weapons/arms/equipment/*clothing/dress, kidneys/fig. inward secret parts (of soul), finish, end/perfection/boundary*'. This is virgo of the Cauldron, *coll* the hazel: wisdom *in a nutshell* (i.e. concentrated). Kaf is the kidneys, where feeling is concentrated (as I found out when someone punched me there by way of greeting); khaf sofit is the bladder.

Being at an angle of thirty-degrees out from straight down, kaf's symbolic meaning is what is gathered close or within reach, its Tifinag character a heap of stones, or perhaps nuts. Thus: כבר, '*multiply/abundance*, formerly, quilt, great/mighty, *many*, sieve, measure (length), lattice-work (of brass), coarse cloth (cogn. חבל to twist)' (A. 'be great/powerful'); כּוּם, 'Pleiades' (A. '*heap up*'); כחה, 'strength/vigor/power/ability, *substance/wealth/riches*' (Syr. 'pant, hence exert oneself (Gesen.)'); כמן > 'treasure' (Syr./A. 'lay up'); כמס, 'lay/treasure up [treasure (pl.)]'; כנס, '*collect/gather together/assemble, collect oneself (wrap oneself up)*, trousers/drawers'; כנשׁ, Ch. 'collect/assemble'; כסס, 'number/reckon, tribute/offering, tax, price'; and כף, 'rocks (only in plural)'. These last six invoke the top of the round—heap or treasure *up* (i.e. collect together in a *pile*)—with either nun or samekh (or both), or with feh sofit (fearn the alder).

Old Hebrew kaf evidently developed from the hieratic of the hieroglyph ***basket with handle***: כּוּל, '*to measure/contain/sustain/nourish*/hold out/endure/maintain/- one's course [*sustenance* (name of *wise* man)]'; כלב ('to clap/to bark'), dog [barker] *fruit-basket*/bird-cage' (A. 'plait/braid'); כמן, 'cumin'; כרכם, 'saffron'; כרם, 'vineyard (w/ זית olive-yard), vinedresser, well-cultivated plain/garden/orchard/field [Carmel]'. And since ***basket with handle*** is shaped like a bowl and could easily pass for a mortar awaiting its pestal: כתשׁ, 'bruise/pound, mortar'; כתת, '*beat*(/down)/hammer/forge, *break in pieces/crush*/rout/be broken, *beaten oil (from olives beaten in mortar)*, Chittim (inhabitants of Cypress/Mediterranean)'—as if *kaf tav* stood for the entire outer half of the Cauldron (which is bowl-shaped, since the outer horizon extends 360 degrees). And once the preparations are done: כרסם, 'devour'.

That last one recalls the rune, an open mouth (filberts in, words out): כדב (= H. כזב), Ch. 'lie/deceive/fail (of water), (be) prove(d) false [lying/false] -hood/lie'; כזב, 'lie/deceive/fail (of water)/(be) prove(d) false, -hood [lying] deceitful/failing'; כחשׁ, 'fail/waste away, *deny/disavow, lie/deceive/flatter*, feign, leanness/deceit, *a lying'*—I believe there is an old saying, 'all poets are liars', probably from frequent use of figurative language—כנה, 'call by (flattering) name(s/titles), companion/associate'; כרז, Ch. 'cry out/proclaim, herald'. Traditionally *coll*, hazel, symbolizes the poet's wisdom and inspiration, so: כהל, 'be able/can'; כנר, (prob. imitating tremulous sound) 'harp/lyre [(pl.)]'; כרן ['harp' (A. כראן)]—indeed the sign for virgo looks very like a harp or lyre.

Then of course there is wisdom's opposite or complement: כסל, '*be foolish* (in derivv. be fat/strong, hence firm/confident (Gesen.)), confidence/hope [ninth month (Chislev)] *folly, fool [-(Orion)] folly* [hope(s, pl.)] loin(s), inward parts/viscera'. VIIII The Hermit (K's trump) lifts a lamp, and one of the two possible names for the rune is *kenaz*, 'torch' (the poet is a *guide* to his people): כוה, '*be burned/scorched, mark burnt in/brand, -ing*, inflamed part (in body)'; כמר, '*be burned/black w/ burning/be warmed/kindled (of love/compassion)*, (in derivv. = כבר plait/braid) idolatrous priests, heat/blackness (fig. calamity), (fishing) net/snare'*, the other name for the rune being *kanō*, 'skiff' (as in the very first root given for kaf, above). (The Nine Hazels of Poetic Art feed the salmon of knowledge in Celtic myth, and virgo is manifested water.) And in order that poets' words be passed on to future poets: כתב, '*(describe/)write (down)/engrave, scripture, ordain/decree, epistle/letter*, register/*record*, Ch. *a writing*/precept/*prescription, ode/composition, a mark*'. Note this has tav in it, which *means* 'one's mark'. Two further ways of guiding one's people: כשד '[s. of Nahor and progenitor of Chaldeans] Chaldeans (inhabitants of Babylon)/fig. *astrologers*'; and כשף, 'practice magic/use witchcraft, incantations/sorceries, magician/wizard, sorceress/witch'.

This is the approach to straight down—the Throne itself in this, the Throne *world*—and Hebrew kaf pictures a curved hand (in addition to kidneys): כבב > '[cake (pl.)] star' (A./Ethiop. '*roll up*'); כדר ['*handful* (of sheaves)'] (coll. w/ A. by Simonis); כמז, '*bracelet* (prob . of gold beads)' (A. '*gather/compress into roundish form*'); כפה, 'cover/extinguish (cogn. כבא/חבא/חפה) only fig. (of anger) appease (or *bend/avert*, cogn. כפף)'; כפף, 'bend/(be) bow(ed) down/humble oneself, (hollow/palm of) hand/paw (kaf), handle (of bolt), pan/spoon/dish/cavity of sling, (palm) branch'; כפל, 'double, *be –d *over*/*fold(ed)*, double/manifold'—three using peh w/ roughly the same meaning—כרס (prob. = כרש 'be curved'), Ch. 'seat/throne'; כרע, 'bend/bow/sink down (of knees)/kneel (in reverence)/(of beasts) bowing (legs to lie down)/make bow down/prostrate/fig. depress/afflict, leg/- bones (also the springing legs of locusts)'; כנע, '*bow down/bring low/(be) humble(/- oneself/submit)/subdue(d)*, bundle/package/bale (from idea of) *folding together [low (s. of Ham)]* Canaanite(s)/merchant [Canaan]'. Continuing with this theme: כבש, 'trample/*tread underfoot*/fig. disregard, *subdue/subject, humble*/force/ravish, *footstool, smelting furnace*'; כמוש, [perh. '*subduer*' (idol of Moabites and Ammonites)]. And here are four that are convex (where the palm of the hand is concave): כבע (= גבע 'be high'), '*helmet*'; כסם, '*shave/poll (the head)* or adorn(?), spelt (a kind of corn)'; כפתר, '*round/spherical knob (on candlestick)*/capital (of pillar)'; כרש ('be curved' cogn. כרס/קרס), 'belly'.

Meroitic kaf is a narrow-necked jar, suggesting liquids (virgo as manifested water): כבס, 'wash (as clothes)/fig. cleanse/purify, wash(er/fuller)'; כדד (= כתת 'beat/strike', A. 'hammer/toil, *draw out of well*') '*earthen jar/pitcher (esp. for drawing water, also for keeping meal)*, spark, -

ling/flashing gem (ruby)' (A. כיד 'strike fire'); כוו (prob. = נקב/קבב 'hollow out'), Ch. 'window'; כוס, 'cup, pelican, bag/purse' (from כנס 'collect' (Gesen.) or כסה 'cover' > 'hide/preserve'); כּוּר, 'dig/pierce, executioner (stabber)/sheriff, *(smelting) furnace [smoking - (pl.)]*, *pot/jar* (dual, so prob. of two compartments), *fire pan/(wash-)basin(/laver)*, *chafing dish*, pulpit, nativity/place of origin, sword'; and כרה, '*dig/*(undermine?)/fig. open (ears), *buy/purchase*, *give a feast, -/banquet*, pit, *well/cistern*'; plus perhaps כבה, '(be) extinguish(ed)/quench'.

The Meroitic hieroglyph can also be seen as a manacle, hence: כבל (prob. = ג\חבל in kindred dialects 'twist/bind together'), '*fetter* [district]'; כלא, '(be) shut up/confine/restrain(ed), prison/separation, pen/sheepfold'; כפת, Ch. 'bind/fetter', virgo being form or cohesion.

Continuing what curves around one: כרבל, 'girded/clothed, Ch. mantle/cloak'; and כרך > '*robe* [כרכמיש fortress of Camosh]' (Syr./Ch. '*surround/wrap around*'), as in *coll*'s own trump, VIIII The Hermit. And note that earlier, in the context of food offerings, we had 'saffron', the color of robe worn by Buddhist monks. Another early name for this trump was Old Man: כלח, 'old age/full age [(a city)]'; כשל, '*totter/stagger, feeble/weary, (cause to) stumble/fall/*fig. seduce, axe, fall/ruin, stumbling block/cause of offence'. Then of course there is the opposite of this: כרב, 'Cherub', an order of angelic beings said to be attendant on God, represented in ancient Middle Eastern art as a lion or bull with eagles' wings and human face but said by rabbinic folk etymology to be from Aramaic *ke-rabya*, 'like a child', hence now represented as innocent little tykes with wings.

Akin to *palm of the hand* is the meaning 'to cover' (as in כפה and כוס above): כחד, '*keep back/(be)conceal(ed)/hide/*destroy/bring to naught'; כנף, 'wing of bird (fig. swiftness)/of army, extremity/corner (as of earth), skirt (of loose flowing upper garment)/pinnacle?, *be removed to a distant part* or *be hid/hide oneself* (coll. w/A.)'—that last being indeed rather hermit-like—כסה, '(be) cover(ed)/conceal/hide, put on/cover oneself, covering/garment'; כפר, '*cover/overlay* (w/pitch), *cover over* (sin i.e. forgive)/pardon, expiate/appease/pacify/avert, be abolished, be expiated, village/hamlet, *cup/bowl*, hoar frost, young lion, henna, ransom, atonement (the *Kippur* in Yom Kippur), *covering of Ark* (בית הכפרת = Holy of Holies, where Ark of Covenant was kept)'; כפש, 'cover over'; כשה, '*covered* w/fatness'; כתם, '*shut up/hide* (cogn. חטמ/חסמ/חתמ) *or* (according to Syr.) spotted/stained (Jer. 2:22), fine gold, -en poem'; כתן ('*cover/hide*', cogn. כתם), 'undergarment/shirt'. All but the first of these invoke the top of the round (soft peh/feh sofit, samekh, shin/sin, mem sofit, nun/nun sofit).

A root touching on these last two groups and introducing the next: כסא (= כסה 'cover'), 'new moon (from A. כשה cover w/ brightness?), seat (of high priest/judge)/(royal) throne'. For, being the Cauldron's manifested water, it is the double best suited to represent the moon, which its shape resembles and its bardic number, *nine*, invokes: כהה, 'become weak/languid/faint, dull/dim (of eyes), become/make timid, admonish, weak(ening/relaxation/mitigation)/faint (of mind)/pale (of spots of leprosy)'; כסף, prop. as in Ch. '*be pale/wan*, hence desire greatly/long after, *silver*, -/money, be ashamed'; כרפס, 'fine *white* cotton cloth/linen'. Plus the twins כבש (by transposition כשב = כסף '*be white*'), '(ewe-)lamb'; and כשב, '(ewe-)lamb'. To which I shall add: כרר, 'leap/dance, *fatted lamb* (from its leaping), *lamb's pasture*, battering *ram*, a cor (measure of capacity containing ten baths), *circuit/circumjacent tract, cake/round loaf*, dromedaries (from their agility and swiftness) > כר הגמל camel's saddle (the haudaj or portable chamber in which Eastern women ride)' (touching also on *enclosing* and *open mouth*). And let us not forget to include her consort, the sun: כּורשׁ/כרשׁ ['sun' (Cyrus, k. of Persia)].

And *inner* paleness: כאב, 'be (in) pain(ed)/fig. grieved, cause pain/sadness, mar/destroy, pain/fig. grief/sorrow'; כאה, 'cause to despond/be dejected/faint-hearted, desponding/dejected'; כבד\כ, 'be heavy/weighty/honored/respected/mighty/abounding/*grievous/burdensome/dull (of senses/mind)*, be/become vehement/violent/great/renowned/glorious, (be) honor(ed), make heavy/grievous/obdurate/harden (the heart), multiply/become numerous, -/abounding/heavy, *grievous/sore/difficult/arduous/slow (of speech)*/the liver, abundance/wealth, heart/mind/soul, honor/glory/splendor/majesty, vehemence/violence, abundance/multitude, heaviness/difficulty, weight'; כדר, 'tumult/warlike tumult' (A. '*be agitated/troubled*'); כוּשׁ, 'Cushite/Ethiopian [*terror (Cush)]*'; כלם, '(be) put to shame/make (feel) ashamed/injure/hurt, shame/ignominy'; כמה, 'long[-ing] for/desire ardently'; כעס, '(be) vex(ed)/irritate(d)/provoke(d/ angry), vexation/grief/sadness, (excitements to) anger'; כפן, 'languish/be languid, hunger (n.)'; כרא, Ch. 'be pained/grieve'; and perhaps כזר, 'bold/daring, cruel/fierce/*deadly (of poison)*' (Syr. 'be valiant/daring'). Four of these involve alef, beyt, or (in one case) both, which are linked to whiteness (inception, a clean slate), alef through *Alphito*, a female bugabear whose name comes from *alphita*, 'white flour', and beyt through birch's white bark.

Three or four of the roots show bleeding over from Q's (Kk's) meaning 'to cut'—could this possibly be related to the nut harvest?—namely: כלף (prob. 'strike'), 'hammers/*axes*'; כסח, 'to cut off'; כרת, '*(be) cut/- off/down(/divided/separated)*/destroy(ed), perish/fail, hewn beams *[cutting (a brook)] separation/divorce* [(portion of Philistines/members of David's bodyguard therefrom) executioners]'; and perhaps כוב ['*thorn*/paliurus' (pl.) (Syr.)].

Sign virgo precedes libra, the present instant: כהן, 'prepare/make ready/adjust/adorn, minister/act/officiate as priest, - (n.), -hood'; כּוּן, 'to stand, set up/fix/confirm/establish, prepare, fashion/form, adjust/direct/aim, strengthen, constitute/appoint, make/be ready [stability (pl.)], be suitable/becoming, (up-)right/true/honest, rightly/well, so/thus, surely/certainly/truly, small cakes (Ch. prepare), but/yet [he shall establish (Jachin)] base/stand (n.), place/habitation, arrangement, foundation/basis, seat' (A. 'exist'); כי (particle) 'which' (rel. pron., Gesen.), rel. conj. '*that, for/because*, (nay) but/yet/nevertheless, *(of time) if/when/so/then*, (כִּי אם but/for/that if/since, unless/except/if not/yet/nevertheless/that)'; כען, 'now (עד כען until now)'; and כלל, '*complete*, Ch. -/(be) finish(ed) [perfection] the whole/- burnt offering, all/every, of all kinds/sorts/altogether*, anything, *complete/perfect, wholly/entirely, bridal state, daughter-in-law, bride/spouse*, splendid things (costly garments)'. For libra is where all four Wheels meet: כפס, 'rafter/crossbeam' (Syr. '*connect/join*'). And it is at the bottom or base: כנן (prob. = כּוּן), '*place/station, base/pedestal (of base or foot of laver)*, lice/gnats, plant?/*stock/root*? [protector]' (A. 'protect'). (Four of these use nun, the sign opposite kaf.)

As what immediately precedes the physical, kaf means *form*—כ, 'as/so', כה, 'so/thus, (of pl.) here/hither, (of time) now, Ch. hitherto/thus far'; ככה, 'thus'. And form implies bounds:

כרכב, *margin/border/ledge (going round inside altar)*'; כשר, 'be right/proper/acceptable, (give) success/prosperity, distaff (n.)'; כתל, 'wall'; כתף, 'shoulder/fig. side (of edifice/sea/city/region), sides/jambs of doors/gates, shoulders (of axle)'; and כתר, *surround/encompass (/in hostile manner), be crowned w/. diadem/crown, capital/chapiter (of column)*'. (Three of these involve reysh and three involve tav; the latter, of course, invokes the *bounds* of conscience.) Regarding both *bounds* (an end) and *to cut*: כיד, 'ruin/destruction, spear/javelin'.

And because old Hebrew kaf looks so much like a make-up brush: כחל, 'blacken/paint (eyes w/ stibium, a kind of powder)'.

I am left with: כרמיל, 'crimson', though red *is* indeed the color associated with summer.

SUMMARY

Kaf, hazel nut: 'round knob', 'shave [*head*]'. **Tifinag** [*cairn marks point on horizon*]: 'rock', 'Chaldeans, astrologers' ['practice magic'], 'heap up, Pleiades'. **To concentrate:** *2* 'lay up, treasure', 'wealth, vigor' ['be great, multiply, abundance, sieve, lattice, coarse cloth, twist']. *Basket* [*bowl-shaped*]**:** 'plait, braid, fruit basket', 'pitcher [*for water or meal*]', 'bruise, pound, mortar', 'beat, break in pieces, beaten oil [*from olives beaten in mortar*]'. **Manifested water:** 'wash'. **Form as containment:** *2* '(jar, wash-basin, fire pan, smelting furnace, sword, pierce) dig (purchase, well, pit)', 'hollow out', 'measure, contain, sustain', *3* 'collect (cup, pelican)', 'connect, join', 'pen, confine, prison', *3* 'bind (-around) (-together)', 'surround, robe', 'girded, clothed, mantle, cloak'. **VIIII Hermit:** *3* '(hide, undergarment, shirt) (garment, covering, conceal) cover (extinguish, bend or avert*?*) ', *2* '(keep back, conceal, destroy) hide (shut up)'. **Old Semitic shape** [*paint brush?*]**:** *2* 'cover over (henna [*used to paint eyebrows, nails*])', 'paint eyelids blue'. **Form as thought's design:** 'write, engrave', 'proclaim, herald', 'number, reckon, compute', 'be proper, success', 'be able, can', *2* '(priest) prepare (direct, true, thus, stand)', 'protect, root, base, pedestal [*of laver*]', *2* '(deceive) lie (flatter)', 'call by name or by flattering titles, thus, in this manner', 'as, like, nearly', '[*rel. conj.*], if, when', *2* 'thus (now, here)'. **Approaching down or libra:** [*as present:*] 'now, so forth'; [*as M-vine:*] 'vineyard, orchard, garden, Carmel'; [*as r-mouth and t-loaf—K as taste:*] 'cummin', 'saffron', 'devour', *2* [*by metathesis*] 'lamb', 'fatted lamb, leap, circuit, round loaf', 'be foolish, fat, firm, Kislev [*9th month*]'. **Sign of 9th Sefirah** [*Divine Throne*]**:** 'be heavy, dull, weighty, honored, majesty [*Kavod*], abundance, heart, mind, soul', *2* '(new moon) seat, throne (be curved)'. **Square-Hebrew:** 'be curved {sun [*Cyrus*]} belly' [*kaf is kidneys*], 'roll up', 'double, double over, fold', 'languish, bend, incline, hunger', *3* '((kneal) bend (hollow, palm of hand)) bow down (bundle [*i.e. fold together*], Canaanite, subdue)'. **Feeling-mind:** 'subdue, trample, disregard', 'cause to despond', 'shame, ignominy', *2* '(cause sadness) be pained (grieved)', 'tumult, be troubled', 'be vexed, provoke', 'bold, cruel', 'become or make timid, faint [*of mind*]' {'terror [*Kush*]'} 'long for, pine'. **Kaf as moon (C):** 'be pale, wan, long for, silver', 'fine white linen'. **Form as limit:** 'margin, border', 'shoulder, side, door jams', 'wall', 'extremity', 'full age', 'totter, cause to fall, axe', 2 'to cut off', 'to complete', 'be completed, ended, pining, vessel, utensil, boat, skiff' [*cf. runic name 'skiff'*], 'calamity, spark'. **Runic name 'torch':** 2 'be burned', 'be extinguished'. **Virgo symbol:** 'harp, lyre'. **Unparsed:** 'cherub', 'eagle [*collated with Pers.*]'.

ר

Reysh

PARSED ROOTS

The hieroglyph whose hieratic form spawned reysh was ***mouth***, which shared libra with ***loaf*** (teyt) and represented Upper Egypt, *consumers* of Lower Egypt's loaf, which suggests a bit of satirizing of Egypt's hungry mouths: רוה, 'be/become satiated w/ drink/w/ fat/fig. w/ unlawful love/be filled/soaked, -/well-watered (gardens), to water, satiate (w/fatness)/fig. satisfy/delight, abundance/plenty of drink, a watering/irrigation' (Syr. 'be drunken'); רון, 'be overcome (of wine)' (A. 'conquer'); רור, 'flow/emit, saliva/spittle/slaver, slime of yoke/white of egg/whey?'; רחב, 'be/become/make wide/large/broad/spacious, extended, *puffed up/proud/arrogant*, make room for/*open wide (mouth*/fig. heart, for instruction), wide open pl./street/square/marketplace, wide pl./fig. freedom/deliverance [enlargement of the people (Solomon's s.-and-successor)]'; רעב, 'be hungry, suffer famine/famish, (w/ ל) hunger after, (cause to) hunger/famine, hungry'. And of course a mouth is still a mouth: רוז, Ch. 'secret' (Syr. רזז/רזו 'hide/keep secret'); רזח, 'outcry (for joy/sorrow)' (A. 'raise voice'); רנן, 'shout for joy/hence sing, call out (invitation), cry out (for help)/wail [rushing/roaring (a river)] rejoice, celebrate/praise'.

Pivoting off the rolled Hebrew (guttural) R is the growl, a vibration or oscillation: רגז, *'(make) tremble/shake/be moved/agitated* (w/anger/grief)/excite (to anger)/*agitate*, Ch. anger, *trembling*/disquiet/perturbation/trouble/*a raging (thunder/horse)*/fury, box/chest/coffer (hanging from side of wagon)'; רגן, 'murmur/rebel'; רגע (cogn. רעש\רעשג\ע\ו), *'be in a commotion/make noise (sea)*, moment/prop. *twinkling* (of eye), in moment/suddenly, *every moment/repeatedly*, *tremble*/shrink?' (Ethiop. 'contract/curdle'); רגש, *'rage/make noise/tumult*, Ch. run together in tumult, bustling crowd/multitude'—it is easy to see in these four how gimel reinforces reysh in this—1. רוף, 'be agitated/shaken'; רחף, *'shake/tremble, flutter*, hover/brood'; רחש, 'boil up/throw up (as fountain), pot/kettle'—in these two, cheyt does the same—רטט, *'trembling*/fear' (Syr./Ch. *'tremble*/be terrified'); רנה, 'rattle'; רעד, *'tremble/quake, shaking*/awe'; רעל, *'be shaken/tremble*, a reeling (from intoxication), veils (prob. *from tremulous motion) [a trembling/quaking]*'; רעם, *'rage/roar (sea)/tremble/quake, to thunder*/irritate/vex, *a trembling/shivering* (fig. for mane of horse), *tumult*/rage/*thunder*'; רעש, 'be moved */tremble/quake* (earth)/*shake*, -/terrify/cause to leap, *earthquake*/tumult/*rattling*/rustling'—and in these four, ayin's closeness to gimel (the phoneticists will know what I mean) gives it a similar effect—רתח, 'make boil, boil/fig. be agitated, a boiling'—cheyt again—רתת (= רטט), *'trembling*/terror'—a *double* dose of conscience (showing the closeness of tav and teyt); and perhaps רהה (spurious root) 'to fear?'.

Reysh represents the body-mind, just as Egypt (**mouth** and **loaf**) represents the sensory realm in *Hymn of the Pearl*. In human beings, the body-mind has 'taken over': ראם, '*be high, oryx?/buffalo? [high] -/sublime things [height of the south (pl.)]*'; ראשׁ, '*head, -/leader/chief, - city/top/summit (of mtn./column), first/chief/principle, head/first/foremost/beginning, firstling,* amount/sum, *body*/band/company, poison(ous plant/hemlock?/poppy?)'; 1. רבב, 'be/become many/numerous, much/many, great/vast, *mighty/powerful*, elder/aged, *chief/captain/leader/*hence *master (of an art)*, greatness, Ch. *chief/head/prince* [metropolis] multitude/abundance, myriad [increase (d. of Saul)]'; רבה, 'multiply/*be/become* many/numerous/*great/-er/*grow up/*be mighty*, increase/bring up/enlarge, Ch. *grow/make great/exalt*, sp. of locust, abundance, amplitude, the greater part/multitude/greatness/increase/*offspring*, interest/usury, *progeny*'—presaging reysh as gonads (see below)—רהב, '*act insolently*, urge/press upon, *insolent/proud, insolence/pride/fig. Egypt*, embolden/*overcome*'—five invoking inception (first-ness) with either alef or beyt—רום, '*be high/lofty, rise*/be lifted up/grow (of worms)/*be exalted (in power/rank)/elated (w/ pride), tall/loud (of voice, i.e. raised)/*fig. *mighty*, Ch. *rise up against*, raise (bldg.)/erect/make grow (plant)/*bring up (children)/*fig. exalt/extol, height/elevation, *a lifting up (of* eyes/*heart i.e. pride/haughtiness)* [lofty (pl.)] praise, high pl. [height] *heap/pile*, offering/gift, (heave-)offering (sacrifice offered by elevating)'; רזן, 'chief/prince' (A. 'be weighty'); רמם (= רום '*be high/lofty*'), '*rise/lift oneself up*, pomegranate/- tree, worm(s)' (A. 'to rot'); רעה, 'feed/pasture (flock)/fig. lead/rule,* part. shepherd(ess)/herdsman, feed/nourish/graze, consume/devastate/feed on (i.e. delight in), associate w/treat as friend/make companion of/*hold intercourse w/*, neighbor/fellow [social] companion/friend, *beloved/lover*, desire/pursuit/striving, thought/will, Ch. -/wish, pastoral, a pasturing/feeding/flock' (Ch. 'to will', Syr. רעא '*think*'); as well as רשׁה, 'grant permission/*authorize' (Ch. רשׁא 'be able/have permission'). Oh, and: רכב (prob. = ברך 'bend'), Ch. 'knee'.

In humans, the sensory lords it over feeling and desire, as portrayed in R's trump, XV The Devil: רבק ['*binding*, i.e. engaging/captivating (Rebecca)] stall (in which cattle are *tied* for fattening)' (A. 'tie/fasten (esp. animals)'); רוע, 'make loud noise, *become evil*/be made worse, suffer evil/injury, cry aloud/shout (in joy/alarm), sound (trumpet/alarm), noise/outcry (of thunder?)'; ריב, 'contend/strive/quarrel, *adversary*, plead/defend cause/decide it favorably'; רכך, 'be tender (of heart)/hence timid/faint/soft (of words) , effeminate/soft/gentle (of words), *tender/young/delicate*, weak/sore (of eyes)faint (of heart), timidity/cowardice'—this last root referring to that 'little devil' that has new parents bound to its endless needs—רכס, '*bind on/to*, difficult/rugged places, conspiracy/plot'; רסן, '*bridle/halter*, inner part of mouth/jaws' (A. רשׁן 'bind'); רעע, 'break/- in pieces, be sad/sorrowful, *make/do evil*, (= רוע) make loud noise/*be evil*/hurtful (of eyes)/envious/*malignant* (countenance/heart), be broken in pieces/destroyed, *evil/bad/wicked*, -ness, worthless/noxious, hurtful/ill-favored/calamitous/sad, harm/calamity'; רעץ, 'break/crush/fig. *oppress*'; רצץ, 'break/bruise/crush/fig. treat w/ violence/*oppress*(ion), be broken/bruised, *struggle together*, fragment/piece'; רשׁע, 'be(/act) wicked(/ly/unjustly/impiously), be guilty/have unjust cause, injustice/fault/guilt, declare/condemn, *impious*/punishable, *cause mischief*/disquiet, *wicked(ness)/ungodly(-iness)*' (Syr. רתע 'be restless/disturb'); רתק, 'be bound, chain(s)'; רתם, '*bind/yoke/harness*, broom?/juniper?'. (I count five here that use sibilents, all at or near the top of the round; and four use ayin, which *takes over* the top of the round.)

The month of *ruis* the elder was the thirteenth and last month of the tree-calendar, hence the death of the Spirit of the Year. In both Tifinag and the Numidian that branched off from it, R was an empty circle, while the B that starts the year in Numidian, and the S that marks the sun's appearance in Nordic Tifinag, are a circle with a dot in the middle, the *empty* circle being the old, worn-out year: רוק, '*to empty (vessel/sack)/(be) pour(ed) out*, draw out (sword/spear), lead out (troops), (in) vain, impoverished/poor/worthless/wicked, *empty-handed*, without cause'; רזה, '(attenuate/cause to) waste away/become lean/barren of land, a wasting/consumption/diminution, destruction/woe'; רחה/רח (root uncertain) 'hand-mill, (only dual) pair of millstones'; רטה (= A. רטא 'throw'?) 'give over' (or < H. ירט 'cast down'); רפק, 'support oneself/lean'; רקב, 'rot/decay, rottenness'; and 1. רקק, 'thin/lean/(adv.) only/alone/surely/certainly/save/except, temple (of head)/fig. cheek [thinness (pl.)] thin cake' (A. 'be thin'). (Four of these involve qof, but I fail to see a connection.) One root reminds us that R's proper place is straight down (libra): רפה, 'hang down (hands)/become relaxed/feeble, let down (wings), decline (of day), sink down (of straw in fire), relax/abate/desist (from someone/something), be remiss/idle/lazy, slacken (hand)/desist (from smiting), relax/loosen/weaken, let alone, leave off/cease, give up/forsake, let go/dismiss, relax/be slothful [n. of ancestor of giants]'.

Before we move on from *ruis*, two things. First, it is clear the death of the Spirit of the Year occurs in the month of sagittary the archer: 2. רבב, '(shoot) arrow(s)'; רטש, 'dash in pieces (against a rock), strike to the ground (w/ arrows)'; רמה, 'cast/throw/shoot (w/ bow), deceive (prop. make fall), Ch. set/place/impose (tribute) [(whom) the Lord sets/appoints (Jeremiah)] slackness/remissness, deceit/fraud/craft'; רצח, 'kill/slay/part. manslayer, dash in pieces/(be a)murder(er), a crushing/a killing/slaughter'; רשף, 'flame?/burning coal?, *lightnings/sparks (of bow, i.e. arrows)*, burning disease'; רשש (cogn. רצץ), '*break in pieces/destroy* [Tarshish] precious stone therefrom (chrysolite?/amber?/*beryl?)'. Four of these involve sibilants (tzaddi or shin).

Second, elder is a medicinal tree (to treat the ailing Spirit of the Year, or ailing humans as winter closes in): 2. רוף (perh. = רפא 'heal'), 'bruised corn/grits, medicine/healing/cure' (cogn. A. רפת 'bruise/pound/Eng. *rub*'); רחץ, 'trust in (someone)'; רפא, 'heal/cure/physician/fig. restore (to prosperity/spiritual also), pardon/console, be repaired/healed/cured/(of waters) be made wholesome, the quiet/languid/fig. the dead (= רפה), medicines [healed] health, cure/remedy/fig. refreshment/recreation/relief (from calamity), calmness/tranquility'; רקח, 'compound/prepare ointment/part. perfumer/apothecary, spice, aromatic herbs'. Three of these involve soft peh: could this be a residue of the Corn Spirit heresy?

Being thirteenth, it has no sign: it is a return to the center to replenish the central dot. Once there, gravity beckons it back to its proper station, libra, the manifested sign of the water triad: רבך, 'mixed/saturated' (A. 'mix'); רהט, 'watering troughs, locks/curls' (Syr. 'run/flow'); רחץ, 'wash (body/flesh)/- away'; רטפש, 'grow moist/fresh/revive'; רסס, 'moisten/sprinkle (in derivv. = רצץ break in pieces), dewdrops, fractures [ruins (pl.)]'; רעף, '(let) drop/distil'; רפסדות, 'floats/rafts' (etym. uncert.); 2. רקק, 'to spit, spittle'. A couple of these point to libra also with teyt; and the two that could relate also to the previous group (healing) have, again, the soft peh.

In the spirit of the second root above—Syr. 'run/flow'—note two things. One, the old Hebrew R was a stick horse, the rune shaped like the animal mask a shaman dons for his or her *journey* (runic name 'ride'). And two, elder was the wood used for Irish witches' magic *horses*. Hence these: רדף, 'follow after/(be) pursue(d)/persecute/put to flight/chase(d/driven away)'; רוד, 'wander/rove, walk/go about (of one in affliction) [a wandering (pl.)] -/erring about, Rhodians' (I suspect from them being wanderers?); רוח, '(prop. be airy/)spacious/wide, relief/enlargement, space/*distance*'; and cogn. רוח, 'smell/fig. -/touch (fire), *scent/perceive (as a horse battle)*, w/ב delight in, air/breeze, breath (fig. vanity/folly), mind/spirit(/soul)/disposition, wind/tempest, side/quarter (of heavens), anger/wrath (from breathing/snuffing, odor/scent/smell, winnowing fan [pl. of fragrance (Jericho)]'; רוץ, 'rush/- for refuge/upon/assail, part. runners/couriers, run swiftly, cause to run/bring quickly/let make haste (hands in work/service), a race'; רחק, 'go far away/recede/be far off/distant/remote, (be) remove(d)/put far away, departing, remote/distant/far above (in value)'; and the source of the word *Merkavah*, רכב, 'ride (beast/chariot)/rider/horseman fig. God being borne on clouds, carry (in chariot), place/put/lay upon, cause to be ridden, (seat of) chariot/vehicle, horses, upper millstone'; רכל, 'go about (as trader), part. -/merchant [traffic (pl.)] trade, talebearing/slandering, market/mart'; רכש, 'sp. of swift horse' (Syr. א— 'horse, esp. stallion'); רמך, 'mare'—that makes four that use kaf, but the only obvious connection is that to *mount up* is similar to being *enthroned*—רפת, 'a stall (for cattle)'; רצא (= רוץ), 'to run'; and the traditional weapon of the horseman, רמח, 'lance/spear'.

Who takes the journey? a shaman, seer, or prophet: ראה, 'see/live (see sun)/seer/prophet, view/regard/observe/visit, look out/provide, choose/have in view, perceive/experience/discern, understand/discriminate, be seen/appear, (be) show(n), kite, seer/prophet/vision, -/revelation, sight/view/spectacle, mirror, -aspect/appearance [behold, a son (Reuben)]'; רמליהו ['(whom) the Lord has adorned' (coll. w/ A.)]; רעמסס ['son of the sun (pl. in Goshen)']; רצד, 'observe/watch narrowly' (A. ditto); רצע, 'pierce/bore through, an awl'; רקד, '(cause to) leap/skip/dance, fig. jolting (of chariot)'; רקם, 'embroider/weave w/ varicolored threads, be curiously wrought/woven [variegated] – work/embroidery'; רשם, 'write down/record', the last few being only *tenuously* connected (shamans *dance*, wear *varicolored* clothing, and we *write down* what prophets say).

And reysh is magical: its bardic number makes it phosphorus, mainstay of chromosomes, quite fitting for the letter whose Hebrew shape is the male erection and the duct that brings it the seed: רבד, 'spread/strew/make up a bed, coverlets, collar/neck-chain' (A. 'bind'); רבל ['fertility' (pl.)] (A. 'be much/fertile/abundant'); 1. רבע, 'lie w/ (carnally), copulate, a lying down'—three that involve beyt or inception—רזם, 'wink (w/ eyes)/*beckon' (= Aram. רמז); רחל, 'ewe/sheep [Rachel]'—whose story pivots on offspring and the lack thereof—רחם, '*love/- tenderly*, have compassion/mercy upon/pity, obtain mercy, the aquiline (small sp. of) vulture, *womb/maiden*, intestines, tender affection/*love*, pity/mercy'; רפד, 'strew/spread, - bed/stay/refresh, support (prob. sides and back of portable couch) [couches]'; and רצה, 'delight/take pleasure in/be well pleased w/accept/associate w/, satisfy/discharge/be paid off/conciliate/make oneself pleasing [delight] will/pleasure/hence wantonness/good-will/favor/grace, benefits [beloved]'.

There is but one category to go (probably the largest), roots telling us libra is manifested earth, where the water triad manifests as the solid dregs on the bottom (throwing cold water on cowboy coffee in a pan to get the grounds to settle): 2. רבע, 'four-sided/-square, four (mostly cardinal) [Arba (n. of a giant)] posterity in the fourth generation'; רבץ, 'lie down (for repose, beasts/fig. men/waters/a curse), to set (precious stones), couching place (for man or beast)'; רגב (cogn. רגם 'heap together'), 'clod of earth [heap of stones]'; רגל, 'foot/track (man/beast), (water) of the feet (i.e. urine), step/pace, go about slandering, explore/spy out/a spy/teach to walk/lead by hand (child), at one's feet, footman/footsoldier [fuller]'—lamedh, of course, pictures learning to walk, seen from above—רגם, 'stone to death, crowd/throng/band [friend] heap of stones'; רגע, '(give/restore/cause to) rest/be quiet, dwell quietly, still/quiet (adj.)'—four that involve gimel yet with no hint of either *growling* or *trembling*, though the letter following is in each case a rather calming one, hence perhaps the meaning is the *alleviation* of disquiet or trembling, albeit not in the third case a particularly *desirable* one—רדד, '(prop. spread out) prostrate/subdue, overlay w/ metal, a wide mantle [subduing]'; רדה, 'tread (winepress)/- upon (w/ ב), subdue/rule over, tread underfoot/break/subdue, cause to rule'; רדם, 'lie in deep sleep/sink down stupefied/senseless, deep sleep, sluggishness/inactivity'—three with dalet in second place, to convey the meaning *spread* or *compass*, plus *dominion*—רמס, 'tread (w/ feet, as potter clay)/- upon (w/ על)/trample underfoot/oppressor, be/something trodden down'; רמש, 'creep (of reptiles)/move (of any living creature), reptile(s), any land animal'; רפס\ש, 'tread/trample upon (esp. water, troubled/made turbid), humble/submit oneself, Ch. trample down/stamp upon'; רפש, 'mud/mire'; רצף, 'range stones artificially (pavement/inlay)/checker(ed/tessellated), - pavement, hot stone/coals'—five involving labial plus sibilant, the reason for which evades my perspicacity—and רקע, 'stamp w/ feet/tread down, stretch/spread out/expand, beat into thin plates/cover w/ same, the expanse (Vulg. firmamentum)'.

Earth's suit is Money (Coins/cycles): רכש, 'get/gain/acquire, substance/property/wealth'; and רפה ['riches']. And its opposite: רוש, 'be(feign oneself) poor/in want, poor/needy, poverty'.

I think the only leftover is ראש ['n. of northern nation, supposed to be Russians']. But to the best of my knowledge, the *Rus* came *many* centuries later (during the Viking Age).

SUMMARY

Reysh as gonads [*semen's path, in square-Hebrew*]**, bottom of round:** 'strew, spread, make up [*bed*], stay, refresh', 'lie with, copulate', 'delight or take pleasure in, satisfy, discharge, object of delight', 'to love, womb, maiden', 'ewe [*Rachel*]', 'run, flow, watering trough, locks, curls'. **Pivot of water triad:** 'wash', 'drop, distil', 'moist, fresh, be wet', 'revive, grow moist', 'moisten, sprinkle, break in pieces, dewdrops, fractures', '(throw up [*as fountain*], kettle) boil (be agitated)'. **"Rrr"** [*growl*]**:** 'to rattle', 8 'tremble, shake (be agitated (rage)) (make noise [*sea*]) (fear) (awe)', 'murmur, rebel', 2 '(make noise, tumult) rage (roar, tumult, a trembling [*poetic for horse's mane*])', 2 '(raise voice) outcry (make loud noise, become evil)'. **XV LeDiable:** 'be wicked, act unjustly, impiously', 'act insolently, embolden, pride', 'be insolent, Egypt', 'flame? burning coal? lightning, burning disease', 'bind to, conspiracy' ['keep secret'], 'wink? be fixed or fastened?', 3 '(a chain) bind (yoke, harness) (halter, bridle, jaws)'. **Rune's name** ['ride'], **old Semitic shape** [stick-horse]: 2 '(fasten) a stall', 'mare', 'swift horse', 'pursue, chase', 'ride [on animal or chariot], chariot [merkavah], seat thereof, cavalry', 'lance', 'smell, delight in, scent [as a horse the battle], air, breath, spirit [ruach]', 'couriers, to run'. **Rune's shape** [shamanic 'seeing']: 2 '(dance) leap (watch stealthily)', 'see, seer, prophet, vision, revelation', 'pierce, bore through, awl' ['embroider'] {'whom the Lord has adorned'} 'be able, permission'. **Body-mind, usurper-demiurge:** 'move, creep', 'foot, pace, teach to walk [RGL]', 'walk, wander', 'traffic, trade, slander', 'acquire, property', 'be or become many or great [grow up]', 3 '(oryx [Sept. unicorn]) be high ((lift up, haughty) rise (pomegranate, worms, rot))', 2 '(head, summit, beginning) chief (prince, be weighty)', 'conquer, be overcome [of wine]'. **Mouth** [as in south Semitic also]: 'be satiated with drink, to satiate', 'be hungry', 'feed, rule, graze, feed upon [i.e. delight, take pleasure in], female companion', 'shout, rejoice', 'contend, plead a cause, strife', 2 '(flow, emit, saliva) spittle'. **Manifested earth** [libra], **fertility** [cf. gonads, above]: 2 '(open wide [as mouth]) wide, spacious (distance)', 'be distant', 'tread down, spread out, beat into thin plates, the expanse [Vulg. firmamentum]', 'tread [winepress], subdue', 2 '(troubled [esp. water], humble oneself) tread upon (tread [e.g. as potter with clay], -under, oppressor)', 'range stones artificially [pave, inlay], hot stones or coals, tesselated pavement', 'clod, heap together', 'mud, mire', 'be muck, fertile, abundant', 'be verdant'; 'four, -sided'. **R-elder** [medicinal]: 'to trust in [someone]', 'heal, cure, physician, restore, the feeble or languid [dead]', 'compound or prepare [ointment], ointment', 'mix', 'bruise, pound, bruised corn, grits, medicine, a cure'. **Tifinag and Libyan** [an empty, burnt-out round], **final month:** 'a hand-mill', 'bruise, break, crush, oppress', 2 '(be evil, calamitous) break in pieces (destroy)', 'pour out, empty, vain, worthless, wicked, poor', 'be poor', 2 '(thin) lean (make to waste away, barren)' , 'be tender, faint, weak, contrite', 'to lean, support oneself', 'relax, become feeble, abate, desist, cease', 'cause to waste away, consumption, diminution', 'rot, decay', 'lie down', 'rest, be quiet' [inverse of **"Rrr"**], 'lie in deep sleep, sink down stupefied or senseless', 'cast, throw, shoot [with bow], deceive, slackness, remissness [properly let fall of the hands]', 'arrow, shoot arrows', 2 '(slay) dash in pieces (strike to the ground [with arrows])', 'stone to death, a crowd, heap of stones'; 'write down or record'.

ג

Gimel

PARSED ROOTS

Hebrew identifies gimel's tarot trump (X The Wheel of Fortune): גדד, 'prop. *cut* hence press upon (w/ על), cut oneself/make incisions, press/crowd together, Ch. '*cut/hew down, good fortune [- - (Gad, tribe/s. of Jacob)]* coriander seed *[fortuna (idol)]* troop/detachment of army/a cutting/furrow [cleft/chink (pl. in desert)]'—for the meaning *cut*, see paragraph after next—גנז ('cover/collect' cogn. כנס), '*treasures*/perh. chests, Ch. *treasure, -y*'; and גרל > '*lot (prop. stone by which determined), -/portion/inheritance*' (A. 'be gritty/stony') . And then there are those who manage fortunes: גדבריא, Ch. 'treasurers'. And of course there is the wheel itself: גב (= כפף '*be curved*', יגב 'dig'), 'back, boss (of shield/buckler), defence/mound, vault, *rim/curvature (of wheel), arch of eyebrow [tax-gatherer] pit/den [hilly]*'; גוז, 'pass over'; גול/גיל, '*prop. move in circle*/hence exult/rejoice/perh. tremble, generation/age, *circle (n.)*, exultation/rejoicing'; גלל, '*roll (e.g. stones)/- along/away/be –ed together*, dung, Ch. heaviness/weight, idols [*circuit*/tract (Galilee)] *rolling/turning/ring*, region, waves/billows [boiling fountain] -/spring, cup/oil-bowl, -/globe (as ornament on top of columns), *heap (of stones)*, -/whirlwind/chaff, skull/head/poll, *wheel*, volume/roll/book', the root from which arose the later term for reincarnation (*gilgul*).

Old Hebrew gimel (a camel's hump) most resembles a pyramid partially buried in sand, hence the following: גאה, 'grow up/increase (plant/water), *be lifted/exalted/majestic, ascending, high/proud/haughty, majesty*, ornament/splendor, pride/arrogance'; גבה, 'be high/lofty, exalted, proud/arrogant, pride [elevation]'; גבח > 'bald(ness) in forehead(/threadbareness)' (Sam. '*be high*', A. '- of forehead'); גבן > 'cheese, hunchbacked, *heights/summits*' (Syr. 'coagulate/be condensed'); גבע (cogn. גבה\הב '*be high*'), '*hill* [-city] goblet/cup, -/bell (of flower, ornament of candlestick), *mitres/bonnets (of common priests, prob. conical)*' > (in my opinion) גבעל, 'in bud/in flower'—here it seems *gimel beyt* (four roots) signifies 'be high', presumably based on beyt's sacredness (two other *gimel beyt* roots mean 'gather together', another 'become strong', the one with two beyts from the previous paragraph can mean *mound, vault, arch of eyebrow*, or *curvature of wheel*, the second beyt thus implying rising up *again?* and the ninth and last means 'bound/limit')—גג, 'roof (of house), top (of altar)'; גדש > 'sepulchral mound, stack of corn' (Ch. 'heap up'); גור, '*sojourn/dwell (for a time, as a stranger)/-ing/residence, congregate/come together, stranger/foreigner*, lion's whelp/- of jackal *[He shall dwell there] granary/fear/terror, garners/storehouses*'; גמם, 'also, yea/truly, yet/nevertheless, troop/host?/desire/longing?' (A. '(be) heap(ed) up/increase'); and גשן ['n. of region in Egypt of Israel's bondage (Goshen)'].

I was surprised to find *to cut* almost as prevalent here as in qof, until I remembered that one of gimel's two runes was named **jēra*, 'year, harvest': גדה > 'banks of river, kid' (A. *'pluck out/off'*, Syr. 'leap'); גדע, 'cut off/down/break/- asunder/(be) in pieces [a cutting down] [cutter]'; גוב, 'plough, board/plank, well/cistern, locust' (A. 'cut/cleave'); גזה, 'cut/- off, hewn stones, quarry'; גזז, 'shear/cut off (hair/wool/etc.), fleece, young grass after mowing [barber]'; גזל, *'strip off, pluck/snatch away*, spoil/rob, young pigeon, rapine/plunder'; גזם > 'sp. of locust [devourer]' (A. 'cut/crop off'); גזע > 'stock/trunk (of tree)' (A. *'cut down'*); גזר, *'divide/cut off/down/in two parts*, decide/decree, Ch. soothsayers, *be cut off*/perish, form/figure (of man, separate pl. in temple), piece/part, separation/solitude, *axe'*—*six* built on gimel zayin! which are the middle two runes of the Elder Futhark, the middle *four* runes being a series in which each Hebrew/Greek number presages the next rune's bardic number—גלב > 'barber' (A. 'scrape/shave'); גלח, 'shave (head/beard)/fig. devastate'; גמדים, 'bold warriors [or n. of a people]' (A. *'cut off'*, Syr. 'be bold'); גרד, 'scrape oneself'; גרז, *'be cut off* [inhabitant of sterile land] *axe'* (zayin again); גרן, 'level pl.at gate of city/the Hebrew forum, threshing floor/fig. grain itself' (A. גרן 'make smooth/level'); גרס, '(be broken/)crush(ed), something crushed/bruised (perh. corn)'; גרע, *'take away (beard)*, draw off, detract/withhold, (be) diminish(ed)/detracted/lessened, narrowed rests/rebatements'—making five built on gimel reysh, I guess invoking the meaning *coming to an end* (R as year's end). And then there is the opposite: גדל, 'be/become great/exalted, *grow (hair/plant/child)/educate*, exalt/extol, lift up, show oneself great, fringes/interwoven chain-work, greatness/majesty/magnificence, pride [overgrown] tower/pulpit/*bed (in garden)*' (A./Syr. 'twist')—note that it ends in lamedh and includes the meaning 'to educate'.

As scorpio is the sign immediately following the physical, we get: גווה\ה (cogn. גבב\ה 'be rising/convex'), 'back, middle/midst, body/person, *corpse/carcass (human/animal)*, a people (prop. body of men)/fig. locusts/other creatures'; גוף, 'be hollow, to shut, *dead body/corpse*'; גפף (= גבב 'be bent/curved'), 'back/hillock, body/person/alone, Ch.wing, -s fig. armies/hosts; and גרם, 'bone, strength, substance/body/framework'. All four involve labials (at times doubled).

In the Cauldron, it is a return to the watery level: גבא > 'cistern, marsh/pool' (A. 'gather together'); גבש > 'crystal (prop. ice), hail [gathering]' (A. 'congeal', Ch. 'gather together'); גיא > 'valley/low plain' (A. גוה 'flow together'); גוח/גיח, 'break/burst forth (water/infant from womb) [a breaking forth (pl.)] bring/rush forth [stream (Gihom, one of the four rivers of Eden)]'; גמא, 'drink in/swallow, give to drink, reed/papyrus'; גמזו, 'sycamores'; גפר, 'tree of whose wood Noah's Ark was made, prob. pitch-pine' (= כפר 'cover over'); and גשם, 'cause to rain, -/heavy shower, Ch. body'. All again involve labials (one only in the Arabic, one only secondarily with waw).

This is *gort* the ivy, but vine-and-ivy (libra-scorpio) run together as the serpent power at the base of the spine and as the season of the Dionysian revels (linked both to ivy and to wine): גחן, 'belly (of any reptile)' (Syr./Ch. 'incline/bend'); גיד > 'sinew/nerve, perh. band' (A. 'bind'); גפן (= כפן/גבן 'be bent/curved'), 'vine'; גת, 'winepress, or rather vat in which grapes are trodden [Goliath's birthpl.] n. of mus. instr.' And given the crux of two of these: גהר, 'bow/bend down'.

Both because it is scorpio, and stimulated by the autumn revels, gamma in Gr. (and in

Numidian) is the male erection seen from the side, while in Berber Tifinag it is a vertical stroke with a pair of dots on either side of it at its base: גוד, 'press upon (cogn. גדד)'; גלד, 'skin'; גלה, 'make bare/open/uncover/disclose/reveal/open/plane, lead away captive, tablet/mirrors'; גלם, 'wrap together, mantle/cloak, embryo (prop. an unformed mass wrapped up together)'; גלמוד, 'sterile/barren, famished'; גשש, 'feel/grope'.

For this is the sign where we choose to climb the closed zodiac back to the head *or* follow the broken-and-extended zodiac down the legs to the feet: 2. גאל, '(be) pollute(d)/stain(ed)/soil, defile oneself'; גיש, 'clod'; גלעד ['hard/rough' (coll. w/ A.)]; גנב, 'steal/fig. carry away (as storm does chaff), deceive, be stolen/brought secretly, steal oneself away, thief, thing stolen [theft]'; גרב, 'scurf/scurvy'; גשפה ['flattery' (coll. w/ Syr.)]. Half of these are only loosely relevant.

Gimel's physiological station is the adrenals, seat of desire, and so: גבר, 'be/become strong/powerful/mighty, increase (of water), make strong/strengthen, confirm, show oneself strong, behave stoutly/insolently, man/husband/warrior, strong/mighty/valiant, hero/chief, valor/courage/mighty acts, master/lord, mistress/lady/queen [man of God (Gabriel)]'; גדף, 'reproach/revile, blaspheme'; גלע, 'grow warm/become angry/irritated'; געל, 'loathe/abhor, be cast away, cast (young, i.e. suffer abortion), a loathing [-]'; גער, 'rebuke/reprove, reproof/rebuke, -/curse'; געש, '(be) shake(n/moved/agitated)/tremble [quaking (pl.)] stagger/reel'; גרה, '(produce grating sound?), excite/stir up (strife), excite oneself esp. to contention/war, strife/contention, throat'. Four of these involve ayin (representing the volatility of mercury).

Gimel's two runes are *jēra*, 'harvest', and *gebō*, 'gift'. They are the two modes of G, desire: the desire to give, and the desire to have (on which the desire to give depends). The rune of the more Christlike of the two choresponds in shape to Greek chi, the initial of Christ: 1. גאל, '*redeem(er)/(be) ransom(ed)/recover (by paying back value for)*, avenge/-er (nearest kinsman, to whom went right of redemption or duty of avenging), *(duty/right/price of) redemption*/purchase, *thing redeemed*, relationship'; גהה, 'heal/cure, healing/cure (n.)'; גלש (prob. = שלג 'be white') hence 'shine/Eng. version appear'; גמל, 'retribute/recompense (good/evil), do/show (good/evil, to anyone), mature/ripen (fruit), wean, camel [- owner] benefit/kindness'; גשור ['bridge (pl.)'].

As the doer's sign, the hieroglyph whose hieratic form spawned gimel is ***alchemical oven*** (which Gardiner, erroneously in my opinion, calls 'stand w/ jar'), hence these roots: גבל, '(set) bound(ary)/limit [mtn. (coll. w/ A.)] bound/limit/border/limited space/territory/margin/edge, a bordering/edging'; גדר, 'wall/fence up, -ed place [folds]'; גוני ['colored (Ch. גון to color/dye)']; גחל '(burning) coal/fig. lightning' (A. 'burn'); גיר, 'burnt limestone/Ch. plaster of lime'; גמץ > 'pit' (Ch. 'dig'); גמר, 'complete/bring to end, come to end/fail, Ch. part. perfect/skilled'; גנן, '*prop. cover/hence protect, garden [-er]* shield/fig. prince, veiling/covering of the heart (w/ לב)'; גפרית, 'brimstone/sulfur'. These form a rather subtly (if loosely) coherent bunch.

This leaves four 'loose ends': גה, prob. for זה 'this'; גוג [—מ (Scythia?)]—although its being dangerous wilds makes it a sort of alchemical oven—גמד, '(a kind of) measure of length'; and געה, 'low (as ox/cow) [-ing (pl.)]', the last two *possibly* relating to *fortuna*.

SUMMARY

Gimel, X Wheel of Fortune: 'roll', 'be curved, rim of wheel', 'move in circle, rejoice' [*rune=harvest dance*]; 'gritty, stony, harsh, lot, portion'. **Old Semitic shape** [*pyramid in sand*]: 2 'heap up (sepulchral mound)', 2 '(hill, mitre) be high', 3 '(tower) be exalted (lifted up)' [*start of ascent of round, at scorpio*]. **Nordic Tifinag** [*roof-beams*]: 'roof'. *Alchemical oven:* 'wall up', 'bound, limit', 'brimstone, sulfur', 'shine', 'burnt limestone', 'burn, coal'; [*geodetically desert:*] 'grow warm, angry' {'hard, rough'} 'sterile, barren'. **Greek, Libyan** [*erect phallus*]: 'make bare', 'skin', 'soil, defile' ['itch, scab'], 'feel, grope' {'flattery'} 2 'body (embrace, bend)'. **G-ivy:** 'be bent, curved, vine', 'bow, bend down', 'incline, bend, belly [*of reptile*]', 'sinew, nerve'. **Adrenals:** 'be or become strong', 'break, burst forth', 'excite, stir up [*strife*], throat, gullet' [*where g-sound is*], 'loathe, abort', 'reel, shake'. **Scorpio** [*leaving the present*]: 'reproach, revile', 'rebuke, reprove' {'a stranger there, expulsion'} 'pass over, away', 'bring to an end', 'die', 2 '(be rising, convex, back) corpse', 'dig, pit', 'clod' [*on earth triad*], 'bone'. **Season, rune 'harvest':** 'fruit, plunder, pasture, expulsion', 9 '(plough) ({<u>fortuna</u>}) cut (-off) (-down) ([*a measure of length*])', 'shear' [3 'shave (diminish)', 'scrape oneself'] 'make level, threshing floor', 'something crushed [*perhaps corn*]', 'treasurer', 2 '(collect, treasury) cover (protect)' ['pitch pine*?*'], 3 '(granary) gather together', 'wrap together, mantle, cloak', 'rain', 'flow together', 'be condensed, heights', 3 '(grain, berries) (clod*?* furrow*?*) carry away (steal)', 2 'pluck (rob)', 'to low [*ox, cow*]'; [*the harvest celebration:*] 'wine vat, musical instrument', 'drink in, reed'. **Rune 'gift'** [X-*shaped*]**, and chi** [*initial of* Christ]: 'heal, cure', 'redeem, ransom', 'bridge', 'recompense, ripen [*fruit*], wean, camel, kindness'. **Unparsed:** 'sycamore' {'to dye'}.

ד

Dalet

PARSED ROOTS

The hieroglyph from whose hieratic form dalet developed was a hand, as if gesturing to point out what is seen on the far horizon, where dalet ended up (in the tree-calendar): דא, Ch. '*this*, —ל — one against the other/together'; דגל, '*be marked/signalized*, set up/be furnished w/, flag/banner/standard'; דן, Ch. 'this/that, —כ thus'; דרע, Ch. = H. זרוע '*the arm* [*strong/mighty/or large pasture?*]' (relating also to oak's strength); דרש, 'visit/frequent/*search for/seek/*- after, ask for/demand back/require, apply oneself to/promote, —מ commentary'. Recalling D's origin at sagittary, thought: 1. דמה, '*be/become like/resemble, liken/compare, imagine/think/meditate*'; and דר [*'pearl of wisdom'*] (A. 'pearl').

The following group of roots relate both to *duir* the oak being the king of trees and to D's original station being sagittary (active side of air): דבר, '*speak* (prim. *range in order/connect* hence in derivv. *lead/guide*/drive subdue/destroy)/- *together/- with/sing (song)*, destroy/subdue, *be spoken, word/command, cause/reason, suit at law, manner/mode/order*, thing/matter/affair, plague/pestilence, float/raft, *word, -s/sayings, (seat of) oracle (Holy of Holies), bee, pasture* (whither flocks are driven)/*desert/wilderness*', this last suggesting the far horizon (and bees are linked to fellow 'moonchild' vav, the heather); דין/דון, '*rule/govern, judge/punish, plead/defend*, contend/strive/- together, (cause for) *judgment*, Ch. -/fig. *tribunal/court, justice/right/punishment*, controversy/strife, (object of) contention/strife [-] Midianite, defender/*judge* [- (Dan)] [- of God (Daniel)] *master/lord (adon, Adonai)*, etc.'; דת, 'law/statute, edict/decree, Ch. judge/lawyer'; plus דריוש [Darius (k. of Persia)]; and דרכמנים 'darics (Pers. coin)'. And as a symbol of royalty: דמשק, 'damask [Damascus]'.

In Meroitic, D is the eye of Horus, our eye on the horizon: דוק > 'watchtower' (Ch./Syr. 'look round/out', A. 'surround'). At its new station, it shares vav's sign—דד, '(only in the dual) breasts (m.!)'—and generates the fiery level of the Cauldron: דלק, 'burn/consume/(fig. of the mind) anguish, kindle/inflame, burning fever'. Moreover: דוץ, 'leap/exult'; and דלג, 'leap/skip', which, as with peh, relate to eyes' ability to leap ahead to the horizon.

Several roots remind us that its new station is early summer: דחן, 'millet'; דרר (cogn. דור), 'radiate/flow freely, (mother of) pearl?, swallow, *spontaneous flowing/liberty, brambles?/weeds? (as growing luxuriantly), the south/fig. - wind*' (A. 'fly around'); דשא, 'spring/sprout forth, send forth grass, tender grass/young herbage'; דתא, Ch. 'tender grass' (= H. דשא). And two remind us the old Hebrew dalet was a boat's jib (which swings, like a door): דגה, 'multiply/be increased, fish [large -] corn/grain/fig. bread'; דִּיג/דָּאג, 'fish, -er'.

Dalet is straight ahead: דהה, 'proceed softly/gently/submissively'; דהר, '*move quickly (horse)/prance, -ings*, n. of tree (Vulg. elm)'; דפק, 'beat/knock, (over-)*drive [cattle-driving* (pl.)]'; דרב > 'goad(s)' (A. 'be pointed'); דרך, '*tread (way*/grapes/olives)/upon (enemies)/bend (bow/arrows *for* bow)/*bend (tongue* like *bow), cause to tread/go/walk/lead, a going/journey/way, -/path*, mode/manner/custom, place trodden upon/footing', three of which involve reysh (which means *head*). Similar, then, to this last, while also touching on the royal status of *duir* the oak: דּוּשׁ/דִּישׁ, 'tread down/underfoot/- out corn/thresh, a –ing, - time, sp. of gazelle/antelope'; דחק, 'press upon/oppressor'; דכא, 'break in pieces/bruise, trample upon, be broken/bruised/contrite, humble'; דכה, 'be bruised/crushed/broken/- in pieces/contrite, a beating/dashing'; דכך (= דּוּך/דָּכָה), 'afflicted/oppressed/poor, a crushing/bruising'; דלח, 'trouble/disturb (water by trampling)'; דקק, '(be) beat(en/ground)/grind small/break in pcs., very small/fine, slender/thin/withered, thin/fine cloth'. Hence: דבל > '[cake] – of dried figs' (A. 'press together'); דּוּך, 'pound/bray (in mortar), mortar'.

In Tifinag and Numidian it is shaped like a doorway, and *dalet* means 'door': דלה, '*draw (as water from well)*, in derivv. *hang down*/deliver (as from prison), *door, -/gate, -/-s/leaves or valves of gates/leaves or columns of roll or book, bucket, boughs/branches*'. Being at cancer, where the round descends, several mean 'hang down'(XII The Hanged Man) or 'flow' or 'drip': דאב, 'prop. flow/melt/hence pine away/languish, anxiety/distress, languor/fainting'; thus דאג, 'be anxious/uneasy/afraid [solicitous] dread'; דבא > 'rest?/fig. death?/affluence/resource/means?' (A. 'rest', Ch. '*cause to flow in*'); דבב, 'go softly/creep along/*only of wine) flow softly*, bear (n.), slander/evil report'; דבה (= דבא\ב 'to flow'), 'doves' dung'; דבק, '*cleave/adhere*, soldering (of metals)/joint (in armor), reach/overtake/follow close'; דבש, 'honey [sweet as –]'; דּוּב, 'cause to waste/pine away [a pining/wasting away (pl.)]'—eight that invoke inception via alef or beyt (seven via beyt or both)—דוה, '*be languid/sick (menses)*, sad/unhappy'; דלל, '*hang down/be languid*/weakened/feeble, brought to/reduced, low/weak (ness)/poor, thin thread/hair/locks, lowness/poverty *[languid/-shing (Delilah)]*'; דלף, 'drop/drip, shed tears/weep, raindrop'; דמן, 'dung/manure, dunghill [- (pl.)]'; דמע, 'weep/shed tears, tear(s), -(s)/fig. juice (of grapes/olives)' (three more that involve labials); and דנג, 'wax'. And the related idea: דחל, Ch. 'be afraid/fear/-ful/terrible/terrify'; דעל [ת— 'fear' (Sam./Syr.)] (or perhaps just a reaction to the 'king of trees'). There is a fly in the ointment, spawned no doubt by the preceding: דרא > 'abhorrence/contempt' (A. 'excite evil'). (I have followed a tangent or two here.)

One of its two forms in south Semitic pictured the bier (or bed) of the sacrificed hero, just as the doorway in Tifinag is also a dolmen (what passed for a tombstone in the megalithic age). For at the station where it ended up, it represents the sacrifice of the god of the waxing year at the summer solstice: דבח, Ch. 'sacrifice, - (n.), מ— altar'; דדה, 'cast out/expel, cleanse/wash away'; דהם, 'be overwhelmed/overcome'; דּוּם (= דמם 'be silent/still'), 'silence/death/fig. the grave, quiet (n.), silent resignation (to will of God), dumbness, silently'; דּוּר, '*dwell*, circle/ball, round pile, age/*generation*/prop. revolution, *habitation/fig. sepulchre*' (A. '*move in circle/go round*'); דחה, 'push/drive/(be) thrust down, Ch. sp. of mus. instr., stumbling'; דחח, 'be thrust down/falling, fall/ruin'; דחף, 'impel/urge/hasten, ruin/destruction', this linked also to *straight ahead*; דיה > 'black vulture, ink' (Ch. דהא 'be dark/obscure?'); 2. דמה, 'be dumb/silent/quiet, fig. reduce to silence/destroy, be –ed/cut off, Ch. be like/similar, similitude/likeness/model/pattern, as/like', recalling gesturing hand, adding the insight that what is at the horizon is not yet within earshot, as also דמם, 'be silent/still, rest/cease/leave off, quiet/rest/silence, - (v.)/quiet/stand still, reduce to silence/(be) destroy(ed)/cut off(/perish), be laid waste, destruction/desolation'—four roots that involve mem (as in *mum's the word*), three of which include the meaning *silence*—דעה [דעואל 'invocation of God'] (A. 'invoke'); דעך, 'go out/be extinguished (as light)/destroyed, dried up/quenched, become extinct'; דפה > 'stroke/ruin/destruction' (A. 'thrust/push'); דקר, 'pierce/(be) thrust through (fig. by want) [a stabbing] piercings (of sword)'. Plus another root that points to sagittary thematically: דכר (= H. זכר '*remember*'), 'Ch. male/(*only by way of eminence*) *ram*, Ch. *memorial/record*', ram being the sign at the apex of the waxing year (over which oak rules).

Speaking of apices (by which I mean apexes), the oak-king's rune is a big belly sticking out (later pointed, thorn-like) named *þurisaz*, 'giant': דבשת, 'bunch/hump (of camel)'; דלען ['pl. of gourds (Ch. דלעת *gourd*)']; and דשן, 'grow/make(/be made) fat(/abundantly satisfied), anoint, regard as fat (offering, i.e. accept it), fat (soil)/(of trees) full of sap, rich/opulent, fat(ness)/fig. fertility, ashes (esp. from altar victims)'. This is the letter of the giant-slayer, Thor or Donar, also known as David, so: דוד (= 2. ידד '*love*') > '*pot/boiler/cauldron*, basket, -s/mandrakes, *love (n.)/friend/beloved [- (incl. David)] uncle*' (Syr. 'disturb/agitate'). Note: in roots דוד *and* ידד, it gives a better view of dalet to view the two dalets as facing one another breast to breast.

It is clear we are speaking here of the hero of the play, hence: די, 'sufficiency/enough (affixed to preps. ב, כ, and מן)'; and די, '(rel. pron.) *who*, what, which, *sign of gen.* (e.g. [די זהב of gold (pl.)]), (conj.) *(so) that*'.

Even flitting about between cancer and sagittary, dalet remains *above* water or form in the Cauldron, on the airy and fiery levels. Hence: דאה, 'fly, sp. of bird (kite/Vulg. milvus)'; דגר, 'hatch/brood over eggs'; דוכיפת, 'sp. of unclean bird (Vulg. hoopoe)'. And to touch on the fiery level of the phoenix's rebirth: דקלה/Ch. דקלא ['palm-tree' (district in Arabia)].

By the way, the *other* form of dalet in south Semitic was an axe, the giant it was to slay being the oak (I presume they had *some* kind of oak in Yemen back then).

Two 'loose ends' (to add to the various 'stretches' above): דהב, Ch. = H. זהב 'gold'; and דרג > ה—מ 'steep pl./precipice' (A. 'ascend by steps')..

SUMMARY

Dalet in Phoenician (jib) [*obliquely*]: {'pearl'} 'fish, fishing', 'hatch, brood over eggs', 'multiply, fish, Dagon, corn' ['millet'], 'disturb water by trampling'. **Sign of breast** [*where one points*]: 2 '(way) tread (thresh, species of antelope)', 'be pointed, goad', 'drive [*cattle*], knock', 'move quickly, prance', 2 '(skip) leap (spring, dance)', 'spring forth, tender grass', 'breast[s]' {'two wells'} 'seek'. **Horizon without,** *hand* [*gesturing*]: 3 'this' {'arm, large pasture'} 'be marked, signalized', 'look round, out, surround', 'move in circle, dwell, generation', 'radiate, fly round, pearl'; [*manifested fire:*] 'burn, consume, inflame'; [*effect of sensation:*] 'abhorrence, excite evil', 'fear, terrify', 'be uneasy, anxiety'. **Cauldron's rim, giant's girth** [*rune*]: 'disturb, love, Beloved [*David*], cauldron, basket' {'gourd'} 'grow fat, fatten, rich, anoint', 'sufficiency' ['darics', 'gold-making']. **XII LePendu** [*hang, drip*]: 'cleave, adhere', 2 (door, page, bough, bucket) hang down (languish)', 2 '(languish, melt) pine', 'be languid, menstruate', 'rest, cause to flow in, affluence', 2 '(drop, drip) weep (a tear, juice)', 'wax', 'honey', 'creep along, flow softly [*wine*], a bear, a slander' ['proceed softly, gently'], 'flow, bird droppings', 'dung, manure', 'cast out, wash away'. **Oak-king** [*sacrificed hero*]: 'sacrifice, altar', 'be extinguished, quenched, become extinct', 'be overwhelmed, overcome', 'grind fine', 'pound, mortar', *2* 'be crushed (oppressed) bruised (contrite)' ['press together, cake of dried figs'], 'thrust through, pierce'; 'be thrust down', *3* '(fall) ruin (destruction)', 'precipice' 2 '(be dark, black vulture) kite (fly)' ['name of unclean bird [*Vulg. hoopoe*]']; 3 '(death) be silent (be dumb, cut off)', 'cause to pine away'. **Tifinag-Libyan** [*dolmen*]: 'remember, memorial' {'invoke'}. **Reason-mind:** 'resemble, compare, imagine, meditate, think, model, as', 'so that, because that'. **Oak as dominion:** 'speak, range in order, cause or reason, commandment, law-suit, bee [*Deborah, prophetess who judged Israel*], pasture', 2 '(law, edict, lawyer) judge ([*Dan, Daniel*], Judged [*Dinah*], govern, rule, master, Lord [*Adonai*])', 'press upon, oppressor', 'Darius'.

בּ

Beyt

PARSED ROOTS

Beyt is the birth of the year. Our B, and the rune as well, both got from Greek, express this as a pregnant woman's profile: בטח, 'cling to/rely upon/trust/confide in/be (over-)confident, security/tranquility'; בטן, 'belly/*womb/inmost part (of heart/mind)*, protruberance (in column), pistachio nuts'; בכר > '*bear early fruit/be first born*, young camel [juvenile] *first fruit*' (A. '*be early*'); בל, Ch. 'heart'; בסר > '*unripe*/sour grapes' (A. '*do too soon*/look sour'); בעת, '*kick/- up*, spurn at'; בצל > 'onions, *nakedness*' (A. '*strip*/peal'); בקע, 'cleave/divide, break/rip/lay open (fortified city)/*hatch (eggs)*, valley, fissure/cleft, rend/tear in pcs. (as beasts), half-shekel'; ברא, '*create/form/make/be born*/cut/- down/fashion, *son/grandson, a new/wondrous thing*, feed/fatten, -ed/fat'; בשל, '*(become) ripe(n), boil*/seethe'; בשׂר, 'flesh/body, all flesh (all creatures), near relation/consanguinity, the secret parts (viri)'; בתל > '*virgin, -ity/tokens thereof*' (A. 'separate'). That meaning 'separate' crops up a couple times before we get to its proper place (near the end). In the above, four involve reysh and four involve lamedh: reysh means 'head' or 'beginning', while lamedh conveys the idea of *nurturing*.

Since ogham B begins its series of five and thus occurs on the thumb: בהן > '*thumb*/big toe' (A. 'shut up'). The vowel in ogham which shares the thumb with B is *ailm*, the silver fir, thus: ברשׁ > '*fir-tree*(/cypress, Gesen.), (anything made of its wood, e.g.) lance/mus. instr.'

Birth implies a household to be born into (beyt's meaning); Sabean beyt pictures walls and flat roof of a dwelling in those parts. Hence: בּ, '*in/within/among*, at/near/by/on/before (*in presence of*), to/unto/upon/against, for (price), -/on account of/because of, w/by/through, (pref, to inf.) *in/when*'; בהט, 'sp. of marble'; בּוֹא, '*enter/come/go in*, have intercourse w/enter into (various things), *entrance*, income/profit/fruit'; בּוּת, Ch. 'pass the night', from which is commonly derived בּית, 'house/dwelling, tent/tabernacle, temple, palace, place/space/inside, household/family'. And how it comes about: בנה, '*build/construct (house/temple)*, repair/restore/fig. establish/prosper/*be built up (obtain children)*, (foster) *son/descendant, daughter*, model/form/resemblance/bldg.' Then there are the environs: בּוּס, '*trample upon/tread underfoot*/down (profane) [trampler] *[pl. trodden down (ancient name of Jerusalem)]* a treading down/destruction'; בשׂס, 'trample upon' (samekh being the top of the round).

Consistent with *within*: בּאר, 'engrave (as on tablet), expound/explain, *well/cistern [-/-]*'; בהה > 'emptiness' (A. בהו 'be void'); בּוּק (= בקק '*to empty*'), '*void, emptiness*/devastation'; בּוּב, '*be hollow*, apple of the eye/pupil'; בקק, '*(make) empty* (as land of inhabitants)/depopulate, (of counsel) *empty*/pour out (deprive one of it), pour itself out (of a tree)/spreading/luxuriant (vine), *bottle* [profusion (of the Lord/of the mtn.)] [effusion (stream)]'.

Concurring with *temple (house)*, B's trump is V The Pope: בדק, '*(repair) breach*/rupture (in bldg.)' (A. 'tear/rend'); בום '(prob. be high), *high pl./hill/-ock usually dedicated to religious worship (whether true or false)*/fig. of waves (of sea)/of clouds, height/strong place' (Syr. בים 'raised pl./*pulpit*'); בי, particle of entreaty (always with אדני, 'pray God') from root בעה (below); בירה, 'castle/palace, *the temple*'; בֵּלְטְשַׁאצַּר [n. given Daniel at court of Ninevah]; ברך, '*bend knee/kneel/worship/bless*/salute/greet, *blessing/gift*/piece, cool of water', hence also ברע ['gift' coll. w/ A. (Gesen.)]; בשׂר, 'announce/declare, *bring/tell/receive good tidings* [cool/cold (coll. w/ A. Gesen.)]' (five that involve reysh, the 'head' or 'start'). Combining this with the swelling of pregnancy: בעה, '*make swell/boil up*, seek/ask/request/*swell out*, be sought out, petition, *prayer*'; and a couple that continue with *to swell*, בוע > 'blains/pustules' (Ch. '*boil/swell up*')'; and בצק, 'swell (feet), dough [elevation]'—interestingly, this last ends in qof (womb), which is from the hieratic of the hieroglyph **hillslope** (a womb-like swelling of the ground).

Growing naturally on this is the white bark (purity, separation from *other*) of *beth* the birch, as well as its clear, sweet sap: בדל, '(be) *separate*(d) *(make division/distinguish/select)*, part/portion, tin, *separation/separate place*, depart, *bdellium (a transparent gum)*/(A. and rabbis, pearls)'; בהק > 'a kind of harmless leprosy (of *dull whitish spots*)' (A. '*be white*/shining'); בהר > 'bright/shining, -/*whitish* scurf' (A. 'shine')—whence comes *Bahir*—בוץ > '*fine linen/byssus*, eggs *[white]*' (A. '*be white*/shining'); בכא (= בכה 'weep') '[a weeping] sp. of shrub distilling a white/acrid gum'; בכה, '*weep/mourn/lament*, -ation/trickling of water'; ברק, '*lighten*/send forth lightning, -/*glitter* of sword, sp. of gem (emerald), threshing sledges'; and בשׂם > 'balsam tree, -/scent/perfume' (Ch./Syr. 'be sweet/pleasant/fragrant').

What surprised me about beyt was its interpretation of 'the horizon behind', which from the Grail we know as the *horizon within*: (1) taking back or *to oneself*; (2) being taken *a*back; and (3) self-*knowledge* (the one I knew about). Hence the following three groups.

To take 'back', meaning *to oneself*: בג, 'food'; בגד, 'act covertly/deal falsely, treacherous, covering/wrapper/cloak/garment, rapine/violence'; בדא, 'devise/feign'; בזא, = בזז 'to spoil'; בזז, 'take as prey/spoil/plunder, prey/spoil/booty'; בחל, 'loathe, *greedily gotten*' (Syr. 'loathe', A. '*be greedy*'); בלם, 'bind/bridle'; בלס, 'pluck/gather figs'; בלע, 'swallow/consume/destroy'; בנט '(prob. bind), girdle (worn by priests)'; בעל, '*have dominion over/possess*, lord (Baal)/(become) husband (of)/*possessor/owner*, mistress, disdain/despise'—five altogether that reach out using lamedh—בצע, 'break (in pcs.)/*cut off/spoil/plunder*, - (n.), *gain/profit*, defraud, finish/complete'; בצר, '*cut off/prune vine/gather vintage/-er*/fig. destructive enemy, inaccessible (cut off)/fortified/fig. incomprehensible, fortress/stronghold, *be restrained*, fold for cattle' (two that invoke tzaddi's strife). Then there is the means, showing how Brazil got its name (through Phoenician): ברזל, 'iron/- instr./fig. hard/inflexible thing [of iron/austere]'. Thus also: בתק, 'cut/pierce' (qof = *cut*).

And being taken *a*back: באשׁ, 'stink/become odious/fig. make loathsome/act wickedly, Ch. be evil, stench, bad grapes, weed'; בהל, 'be agitated/terrified/amazed, hasten/confound, be ruined, Ch. haste, terrify/alarm, fear/terror'; בהם > 'cattle/wild beast/Behemoth (hippopotamus?

perhaps elephant?)' (A. 'be dumb'); בזה/בוז, 'despise/condemn'; בוך, 'perplexed/confused'; בּוֹשׁ, 'be ashamed/disappointed/confused/perplexed, shame/confusion/ignominy, delay/cause disgrace, idol, secret parts'; בטא, 'talk rashly, rash utterance'; בטה, part. 'idle talker'; בלה, 'harass/trouble, terror/calamity [feeble]'; בנס, Ch. 'be angry'; בער, '*consume/burn/- up (w/ anger), be/become brutish, -/stupid, feed upon, a burning [torch] cattle/beasts, - (of burden)*'; בעת, 'be terrified, terrify/alarm, come upon suddenly, terror'; ברד, 'to hail, - (n.), spotted'; ברח, 'pass/shoot along (as bar), *(cause to) flee(/put to flight), fleeing/fugitive*, (cross-)bar/bolt'; ברם, Ch. adv. 'but/yet, nevertheless'. To which we might add: בטל, 'rest from/cease, Ch. cause to -/hinder'; and בלה, '*grow old/waste away/consume*, destroy, old/worn out, custom/tax, old clothes/rags, not/nothing, consumption/want/without, besides, worthlessness/*wickedness/injury*/destruction'. That makes six that involve heh, partaking of *eadhe* the aspen's sensitivity to the slightest breeze. Four involve reysh and four lamedh: one takes with one or the other (the right or the left).

The goal is self-knowledge; so let us begin with solitude: בדד, '*(be) separate/solitary, -/alone [separation]* (in derivv. devise/feign), part/members/limbs/branches/staves/poles/fig. princes/*fine linen/- garments/lies, separately/alone*'; בדר, Ch. 'scatter'; בזק > 'lightning [-]' (Syr./Ch. 'scatter'); בזר, 'scatter/disperse'; בתר, 'cut in pieces/divide, piece/part, *separation* [section]'. And as transition to knowledge itself: ברר, '*separate*/select/choose out/*purge/purify, show oneself pure (morally), -/chaste*, cleanse/clear (as corn), polish/furbish (sword), corn/grain (purified from chaff/or growing), open fields/country, *pure/clear*/empty, *cleanness/purity*, (Vulg. birds/fowls)/geese (Gesen. *from their whiteness*), soap, *examine/prove*, chosen/beloved', which hearkens back both to birch's white bark and the sacred. Then: בור, 'examine/prove' (cogn. בּרר); בחן, 'try/prove/test, watchtower, tryer/assayer'; בחר, '*prove/examine* (as Syr.)/choose/select, elect, choice/excellent, youth (choice age)'; בון/בין, 'distinguish/discern, mark/attend/understand, know/be wise/explain/teach, interval/midst, between/within, prudence'; בלג, 'open/cause to break out, make(/be) cheerful(/glad)/enliven [joy] exhilaration/cheerfulness'; בעשׂיה [perh. for מעשׂיה 'work of the Lord']; בקר, '(in derivv. plow/*break forth (as light))/search/look after/take care of/consider/observe, search/examine*, oxen, herdsman, *dawn*/daybreak/(to)morrow, *a looking after/caring*, chastisement'; בקשׁ, '*seek/- after*, require/demand, act/request, -/petition'; ברה, 'eat, choose/select (prop. cut), food/fat, agreement/league/*covenant*, sign thereof (i.e. circumcision)'; בתת, 'bath (liquid measure), excision/desolation, clefts/fissures' (A. '*cut/mark out/define*'). A total of *eight* involve reysh, thus setting off the whole year (by its first and last month) for the pursuit of knowledge.

And then there is its opposite: בלל, 'suffuse, mingle/mix/confound, give fodder, mix oneself/be mixed, Babylon, Ch. -ians, mixed provender/fodder, mixture/confusion (of sp. by bestiality/of relations by incest), disorder/blemish (in eye)'; and ברם > 'cloth interwoven w/ various colors' (A. 'twist threads together').

SUMMARY

Beyt as hollowed-out dwelling: 2 '(house) temple (palace)' ['porphyry, species of marble'], 'shut up', 'enter', 'in, at', 'hollow', 'void', 2 'to empty out (lay waste)', 'engrave, pit' ['light, sandy soil'] 2 'trample upon ({*Jerusalem's old name*})', 'build, son'. **Birch [*1ˢᵗ month*]:** 'do too soon, unripe', 2 '(unripe) early (first born)'. **Beta, a pregnant profile:** 'flesh, body, privates', 'belly, womb', 'kick', 'boil, ripen', 3 '(boil) swell up', 'devise, invent', 'create, cut, form, be born, son, a new and wonderful thing [*Beriyah*]', 'cling to, trust'. **Birch's white, peeling bark:** 3 'be white, shining', 'shine, be glad', 'lighten, flash [*lightening*]'; 'strip, peel, onions'. **Song of Amairgen's 'I am a drop in the air'** [*from its sap?*]: 2 'weep (gummy shrub)', 'trickle' ['hail']. **V LePape:** 'repair breach', 'bless', 'good tidings', 'sweet', 'pulpit, high place', 2 '(pure) to separate (virgin)'. **Inner horizon:** 'separate oneself', 4 'scatter (be alone)', 'act covertly', 'seek', 3 'examine, prove', 2 '(examine, daybreak) distinguish (know)', 'cut, define', 'cleave, divide', 2 '(divide) pierce (iron [*Brazil*])'; [*take for oneself:*] 2 'plunder (cut off)', 'cut off', 2 '(select) food', 'pluck figs', 2 'consume', 'engulf', 'be greedy', 'possess'. **Horizon behind:** 'behind, be distant'; [*pulled back:*] 2 'bind, bridle', 'but, yet, nevertheless', 'cease, rest from'; [*taken aback:*] 'flee', 3 'terror', 'be dumb, Behemoth', 2 'be perplexed', 'mix, confuse, *Babel*', 2 'talk rashly', 'be angry', 2 'despise', 'stink, sour grapes'. **Unparsed:** 'gift', 'gay-colored cloth', 'cypress or fir, lance or musical instrument thereof'.

The
Three
Mothers

אשמ(ם)

Dark Mood of Yesterday

Fly away, fly away,
Dark mood of yesterday.
You are no-longer welcome here.
This is no place for you to stay.

My ungraceful heart is full,
Allowing me to strive to pull
My life from underneath the wool:
      We've passed your part of the play.

You serve no purpose anyhow:
Where once you heralded the truth,
The truth of life is different now.
You're but a vestige of my youth
That once resided on my brow
And made my attitudes uncouth,
      But not anymore, I pray,

For while your back was turned to me,
I healed my wounds and set you free
To prey on someone else's glee
      Like an unwanted stray.

א

Alef

PARSED ROOTS

One of the reasons alef is shaped like a whirlwind or 'pillar of fire' is that it comes from the hieratic form of the hieroglyph ***Egyptian vulture***, an eagle-like, tool-using bird that soars to great height by spiraling up thermals. Hence: אבר, 'be strong, fly, soar, wing/feather'; אדליא [Pers. 'heart?/eagle?']; איה, 'n. of bird of prey (Sept. & Vulg. vulture/kite)' (see root 2. אוה below); plus אנפה, 'n. of unclean bird/sp. of eagle (Bochart)', excerpted from root אנף, below.

The most striking thing about *ailm* the silver fir is that it limits the outward growth of its limbs in order to put its all into growing tall: אזר, 'bind/gird about (as garment/fig. strength), gird up (loins)/oneself, girdle/belt, fetters'; אטם, 'shut/close'; אטר, '*shut/close*, shut up/*bound*, impotent'; אסר, 'bind, put in bonds/fetter, harness (chariot), obligation/vow of abstinence, be bound/imprisoned, captive/prisoner'; אפד, '*gird*/put on, ephod (esp. of high priest)/perh. idol (dressed in one), vestment'; אפף, 'surround/encompass'; אפק > '*restrain(/constrain) oneself (to act)* [fortress] *mighty/eminent*, boss (of shield), brook/torrent/channel/fig. tube (*spoken of the bones of the Behemoth*)'; אצל, '*(with-)hold (back)/reserve, be contracted, withhold*, (prop. select/)noble(man/remote part), juncture/joint, *side/by/near*'; אצר, 'lay/treasure up, appoint as treasurer, store(-house/treasury)'; אשׂר '(prob. = אסר bind) [(whom) God has bound] [vow of God]'—five with reysh as third letter, four of which mean *bind*, which is what R's trump Le Diable *does*. Plus: 2. אזן, 'weigh/consider, a balance', which is the same thing *in spirit*.

Alef is the one letter whose bardic number equals its Hebrew number, representing unity: אגד, 'Ch. bind together, bands/knots/bundle/bunch/troop/vault (of heaven)'; אגר, 'gather/collect [-ed] a small coin, letter/epistle/edict'; אח, 'brother/kinsman/countryman/friend/fellow, kinswoman etc./ally'; אחד, 'one/first (in time)/a, joined into one'; אך, 'only(/but)/just now, surely/certainly'—five built on alef plus a guttural, signifying what is drawn in close to the vertical axis or throat—אל/אלה, 'these'; אלשׁ ['crowd (pl.)']; אמם '[union?] people/nation' (A. 'be related (cogn. עמם)'); אנון, Ch. 'they'; אנחנו, Ch. 'we'; אסף, '*collect/gather/assemble*, take (in)/receive to oneself/draw back (as hand), take away/hence destroy, gather in/up (as rear an army)/receive (as guest)/*be gathered/- together [collector]* stores/storehouses, *ingathering/harvest of fruits, collection, assembly*/council'; אף, 'also/moreover/indeed/yea'; ארב, 'lie in wait/ambush, fraud/plot, network (over window/chimney hence) *the visible heavens*'; ארה, 'pull/pluck off, *gather*, stall/stable, *ark*, coffin, lion, *hero*'; ארשׂ, '(be) betroth(ed)'; 3. את/-את, '(in company) with/by/near [-] towards, from w/'.

Alef as ox: אבס, 'feed/fatten (cattle), crib/stall (in which animals are fed), barn/granary'; אין/און' '(in derivv. *be nothing*/be light/easy, *be strong*), nothingness/falsehood/vanity, idol(s), wickedness/iniquity, adversity/calamity/sorrow *[strong] power/strength/vigor*, wealth/riches [sun (On-Heliopolis in Egypt)] *not/none*'; אחשתרן, 'mules (Pers. orig.)'; אכד ['fortress (= עקד/אגד bind/*strengthen*)']; 2. אלה > '(large) tail (of eastern sheep)' (A. *'be stout/fat'* cogn. אול); אלל '(in derivv. *be nothing*/*be strong* (cogn. אול)/howl (cogn. ילל)), *nothing*/nay, not so, terebinth/oak, nought, vain/idols/vanity, sixth mo., wo!/alas!'; אלף, 'learn (in derivv. accustom oneself/become familiar, join together/associate)/teach/bring forth thousands, *tame/gentle*, familiar/friend, head of family/tribe, *ox/bullock*'; אמץ, '*be/make strong*/courageous, repair/restore/harden (heart), *powers/forces*, *active*/fleet/*vigorous*'; ארך, '*be/become long* (boughs/*time*), a healing, tardiness, *forebearance*, meet'; אשן ['fortified' (A. *'be strong'*)]; 2. את/-את, 'sign of accusative/nominative w/ certain passive verbs'; אתן > 'she-ass' (A. *'step slowly'*). Possibly: ארד '(perh. = ערד flee) [mushroom?] [flight?] [fugitive] [*strong* (coll. w/ Pers.)] Ch. ארדא mushroom'.

The related subject of ploughing: איפה, 'an Ephah (corn measure)'; אכל, 'eat, food'; אכר > 'ploughman, husbandman' (A. 'dig'); אלם, 'bind, be dumb/silent, sheaf of corn, widow'; אסם > 'storehouses'; 1. את, 'ploughshare'; and from Egyptian, אחו, 'grass, reeds/bullrushes'; and אטון, 'thread?/linen?'. Then there is the ploughman's 'foe', The Mother of the Wood: אטד 'blackthorn [(region beyond Jordan)]'; אסנה ['thornbush']; and אשל, 'tamarisk (a middle-sized prickly tree)'.

Another task the ox helps with solved a long-standing puzzle for me: what do ***Egyptian vulture***, silver fir, and ox have in common? All uplift something (themselves in the first two cases) to great height: the first spirals up thermals, the second shoots upward forsaking breadth, and the ox turns the pump that raises water up from the water table to the arid surface. Hence: אבל > 'grassy pl./meadow' (A. 'be moist, i.e. moisture of grass'); אגל (A. 'flow together'); אגם > 'pool/marsh, Ch. grieve, cauldron, reed' (A. 'be hot/warm/stagnant'); אגן, 'basin/bowl'; אשד, 'pour out, Ch.(/Syr.) ravine'.

Earth and careful measurement constitute another subject to which the ox is relevant: אות, 'consent/agree to'; אנך, 'lead/plummet'; ארע, 'Ch. earth/low/inferior/bottom'; ארץ, '(the) earth/land/ground, country(-ies, esp. Gentile)'; ארק, 'Ch. the earth'; אתר, 'Ch. place/—ב after'. And perhaps: אבן, 'stone, gem, weight'.

This is the A of the Logos, thus the creative beginning of the Word: 1. אזן, 'listen/give ear/attend, kind of instr./weapon, Ch. be armed, ear(s)/fig. hearing [- well]'. The doer, creator of thoughts, signifies inception: אב, 'father, fore-/ancestor, author/inventor, father (honorary of priests/prophets as teachers)/hence advisor'; אבב, 'Ch. bear fruit, greenness/verdure, Ch. fruit, green ears of corn'; אדם, 'be red/ruddy, made/dyed red, be sparkling, man (human being)/men [Adam] red/-ish brown, Edomite(s), ruby/cornelian, ground/soil/land/region/country [human (pl.)] red-haired, blood/-shed/-guiltiness/- of grapes (i.e. wine)'; איל/אול > '*prince/chief*, body, *vestibule/porch*, *ram*, stag/hart/hind [deer-field (pl.)] strength/force, the mighty/*noble* hence oak/*pine*/terebinth/etc. [oak] Ch. tree [my God is Lord (Elijah)] terebinth'—*ailm* can mean fir or pine—איש, 'man/husband, woman/wife'; אם, '(grand-)mother, -city/metropolis, forearm (prop. mother of the arm)/cubit, basis/pedestal'; אמה, 'maidservant'; 2. אנה > 'make happen/befall, seek occasion (against anyone), ship(s/fleet), sexual impulse, occasion/cause' (A. 'meet/be in good time'); אפן (cogn. פנה 'turn/revolve'?), 'wheat-season'; אשה (= אשש 'found'), 'foundation [whom the Lord heals]' (A. 'heal'); אשך, 'testicles'; אשש > 'foundation, cake' (A. 'found/make firm'); אתה\א, '(things) to come, entrance, Ch. bring'; אתק ('Sept. peristyle/Vulg. portico'). Then there is the opposite: אפס, 'cease/fail/have an end, -/extremity/soles (of feet)/ankles/no more/none besides/nothing but/only/except/unless'. Every root but one references *inception*: either mother letter mem (3 roots) or shin (4), or nun (3), or beyt (2), or samekh (1), or qof the womb (1), or an alternate ending in alef (1), soft peh (*fearn* the alder) being twice used as reinforcement (once of nun, once of samekh)—and the exception involves lamedh, *also* a setting-forth (from self).

Then there is action, the doer itself, thus: אבד, '(cause to) stray(/disperse)/wander/be lost, (cause to) perish(/destroy), be –ed, ruin/(pl. of) destruction(/abyss)'; אבצן ['labor']; אבק, 'fine dust, wrestle/prop. dust each other, (aromatic) powder'; אדד ['befall'] (A. הדד '-'); אדין, Ch. 'then'; אדרזדא, Ch. 'quickly/diligently'; אדרכנים, 'darics (Pers. gold coin)'; אדש, 'thresh?'; אוז [A. 'quick']; אול, 'be foolish'; אוץ, 'be narrow, urge/hasten'; אז, 'then/at that time'; אזד, Ch. 'depart'; אזל, 'go away/depart, weaver'; אחר, 'stay/tarry, behind/after, west'; אל, 'to, about, for, into'; אלץ, 'urge/press'; אמר, '*say/command, think/word/matter*, bough/summit? [Amorites]'; אנא\ה, 'Ch. I'; אני short for אנכי, 'I'; אנש, 'incurable, *mortal*, grievous (pain/day), malignant (heart), *mankind, common people*'; אנס, 'urge/compel, Ch. to trouble'; אספרנא, Ch. 'diligently'; (א)אפו, 'now/then'; אפתם, Ch. 'at last'; אפר > 'ashes/anything worthless, (sp. of) headband/turban (= עפר to cover) [double fruitfulness (Ephraim)] [fertility]' (A. 'be light/fleet'); אקו, 'sp. of wild goat or gazelle'; ארח, 'go/travel, way/road/manner'; ארן, 'be active/nimble [wild goat] mtn. ash?'; and surely related to that last, ארנבת, 'hare'. I guess this goes here: אשר, '(rel. pron.) who/which'. Grouped thus: built on *ab* the father, 3 (all of which raise dust); on alef dalet, 5 (mostly concerning time); on alef vav or waw, 3 (expressing precipitous haste, vav being *forward*); on alef zayin, 3 (time and departure, zayin being the old moon); on alef nun, 3+ (troubled, mortal *us*); on alef *fearn* or soft peh, 3 (timing, quickness), and on alef reysh (the shaman), 3 (mobility, nimbleness).

It is thus the fire triad, meaning the old Hebrew form is most correct when it points up: אבך, 'roll/swell up (in the mounting up of smoke)'; אגג [A. 'to burn']; אהל, 'shine' (= הלל); אוד > 'mist/vapor (exhalation arising from earth), wooden poker/firebrand, causes/prop. turnings, straitness/calamity/destruction, might/power/excess' (A. 'bend/turn/surround, be strong'); אור, 'become/give light/shine/(be) enlighten(ed)/illuminate/fig. cheer/enliven, kindle, fire/light [-/- (Ur)] (the Urim of Urim va-Thummim) lightning/luminary/fig. prosperity(/herbs)/knowledge [light of God] [light of the Lord] [he shall enlighten] light/luminary (sun/moon), candlestick (in tabernacle), glorious/shining'; אזא\ה, Ch. 'kindle'; אחח > 'fire-pot/pan' (A. 'be warm/hot'); אע, Ch. (= H. עץ) 'wood/*timber'; אפה, '(be) bake(d), baker, something baked, - pieces'; אפח [perh. = פוח 'breathe']; אפע (prob. cogn. פעה/פאה 'breathe'), 'breath/nothingness/vanity'—three built on alef soft peh (*fearn* the alder), of which two mean life and one involves grain—and אש, 'fire (used of lightning/sun/fig. anger, shining/brightness, burnt-offering, incense-offering'. And then there is the converse: אמש, 'prop. past night/adv. last night/yesterday, night/darkness'; אפל > 'late, dark/obscure, thick darkess/fig. misfortune' (A. 'set/go down (as sun)').

Of the self's three parts, the doer or *nefesh* is the level on which the emotions swirl and eddy, muddying things: אבה, 'be willing/inclined/desirous, reed/bulrush, desire, poverty/misery, miserable/wretched, wishing/hence poor/needy'; אבל, '(cause to) mourn, -ing/lamentation'; אבח > 'threatening (of sword)'; אגא ['fugitive' (coll. w/ A.)]; אהב, 'love(ly/amiable), friend, lover, amours/loves, loveliness, (be)love(d), delightfully'; אהה, 'ah/alas! (in grief)'; 1. אוה, 'long for/desire, -/longing/lust, (object of) desire(/delight)/appetite/lust, habitable earth/land/(sea-)coast/island' (A. 'bend/inflect, turn aside/dwell/take lodgings'); 2. אוה > 'wailing, wo!/alas! (in grief), ho! (in threatening), jackal, n. of bird of prey (Sept. & Vulg. vulture/kite)'; אים, 'Ch. terrify, terrible, terror/dread, idols [Moabites]'; אח, 'ah/alas! (in grief), sp. of howling animal'; אחלי, 'O that! (adv. of wish)'; אי, 'where?' and איכה/איך, 'how? (also of grief)'; איב, 'hate(/be an) enemy/adversary [persecuted (Job)] enmity'; איזבל ['uninhibited (Jezebel)']; אלח, 'be corrupt (morally)'; אמל, 'droop/waste away/languish/be sick, feeble'; 1. אנה, 'sigh/mourn, -ing/sorrow'; און, 'complain/murmur'; אנף, 'breathe through nose/snort/hence be/become angry, n. of unclean bird/sp. of eagle (Bochart), nose, nostrils/fig. face/countenance, anger'; אנק, 'groan/moan/lament, groaning/lamentation/a kind of lizard'; אסה > 'hurt/injury, mischief [injurious]' (coll. w/ A. אזה '(be) hurt/injure(d)'); ארש > 'desire/request (n.)' (A. 'to desire'); אשם, 'feel/bear guilt/be/become guilty/transgress/suffer punishment/be laid waste/destroyed, bring consequences of sin (on anyone), guilt/damage, trespass-offering, guilty'. Six involve beyt (broken front-column) and two vav (same thing), four involve heh (desire's sensitivity), and four have nun second (for negation), one even including nun's proper function, *anger*.

Its trump is I Le Bateleur (Magician/Mountebank): אדב > 'faint [אל— miracle of God]'; אה, 'where!/ha!'; אוב, 'leather bottle, spirit, conjurer'; אוה, 'mark/sign, portent, miracle'; אחז, 'seize, catch, join, overlay/cover, fasten/hold, possession'; אטט > 'necromancer' (A. 'utter gentle sound/murmur'); איחי [Ch. = H. יש 'there is']; אלו, 'see/behold, if/though'; אם, 'if, supposing, that, though, surely, whether/or'; ארג, 'plait/weave/web'; ארו, 'Ch. lo/behold!'; ארר, 'curse/execrate'; אשף > 'cover, enchanter/magician, quiver (sons as arrows)'.

As the fire triad, alef points up and thus ultimately stands for Uprightness—for the Logos, for the divine Form (Unmoved Mover). In other words, A, the first vowel, shares the quality of sacredness with the first consonant, B: אדן, 'base of column/fig. foundation'; אדר, '*become/make glorious/honorable*, great/mighty, noble/excellent/hence prince, n. of twelfth mo., cloak/mantle, greatness/*splendor/magnificence*, Ch. chief judges'; אהל, 'tent/*tabernacle*/dwelling, to pitch/live in tent(s)'; אזב > 'hyssop [dwarf?]'; אחשדרפן, 'chief satraps (officers of Pers. court)'; אהלים\ות, 'lign aloes/- wood (a perfumed wood)'; אכף, 'bow down (cogn. כפף compel)'; אלה, '(G)god/idol' (A. 'worship/adore'); אלה, 'denom. of אל prop. invoke God, swear/curse/howl'; אלמגים, 'almug trees (red sandalwood)'; אמן, 'stay/support, nurse/bring up/part. nursing-(i.e. foster-)father, multitude, be firm/true/faithful, be borne (? Isaiah 60:4), be firm/established/sure, trust/confide, believe in/rely on, constant/unwearying, steadiness/truth/faithfulness, artificer, Amen/so be it, covenant/fixed allowance, beam/lintel, education/nursing/truly/indeed'; אנא\ה, 'I pray, etc.'; (ה)אנת(ה)/(ה)את, 'Ch. thou, you/ye'; אסנת [(w. of Joseph) 'belonging to Neith (Athena)' (coll. w/ Egyp., Gesen.)]; ארגמן, '(reddish) purple'; ארז, 'be firm/fast, cedar [built of -] - wainscot'; ארם (=

ראם/רממ/רוּם ‘be high’) ‘[lofty (pl.)] [high] Aramea(n)/Syria(n), language of same, castle/palace’; אשׁר, ‘go straight on, (be) guide(d)/direct aright, (be made/)pronounce(d) happy/call(ed) blessed [-/happy(Asher, tribe, s. of Jacob)] fortune (goddess), (Asherah, God’s consort)/images/shrines, happiness/blessedness, step/going/wood of box tree [step (Assyria)] Ch. wall [upright towards God]’. I would say ‘Asherah’ more than justifies alef being a ‘mother letter’. (Six involve reysh and five lamedh, which leads me to want to say that that means both hands are sanctified.)

One leftover: אגוֹז, ‘a nut’ (A. גוֹז, Syr. גוֹזא), though one might well suggest it points to the nut harvest at virgo, hence to A’s original place in the array of vowels across the Egg’s lower half.

SUMMARY

Alef *eagle***:** {‘heart*?* eagle*?*’} ‘name of bird of prey’, ‘soar’, ‘be high’. **Fire triad:** ‘go up in smoke’, ‘ashes’ [‘fine dust, aromatic powder’] ‘sandalwood*?*’ {‘burn’} 2 ‘(burnt offering) fire (kindle, light, Ur)’, ‘kindle’, ‘shine’ [‘night’, ‘dark’] ‘bake’, ‘be warm, hot’. **Seated torso’s (3rd) wheel:** ‘wheel’, 3 ‘(red) man (woman (mortal))’. **Beginning, origin:** ‘then’, ‘mother’, ‘father’, ‘testicles’ [‘hare’], ‘entrance’ [‘portico’], ‘found, make firm’. **Fir:** [*limits its lateral growth to soar higher:*] ‘constrain oneself, eminent’, ‘be contracted’, 3 ‘bind (gird about)’ [‘gird on’], 2 ‘surround (encompass)’, 3 ‘close (shut up)’ [‘tent, tabernacle’] ‘worship’ [*rune is named ‘god’*] ‘invoke’, ‘guide, go straight’, 2 ‘be firm (cedar)’, ‘base of column’, ‘command’, ‘chief satraps’, 2 ‘prince (strong [*for pine, oak, etc.*], terebinth)’. **Unity:** ‘one’, ‘only’, ‘I’, ‘betroth’ {‘union’} ‘brother’, ‘gather, lion, ark’, ‘agree to’, ‘these’, ‘also’, 3 ‘collect (draw back [*as the hand*])’, ‘bind together’. **Ox:** ‘ox, join together’ {3 ‘cattle’} ‘feed cattle’ [‘eat’], 3 ‘(bend) be strong (nothing (terebinth))’ {‘be strong’} ‘step slowly, she-ass’ [‘mules’] ‘slowness, prolong’; [*use in land-measure:*] ‘place’, ‘stone’, 3 ‘the earth (low)’; [*power to irrigate:*] ‘ravine, pour out, low place’, ‘be moist [*grass*]’ [‘mushroom’, ‘bear fruit’, ‘lead, plummet’, ‘weigh’]; [*plowing:*] ‘dig, ploughman’, ‘ploughshare’, ‘[*corn measure*]’ {2 ‘grain’} [‘thresh’], 2 ‘storehouse’. **Doer** [*emotions*]**:** ‘terror, dread’, ‘hate’, ‘curse’, ‘howl’, *10* ‘lament [*and sounds thereof*]’, 3 ‘urge (be narrow)’, ‘O that!’, ‘love’, 3 ‘desire (bend)’ [‘weave’, ‘net, ambush’, ‘injury’] 3 ‘befall’, ‘cease, fail’, 2 ‘depart’, ‘be active, nimble’ [‘goat-antelope’], ‘towards’, ‘go, way’ [*like ox*] ‘stray’, ‘transgress’, ‘folly’, ‘vanity’, ‘be corrupt’. **I LeBateleur:** ‘magician’ [{‘belonging to Neith’}], 2 ‘necromancer’; [*captures attention:*] ‘behold’, ‘mark’, ‘where’, ‘finger’, ‘attend’, ‘tarry’ {‘crowd’}. **Unparsed:** *2* ‘if, or’, ‘blackthorn’ {‘thorn-bush’} ‘tamarisk’, ‘hyssop, dwarf*?*’.

שׁ

Shin

PARSED ROOTS

Roots from shin are extensive, as befits S, which the Irish call the queen of consonants, as it alone does not rhyme with any other consonant (e.g. *m* with *n*, or *p* eith *t*). What surprised me was how the roots extend spring's plenty—this being *saille* (sal-yuh) the willow—into the plain of Shinar, the captivity, and the Tower of Babel: the Bible mentions how in Babylon during the captivity Jews hung their harps on the willows (thought to actually be the Euphrates poplar).

Let us begin with shin's shape in square Hebrew, which is a crown. Thus: שְׁבוֹ, 'agate'; שֵׁבֶט, '*staff/rod (for punishment)*/measure/fig. portion, *sceptre/tribe*, spear/lance, eleventh mo.'; שׁגל, 'lie w/ (woman), hence queen'; שׁוּע (= ישׁע), 'rich/opulent, liberal/noble, riches/wealth, salvation/deliverance'; שׂוּר, '(= שׂררה\ה) contend/strive, *be prince/have dominion, appoint princes*, to saw, (= סוּר) go away/depart'; שׁחה, '*bow/stoop down*/depress/*prostrate oneself/worship*, a pit'; שׁחח, '(be) bow(ed)/stoop down/brought low/be depressed, bowing down/submission, bring low/cast down'; שׁטר, 'officer/*overseer/magistrate*, Ch. a side [writer] *dominion*' (A. שׁטר 'to write'); שׁלט, '(let) rule/have dominion/power over, give permission/permit, Ch. get mastery of/seize, a shield, imperious/impudent, ruler/magistrate/prince, Ch. empire, authority/power, potent, Ch. -ful/mighty/lawful'; שֵׁם, 'name, fame/renown/reputation, Shem (s. of Noah)'; שׁמשׁ, 'Ch. attend/serve'; שׁפט, 'judge/administer justice, do - to/defend/vindicate, litigate/be judged, *rule(-r/judge)*, condemn/punish, judgment/punishment, justice/equity/right/privilege, cause/suit, custom/usage, law/institution, mode/manner'.

Willow's thin, drooping boughs: שׁוּל, '(only in plural) *train (of robe)*/hem (of garment)'; שׁחף > 'thin board, seagull, consumption' (A. '*be thin*'); שׁלח, 'send, - word/message/charge, send away/let go, put forth/*stretch out/extend*, dismiss, set free/*let hang down (the hair)*, cast down/off [a sending forth] *stretched out/slim/slender*, missile weapon/shoot/*sprout* [armed men (pl.)] a sending forth (cattle for grazing)/putting forth (hand), table, divorce/presents/dowry'; שֵׂעָר, '*hair, barley, hairy*/he-goat/demons, she-goat'; שׁקף, '*prop. bend forward to see*/look out/*abroad* (e.g. through window/(of mtn.) overhang/*look towards*/fig. impend/threaten, covering/coping/*frames (1 Kings 7:5), coped/having copings/*embrasure/*opening w/ beveled jam, lintel' (A. שׁקף 'cover, *be long and bending from length* (Gesen.)'); שׂרע, '*part. stretched out/prolonged*, i.e. having any member too long/unnaturally grown out, stretch oneself out'.

Its long, flexible boughs are woven into wicker work. Hence: שׂבך '(= סבך *interweave*), (ornaments of) net(work ornamenting capitals of pillars)/*lattice* (of window), thick(et) branches';

200

שבס ‘(perh. = שבץ mingle/*interweave*), cap of network/cauls (Isaiah 3:18)’; שבץ, ‘*weave in checkerwork/embroider*, be set/encased (of precious stones), perplexity/terror, giddiness/the cramp?, *textures/cloth interwoven/embroidered* (w/ gold threads), settings/bezels (for precious stones)/checkerwork/*embroidery*’ (Syr. ‘mingle/*interweave*’, A. ‘be *interwoven*/intricate’); שזר, ‘part. twined linen’ (A. ‘to twist’); שעטנז, ‘cloth of different threads (wool and flax together)’; שפן, ‘jerboa’ (zig-zag trajectory); שרג, ‘be interwoven [branch] –es (of vine)’; שרך, ‘part. twisting/winding (her course) (Jer. 2:23), shoe-latchet’; and שרק ‘(= שרך\ג interweave), vine (of choice quality), shoots/tendrils (of vine), combed [vineyard]’ (Syr. סרק ‘comb/prop. disentangle (flax)’). Four of these involve reysh, an oscillation (being rolled). (R has many masks.)

Continuing in this vein, Greek, Numidian, and runic S all picture a lightning bolt, that is, a zigzag: שאג, ‘roar (as lion/thunder)/groan, - (n.), a roaring’; שחק, ‘bruise/pound/reduce to dust, wear away, dust/cloud(s)/sky’; שער, ‘shudder, fear/reverence, sweep/tear away w/ a tempest, rage against/rush upon like a tempest, -/storm, a shuddering/horror, showers’.

This zigzag, turned on its side as in old Hebrew, becomes a molar, thus representing the cerebrospinal nerves: שנן, ‘sharp(en, e.g. sword)/fig. (the tongue, utter sharp/insulting words), inculcate/teach diligently, be pricked/pierced (w/ pain), tooth/ivory/prong (of fork)/sharp cliff, sharp/pointed saying/taunt’. Some toothlike things: שוש ‘(prob. be white), white marble/fine linen/byssus [white] lily/artificial -/n. of mus. instr./Susa (capital of Persia)’; שיד, ‘(cover w/) lime/plaster’; שית, ‘thorn/s (always coupled w/ שמיר)’, etym. unknown; שכך, ‘cover (in derivv. = שוך weave/hedge, but perh. also cut, cf. Latin *secare*) thorn, hedge/fence, spear > שכין knife (Ch. סכין)’; שלג, ‘(be white as) snow (of bones of slain)’; שלף, ‘draw (sword), pull off (shoe), pluck up (grass)’; שקד, ‘(formed like) almond(s), - tree’; שרט, ‘cut/make incisions (in body), tear/hurt oneself (by lifting), an incision’.

In the *Sefer Yetzirah*, shin is equated with fire, which give us: שאף, ‘draw in (air/wind cogn. שאב), pant/gasp, breathe hard/puff/hasten, breathe in/snap/snuff up (air/wind)/fig. pant for/desire eagerly, fig. (of savage enemies) swallow up/destroy’; שש\שאר > ‘leaven, kneading-trough’ (A. שאר\ת ‘*be hot/boil up*’ Gesen.); שבב > ‘*flame*, fragments’ (A. ‘*kindle*, Ch. ‘break’); שחן > ‘boil/sore/ulcer’ (A. ‘be hot/inflamed’); שרף, ‘burn/consume (lamps/torches for the dead), bake (bricks), be burned, sp. of venomous serpent/seraphim (order of angelic beings), funeral burning, -/conflagration’; שרת (doubtful root) > ‘frying-pan’; שתר [‘star (n. of Pers. prince)’]— four involve reysh (Le Diable, what glows in the dark).

Fire’s sense is sight: שבר, ‘view/examine, look/wait for/hope’; שגה, ‘look’; שהד > ‘a witness, testimony (a Ch./Syr. word)’ (Syr./Ch. ‘testify/bear witness’); 1. שור, ‘see/view/behold, watch for, lyer-in-wait/enemy’ (pointing to the last category); שזף, ‘see/look upon/behold/fig. the sun has scorched me (i.e. = Ch. שרף scorch/burn)?’; שחר, ‘be black, prop. do early/hence seek early/diligently, black, -ness, dusk (of morning)/hence the dawn (— בן son of dawn/Morning Star/Lucifer, at dawn/early, dawn/light/fig. sense/reason, dawn of life/youth, blackish/swarthy [whom the Lord seeks] [two dawns/twilights] [black/turbid (H. appellation for the Nile)]’; שכה > ‘[watchtower (pl.)] intelligence/only fig. heart/mind/epithet of cock?, a sight/object gazed upon, image/figure/imagination/idea/thought’; שמר, ‘keep/guard/*watch*/-man, keep/retain/reserve, *observe/mark*, preserve/protect, take heed/beware, *regard/reverence*, be kept/preserved [keeper] (שָׁמִיר) thorn(s)/diamond, sediment/lees (of wine), *a watching/fig. eyelid*, observance/keeping of a festival [*watch-hill*/height (Samaria)] *[watchful] night-watch*, a *watching*/guarding/*watch*/guards, *pl. of watching*/post/station/fig. object guarded, a keeping/preservation, observance/performance, what is to be observed/charge/law/usage/rite, adherence to (anyone)'; שָׁעָה, 'look at/regard w/ attention/look at w/ favor/regard graciously, look out/about (for help), look away from/allow respite to, look about w/ alarm/be dismayed?/look at/face one another?, Ch. hour/ moment of time'; שָׁפָה, 'part. *conspicuous*/lofty, become prominent/stand out (of bones), cheese (Syr. שְׁפָא cleanse from dregs) [eminent/excellent] elevated pl.'; שָׁקַד, 'wake/be sleepless, watch (w/ עַל over/for any thing/lie in wait for)'; שָׁקַר, 'Ch. look, Ch. stain/paint, wink (w/ eyes)/paint (eyes)?'; שָׁתַם, 'open/only part. הָעַיִן — having his eyes opened, Ch. bore through'. Five of these end in reysh, which makes sense since phosphorus glows in the dark.

The current of the Serpent Adversary is strong here: שָׁאַט '(prob. = שׁוּט condemn/despise) contempt'; שָׁגָא '(= שָׁגָה to err), error/sin through ignorance'; שָׁגַג, 'err/commit error, -/sin through ignorance'; שָׁגָה, 'wander/(cause to)go astray/err/sin through ignorance, a psalm, error/mistake'; שְׁדַר, 'Ch. exert oneself [Shadrach] Ch. *rebellion*'; שׁוֹא '(= שָׁאָה make noise/crash), *storm/tempest*, *destruction/ruin, -s/desolate places, evil/iniquity/wickedness, calamity/destruction, falsehood/lie*, worthlessness/vanity, noise/tumult/clamor' (A. שָׁו *'be evil'*); שׁוּד, '(= שָׁדַד) lay waste, demon'; 1. שׁוּט, '*prop. lash (water w/ oars)*/rower, go/run to and fro/fig. through/over (book i.e. examine it thoroughly), *whip/scourge/fig. calamity*, oar(s)'; 2. שׁוּט, 'condemn/despise'; שׁוּם, 'garlic'; שׁוּף, 'bruise/wound/cover w/ darkness'; שָׁטָה, 'turn aside/go astray'; שָׂטַם, 'hate/persecute/lay snares for, hatred/persecution or snares/destruction'; שָׂטָן, 'be hostile/oppose, opponent/adversary/devil (Satan), accusation'; שָׁכָה, '(perh. = שָׁגָה/Ethiop. שְׂכִי wander/rove)/wander about lasciviously'; שְׂמֹאל/שְׂמאול, '(on/to the) left/- side/hand/the north, turn/go left, use left hand'; שָׁמַם > 'sp. of poisonous lizard' (A. 'to poison'); שָׂנֵא, '(be) hate(d)/-r/enemy, hatred'; 2. שָׂעַר '(prob. = שָׁעַר to shudder), horrid/bad (of figs)/blighted, horrible' (A. שָׁעַר 'infect w/ contagion'); שְׁפַף > 'sp. of serpent [-]' (Syr. 'to creep', A. שָׁף 'speckled serpent'); שָׁקַץ, 'contaminate/pollute, loathe/abhor, abomination/-able thing'; שָׁקַר, 'act falsely towards (w/ לְ)/lie/speak falsehood/deceive/violate (covenant), lie/falsehood, in vain, -/deceitful thing'; שָׂרָה, 'contend/wrestle [contentious (Serai)] government, (in a) row [wrestles w/ God (Israel)]'; שָׁרַץ, 'to creep (of reptiles/smaller aquatic sp.)/abound/swarm w/, multiply/produce abundantly, reptiles/creeping things/smaller aquatic sp.'; שָׁרַק, '(lure by) hiss(ing/whistling) at (in contempt), a hissing/derision, object of contempt, whistling/piping, pipe/flute'; שָׁרַר, '(*twist*/press together/*oppress*? Gesen.) part. *adversary/enemy* [firm] (prop.) navel(-cord), -/sinew/muscle, chain, firmness *(w/ לֵב stubbornness/obstinacy of heart)*'. And perhaps: שׁוּט, 'go/turn aside, one who turns aside'. Seven build on shin waw (the Light trapped in thoughts); seven invoke teyt (earth, the senses), seven invoke reysh (Le Diable, no surprise there), and five invoke alef, this last telling us we doers are the actual perpetrators.

In shin's trump, XVI La Maison Dieu—often called (Lightning Struck) Tower—a crown is being unseated from it by fire and cannonball (representing 16-sulfur): שָׁאָה, 'be desolate/prob. fall w/ a crash, make noise/rushing, be confused/astonished?/gaze at?, be laid waste, tempest, noise/tumult/bustle/shouting, a crash/destruction, desolation'; שׁבר, 'break/- in pieces/quench (thirst)/afflict (heart)/tear (as wild beast)/break down/destroy, define/assign, buy/sell corn, cause to break through (of fetus), be broken/afflicted/oppressed, breach/fracture/fig. sorrow/vexation, solution/interpretation, destruction/ruin/terror, grain/corn (etym. uncert.), pain/ruin, matrix, waves/breakers'; שׁדד, 'treat w/ violence/oppress, attack/invade, plunder(er), lay waste/destroy, spoil/waste/ruin, violence/oppression/devastation, mistress/lady/wife? (A. שׁידה mistress)/female cupbearers? (Ch. שׁדא pour out)/mus. instr. (A. שׁדא sing), Almighty (A. שׁדיד strong/vehement) [stronghold (Ashdod)]'; שׁדם > 'blasted corn, fields/esp. corn fields (also vineyards)'; שׁדף, 'to blight (as east wind corn)'; שׁוע, '(a) cry for help'; שׁחט, '(be) slaughter(ed)/kill/slay, alloyed (gold)' (A. שׁחט 'dilute wine'); שׁחת, 'be marred/spoiled by rotting/be corrupted (morally)/be laid waste, destroy/ruin, (act) corrupt(ly/wickedly)/pervert, be spoiled, corrupt deed/crime, putridity, snare/trap, defilement'; שׁכל, 'lose children/become childless, -, make -/bereave(d/ment/childless state), abort/miscarry, (of vine) be unfruitful, cluster/bunch of grapes/flowers' (A. 'to bind'); שׁלך, 'throw/cast/- off (as plant its flowers)/cast out/expel/banish/cast down/overthrow/destroy, be thrown/cast down/overthrown, gannet (a sea-fowl), felling (of tree)'; שׁמד, 'destroy/lay waste, cut off (persons/nations), destruction'; שׁמם, '(be) desolate/laid waste, wasted/perishing/solitary, lay waste/make desolate, -tion, be astonished/amazed/confounded, destroy oneself [desert]'; שׁסע, 'cleave/divide (e.g. a hoof)/rend/tear asunder, chide/rebuke/keep off/withhold/stay, cleft/division (in hoof)'; שׁסף, 'cut/hew in pieces'; שׁעט > 'stamping (of horse hoofs)' (A. תעט 'stamp/pound in pieces'); 1. שׁער, 'estimate the value/prob. prim. cleave/divide, gate (of camp/palace/temple/but esp. city/fig. the city itself/fig. those assembled at gate, measure [two gates (pl.)] gate-keeper [whom the Lord values]' (A. תער 'be cleft'); שׁתר, 'break forth' (A. שׁתר 'split/burst' Gesen.). (Four involve dalet, lightning's tree; and four involve ayin, mercury's volatility.)

Hence, the Tower of Babel, and confusion of tongues: שׁבשׁ, 'Ch. be perplexed'; שׂגב, 'be lifted/raised up/high/inaccessible, exalted/secure/safe/difficult to comprehend, hill/rock/strong place/refuge, make powerful/strengthen'; שׂום/שׂים, 'put/set/place (someone or thing) to stand erect/hence set (plant)/set in array (an army)/constitute/appoint/set up (pillar)/hence found, and so on'; 3. שׁור, 'wall (perh. from 2. שׁור go round)'; שׁחץ > 'elation/pride [heights]' (A. 'lift up oneself'); שׁית, 'put/set/place (someone or thing made/regarded as erect), set in array/constitute, appoint, set (limit/term), put/lay (hand on anyone), direct/turn (face/eyes i.e. intend), put/lay on (ornament), cast/throw?/lay up?, render/give, attire, foundation?/pillars?, buttock, gift [Seth]'; שׂפה, 'lip, speech/words, language/dialect, brim (of vessel), shore (of sea)/bank (of river), edge/-ing/border/boundary, lower part of face/chin/beard'; שׁתת, (= שׁית) 'set/place/put'. And the more generic: שׁלב, 'join(ed) together, joining, edges/borders'; שׁפה '(perh. join/associate cogn. ספח), female servant/handmaid, family/household/clan, tribe/nation, race/kind (of beast)'—that makes six that involve labials (the most visible speech-sounds). Then there is the mason's tool: שׁקל, *weigh (out/pay)/fig. examine/try, shekel (gold/silver standard wt.) [migration (Askelon)] act of weighing/weight, plummet/Sept. balance'.*

Captivity: שׁאר, 'remain/be left over/left behind, let remain/leave behind, have left/retain, remainder/remnant'; שׁבה, 'take prisoner/carry away captive/carry off, captivity/fig. captives/fig.

state of great affliction/misery'; שבק, 'leave/be left [forsaking]'; שׁוּב, 'turn/- back/return/- to God/be converted, go back/be restored (as field to former possessor/thing to former state), turn away/cease/desist, return to doing, lead/bring back, restore/renew, etc., a return/those that return, turning away/rebellious [restored] a returning/defection/apostasy, return/answer'; שׁוּג, '(= סוּג) *hedge about?/cause to grow? (= שׂגה\א)*'; שׁוּח, 'sink/*be bowed down/depressed* [pit] [-digger] pitfall/*dungeon*/grave/sepulchre'; סוּךְ/שׂוּךְ, '*hedge in/fence (prop. w/ thorn hedge)?/*twist/weave?, bough *[hedge/fence] thorn-hedge*'; שׁכך, 'bow/stoop down/lower itself/(cause to) abate/quiet/still (*sh*), Sheshach (a name for Babylon)'; שׁלל, 'draw out (as in A.), *plunder/spoil/carry off (spoil)*, *become prey*, *plunder/booty*, gain/profit, stripped/naked/Sept./Syr. barefoot, *captive/prisoner*'; שׁלמאסר/שׁלמן [(king of Assyria who carried off the ten tribes into captivity)]; שׁסה, 'plunder/spoil'; שׁסס, '(be) plunder(ed)/spoil(ed), prey/booty'; שׁפל, '*be made low*/depressed (of voice)/*humbled (in spirit), bring low*/throw down/*humble/- oneself*, low/-ly/mean/contemptible/*humble, low place/condition*, low country, lowness (of hands)/remissness/idleness'; שׁקד, 'be bound/fastened'; שׁרד, 'flee/escape, remnant, one left/escaped'; שׁרה, '*loose/set free/untie*/solve/lodge/dwell/begin, be loosened, beginning [pleasant lodging] solution/maceration, coat of mail' (A. שׁרי 'glitter'); and שׁשׁא, 'lead (*as on a rope)'. Plus: שׁכם, 'shoulder/part/portion [Shechem]', substituted for Jerusalem during the captivity (for the Jews that remained behind).

The plain of Shinar: שׁדד, '(coll. w/ A.) be straight/even [plains]'; שׂדה, 'plain/level tract of country, field/piece of cultivated ground, fields/country/territory'; שׁוה, 'be equal (in value), countervail/be sufficient (for a damage)/enough, be fitting/proper, be like/resemble, *make level/even*, make (oneself) similar/like, put (forth/yield)/set/place *[plain]* [like/similar] liken/(be) compare(d/considered like)/feared (as in Ch.)'; שׁנער [Shinar (the country round Babylon)]. Some things likely found there: שׁוֹר, '(herd of) ox(en)'; שׂיה, 'one of flock/sheep/goat'; שׂיח, 'plant/shrub/bush'; שׂלו, 'quails'; שׁפת, 'set/put/place/give, stalls/folds (for cattle)?/pots/cooking vessels?, folds/enclosures for cattle'; שׁקמה, 'sycamore trees'; שׁקק '(prob. = זקק to strain, Gesen.), sackcloth/sack (for grain)'. Then there is the process of getting there: 2. שׁוּר, 'go/travel (esp. for traffic)/part. traveling company/caravan, gift/present'; שׁכח, 'Ch. be found, find/get/obtain'.

Then there is the *sh* sound itself, shushing, resting: שׁאן, '(= שׁען lean/*rest)/be(/live) quiet(ly) [quiet] at ease [two resting places], (living in) quiet(/peace), at ease/careless/proud, wantonness/pride'; שׁבח, '*soothe/quiet/calm, -/still*, praise/laud, pronounce happy *[soothing] praise oneself/boast of*'; שׁבן ['tender(ness)'] (A. 'be tender/delicate'); שׁבת, '*rest (from labor)/*lie uncultivated/cease/desist/(be) interrupt(ed)/*keep Sabbath, day of rest/Sabbath, make/let rest (from labor), restrain/still*, put away/remove, *a ceasing/cessation*, interruption/loss of time [-born] destruction/ruin'; שׁהה, 'prob. A. שׁהא forget/neglect'; שׁוּח, '*meditate* (= שׂיח)'; שׁכב, 'lie down esp. to sleep/rest, lie/keep one's bed, lie (of one slain), lie w/ (carnally), be ravished, lay down, stop?/pour out?, layer (of dew), act of lying w/, *couch/bed/bier*'; שׁכח, '(leave from) forget(fullness)/disregard/(be) neglect(ed/forgotten), forgetting/neglecting'; שׁכן, '*lie down/rest*, abide/continue/dwell(ing/settled)/inhabit, place/fix, cause to dwell, inhabitant/neighbor, dwelling (also of God, a temple)/tent/sacred tabernacle/lair of beasts'; שׁלה, '*be quiet/at ease*/enjoy prosperity/make prosperous/draw out, become negligent/go astray/err, deceive (from idea of quieting/flattering, by promise of happiness, or leading astray), fault/error, careless/unmindful (of God), *quiet*/prosperity, failure/negligence, *quiet/stillness*, the after-birth, *pacificator/bringer of peace (i.e. Messiah)/Shiloh*'; שמט, 'let go/release/remit (debt)/*let lie uncultivated, cease from, set oneself free/break loose* or kick (A. שמץ strike/smite) or stick fast or drop/slip/stumble, *(be) throw(n) down*'; שמץ > '*short/gentle sound/hint/a whispering*, a -/muttering?/rout/overthrow/ill fame/reproach?' (A. 'impel/drive/thrust, speak rapidly'); שען, '*lean/rest*/rely on/trust in, *recline*, touch/border upon/be adjacent to [support (pl.)] a stay/support, staff'; שעע, '*be closed/(of eyes) blinded/be overspread, cover/blind (eyes)*, delight (oneself/be –d)/rejoice, be fondled/caressed, delight/indulge oneself (ב w/in anyone)/be dazzled/blinded?, delight/pleasure' (Syr./Ch. —/שוע 'spread over, stroke/caress/flatter'); שפן, 'cover/hide'; שקט, 'rest/be quiet/undisturbed, rest/be free from (w/ מן), be inactive/silent, give rest, (keep/be) quiet/still/part. rest/quiet'; שתק, 'be still/rest/abate (of waves/strife)'. (Four involve motherly beyt.)

In fact, *sh* is the sound of the fount of spring (*saille* the willow): שאב, 'draw (water), watering troughs/places'; שבל > '*train (of robe)/locks (of hair) (from idea of flowing)*, snail (from its slimy trail), *ear of corn/branch/stream/flood [shoot]* way/path' (coll. by Gesen. w/ A. 'go, *rise/grow, flow copiously*')—here beginning very close to where we began with those willowy boughs, earlier—שבע, 'be/become satiated/satisfied/filled (esp. food, less freq. drink), satisfy/satiate, abundance/plenty, satiated/satisfied/full, enough/abounding/rich, satiety/fulness'; שגא, '(= שגה) be/become/make great, magnify/laud, Ch. become great/increase, much/many, great/-ly'; שגה, 'become great/increase'; שגר, 'the young/offspring, Ch. cast forth/eject'; שדה, 'Ch. *cast/shoot/pour out, breast/teat* [shedding/darting light]' (A. שדא '*moisten/irrigate*'); שון > 'urine' (Syr. תון 'urinate'); שוק, '(cogn. שקק run) hence run after/desire, *run over/(cause to) overflow*, leg (man/beast), street, desire/longing'; שחה, '(a) swim(ming), make to -/overflow'; שחה, 'squeeze/press out'; שטח, 'spread abroad/expand/enlarge, strew/scatter'; שטף, 'wash (away), -/rinse/cleanse, overflow/inundate/overhelm/fig. sweep away (as flood), be washed/rinsed, an overflowing (of water, fig. effusion of anger/devastation by an army)/flood/inundation'; שמן, 'be/become fat, stout/robust/(of land) fertile/(of food) nourishing, fatness/richness/delicacy, (of land) fertility/fig. prosperity, oil, ointment, rich production (of earth), rich/delicate food, fertile fields'; שמנה, 'eight/y, -th/mus. instr.?/the octave?'; שנב > 'latticed window' (A. '*be cool*'); שפח, 'pour out, make fall off (as hair by disease/scab)/make bald, a shedding of blood (A. shed blood)/or perhaps confusion?'; שפך, 'pour out (fig. prayer/soul/heart before Lord/anger on anyone, (be) pour(ed) out (spirit, i.e. God), shed (blood), throw up (mound), be profusely expended, slip (of steps), pl. of pouring out, male organ (f.!) [effusion/increase]'; שפע, 'an overflowing/abundance [-] - (of water)/multitude (of camels)'; שצף, (= שטף) 'an overflowing'; שקה, 'give to/let drink/water (cattle)/irrigate (ground), be overflown, be moistened/refreshed, cupbearer/butler, drinking-trough, drink/refreshment, well-watered country'; שקע, 'sink in water, *be overflown/submerged*, subside/abate (fire), cause to sink/subside/depress'; שרח ['abundance']; שרש, 'root, what springs up from the root/shoot/sprout, foot (of mtn.)/bottom (of sea)/sole (of foot), take root, origin/source/cause, root out/extirpate'; שתה, '*to drink/to banquet*/be drunk, a drinking/warp (of web), *banquet/feast*' (A. שתי 'fix warp to loom', Syr. '*weave*'); שתל, 'to plant, shoot/branch'; שתן, 'make water'. Eleven of these involve labials, four beyt and five soft peh (*fearn* the alder, the Corn Spirit).

Given the prosperity of the season, we should add these: שחד, 'give presents/bribe, -(ry)/gift/present'; שי, 'present/gift'; שכר, 'bribe/hire, - out oneself, wages/reward, laborer/hireling [he brings reward?/gotten by hire? (Issachar)]'; and שכר, 'drink to hilarity/be intoxicated/fig. giddy, make/act like one drunken, strong drink, intoxicated/drunken, -ness, *gift/present*' (A. *'give reward/present'*).

In Nordic (and Berber) Tifinag, S was the sun-symbol (circle with central dot), since spring was when it first appeared (north of the Arctic Circle), and the rune S, a vertical zigzag, bears the name *sōwilō*, 'sun' (the same word as *sol* in Latin): שחל, 'lion, onyx/an odoriferous shell' (A. שחל 'to peel/shell'); שטה, 'acacia/- wood [- (pl.)]'; שכם, 'rise early (in morning), get early (to a pl.), in the morning, early/without delay'; שמח, 'shine cheerfully (of a candle), express joy, be -ful/glad, cheer/gladden/make rejoice, -ing/joyful/glad, festivity/mirth'; שמש, 'sun [-like (Samson)] windows/notches/battlements'; שפר, 'prop. be bright/pleasant/acceptable to (w/ על), make bright/beautiful/brightness/beauty, Ch. to please [pleasantness (pl.)] trumpet/curved horn [fair (pl.)] royal canopy, Ch. dawn, measure (etym. uncert.)'; שרב, 'heat (of sun)/drought, mirage [heat of the Lord]' (Syr./Ch. 'be hot/dry'); שרק, 'bay (of horses)'; שש, 'six(-th/-ty)'; שת, 'Ch. six(-ty)'.

Shin is the initial of the word *Shekinah* (divine Presence) and stands for the Holy Spirit—Sophia (Wisdom) and alter-ego Prunikos. Related to sight: שכל, 'act wisely/prudently/wittingly, look at/consider/attend to, be/become intelligent/wise/prudent, part. wise/prudent/godly/pious, intelligence/wisdom, (cause to) prosper/have success, make wise/teach/instruct, understanding, regard/estimation, craft/cunning'. Other relevant roots: ש, 'rel. pron. who/which/what, that/so that/for'; שאל, '*ask/inquire of/interrogate*/demand/require/request/petition, ask as loan/borrow, ask leave/beg/lend, request/petition/thing lent/loan, *subject of inquiry*/matter/affair, grave/*abode of departed souls*/Hades (from demanding? or = שעל be hollow) [asked for/lent (Saul)]'; שבע, 'seven(-fold/-ty), - times, -th, - days/week, swear/promise by oath (often confirmed by seven victims), cause to swear/charge solemnly, oath/curse'; שיש/שוש/שיש, 'exult/be glad/rejoice, (object of) joy/gladness, rejoicing'; שזב, 'Ch. deliver/rescue'; שחק, '*laugh/(w/ אל) smile upon/approve*, (w/ ל/על) laugh at/deride/scorn, make sport/play, - *mus. instr.*, skirmish'; שיח, 'speak, tell/declare, complain/lament, meditate, speech/talk/discourse/complaint, meditation, thought/purpose, pious meditation'; שור/שיר, 'sing(er), to be sung, a singing/song, sacred -/hymn'; שלם, 'be entire/i.e. sound/safe, (be) complete(d)/finish(ed), be at peace, preserve/keep uninjured, restore/make good, repay/pay (debt), perform (vow)/recompense, be perfected, make peace w/, Ch. make an end of/restore, whole/perfect/full/complete/finished, safe/uninjured, peaceable [Salem (Jerusalem)] sound/well, wholly, safe/secure/enjoying peace, -ably disposed, health/welfare/prosperity/peace, friendship, peace-/thank-offering, retribution [peaceable (Solomon)] reward/gift'; שמה, 'heaven/-s, -ward' (A. 'be high'); שמע, 'hear/listen/give attention/accept prayer (God)/hearken/understand, be heard, obey/show oneself obedient/submissive, be understood, cause to hear /summon/proclaim/play aloud/sing/call, rumor/report [-] sound/music [a hearing/accepting

(Simeon)] [renowned] [etc.] [heard of God (Samuel)] [God hears (Ishmael)] news/tidings/information/teaching/doctrine, a hearing/audience, obedience/subjects'; שׁקק, '(a) run(ning) to and fro/be greedy/eager [-ness]'; שׁרת, 'wait upon/serve/minister/perform service of sanctuary, service/ministry, attendant, worship'. As a sign of wisdom: שׁיב, '(be) grey-headed/old man, grey hairs/old age'. And in the spirit of shamanism: שׁגע, 'mad/dened (applied contemptuously to prophets), act/behave like madman, madness/impetuosity'.

The following seem symbolically related to the above: שׂמל '(wrap oneself in garment, Gesen.), garment' (A. 'cover w/ garment'); and שׁנס, 'gird up (loins)'.

There is one remaining category, namely the Rubedo or reddening, third and final stage of alchemy and thus up there with the Holy Spirit in terms of sacredness. It arises from the fact that the 'father' properly matched with shin as mother is vav, bardic U, the full moon, associated thus with the color *red*: שׁהם, 'onyx/sardonyx'; שׁנה, '(be) repeat(ed)/do again, be different from, alter/(be) change(d), -able/unsteady, change (garment)/alter (promise/one's way)/disfigure (the countenance)/transfer (location), disguise oneself, be changed/altered/different from (w/ מן)/part. different, violate/transgress, year/fig. produce of same, two/both/(a) second (time/again), angels (perh. changed/glorified ones)?, second (in) rank (in succession/dignity/quality/(the) next/a doubling/duplicate/copy/division (of Jerusalem), *bright scarlet color (from the coccus)/scarlet clothes/garments*' (A. שׂנא '*shine/be bright*'); שׁרד, '*(prob. color)ed (garments), red chalk/ochre or style/graver (Gesen. coll. A.)*'; שׁשׁר, 'red color/red ochre'. Being as it is the third stage: שׁלושׁ/שׁלשׁ, '(they) three/thrice/thirty, divide in three/do a third time/on third day/threefold/three yrs. old [triad] third/- part/- yr., one-third of an Ephah (measure)/mus. instr. (triangle?/harp w/ three strings?)/chariot warriors (three to a chariot)/officer of third rank, descendants of the third generation/great-grandchildren [in a triangle (pl.)] three days ago/day before yesterday'.

The following is interesting in and of itself, for it shows the mother shin giving birth to the mother alef giving birth to the fourth Wheel or womb, where reysh (heredity) stands for the fourth Wheel and the four smaller Wheels it contains: שׁאר, 'flesh, blood-relation/kindred, food, blood-relationship, near relative'.

I am left with: שׁעל > 'hollow hand/palm, handful, fox [-es (pl.)] narrow path/hollow way'; and שׁתם, 'stop/shut out'.

SUMMARY

Shin *is the most difficult to parse, because the categories tend to bleed into each other indiscriminantly.* **Square Hebrew** [*3-pronged crown*]: 'three, divide in three, three-stringed harp'; 'ask leave {asked for [*Saul*]}', 2 '(judge) rule', 2 'be prince, have dominion (contend [*Israel*=wrestler with God])', 'dominion, magistrate [*Arab.* write]', 'to lead', 'sceptre, tribe', 'queen, to lie with [*a woman*]'. **Shekhinah** [*Holy Spirit*]: 'name, renown, the Name' {'*fame?*'} 'hear, listen, accept prayer [*God*], understand, proclaim', 'sing, sacred song', 'exalt, rejoice, be glad'. **'Shsh':** *3* '([*ShKN*] lie down, abide, continue, sacred tabernacle) (be still, abate [*waves,* *strife*]) rest (be quiet, undisturbed, to quiet, to still)', 2 '(bow down, to still) to quiet (to calm, soothe [*ShBCh*])', '[*ShBTh*] rest from labor, keep sabbath' [*ShBO:* 'seven, week'], '[*ShLM*] be entire, be at peace', 2 '([*ShLH*] be at ease, Shiloh [*i.e. pacificator, Messiah*], fault, error [*i.e.* become negligent?]) be quiet (rest on, recline, careless, proud, wantonness)', 'meditate, speak, complain, lament, thought', 'cry for help' [*in child, calls for "shsh"*], 'be tender, delicate', 'a whispering, a hint'. **Fire's hisss:** 'draw in [*air, wind*], gasp', 'hiss', 'stop, shut out', 'laugh, deride, scorn, smile upon', 2 '(leaven, boil up) be hot (inflamed, a boil, a sore, ulcer)', 'frying pan', 'kindle, flame', 2 '(scorch) burn (consume, bake bricks, species of venomous serpent, Serafim)'. **S-shape** [*serpent, Adversary*]: 2 '(species of serpent) to creep (swarm with, multiply, reptiles, creeping things)', 'species of poisonous lizard', 'be lowered, low, mean, contemptible, lowly, humble, low country', 'lie down, lie [*slain*], -with carnally, be ravished, couch, bed, bier', 'wander about lasciviously', 'run to and fro, be eager, greedy', 2 '(turn aside) go astray (err, sin through ignorance)', 'be intoxicated, strong drink', 'be corrupted [*morally*] or spoiled by rotting, be laid waste', 'to blight [*as the east wind corn*]', 'horrid, bad [*of figs*]', 'contaminate, pollute, loathe, abominate, abhor', 'contemn, despise', 2 '(be hostile, oppose, the devil, Satan, the A-) adversary (enemy, firmness, chain, sinew, navel)', 2 '(enemy) hate (persecute)', 'deceive, violate [*covenant*], falsehood', 'rebellion', 'left, north'. **Fire's sense:** 2 '(view, watch for, layer-in-wait, enemy) see, behold (look upon)', 'be sleepless, watch [*-over, -for*], lie in wait', 2 '(keep, watch, guard) regard (look at)', 'act wisely, look at, consider', 2 '(examine) view (regard, look for {watchtower} a sight, image, idea)', 'wink, paint the eyes [*Chald. SQR,* look; *also* stain, paint]', 'look', 'testify, bear witness, a witness', 'open [*as eyes*], bore through', 'become visible, appear, conspicuous, lofty' {'star'} 'cover, hide'. **Sun** [*Lib. shape, runic name*]: 'lion' [*its sign*]; 'sun', 'heat [*of sun*], drought, mirage', 'shine cheerfully [*a candle*], gladden', 2 '(bright scarlet, shine) be bright (pleasant, trumpet, dawn, royal canopy)', '[*of horses*] bay', '[*Arab.* to glitter] coat of mail'; 'six', 'year, two, second, repeat, alter, changeable, unsteady'; 'acacia' [*yellow globular flowers; WG, p. 264*]. **Old Semitic shape** [*molar*]: 'almond'; 'to cut? thorn, spear', 'thorn(s)', 'knife', 'draw [*knife*], pull off [*shoe*], pluck up [*grass*]', 'sharpen, teach diligently, tooth [*ShN*], ivory, pointed saying or taunt', 'snow, be white as snow', 'be white? white marble, fine linen, lily', 'garlic' [*lily family*], 'lime, plaster', 'forget, neglect'. **Lightning** [*in Greek, Libyan, runic*]: [*cleaves wood:*] 'to saw?' [*saw-toothed symbol*], 'cut or hew in pieces', 'cut, make incisions, tear or hurt oneself', 'cleave, divide, rend or tear asunder, cleft [*in hoof*]', 'break forth, split? burst?', 'storm, shuddering, showers', 'roar [*lion, thunder*], groan'. **XVI LaMaisonDieu** [*lightning-struck tower*]: 'clap hands, suffice, a smiting, chastisement', '[*Arab. ThOT,* stamp, pound in pieces] a stamping [*of hooves*]', 2 '(fall with a crash? tempest, tumult) lay or be laid waste (be desolate, astonished)', 3 '((oppress, attack, plunder) lay waste) destroy (break in pieces, a breach or fracture, calamity)', 'to plunder, spoil', 'to row [*properly* lash with oars], a whip or scourge', 2 '(wound, cover with darkness) bruise (pound, reduce to dust, wear away)', 'slaughter, kill, slay'; [*dislodged crown:*] 'be grey-headed'; [*tower ejecting twins:*] 2 '(send, -away [*let loose*], let down [*by a cord*], shoot, sprout, missile weapon) throw, cast (-off [*as plant its flowers*], -out, expel, banish, destroy, cast down, overthrow, a felling [*of a tree*])' [*cf.* **fount of spring** *below*], 'eject, cast forth', 'become or make childless, miscarry', 'flee, escape'. **Tower of Babel** [*from trump*]: 2 'set, place [*standing or erect*]', 2 '(be lifted, raised up, or exalted) be high (heavens)', 'elation, pride', 'impetuosity, madness', 'be perplexed', 'lip, speech, language, dialect, brim [*of vessel*], shore, border', 'wall'. **Babylon** [*from Babel*]: {'[*ShLMNASR, Assyrian king, carried away ten tribes into captivity*]'} 'take prisoner, carry away captive', 'carry off [*spoil*], stripped, naked, captive, prisoner', 'be bound, fastened, 2 '(attend) serve (wait upon, worship)' {'Shadrach [*Daniel's companion*]'} 'remain, remnant', 'leave, be left', 'go away, depart', 'travel, caravan, gift', 2 '(gift) bribe (hire)', 'weigh, -out [*pay*], examine, a plummet', 'estimate value, gate [*also poetic for* city], a measure' {'Sheshach [having brazen gates, *for Babylon*]'} 'there, thither, then', 'to loose, set free, solve, dwell, begin, -ning, solution, maceration', 'deliver, rescue', 'return, lead or bring back'. **Plain of Shinar** [*settled life near Babylon*]: 'Shinar', 'fields, cornfields, vineyards', 'plain, level tract, field, cultivated land', 'be straight, even, a harrow', 'make level, even, put forth, yield [*fruit*]', 'let lie uncultivated, set oneself free', 'flesh, kindred, food', 'one of the flock', 'ox, herd of oxen', 'stalls, folds [*for cattle*]'. ***Lotus pool*** [sh—*replaced* ***quail chick***, w *(to shush U of Logos)*]: 'quails', 'sink in, be submerged, pond, pool'. **Willow's proverbial thirst:** 'draw [*water*]', '[*Arab.* fill with water]'. **As fount of spring:** 2 '(to water [*cattle*], drink, well-watered country) irrigate (moisten, cast, shoot, pour out, breast, teat)' [*cf. old Semitic (table 2)*], 'pour out, shed [*blood*]', 'make water', 'urine', 3 '(swim) (wash, -away, inundate) overflow (run after, desire)', 2 '(satiate, plenty) abundance (-of water, an overflowing)' {'abundance'} 'flow copiously, train [*of robe*], locks [*of hair*], stream, flood', 'hair, barley, hairy, goat, demons', 'a plant or bush', 2 '(root, shoot, sprout, cause, source) origin (be black, at dawn, early)', 'rise or arrive early', 'to plant, shoot, branch', 'become great, increase', 'become fat, fertility [*of land*], oil', 'rich, opulent, liberal, noble' ['hollow hand, palm, handful, narrow path, fox', 'find, get, obtain'] 'squeeze, press out', 'spread abroad, expand, enlarge, strew, scatter'. **Its thin, droopy boughs:** 'be thin', 'be bowed down or depressed', 'cover, be long and bending from length, [*of mtn.*] overhang or look towards', 'stretched out, prolonged [*having a part too long, unnaturally grown out*]', 'train [*of robe*], hem [*of garment*]', 'be overspread, closed' ['sycamores']. **Wicker or weaving, 'lurch to and fro'** [*in 'Orphic' hymn*]: 'be cool, latticed window', *3* '(mingle) interweave (tendrils [*of vine*], combed [*Syr. SRQ* to comb *(flax)*]) (net, network, lattice)', 'sackcloth [*prob. ZQQ* to strain *(cogn. Lat. saccavit) or Ethiop. SQSQ* lattice]', 'twisting or winding her course, shoe-latchet', 'a drink, banquet, warp of web [*Arab.* fix warp to loom, *Syr.* weave]', 'join together, joinings, edges, borders', 'join or associate*?* family, handmaid, household, clan, tribe, race, kind [*of animals*]', 'hedge in*?* twist or weave*?* a bough', 'gird up [*loins*]', 'garment, wrap oneself in same', 'a cloth made of different threads of wool and flax together', 'twist, twined linen'. **Spring's 4-8-16:** 'eight'. **Fire's color** [*alchemy's Rubedo, associated with U of Logos*]: 'red ochre', 'color*?* colored garments, red chalk or ochre*?* a style or graver*?*', 2 '(oderiferous shell [*Arab.* to peel, shell]) onyx (sardonyx)' [*the sard in sardonyx is deep orange-red*]. **Unparsed:** 'agate', 'shoulder, part', 'jerboa'.

מם

Mem

PARSED ROOTS

Mem is *water* in *Sefer Yetzirah*, from its calendar position at libra, the dregs of the water triad: מאן, 'Ch. vessel/*utensil/*goblet'; 2. מאס, '(= מסס) *melt*/*dissolve*/waste away'; מואב ['*water (i.e. progeny) of the father (Moab)*']; מוג, '*melt (away)/flow down/(be) dissolve(d/undone)* (fig. from fear), *cause to melt*/despond/waste away'; מטר, '*(cause/give) rain* (as lightning/fire and brimstone/hail/manna), *be –ed upon*'; מי, '*water/s/fig. juice* (e.g. of poppies) (emblematic of abundance/danger/terror/arrogance)'; מיכל, 'brook (R. uncert.)'; מסה, 'cause to flow down, dissolve/melt'; מסס, '*flow down/melt*, become weak/faint (heart, from fear/grief/sorrow), cause to faint/make -hearted'; מקק, '*(be) melt(ed)/flow/run*, (cause to) waste/consume away, rottenness'; מרק, 'make clean/bright by rubbing/polish/furbish, purification/fig. precious ointments/perfumes, *broth, be cleansed, cleansing*/remedy'; משע > 'a cleansing/clean' (A. 'cleanse').

Physiologically, this translates into blood: מאם > '*spot/blemish* (physical/moral)'; מאר, 'irritate/pain(ful)'; מחה, '*strike*/wipe out/away, (be) blot(ted) out/destroy(ed), *part. taken from the marrow*, destroying/corrupting, a striking (of battering rams)' (A. מחח '*take out marrow*'); מחח '*(be marrowy)*, fat/rich, *marrow*'; מחץ, '*dash/plunge (as foot in blood)*/break in pieces/fig. crush (of wisdom), *contusion/bruise*'; מחק, 'strike/smite'; מרדך ['Merodach (Babyl. Mars)']; מרדכי ['Mordecai'] (very bloody story); מרח, 'rub/bruise/crush'; מרט, 'make smooth/polish/*sharpen (sword)*/pluck out hair/make/become bald, *be sharp(ened)*, Ch. be plucked'—four built on mem cheyt (shoulders, bulk), and four on mem reysh.

As long as it is at its calendar-station libra, it represents blood drawn to the loins: מול, '*(be) circumcise(d)*, (be) cut off/destroy(ed), *circumcision*'; מזיח/מזח, 'girdle/*belt'; 2. מלל, '*(be) circumcise(d)*, be cut off (as grass/etc.), ear of corn'; ממזר, 'bastard (from adultery/incest, etym. uncert.)'; מע, '*intestines/bowels/fig. belly/womb/viscera*/fig. heart/mind [compassionate]'; מעך, 'press, *bruised/castrated* [oppression]'; מתן > '*loins*, Ch. strong' (A. 'be firm'). Association with the loins may be why as a prefix מ (standing for מן from root מנן) means 'from/of'.

Mem is a stand-in for reysh at libra, and the following is perfectly placed to be roughly where reysh is in the geodetic model based on a *Giza* fulcrum (libra): מף [Memphis (Egyp.)], which is slightly south from Giza, towards Upper Egypt (*mouth* reysh, consumers of *loaf* teyt). And as manifested earth, libra represents touch (Egyptians' fourth and last sense), symbolizing the sensual (in Hymn of the Pearl): 2. מוש, '(= משש) feel/touch [tried]'; משש, 'touch/(examine by) feel(ing)/- one's way/grope'.

Let me introduce this this way: old Hebrew mem shows a mother gathering us to her bosom with her left arm. Here are some of the things that might arouse that compassion: מאן, 'refuse/be unwilling, -/refusing'; 1. מאס, 'reject/despise/lightly esteem, aversion/contempt, be condemned/despised'; מגר, 'fallen/delivered up, cast down/overthrow [precipice (pl.)]'; מוט, 'totter/shake/(of foot) slip/slide/(of hand) be weak/fail (fig. of prosperity), be moved/shaken, cause to fall/come down, a tottering/shaking/pole/staff/yoke'; מוך, 'become reduced/wax poor [reduced/thin]'; מזה ['fear']; מכך, 'waste/pine away/sink/decay, -/perish'; מלח, 'pass away/vanish, decay/rottenness'; מעד, '(make/be made to) vacillate/totter'; מעל, '*act perversely/treacherously/be faithless, perverseness/treachery/sin*, robe/mantle/long full upper garment (of men and women of dignity)'; 1. מרא, '*be rebellious* (cogn. מרה), fly (from idea of rising?)'; מרד, 'rebel/revolt/cause sedition [(let us) rebel (i.e. Nimrod, prob. builder of Babel)] rebellion/defection/contumacy, Ch. rebellious'; מרה, 'rebel/be disobedient, (= מרר) be bitter, resist/contend w/, be rebellious, grieve, embitter [refractory] [rebellion (Miriam)] -/contumacy/bitterness, razor [double rebellion (fig. Babylon)]'; מרץ, 'be weak, diseased/pernicious/foul, make weak/foolish' (A. 'be diseased/weak (in body/mind)'); מרר, 'be (em)bitter(ed/exasperated), embitter/irritate/provoke, weep bitterly, a drop (in the bucket), bitter/ness/fig. sad/sorrowful/sadness/grief, lamentable, deadly/pernicious, violent/cruel, bitterly (of lamentation), myrrh [bitter/sad (Ruth)] [bitter fountains] gall, severe things/poison, -ous, grief/sorrow/trouble'—*six* built on mem reysh, since this is *essence* of reysh.

The converse, expressed in sound as *mm*: מגד > 'what is most precious/excellent/pleasant [noble of God] choice/precious things' (A. 'be honored, be noble/excellent'); מוץ, '(o)press(or), chaff, pressing (of cream to make butter)/churning'; מלץ, 'be smooth/agreeable'; מלצר, '(officer in Babyl. court) master of wine/chief butler?/treasurer? (coll. w/ Pers.)'; מן, 'manna/miraculous food w/ which God fed the Israelites in the wilderness (etym. uncertain)'; 2. מרא > 'fat(tened), fatling/esp. fatted calf [fattening?/causing rebellion? (Mamre)] crop (of birds)'; משרת, 'frying pan (etym. uncert.)'; and its essence, מתק, 'be/become/make sweet, (= Syr.) suck/feed upon w/ relish, sweet(ness/pleasantness)'; hence perhaps also מזה '(= מצץ/מצה suck/- out), sucking (famine)'.

And sound *m* conveys the idea *mum's the word*, mem's corresponding hieroglyph being *owl*, renowned for silent flight. Hence: מות, 'die/dead person/perish/be destroyed (of a state), (be) put to death/kill/slay, the dead/the slain, death/grave/pestilence/destruction/ruin'. And its converse: מחא, 'clap/strike (hands, exultingly), Ch. -/smite (e.g. hand, i.e. hinder/restrain)/be fastened/nailed to'—starts with mem then erupts with the contrasting harsh sound cheyt. And as apex of the waning year of the holly king and his satire: מוק, 'mock/deride'—almost our *mock*.

In the early Greek 'hymn' reconstructed from the Boibel Loth letter-names, M, *moiria*, becomes *moiraō*, 'I distribute': מאה, 'hundred(s/th)/- times'; מג, 'magian/Pers./Median priest (only in expression רב־מג chief of the magi)'; מגן, 'give over/deliver, make one to/as (any thing), give/make?/else denom. of מגן shield (R. גנן) hence protect/surround/deprive of shield/disarm'; מדי, 'Mede(s)'; מה, 'what?/why?/how?, Ch. whatever/how very!, something/anything whatever'; 2. מהר, '(cogn. מור) purchase (wife), price/dowry (paid to her parents)'; מור, 'be changed/altered, exchange, exchange/transfer/restitution/equivalent/recompense'; 1. מוש, 'move/withdraw/depart, remove/put away, let go/escape'; מחר '(prob. = מכר sell), price/wages'; מי, 'who(m)? [who is like unto God? (Michael)]'; מימין ['at right hand']; מכר, 'sell/give in marriage (for price)/deliver/give up (into power of another)/be sold/delivered up/sell oneself/give oneself up (to do evil) [sold] ware/merchandise/price/value/sale/thing sold [price of the Lord]'; מלט, 'let escape/slip/(be) deliver(ed/escape), lay eggs/bring forth, mortar/cement [whom the Lord delivers]'; מלך, 'reign/be (made/make) king, consult/take counsel, king (applied to God/false gods) [Moloch (idol of the Ammonites)] advice/counsel, queen [counselor] dominion/reign/rule, kingdom/realm [king of righteousness (Melchizedek)] kingship/royalty [queen of heaven (epithet of Astoreth, Phoenician Astarte/Diana/Venus)] etc.'; 1. מלל, 'speak/declare/announce [eloquent] word/saying/(object of) discourse, word/esp. order/mandate, thing (matter?) [I spoke]'; מלק, 'wring/pinch off'; מן, 'Ch. who?/what?/whoever/whatever'; מנה, 'separate/appoint/(be) number(ed)/constitute/destine (w/ ל assign), Maneh (H. weight 100 shekels), part/portion, times, Ch. number [n. of idol (prob. god of destiny/fortune)] [portion/possession (pl)]'; מנח > 'gift/present/tribute/offering to God/sacrifice' (A. 'give'); מנן > 'part/portion/strings (of instr.), of/from/out of/before/in presence of, according to, by/through/because/on account of, about/concerning, away from/without/besides, more than, at/in/on, since/after [perh. allotted (pl.)]'; מנע, '(be) restrain(ed/hindered/withdrawn)/hold/keep back/withhold/refuse [whom He withholds] [restraint]'; מסר, '(as in Ch.) deliver/offer up/hence teach/stir up/be delivered/given up'; מעט, 'be/become little/few, make small/few/diminish, make/do/give little, -/few/small, -ness/fewness/, nearly/almost/shortly/soon, naked/drawn (of sword, Gesen. polished/sharp)'; מצה, 'suck/drain/wring out'; מצץ, 'suck, unleavened bread (from idea of pressing/extending by pressure, or sweetness supposed contained in R.), feast thereof'— relating either to 'I distribute' or to *stretching out* (below)—מצר '(prob. to shut) [fortified/border (Egypt)] [n. of s. of Ham/Egypt/-ians]' (A. 'limit/border'); מרא, 'Ch. lord'; מריה ['shown/chosen of the Lord (Moriah)']; משח, 'prop. (as in A.) draw hand over/smear/rub over (w/ oil)/anoint, paint, consecrate (by unction), appoint/constitute, (be) anoint(ed) oneself, Ch. oil, (the) anointed (applied to priests/kings)/Messiah, an anointing/unction/portion, -/part, extension/spreading out' (Syr. 'measure') (thus bleeding into the next category); משל, 'rule/have dominion/power, cause to rule/give dominion to/appoint ruler, -/prince, dominion/kingdom, rulers/lords'; משר > 'measure (for liquids)' (A. 'divide'); מתג, 'a bridle'. That makes nine involving reysh (*head* distributor); only five involving lamedh (an actual reaching out). Five are built on mem nun, making use of nun's ability to hold back (being one back from aries the head).

Finally, there is a stretching out towards the eternal with regard to this mother of all mothers: מדד, '(be) measure(d)/apportion/extend/stretch oneself, measure/extension/tribute, vestment/garment, covering/carpet' (A. 'extend'); מדה '(= מדד extend), vestment/garment, extension'; מהה, 'delay/tarry, wait'; מוד, 'perh. move/shake (but see מדד), continuance/perpetuity, constantly/continually/always'; מחר, 'tomorrow/in future time/- to come, the day after'; מטא/Ch. מטה, 'come on/to/arrive at/happen/reach to'; מלא, 'be ful(l)filled/completed (of time), fill/make full, fulfil (of time/promise/desire), complete (number/words)/fully, fill(ed) in/insert(ed)/set (of gems), filling/full(y), fullness/plenty (of grain/wine), consecration (to priestly office) [God will fill him] insertion/setting (of gems), bezel (of ring)/fig. socket (of eye)'; מלח, 'salt, ברית מלח covenant of salt (i.e. lasting covenant, salt as emblem of perpetuity), to salt/be salted/washed w/

salt water, Ch. eat salt, seaman/mariner, sea-purslain (marine plant leaves of which are eaten by the poor), salt/barren land'; מצא, 'come to/reach to/arrive at/(be) obtain(ed)/acquire(d), come upon, find/discover, befall/happen/be sufficient/enough, be found/present/at hand, cause to come to (i.e. deliver/give up), cause to obtain/offer/present'; מקל, 'shoot/twig/staff/stick/mace (badge of authority) [shoots]' (coll. w/ Ethiop. 'shoot/sprout'); מרג > 'threshing-sledge'; משה, 'draw out [draw(ing/n) out/deliverer (Moses)] silk'; משׁך, 'draw (one to a pl.)/- out (esp. bow/also trumpet), stretch/hold out (hand in fellowship), prolong/continue/make durable/strengthen/scatter (seed), spread out, seize/take/hold/take away/remove, be delayed/protracted, -/deferred, cords/bands, acquisition/a scattering'; משׁק (= משׁך), 'possession/overspreading'; מתה > 'man/prop. adult/men מתי מספר men of number/i.e. that can be numbered/few מתי אהל men of tent/i.e. domestics [man of God] when?/when, all/every one' (A. מתא/מתי 'extend' cogn. מתח); מתח, 'stretch out, sack/bag'. To extend and stretch out wine: מהל, 'adulterated (of wine)'; מזג '(= מסך mix), mixed wine'; מסך, 'mix/mingle, mixture (i.e. mixed/spiced wine)', these last two hearkening back to 'I distribute'.

And then there is its converse (time compression): 1. מהר, '(make) haste(n/be quick), be hasty/rash/inconsiderate/impetuous, quick(ly/speedily)/ready/skilful'; מול, 'over against/opposite, before/formerly/yesterday'.

Mem sofit is the ultimate unity, being the Monad; and also the teffilin on one's brow, to commemorate Adam Qadmon. Hence: מכבנא ['circuit/band (Syr. bind round)']; מכבני ['binder']; and מצח, 'forehead/brow/front, greaves'.

Mem sofit ultimately stands for self-knowledge: מין/מון '(perh. = מנה appoint/define), species/sort/kind, image/likeness/form/appearance'; משל, '(utter comparison/)similitude/parable, sentiment/sententious saying/maxim, proverb/by-word/subject of taunting proverb, part. using similitudes (i.e. poets), be/become like/similar, compare, something like/similar, taunting/by-word'. Indeed according to both Graves and me, the line from the Song of Amairgin for M is: *I am a hill of poetry*. To the light thus shed can perhaps be linked the following: מתרדת [(Pers.) 'given/dedicated to Mithra (the genius of the sun)'].

I am left with: מטל > 'bar of iron' (A. 'forge iron'), though this may simply be a concrete leftover from what is stretched out in time (i.e. sturdy).

SUMMARY

Mem, the closed mouth: 'speak, word', 'similitude, parable, proverb, poets', 'magi'. **M-vine:** 'smooth [*of speech*], wine steward', 'mix liquids [*esp. wine*]', 'mixed wine', 'diseased, weak, foolish', 2 'totter', 'mock'. **Blood:** *2* 'strike, smite', 'dash, plunge [*as foot in blood*], bruise', 2 '(castrated) bruised (rub)' ['polish, sharpen, make smooth, pluck hair'] 'spot, blemish', 'irritate, painful', 2 'circumcise, cut off', 'forge iron' {'Mars*?*[*Merodach*]'} {'Mordecai' [*a bloody story*]}, 'wipe out, take out marrow, marrow'. **Mmm:** 'be excellent, what is most pleasant, choice things', 'salt [*BRYTh MLCh, 'covenant of salt'*]', 'matzah [*from pressing? or sweetness?*]', 'pressing or churning [*of cream*]', 3 '(sweet) suck'. **Old Semitic shape** [*drawing* *to bosom*]: 'touch, feel', 'over against, opposite, before', 'belly, womb, compassionate'. **'I distribute'** [*in 'Orphic' hymn*]: 2 '(shield) deliver up (sell, give in marriage)', 'purchase-price for wife', 'exchange, equivalent, recompense', 'hundred', {'chosen of the lord [*Moriah*]'} 'lord', 'reign, advice, counsel', 'rule', 'a bridle', 'what? which, why?' 2 'who?', 'reject', 'withhold', 'pinch off', 'threshing sledge', 'diminish, give little', 'let slip', 'gift, tribute, offering', 2 '(let slip) deliver (offer)', *3* '(appoint) (apportion, manna) portion (measure, extension, anoint, Messiah)', 2 '(all, everyone) extend (measure, apportion)', 2 '({deliverer [*Moses*]}) draw out (acquisition, stretch, prolong, continue)'. **Mem-sofit:** [*stretched out, eternal:*] 2 'reach, arrive', 2 'come or reach to (offer)', 'extend,', 'delay, tarry', 'the future', 'perpetuity, continually', 'to shoot, twig, staff'; [*on AQ's 'brow':*] 'forehead, brow', 'species, sort, kind, form, image'. **Calendar's libra:** 'loins', 'belly, bowels', 'girdle', 'well fed'. **Water:** 'filled, full', '[*liquid measure*]', 'vessel', 'waters', 'rain', 'a brook', 'cleanse', 3 'melt, flow (-down, dissolve)', 'flow, a drop, weep bitterly, be bitter'. **'Fallen'** [*intermediate*] **mem:** 'be unwilling', *3* 'to rebel (Nimrod)' [*all 3 begin with MR*], {'Egypt', 'Memphis'} 'act perversely, be faithless, sin', 'fallen, cast down {precipice}', 'become reduced', {'fear'}, 2 '(decay) perish (ruin)', 'vanish', 'depart'; [*the present:*] 'be hasty, rash, ready' {'given to Mithra'} 'daily burnt offering'.

Afterword

It is somewhat surprising to me *how* coherently the clusters of meaning reinforce the underlying bardic corpus. There is little doubt that I have at times rounded up rather broadly; certainly the reason for certain inclusions will not be acceptable to every reader. Overlooking the occasional wild inclusion, though, there is still general coherence to the currents uncovered.

It has taught me two very important lessons (amongst others). One is the association of *cutting* with fruit and nut harvest, qof and kaf. (*Duh*, you say.) Second is the several varieties of the meaning *back* or towards the inner horizon, beyt: *taking for oneself* and *being taken aback*, in addition to *self-knowledge*.

At the very least this study has confirmed the reordering of the twelve simples, since their meanings appear consistent with their corrected placement on the round. But I think for those who value Scripture and study it more seriously than I do (for either its religious or its historical content), what is revealed herein may well deepen understanding of underlying poetic meanings. I would certainly value the results herein more than I would the permutations of Gematria based on Hebrew numbering, which is a later strata than the original bardic numeration and what tree-letters reveal about the root meanings (such as rowan's sheltering of other species that eventually displace it, as befits its meaning *to teach*).

I hope scholars, rabbis, and the merely inquisitive will find this study as useful as I have. May it serve to enhance, rather than upset, the reverence in which Scripture is held by moderns who have *not* been tricked by materialism and Darwinism into thinking it 'old hat'.

G.K.Spain
15 February 2024

Appendix:
Carian Inscriptions in Egypt

No Rest for the Wicked

All mankind does frailly mends
askew ends, wild since childbirth.
Therefore, one strikes ore who asks
that our tasks teach us true worth.

In *The Carian Language* (Leiden, London: Brill, 2007), a certain (seemingly) Ignacio-Javier Adiego claims to have finally solved the mystery of Carian: he claims the language is Indo-European, of the Anatolian type. His approach to translating these troublesome inscriptions depends almost *entirely* on supposed transliteration of names in certain bilingual inscriptions in Egypt, yet it has been dubbed the *definitive* decipherment (by Adiego and others). But as his sound-values mostly vary wildly from what shared letter-shapes signify in Semitic, Greek, or other neighboring alphabets, it has never seemed very likely to me. He transliterates C as *d*, Greek delta as *l*, vau digamma as *r*, a crossed circle (or circle with dot in it) as *q*, Greek lambda as *b*, Greek nu as *m*, Greek qoppa as *t*, Greek rho as *š*, Greek phi as *ñ*, and Ψ (psi, or 'western' chi) as *n*. The article I cite below states (on page 2): "In all cases, Adiego's claim to have deciphered Carian was fairly strange as he was *still about completely unable* to translate any single sentence or inscription written in Carian." Indeed it seems presumptuous to claim success behind such a sketchy 'solution'.

To my perception, it smacks of *elitist consensus*, something similar to the early twentieth-century shift from seeing Canaanite letters as originating in Egyptian hieratic—including 'group-writing', use of certain two-sound signs for individual sounds when transcribing non-Egyptian words or names—to seeing them as originating in 'proto-Sinaitic' scratchings: it simply became the new fad, perhaps because many scholars felt 'stuck' (by a not-quite-complete theory of letter origins)—which is even more true with regard to Carian.

I just read (online) an anonymous (though meticulously referenced) study of the Carian inscriptions at Abydos illustrating a method of analysis that is only occasionally tenuous and at the same time *much* more fruitful. The language turns out (according to the article) to be akin to Hurrian, a language that was thought to have died out half a millennium earlier (than mid-first millennium BCE). Quite a few inscriptions appear to be *in* Hurrian, as if a significant faction among the mercenary Carians serving in Egypt spoke an archaic dialect. Perhaps *Carian* is even how the word *Hurrian* had evolved by then.

Though the article itself was unattributed, two works were referenced for the translations offered: Jean Catsanicos, "L'apport de la bilingue Ḫattuša à la lexicologie hourrite", in Jean-Marie Durand (ed.), *Amurru 1* (Paris: Éditions Recherche sur les Civilisations, 1996), pp. 197-296; *and* Emmanuel Laroche, *Glossaire de la langue hourrite (= Revue Hittite et Asianique*, 34/35) (Paris: Éditions Klincksieck, 1980).

Oddly enough, though the article claimed Adiego's only correct transliteration was alpha, its own transliteration seems to agree on several others: *n* for Ψ (trident of ash-god Poseidon); *r* (if only sometimes) for F—as if truncated from Greek P (rho)—*s* for M (Greek san); and V or Y (Greek upsilon) for *u*. And O is variously transliterated. Of course, since the inscriptions are graffiti, many damaged or incomplete, the transliterations seek to correct the occasional defective letter (such as adding a line to a seemingly empty circle?).

What has long seemed ridiculous to me about the *Adiego* approach is that it completely overlooks the repeated occurrence of the name of the sun-god, *Ra*, when read with *obvious* values (in this case Greek)—often with word-separators separating out the name! Another recurring combination is *b-w* for *biwa*, 'for you' or 'to you' (in Carian), in graffiti dedicating gifts *to* Ra. The article pictures inscriptions as Adiego illustrated them, whose interpretation is given for a couple of them *not* from Abydos, then for those and thiry-nine inscriptions from Abydos (Egypt) gives its own transliteration and translation, making sense out of most of them. Then near the end it treats of a bilingual inscription from Kaunos, and there, I must admit, they lose me a little: there is just too little consistency in the use of the letter-shapes; but I am perhaps missing something. There are also a few places earlier on that I stumbled over, but I do believe the basic approach is a much sounder one than Adiego's, that is, if the Hurrian and Carian shown represent a valid vocabulary. It certainly does not seem like a hoax.

In dealing with the Kaunos inscription, the article points to something which might help explain why direct transliteration from names in bilinguals misses the mark: ". . . the Greek Person names seem to be half-translated into Carian, instead of being just rephonemicized in Carian." Imagine future archaeologists finding a bilingual inscription, all-consonants, with the Lakota name *Thashunke Witko* transcribed *Crazy Horse*: they might think our C meant *Th*, our *r* meant *sh*, our *z* meant *nk*, our *H* meant *W*, our *r* meant *t* (as well as *sh*?), and our *s* meant *k*.

What is apparent (as the article asserts and shows) is that the Carian letters are primarily a consonantal alphabet, like Semitic, with A (*'a*), F (*w*), and Y used to indicate *lengthened* vowels. It is my humble opinion that the article presents a much more plausible approach to Carian than the supposedly definitive solution of Adiego's. Hence I shall end my remarks by giving the link for the article, so that readers who are interested may investigate it for themselves:

www.scribd.com/document/70863875/The-Issue-of-Deciphering-Carian

Signs & Abbreviations

Italics call attention to certain meanings in roots where not all the meanings are to the point.

Numbered roots are instances of similarly vocalized root with different meaning (I omit vowels).

( )	Alternative sense, sometimes context (unexpressed); if the first meaning, and not separated from the root by a comma, it means the root itself is not used, only derivatives (though not all unused roots are so indicated).
[ ]	In proper name.
{ }	Root in ו also referenced under י or (in one case) ק.
?	Meanings on which scholars have differing opinions.
>	From which is derived (can point either way).
*	Definitions imported from other sources.
- *[alone or w/ suffix]*	Previous word-meaning.
—	With prefix or suffix, the (Semitic) root being discussed.
w/	with
/ *[otherwise]*	or
\	Alternative first or last letter (Hebrew).
A.	Arabic
adj.	adjective
Aram.	Aramaic
Assyr.	Assyrian
Babyl.	Babylonian
bldg.	building
cf.	compare
Ch.	'Chaldean' (language of Book of Daniel)
coll.	collated
conj.	conjunction
d.	daughter
derivv.	derivatives
Egyp.	Egyptian
Eng.	English
Ethiop.	Ethiopian
etym.	etymology
f.	feminine
fig.	figuratively
Gesen.	Gesenius
H.	Hebrew
incl.	including
inf.	infinitive

instr.	instrument
k.	king
m.	masculine
mo.	month
mtn.	mountain
mus.	musical
n.	noun *or* name (should be clear from context)
onom.	onomatopoeia
orig.	origin
part.	participle
pcs.	pieces
perh.	perhaps
pers.	person
Pers.	Persian
pl.	a place
pref.	prefix
prim.	primarily
prob.	probably
pron.	pronoun
prop.	properly
R.	root
r.	river
rel.	relative
s.	son
Sam.	Samaritan
Sept.	Septuagint
sp.	species
subst.	substantive
Syr.	Syrian
v.	verb
Vulg.	Vulgate
w.	wife
yr.	year

Night Watch

keep watch, my spirit
do not slag
let no injunction
bend your course
relax and nature
will prevail
and turn all purpose
into rust

close not the eyelids
when you sleep
for even dreamland
needs man's skill
even in death
take with you there
the things that serve you,
nothing more

Endnotes

[1] B. Davidson, *The Analytical Hebrew and Chaldee Lexicon: Consisting of An Alphabetical Arrangement of Every Word and Inflection Contained in the Old Testament Scriptures, Precisely as They Occur in the Sacred Text, with a Grammatical Analysis of Each Word, and Lexicographical Illustration of the Meanings* (London: Samuel Bagster & Sons, 1966).

[2] Kieren Barry, *The Greek Qabalah: Alphabetic Mysticism and Numerology in the Ancient World* (York Beach, ME: Samuel Weiser, 1999).

[3] Gershom Scholem, *Major Trends in Jewish Mysticism* (New York: Schocken Books, 1974), p. 100.

[4] Ibid.

[5] Loeb Classical Library, Plato vol. V, *The Republic, vol. 1* (Cambridge: Harvard University Press, 1982), pp. 521*ff*.

[6] Robert Graves, *The White Goddess: A historical grammar of poetic myth* (New York: Farrar, Straus & Giroux, 1948)—hereafter referred to as *tWG*.

[7] Michael A. Cremo and Richard L. Thompson, *Forbidden Archeology: The Hidden History of the Human Race* (Los Angeles: Bhaktivedanta Book Publishing, 1996), especially pp. 454-8, 297-9, 805-814 (summarized 815*f*).

[8] J. Williams ab Ithel, ed., *The Barddas of Iolo Morganwg: A Collection of Original Documents, Illustrative of the Theology, Wisdom, and Usages of the Bardo-Druidic System of the Isle of Britain* (Boston: WeiserBooks, 2004), p. 79.

[9] *tWG*, p. 295.

[10] Max Freedom Long, *The Huna Code in Religions: The Influence of the Huna Tradition on Modern Faith* (Marina del Rey, CA: DeVorss & Co., 1965), pp. 33*f*.

[11] Long, op.cit., pp. 30, 48, 68*ff* (see also Hawaiian dictionary at the end).

[12] Long, op.cit., pp. 47, 49.

[13] Harold W. Percival, *Thinking and Destiny* (Dallas: The Word Foundation, Inc., 1974 [orig. 1946])—a more recent edition (eleventh) includes the book *Masonry and Its Symbols* as a chapter, thus altering the page numbers, which for that later edition you will find in brackets after each citation, thus—p. 419 [p. 367]. It will hereafter be referred to as *T&D*.

[14] S. Mahdihassan, *Indian Alchemy or Rasayana: In the Light of Asceticism and Geriatrics* (Delhi: Motilal Banarsidass Publishers, 1991), pp. 81, 96.

[15] Martin Bernal, *Cadmean Letters: The Transmission of the Alphabet to the Aegean and Further West before 1400 B.C.* (Winona Lake: Eisenbrauns, 1990), pp. 121f.

[16] Ralph J. Fessenden and Joan S. Fessenden, *The Basis of Organic Chemistry* (Boston: Allyn & Bacon, 1971), p. 326.

[17] John Gardner and John Maier, tr., *Gilgamesh: Translated from the Sîn-leqi-unninnī version* (New York: Vintage Books, a division of Random House, 1984), Tablet I, column ii (p. 67), and Tablet IX, column ii (p. 198).

[18] C. Kerényi, *The Gods of the Greeks* (London: Thames & Hudson, 1951), p. 114.

[19] Harold Waldwin Percival, *Masonry and Its Symbols: In the Light of Thinking and Destiny* (New York: The Word Publishing Company, 1952), pp. 18*f, 35* [*T&D*, later edition, pp. 676, 685].

[20] See Betty Jo Teeter Dobbs, *The Foundations of Newton's Alchemy, or "The Hunting of the Greene Lyon"* (New York: Cambridge University Press, 1975).

[21] C. Scott Littleton, The New Comparative Mythology: An Anthropological Assessment of the Theories of Georges Dumézil (Berkeley: University of California Press, 1973), its main theme.

[22] *T&D*, pp. 499, 459 [pp. 438, 403].

[23] Gershom Scholem, *Kabbalah* (N.Y.: Meridian, 1978), p. 110.

[24] Ibid.

[25] Ibid.

[26] Grimm, *Teutonic Mythology*, Vol. II, p. 651. He says: "According to the Ostgota-lag (bygdab. 30), any one may in a common wood hew with impunity, all but *oaks* and *hazels*, these have peace, *i.e.* immunity. In Superst. I, 972 we are told that oak and hazel dislike one another, and cannot agree, any more than haw and sloe (white and black thorn; see Suppl.)."

[27] *Bulfinch's Mythology* (New York: Modern Library, Random House, no date), p. 263 (in chapter XXXVIII's initial section, called "Northern Mythology"); G. A. Gaskell, *Dictionary of All Scriptures and Myths* (New York: Gramercy Books, 1981), p. 75 (identified as symbols of desire-nature and instinct-nature); also Marijane Osborn and Stella Longland, *Rune Games* (Boston: Routledge & Kegan Paul, 1982), identifies Embla (the first woman) with alder, p. 88.

[28] *tWG*, p. 168.

[29] *tWG*, p. 278.

[30] *T&D*, p. 658 [p. 577].

[31] See, for instance, *The Zohar*, tr. Harry Sperling and Maurice Simon (London: Soncino Press, 1934), vol. 1, pp. 158*f*.

[32] *T&D*, pp. 480*f* [p. 421*f*].

[33] *Zohar: The Book of Splendor (Basic Readings from the Kabbalah)*, selected and edited by Gershom Scholem (New York: Schocken Books, 1949), p. 40.

[34] Barry Fell, *Bronze Age America* (Boston: Little, Brown & Company, 1982).

[35] Barry Fell, *America B.C.: Ancient Settlers in the New World* (N.Y.: Pocket Books, Wallaby, 1978), chapter 12.

[36] Grimm, *Teutonic Mythology*, vol. 2, pp. 713*f*.

[37] *tWG*, pp. 85*f*, 120, 137*f*.

[38] See Mircea Eliade, *The Forge and the Crucible: The Origin and Structures of Alchemy* (New York: Harper & Row, 1962).

[39] Sir Alan Gardiner, *Egyptian Grammar: Being an Introduction to the Study of Hieroglyphs*, third edition (Oxford: Griffith Institute, Ashmolean Museum, 1957), p. 27.

[40] Ibid., p. 471.

[41] Peter Berresford Ellis, *The Druids* (Grand Rapids, MI: William B. Eerdmans, 1994), p. 224.

[42] *The World's Writing Systems*, Peter T. Daniels and William Bright, editors (New York: Oxford University Press, 1996), p. 85.

[43] Bernal, *Cadmean Letters*, pp. 92*f*.

[44] *tWG*, p. 170.

[45] *tWG*, pp. 172, 184, 233, 372.

[46] Bernal, *Cadmean Letters*, p. 106.

[47] *tWG*, pp. 226*f*.

[48] Gardiner, *Egyptian Grammar*, p. 482.

[49] Ibid., loc.cit.

[50] Ibid., loc.cit.

[51] Fell, *Bronze Age America*, p. 127.

[52] Alwyn Rees and Brinley Rees, *Celtic Heritage: Ancient Tradition in Ireland and Wales* (New York: Thames & Hudson, 1961), p. 198.

[53] Peter Berresford Ellis, *The Druids* (Grand Rapids, MI: William B. Eerdmans, 1994), p. 234.

[54] Patai, *The Hebrew Goddess*, pp. 166*f* (from a popular short version of Luria's own formula), p. 172 (from Nathan of Hannover, sixteenth to seventeenth century), pp. 189*f* ("to unify the Name—yud-kei with vav-kei," from modern Hasidic-American *Complete Art Scroll Siddur*, pp. 4*f*), and p. 191 (from the modern Sephardic *Siddur Bet Yosef v'Ohel Avraham*, p. 129).

[55] Grimm, *Teutonic Mythology*, vol. 2, pp. 709, 713*f*.

[56] Ibid.

[57] Ibid.

[58] *Clement of Alexandria*, G. W. Butterworth, tr. (New York: G. P. Putnam's Sons, 1919), p. 45.

[59] Grimm, loc.cit.

[60] Ibid.

[61] Aryeh Kaplan, *Sefer Yetzirah: The Book of Creation* (York Beach, ME: Samuel Weiser, 1990), p. 73.

[62] Giorgio de Santillana & Hertha von Dechend, *Hamlet's Mill: An Essay Investigating the Origins of Human Knowledge and its Transmission through Myth* (Boston: David R. Godine, 1992), pp. 322*f*.

[63] Grimm, loc.cit.

[64] Gardiner, *Egyptian Grammar*, p. 80 (see also pp. 179, 572, 574, 619).

[65] C. Scott Littleton, The New Comparative Mythology: An Anthropological Assessment of the Theories of Georges Dumézil (Berkeley: University of California Press, 1973), its main theme.